PURCHASING:
A GUIDE FOR HOSPITALITY
PROFESSIONALS

David K. Hayes
Panda Pros Hospitality Management and Training

Jack D. Ninemeier
The School of Hospitality Management Michigan State University

Prentice Hall
Upper Saddle River, New Jersey
Columbus, Ohio

Library of Congress Cataloging-in-Publication Data

Hayes, David K.
  Purchasing : a guide for hospitality professionals / David K. Hayes
Jack D. Ninemeier. — 1st ed.
    p. cm.
  ISBN-13: 978-0-13-514842-6
  ISBN-10: 0-13-514842-1
  1. Purchasing—Management.   2. Hospitality industry.   I. Ninemeier,
Jack D.   II. Title.
  HF5437.H35 2010
  647.94068'7—dc22

                                            2008054691

Editor in Chief: Vernon Anthony
Acquisitions Editor: William Lawrensen
Editorial Assistant: Lara Dimmick
Production Manager: Wanda Rockwell
Creative Director: Jayne Cone
Cover Designer: Bruce Kenselaar
Cover Photo: Getty Images Inc.
Director, Image Resource Center: Melinda Patelli
Manager, Rights and Permissions: Zina Arabia
Manager, Visual Research: Beth Brenzel
Manager, Cover Visual Research and Permissions: Karen Sanatar
Image Permission Coordinator: Ang'John Ferreri
Director of Marketing: David Gesell

This book was set in Palatino by Aptara®, Inc., and was printed and bound by Bind-Rite. The cover
was printed by Demand Production Center

Pearson Prentice Hall™ is a trademark of Pearson Education, Inc.
Pearson® is a registered trademark of Pearson plc
Prentice Hall® is a registered trademark of Pearson Education, Inc.

Pearson Education Ltd., London
Pearson Education Singapore, Pte. Ltd.
Pearson Education Canada, Inc.
Pearson Education—Japan
Pearson Education Australia Pty. Limited

Pearson Education North Asia, Ltd., Hong Kong
Pearson Educación de Mexico, S.A. de C.V.
Pearson Education Malaysia Pte. Ltd.
Pearson Education Upper Saddle River, New Jersey

Prentice Hall
is an imprint of

www.pearsonhighered.com

10 9 8 7 6 5 4 3 2 1
ISBN-13: 978-0-13-514842-6
ISBN-10:   0-13-514842-1

CONTENTS

PREFACE

Successful hospitality operations require staff members at all organizational levels with a vast array of knowledge and skills relating to many specialized areas. Each area is important, and none can be singled out as the most critical. However, the need to assure that production personnel have the resources required to serve customers must receive significant attention.

This book, *Purchasing: A Guide for Hospitality Professionals*, presented an exceptional planning challenge in its early developmental stages because the authors determined that the subject matter to address all aspects of the topic was so extensive. The solution: applicable subject matter was identified, and two hospitality-specific books were written.

This book considers basic topics important to understanding the management of the purchasing process, and it presents information helpful in developing quality descriptions (specifications) for commonly purchased products. It focuses on product purchasing in restaurants and provides a comprehensive overview of the topic with an emphasis on the basic functions of purchasing: obtaining the right product at the right time in the right quantity from the right supplier. (*Note:* The second book written from the earlier content outline addresses the broader topic of procurement, the entire process of acquiring and evaluating goods and services.) Its scope extends beyond that of the present book and identifies information important in the purchase of services, products used by lodging properties, and global procurement concerns, among other specialized topics.

This book will be useful for readers who want to learn the essential elements of purchasing with an emphasis on managing the process, identifying quality characteristics of necessary products, and understanding the ever-increasing role of technology in the process. The authors have made it especially reader-friendly with understandable descriptions of how purchasing works and definitions for more than 450 industry- and purchasing-related terms. Several other elements are included in each chapter (these are described below) to help ensure that readers will understand the basic information described and will know how it can be applied in the hospitality workplace.

BENEFITS TO READERS

The authors believe that this book will benefit students, faculty members, and industry professionals in several ways.

STUDENTS

Students interested in hospitality careers will benefit from this book as it is used in purchasing courses and as they participate in project-based instruction in other courses where information about purchasing is important to fully address operating problems being considered.

Each chapter presents practical concepts that are in common use in successful foodservice operations. The first part of this text's emphasis is on clearly identified process and procedure benchmarks that can be incorporated into the way things are done by foodservice organizations as products are purchased. While there is some emphasis on the "why", details about the "how" of each procedure are thoroughly explained. The second part of the book relates to the items purchased by foodservice operators. If you are interested in knowing more about the food, beverages, and related products needed to make restaurants successful, you will be keenly interested in this portion of the book.

FACULTY MEMBERS

Hospitality faculty members want their students to have the very best learning resources. This book meets their expectations by presenting content that is up to date and accurate and by helping to ensure that jargon, complex discussions, and less-relevant information does not get in the way of education. The authors recognize that, while a textbook is very important, the role of the faculty member is even more critical. This book and its supplemental teaching materials (see below) will be of significant assistance to faculty members who want their students to learn about purchasing management and the quality aspects of commonly purchased products. The more than three hundred Web sites noted throughout this book provide fertile ground for projects, additional reading, class discussions, and other educational activities to best ensure that students understand and can be successful in the real world of hospitality purchasing.

INDUSTRY PROFESSIONALS

Those currently working in hospitality industry positions with purchasing responsibilities will also find this book valuable. Its content can answer questions, provide solutions, confirm that existing procedures are appropriate, and provide tactics helpful in ensuring that optimal value is received for the purchase dollars being spent. Managers can share their professional resources, including this book, with others who are aspiring to positions with increased responsibilities. Educational and training experiences related to purchasing are easily justified with regard to cost when one considers that at least 30 percent of the revenue dollars generated by a property are routinely used to purchase the products required to serve guests.

ORGANIZATION OF BOOK

This book is divided into two parts. In the first, management of the purchasing process, a ten-step purchasing process is detailed in six chapters. The steps describe how to

- identify product need.
- determine quality requirements.
- conduct make or buy analysis.
- determine the quantity of products purchased.
- identify supplier sources.
- select suppliers for specific orders.
- order products.
- receive and store products.
- process payments (the accounting function).
- evaluate the purchasing process.

In the second part of the book (seven chapters), detailed information addressing the purchasing of common food, beverage, and other products used by foodservice operations is presented. The chapters include product quality-related information about

- meats, poultry, and seafood.
- produce, dairy, and eggs.
- groceries.
- alcoholic and nonalcoholic beverages.
- nonfood items.
- technology and services.
- capital equipment items.

Information helpful in understanding how to purchase these common food products and other items is made easier by references to numerous Web sites that provide detailed information useful to foodservice buyers (and to those learning how to purchase these items).

CHAPTER EDUCATIONAL COMPONENTS

Each chapter contains numerous elements to help retain the readers' interest, to review application of the subject matter to the workplace, and to reinforce the major learning principles that are presented. Taken in total, they help to make the subject matter real, and they reinforce the importance of procedures to implement an effective purchasing system. These supplemental elements are as follows:

- *Purchasing Pros Need to Know!*—This chapter introduction previews the most important topics that will be discussed, and it defends their importance in understanding a comprehensive overview of the purchasing process.
- *Chapter Outline*—A detailed outline is provided to summarize important chapter points, identify the context of each chapter section relative to the entire chapter, and to help busy readers identify specific areas in which subject matter is addressed.
- *Buyer's Guide to Purchasing Terms*—Key terms important in understanding the hospitality industry in general and purchasing concepts more specifically are presented in bolded terms and defined where first used in the chapter. There are approximately 450 of these keys terms identified throughout the book in efforts to incorporate an understanding of language and industry jargon into the book's educational goals.
- *"Buyers at Work"*—Each chapter contains approximately two to three case studies that allow readers to apply what they are learning in business situations that commonly confront managers and purchasers. After each case study is presented, several questions are posed to allow readers to make decisions in ways that incorporate information presented in the text.
- *"Professional Purchasing Prevents Problems"*—Each chapter contains several of these elements that identify specific purchasing-related problems and present information useful in preventing the problem. This information supplements that in the chapter and helps to defend the premise that problems can be prevented by applying the basic principles of purchasing described in the chapter.
- *"Did You Know?"*—These elements provide supplemental information applicable to the chapter's topic. Their purpose is to provide additional material and to retain readers' interest with good-to-know and anecdotal information that helps to round out the readers' understanding of the topic.
- *Buyers Guide to Internet Resources*—Each major section in the chapter is concluded with a list of Web sites providing supplemental information about the topic discussed in the section. In total, there are approximately three hundred Web site notations.
- *Purchasing Terms*—Each of the terms defined in the "Buyer's Guide to Purchasing Terms" throughout the chapter is listed at the end of the chapter in the sequence in which they are used in the chapter.
- *Make Your Own Purchasing Decisions*—Questions posed at the end of each chapter encourage the readers to apply what they have learned. They are general questions that can be addressed individually or in groups. As the latter tactic is used, students can further develop interpersonal skills and learn firsthand about group dynamics and teamwork.
- *Chapter Photos*—Each chapter contains several photos that illustrate common restaurant situations applicable to the chapters' topics. These photos help to make each chapter more hospitable, and they provide a complement to extensive verbal discussion in each chapter.

SUPPLEMENTAL BOOK MATERIALS

An extensive set of instructor and student learning resources have been developed to accompany this book:

- PowerPoint lecture aids for each chapter
- Vocabulary quizzes (one per chapter)
- Two hundred question exam bank
- Instructor's notes for each "Buyers at Work" mini case

ACKNOWLEDGMENTS AND DEDICATION

The authors wish to thank Vernon Anthony, Editor-in-Chief, and William Lawrensen, Acquisitions Editor, for the help they provided in developing the subject matter for this book. We would also like to thank Lara Dimmick, Editorial Assistant and other production personnel who contributed to this project.

We would like to extend a special thank-you to those educators and other experts who reviewed and contributed helpful suggestions to this book: Steven F. Bergonzoni, Burlington County College; Jennifer DeRosa, Eastern Iowa Community College; and Paul Glatt, Cuyahoga Community College.

Stephen Marquardt, account manager, American Restaurant Supply, Kailua-Kona, Hawaii, reviewed several of the management chapters and provided anecdotes and other specific comments, and his assistance and input are sincerely appreciated. As she has previously, Allisha Miller of PandaPros Hospitality Training did an excellent job coordinating the photo selection for this text, and we thank her for her hard work. Also, a very special "Thanks" for his insightful guidance goes to Beat Müller, the talented and gracious Gerente General (General Manager) of Real Resort's "The Royal Playa Del Carmen".

As always, our wives, Leilani Sill Ninemeier and Peggy Hayes, supported and encouraged us during every step in the planning, writing (and rewriting—many times), and follow-up activities required to prepare this book for publication. We thank them once again for their assistance and support.

The authors dedicate this book to several members of the Hospitality Education Academy who are no longer with us: Eddystone Nebel III, Henrietta Becker, Stephenson Fletcher III, Anthony Marshall, Beatrice Donaldson David, Marjorie M. McKinley, Lewis J. Minor, Arthur Avery, Raphael R. Kavanaugh, and Joseph J. Cioch. These individuals, who were the authors' major professors, instructors, department heads, mentors, and colleagues, provided benchmarks of professionalism and wisdom. If this book influences subsequent generations of hospitality managers and educators, it will be because of those who have affected our own experiences.

David K. Hayes
Okemos, Michigan

Jack D. Ninemeier
Hilo, Hawaii

Introduction to Purchasing Management

Purchasing Pros Need to Know!

In this chapter you'll see why purchasing is important as you learn about its objectives. You'll also discover the basic steps in an organized purchasing system, which if followed, can help you to be a professional purchaser.

Who performs purchasing tasks in hospitality operations, and exactly what do they do? You'll learn about the roles, responsibilities, and specific tasks of persons with purchasing responsibilities in several types of hospitality operations.

Purchasers must comply with numerous laws, many of which are enforced by agencies of the federal government. This chapter will help you to understand their affect on purchasing: to identify what purchasers can (and cannot) do. Also, you'll learn about the Uniform Commercial Code and see how it affects the buying process.

Buyers and sellers make purchasing agreements in which, for example, the buyer says, "I will do this, if you will do that." These buying/selling contracts can be complex, and as a professional purchaser, before you enter into a legally binding contract, you must know their basic types, the elements they must contain, and specific contractual terms and clauses that are used in them. You will learn details about these and related concerns in this chapter.

Professional buyers follow basic ethical principles. While these will be based on your moral standards and beliefs, you'll learn one approach to determine if a course of action is ethical in the final section of this chapter.

■ ■ ■

Outline

WHAT IS PURCHASING?

What is purchasing, and why is it important? You'll learn the answers to these questions in this introduction.

Definitions

Many hospitality managers use the terms **procurement,** and **purchasing** to mean the same thing, and we will also. However, technically, procurement relates to the entire process of acquiring and evaluating goods and services needed by the hospitality organization. It begins when needs are determined and ends after products are used or contracted services are provided. Also, there is an emphasis on supplier interactions to provide greater value. By contrast, purchasing relates to "buying" activities such as determining purchase quantities or service requirements, placing orders, and paying suppliers for them. Many aspects of the broad scope of procurement will be discussed throughout this book, although its emphasis is on buying procedures.

Purchasing Is Important

As a purchaser, you will have one primary concern: to identify and obtain the products and services that best allow your organization to meet the wants and needs of its customers at a fair price.

The purchasing process is never-ending. Customer preferences change and new product and service alternatives are continually introduced. Price concerns require ongoing attention, and you will need to continually learn about the marketplace and its suppliers, revise your purchasing procedures, and evaluate your success.

Buyer's Guide to Purchasing Terms

Procurement   The process of acquiring and evaluating goods and services beginning with determining needs through product use, conclusion of contracted service, or end of the useful life of an equipment item.

Purchasing   The process of "buying": placing an order, receiving a product or service, and paying the supplier.

There are numerous ingredients necessary to prepare all of the required food items for this buffet. Each ingredient must be purchased, and detailed procedures help to ensure that the right ingredients are available at the right time, in the right amounts, and at the right price.

Richard Embery/Pearson Education/PH College

OBJECTIVES OF EFFECTIVE PURCHASING

Purchasing objectives are simple to state, and they are shown in Figure 1.1: to obtain the *right* product or service at the *right* price from the *right* source in the *right* amount at the *right* time. Unfortunately, it is more different to attain these objectives than it is to write them down or to read them.

When you review Figure 1.1, you'll see that attainment of purchasing objectives helps customers and the hospitality operation. Changes in the needs (desired benefits) of the customers and hospitality operation may lead, in turn, to revisions in purchasing objectives.

Purchasing objectives help to determine what purchasers should do. For example, they must help to determine their organization's specific needs for products and services and to identify the best sources for them. Purchasers can assist in decision making about the products and services to be provided by their own employees and those that should be obtained from suppliers. They can also help to assess how technology can improve the purchasing process.

Purchasing objectives also drive activities that are part of a purchaser's day-to-day responsibilities. For example, they must

- ensure that products and services are available when needed.
- develop purchasing policies and procedures.
- use purchasing practices that yield the best **value.**
- ensure on-time supplier payments and maintain appropriate supplier relationships.

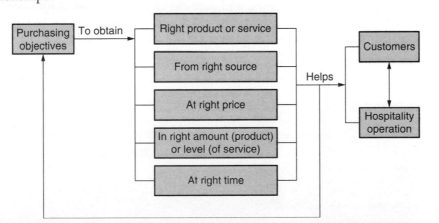

FIGURE 1.1 Purchasing Objectives

Buyer's Guide to Purchasing Term

Value   The relationship between the price paid to a supplier and (a) the quality of product or service received and (b) the usefulness of the information and service provided.

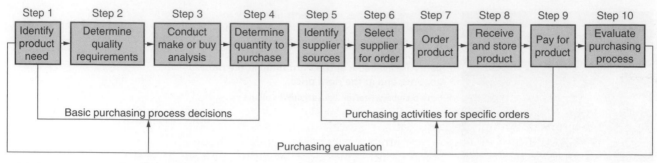

FIGURE 1.2   Steps in Effective Purchasing

STEPS IN PURCHASING PROCESS

Several steps are required for effective purchasing, and they are reviewed in Figure 1.2.

Let's review the purchasing steps outlined in Figure 1.2:

- *Step 1: Identify Product Need.*   Need is driven by what the customers want. If many guests visiting a hotel's bar request a particular "**call brand**" of liquor, it must be purchased. If the owner of a hotel has landscaping needs, this service must be purchased unless the employees can perform these tasks at the required level of quality and at an acceptable cost (see Step 3).
- *Step 2: Determine Quality Requirements.*   "**Quality**" considers how suitable a product or service is for its intended purpose. Ground beef can be purchased with different percentages of fat content, and it can be purchased fresh or frozen. Hotel owners can purchase window-washing services that provide all or part of their total needs, and as often as they wish to pay for them.
- *Step 3: Conduct Make or Buy Analysis.*   Some products can be prepared on-site or can be purchased partially or completely prepared. Should hamburger be purchased in bulk, then be portioned and shaped into patties by cooks, or should the product be purchased in a patty of specified weight? Decisions such as these must consider the availability of (1) alternatives, (2) quality concerns, and (3) costs.
- *Step 4: Determine Quantity to Purchase.*   Products can be purchased in large or small volumes, and services can be purchased for short or longer time periods. Important factors include available space and possibility of theft (for products), assessment of quality requirements (for services), and **cash flow** concerns.

Buyer's Guide to Purchasing Terms

Call brand (liquor)   A specific brand of liquor that is more expensive and of higher quality than other brands offered by the operation.

Quality   Suitability for intended use; the closer an item comes to being suitable for its intended use, the more appropriate is its quality.

Make or buy analysis   A process to determine whether products should be prepared on-site or be purchased from an external supply source. Sometimes called "Do/Buy Analysis" when services are analyzed.

Cash flow   The total amount of money received and spent by a business during a specific time period.

- *Step 5: Identify Supplier Sources.*   Hospitality purchasers often have several suppliers who can provide products and services. Their experience, supplier references, and "trial orders" with potential suppliers can help to determine a "short list" of those with whom orders will be placed.
- *Step 6: Select Supplier for Order.*   Which potential supplier (Step 5) should provide products/services? The answer depends, in part, on the type of purchasing system used. Supplier selection decisions may be based on best prices determined through **price quotations** for each specific order, or pricing may be established in long-term **contracts** that enable a supplier to provide products or services for several months (or longer) at a price agreed upon before the first delivery is made.
- *Step 7: Order Product.*   Products can be ordered after the proper quality and quantity are known (Steps 2 and 4) and after the supplier has been selected (Step 6). Legal concerns, the possible need for **expediting** to ensure on-time delivery, and confirmation that services meet the buyer's expectations then become important.
- *Step 8: Receive and Store Product.*   Products must be delivered, and services must be provided. Procedures must ensure that the proper quality and quantity of products and services are delivered, and products must be properly stored to minimize quality or theft problems. Record-keeping tasks applicable to product storage are needed.
- *Step 9: Pay for Product.*   The timing of payments, concerns about fraud as payments are processed, and basic accounting concerns to identify and assign costs to the specific operating departments that incur them become important when payments are made.
- *Step 10: Evaluate Purchasing Process.*   Evaluation is useful to ensure that each step in the purchasing process is done correctly. This concern applies to the way that basic purchasing process decisions are made (Steps 1–4) and to activities undertaken for specific orders (Steps 5–9).

The purchasing overview just described drives the discussion of purchasing management in this book. Specifically, you will learn about the first three steps of

The manager, chef, and others responsible for purchasing at this small restaurant must never forget about the guests being served when purchasing decisions are made.

Colin Sinclair © Dorling Kindersley

Buyer's Guide to Purchasing Terms

Price quotation   A request made to a supplier for the current price of a product or service meeting the property's quality requirements.

Contract   An agreement made between two or more parties that is enforceable in a court of law.

Expedite   Following up on both product orders to ensure timely delivery and service contracts to ensure compliance with their terms.

Buyers at Work (1.1)

"The way I see it, we lose regardless of what we do!" said Kendrick to Molly.

"Yes, I agree," replied Molly as they chatted during a fast lunch break at the Kansas Palms Restaurant.

Kendrick was the chef, and Molly was the head bartender at the busiest restaurant in town. They were reacting to their general manager's statements about the need for a more formalized purchasing system that moved beyond department heads purchasing what they wanted when they wanted it.

"We lose if we suggest that one person should purchase all items," said Kendrick, "because neither of us have time to educate a new purchasing manager about what we need and who the best suppliers are."

"Yes," said Molly, "and we also lose if we spend additional time in formalizing purchasing procedures. We know what products we need, what quality they should be, and whether we should make them or buy them. We know our best suppliers, and we know the procedures to receive and store items. Also, I'm worried about payment or accounting issues; that's the job of people in the office."

"Well," said Kendrick, "what should we do? Take on more work, lose control, or fight this new idea?"

1. What are the advantages and disadvantages to the Kansas Palms Restaurant continuing the existing purchasing system?
2. What are the advantages and disadvantages to the Kansas Palms Restaurant adopting a more formalized purchasing process such as that reviewed in Figure 1.2?
3. What should the restaurant manager do when he or she learns about possible resistance to revised purchasing procedures? (*Note:* Be sure to consider examples of compromise between the current and proposed systems.)

PROFESSIONAL PURCHASING PREVENTS PROBLEMS (1.1)

Time and Accuracy Concerns Must Be Addressed

A common problem: Purchasers are busy and cannot perform all required work.

In the not-too-distant past, the basic purchasing process involved a manual system with lots of paperwork, and inaccuracies caused many problems for buyers and their suppliers. For example, when additional products were needed, storeroom personnel sent a purchase requisition (paper) to alert the purchasing department. Purchasing staff then sent a Request for Price Quotation (paper) to eligible suppliers who responded (on paper) with their "best" price. A purchase order (on paper) was issued, and the supplier delivered products listed on a delivery invoice (paper). This moved from receiving or storeroom personnel to the purchasing and/or to accounting department with copies (paper) perhaps going to others in the user department. Then purchase orders (paper) were matched with delivery invoices (paper), and the payment (paper check) was prepared and mailed to the supplier.

As you'll learn, all the above and other buying tasks can be automated. It is no longer even necessary for storeroom personnel to prepare a paper list of items to be removed from inventory for issuing. Instead, notebook computers and/or other technologies allow this physical task to be automated.

The proper use of technology can reduce errors and increase the time that purchasers can use to provide creative (and less clerical) assistance to their employer.

purchasing (identify product need, determine quality requirements, and conduct make or buy analysis) in Chapter 2. In Chapter 3, you will learn about purchase quantity issues. Chapter 4 will explain Step 5 (identify supplier sources), and Chapter 5 will detail Steps 6 and 7 (select supplier for order and order product). Chapter 6 will conclude our discussion of purchasing management as it explains Steps 8, 9, and 10 (receive and store products, pay for products, and evaluate the purchasing process).

CLOSE LOOK AT PURCHASING TASKS

When products or services are purchased by large hospitality organizations, a **purchasing director, purchasing agent,** and/or other members of a purchasing department are needed. In small organizations, persons with numerous responsibilities not limited to purchasing will perform purchasing tasks.

Purchasing Volume Affects Purchasing Duties

Hotels with five hundred or more guest rooms will likely have a full-time purchasing director and, perhaps, clerical or other staff members who assist with the purchasing function. These and smaller properties also have clerical and accounting staff assigned to accounting and bill payment activities who assist with purchasing-related activities.

As hospitality organizations become larger, one or more purchasing agents may be needed. Multi-unit hospitality organizations may have specialized purchasing staff in district, regional, or other offices to help individual operating units with their purchasing activities. These organizations may use a **centralized purchasing system** in which purchasing requests are routed to those with specialized responsibilities who then assist property personnel with their purchasing needs.

Smaller, single-unit hospitality organizations typically use a **decentralized purchasing system.** Department heads become more responsible for each purchasing step, often with input and/or approval by the general manager, especially for high-value and/or large-quantity purchases.

Purchasing System Affects Purchasing Duties

Figure 1.3 reviews a possible purchasing process in a large hotel and identifies departments and personnel who may be involved.

Buyer's Guide to Purchasing Terms

Purchasing director   The top-level manager in a large hospitality organization who is responsible for the organization's purchasing function; also called purchasing manager.

Purchasing agent   A staff member in a large hospitality organization with responsibilities to purchase specific lines of products, services, supplies, or equipment; also called buyer.

Purchasing system (centralized)   A purchasing system in which all (or most) purchases are made by a purchasing agent for the entire organization.

Purchasing system (decentralized)   A purchasing system in which all (or most) purchases needed by a department are made by department heads or someone within their department who is designated to do so.

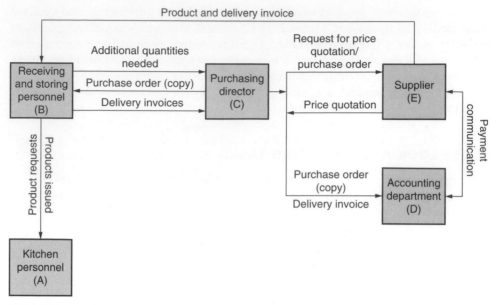

FIGURE 1.3   Purchasing Process in Large Hotel

Let's review Figure 1.3:

- **(Box A) Kitchen personnel.**   Kitchen personnel request required food products from receiving and storing personnel, who **issue** the products from the central storage area.
- **(Box B) Receiving and storing personnel.**   These employees inform the purchasing director (Box C) when additional product quantities are required to maintain inventory levels. They also receive incoming product deliveries from the suppliers and route the applicable **delivery invoices** to the purchasing director.
- **(Box C) Purchasing director.**   Purchasing directors serve in a **staff position** as technical "purchasing experts," and they assist persons in user departments who are in **line positions.**

  When additional products must be purchased, the purchasing director requests price quotations from suppliers, makes the supplier selection decision,

Buyer's Guide to Purchasing Terms

Issue (product)   The task of transferring products from storage areas to user departments so user personnel can meet production needs.

Delivery invoice   A document signed by a representative of the hospitality operation when products are delivered to transfer product ownership from the supplier to the property.

Staff position   Organizational roles (positions) occupied by technical, advisory specialists such as purchasing agents who provide advice to, but who do not make decisions for, those in the chain of command.

Line position   Organizational roles (positions) occupied by decision makers in the chain of command. Line decision makers have authority that flows from one level of management to the next.

and places product orders. A copy of the **purchase order** is routed to the receiving and storing personnel for use during the receiving process, and a copy is also sent to the accounting department for later verification with the applicable delivery invoice.

- *(Box D) Accounting department.* The purchasing director notifies the accounting department that an order has been placed by routing a copy of the purchase order. When the order is received, the delivery invoice sent by receiving and storing personnel to the purchasing director is forwarded to the accounting personnel. Processing (matching) purchase order and delivery invoice documents, making payments to the suppliers, and administering other purchasing, record-keeping, and related tasks are additional examples of the accounting function.

- *(Box E) Supplier.* The supplier normally works with all property personnel involved in the ordering process except those in the user department (kitchen). (*Note:* Supplier representatives may interact directly with foodservice personnel when, for example, they provide information about product use and address problems applicable to the items they sell.) Suppliers send information to the purchasing director in response to a request for price quotation and, if they receive the order, delivery personnel transport products to the property and unload them for receiving and storing personnel. Suppliers also interact with accounting staff as payment and record-keeping processes evolve.

There can be many variations of the process outlined in Figure 1.3. For example, the chef and/or food and beverage director may communicate directly with the purchasing director, and receiving and storing personnel may route copies of delivery invoices to the chef and/or food and beverage director before

Buyers at Work (1.2)

"Bad news!" said Jacelyn, the general manager, as she met with the department heads at the Broad Beach Hotel. "We're over budget in almost every category of expenses, and we must cut costs. We can't do much about our rent and taxes, but we can reduce the costs of what we purchase. How can we do more with less? We can begin by reducing purchasing costs. Be creative and consider the use of less expensive items, and I've asked Henry to try to get better deals from our suppliers."

After the meeting, Sandy, the executive housekeeper, talked to Henry, the purchasing director.

"Henry, you're under pressure to get us out of this financial mess by saving money, huh?"

"Yes, Sandy, and I'll do what I can. However, purchase costs are only one thing. I can buy products at a reasonable cost, but if they are not used correctly, inexpensive products can become costly. Resolving our financial problems must be a team effort; I can't do it all by myself."

1. How should a product's quality be considered when there is an emphasis on purchase cost?
2. How can Henry work with each department head to determine what products are required and how to ensure that correct quantities are purchased?
3. If the hotel's expenses remain high, how can the management staff determine whether the "problem" rests with the purchasing department, the user departments, or both?

Buyer's Guide to Purchasing Term

Purchase order A document used to obtain prices from suppliers, and to inform suppliers whose price proposal is accepted that a shipment should be delivered.

Did You Know? (1.1)

Effective purchasing requires that many activities be undertaken and performed correctly. Each is necessary and is required regardless of the organization's business volume and number of employees. Persons such as a department head in a small hotel property or a restaurant's owner/manager will likely need to assume purchasing responsibilities in addition to operating duties that in a larger property would be done by one or more persons in specialized purchasing positions. The old saying "Hospitality managers are very busy" is correct and, in small properties, they often perform a wider variety of tasks than do managers in larger properties with more specialized positions.

they are sent to the purchasing director. Additional copies of one or more purchasing documents may be routed to an external entity, such as a regional purchasing office in multi-unit organizations. Also, all, some, or none of the above steps may be accomplished electronically with little or no face-to-face or hard-copy communication being necessary.

Purchasers working for small chain organizations may combine product order requirements from each unit, obtain price quotations, select suppliers, and arrange for product delivery to the individual properties.

What Does a Purchaser Do?

Figure 1.4 shows an extensive list of tasks that might be included in a **job description** for a purchasing director. Someone (or several persons) in small operations without a full-time purchasing specialist must do most, if not all, of these tasks.

Did You Know? (1.2)

Wise purchasers ask for, require, use, and are willing to pay for the information they receive from their suppliers. They prefer suppliers who are experts in the products and services they sell, and they know the cost of supplier information is one element in the price they pay for products and services. They also know the limitations of their responsibilities.

Assume that a property's wine merchant (supplier) informs the buyer that the price of several wines will be increasing and there is an advantage to purchasing in larger-than-usual quantities to take advantage of the current lower prices.

Purchasers should not participate in **speculative purchasing.** They may not know about their organization's cash flow (Does it have funds to pay for additional wine purchases?) or even about forthcoming menu changes that may influence wine preferences of the customers. The best purchasers inform the appropriate manager about the pending price increases, so the manager can make a decision about larger-than-usual quantity purchases. This is in line with the role of a staff purchasing specialist who provides advice to, but does not make decisions for, line managers.

Buyer's Guide to Purchasing Terms

Job description   A list of tasks performed by an employee working in a specific position.

Speculative purchasing   The act of determining the quantities of products to purchase based on forecasted future prices. If prices will be increasing, larger quantities of items may be ordered. If prices will be decreasing, smaller quantities with more frequent deliveries may be purchased.

- Identifies potential suppliers.
- Selects suppliers; negotiates prices and contract terms.
- Coordinates the purchase of products, services, equipment, and supplies.
- Reviews purchase requisitions (requests for product purchases).
- Communicates with suppliers to obtain product or service information including price, availability, and delivery schedules.
- Selects products for purchase after testing, observing or tasting, and examining items.
- Estimates product prices using knowledge of current market prices.
- Determines purchase method such as direct purchase or bid.
- Prepares purchase orders or bid requests.
- Reviews suppliers' price proposals and negotiates contracts within scope of authority.
- Maintains manual or computerized purchasing records, as necessary.
- Discusses defective or unacceptable goods or services with property personnel and suppliers to determine problem and to take corrective action.
- Approves invoices for payment.
- Expedites delivery of products to users.
- Recommends improvements in overall purchasing procedures.

- Determines correct purchase quantities.
- Analyzes changes in customer demand.
- Keeps current with suppliers to forecast costs and availability of required products.
- Meets with managers to establish **bartering** requirements and specific purchasing guidelines.
- Interacts with distribution channel members to determine best supply sources.
- Stays informed about new product developments.
- Develops and monitors purchasing department's budget.
- Manages purchasing policies and procedures, systems, best practices, and goals for the purchasing department.
- Reviews, revises, and maintains product purchase specifications.
- Evaluates competitive bids.
- Ensures that all purchasing files are kept current, complete, and available.
- Resolves supplier problems.
- Maintains supplier handbook and vendor information.
- Establishes and maintains proper supplier relationships.
- Interacts with property managers and suppliers to establish, improve, and maintain electronic purchasing systems.
- Assists in the training of property personnel about purchasing procedures.

FIGURE 1.4   Possible Job Description Tasks for Purchasing Director

Meat items are expensive and require special purchasing attention. Yield testing helps buyers determine the quality standards for the meat products they order from their suppliers.

Vincent P. Walter/Pearson Education/PH College

Buyer's Guide to Purchasing Term

Bartering   A business transaction in which goods or services are exchanged for other goods and/or services without money changing hands.

Buyer's Guide to Internet Resources: Introduction to Purchasing

Web Site	Topic
www.hotel-online.com	Hotel purchasing (Type "hotel purchasing" in the search box.)
www.ofee.gov/gp/gp.asp	Green (environmentally friendly) purchasing (Enter **"green purchasing"** in the site's search box.)
www.nfib.com	The National Federation of Independent Businesses (Enter "purchasing" in site's search box.)
www.careeroverview.com	Career information for purchasing managers (Click on "Management" then "Purchasing Manager.")
www.looksmart.com	Access to hundreds of purchasing articles (Enter "purchasing" in the site's "find" box.)
www.mcdonalds.com/usa/good/products.html	The concept of "responsible purchasing" as practiced by McDonald's Corporation.
www.eatec.com	Purchasing Technology Systems
www.ishp.org	International Society of Hospitality Purchasers

REGULATORY CONCERNS AFFECT PURCHASING

There are several U.S. federal agencies that issue rules and regulations that buyers and sellers must follow. Also, Congress itself has passed laws that affect the purchasing process. Various states and some local governments also have agencies and regulations related to purchasing. In this section you'll learn about some of the most important of these regulatory organizations and how they affect purchasing.

Role of Federal Agencies

FEDERAL TRADE COMMISSION (FTC)   When Congress created the FTC in 1914, its purpose was to prevent unfair competition in commerce. In 1938 Congress passed a broad prohibition against "unfair and deceptive acts or practices." Since then, the FTC has begun to administer a wide variety of other consumer protection laws. All hospitality buyers should be familiar with the FTC because one of its current responsibilities involves truthful advertising. If, for example, a hospitality buyer purchases "Colorado" trout for a restaurant that advertises this menu item, the FTC is responsible for ensuring that the buyer selects, and the restaurant serves, trout that is from Colorado. To serve trout from another location would be a deceptive and illegal trade practice.

FOOD AND DRUG ADMINISTRATION (FDA)   Formed in 1906, the FDA is an agency of the U.S. Department of Health and Human Services. It is responsible

---

Buyer's Guide to Purchasing Term

Green purchasing   The placement of purchasing priority not only on price and quality, but also on a product's affect on the environment.

These guests looking at a menu are learning that the restaurant serves fresh Gulf of Mexico shrimp. Purchasers must take care to ensure that, in fact, fresh Gulf of Mexico shrimp are purchased.

Picture Press/Corbis/Bettmann

for regulating food, dietary supplements, and other products to ensure the safety of the American public and the effectiveness of marketed foods. Its regulations can include bans of items considered unsafe. The FDA has the broad authority to ensure that the foods and beverages sold in the United States are safe, wholesome, and truthfully labeled.

U.S. DEPARTMENT OF AGRICULTURE (USDA)   The original purpose of the USDA was to meet the needs of American farmers and ranchers, but over the years, it responsibilities have expanded. For example, the USDA Food Safety and Inspection Service ensures that all meat, poultry, and processed egg products are safe to consume and accurately labeled. As you will learn in later chapters, the USDA and its inspection and food grading programs play a very important role in the marketing and purchasing of many food products used in the hospitality industry.

ENVIRONMENTAL PROTECTION AGENCY (EPA)   The EPA protects human health and safeguards the environment. It sets several standards related to food. One is enforcement of the Food Quality Protection Act that limits the type and amount of pesticides used in food for human consumption.

OCCUPATIONAL SAFETY AND HEALTH ADMINISTRATION (OSHA)   This agency is part of the U.S. Department of Labor. It prevents work-related injuries, illnesses, and deaths by issuing and enforcing rules (standards) for workplace safety and health. Among the changes in safety regulation brought about by OSHA are several that affect equipment purchases for hospitality employees:

- Guards on all moving parts: Guards to prevent contact with equipment blades such as those on food slicers and meat saws are required whenever contact is possible.
- Personal protective equipment (PPE): The use of gloves, coveralls, and other protective equipment when handling hazardous chemicals and blood is required by OSHA.
- Lockout/tagout: OSHA has developed requirements for locking out energy sources in an "off" condition when equipment repair or maintenance is performed.
- Hazard communication: This rule requires that employees receive information about the hazards of chemical products used in the workplace.

• Blood-borne pathogens: OSHA has issued a standard designed to prevent hotel, health-care, and other workers from being exposed to **blood-borne pathogens** such as **hepatitis B** and HIV (the AIDS-causing virus).

INTERNAL REVENUE SERVICE (IRS)   The IRS works with the Bureau of Alcohol, Tobacco, and Firearms (ATF) to regulate the production and sale of alcoholic beverages in the United States. The IRS has administrative oversight of alcohol sales, and it requires alcoholic beverage sellers to follow tax laws by identifying unreported income and monitoring product usage (costs) and unreported tip income. These activities affect purchasing because it is necessary to develop record-keeping systems that ensure compliance with tax payments and to select **revenue**-recording systems that confirm actual **sales** levels.

BUREAU OF ALCOHOL, TOBACCO, AND FIREARMS (ATF)   The ATF controls the production, labeling, and advertising of alcohol and the relationships among **producers, wholesalers,** and **retailers.** The agency's efforts are directed mainly at protecting consumers against products that are impure, mislabeled, or otherwise potentially harmful.

Other federal agencies and departments also affect the purchasing process. However, even with all the oversight and assistance, professional buyers must use their own judgment and knowledge and recognize that the philosophy of **caveat emptor** remains important.

The Uniform Commercial Code

The **Uniform Commercial Code (UCC)** is not a federal law. Instead, it is an effort by the individual states to standardize commercial laws across their borders. Its necessity becomes clear when, for example, a buyer in one state purchases food items grown in another state that are manufactured in yet another state from a seller located in still another state. The UCC, in its entirety, has been adopted in forty-nine states (Louisiana has enacted most, but not all, UCC provisions), the District of Columbia, Puerto Rico, Guam, and the U.S. Virgin Islands.

The UCC requires that a supplier sell only goods that are fit for their intended use and that are free of defects. This means, for example, that a food-service buyer selecting a food product can be assured the product is wholesome

---

Buyer's Guide to Purchasing Terms

Blood-borne pathogens   Disease-causing microorganisms (germs) that are transmitted by blood.

Hepatitis   A liver disease caused by a virus that attacks the liver.

Revenue   Money generated from the sale of products and services.

Sales   Number of units (such as a specific type of sandwich or number of drinks) that are sold to guests.

Producer   One who manufacturers a product.

Wholesaler   One who sells products to retailers; see *retailer*.

Retailer   One who sells products to end users (consumers).

Caveat emptor   Latin for "Let the Buyer Beware"; the commercial principle that the buyer must check the quality and suitability of goods before purchasing them.

Uniform Commercial Code (UCC)   A model set of laws regulating commercial transactions, including banking and credit, but especially those related to the sale of goods.

Did You Know? (1.3)

Food labeling (including the current interest in labeling restaurant menu items) is of concern to federal legislators and regulators. A history of some important food-labeling legislation includes the following:

1906—The Federal Food and Drugs Act and the Federal Meat Inspection Act authorized the federal government to regulate the safety and quality of food.

1913—The Gould Amendment required food packages to state the quantity of their contents.

1938—The Federal Food, Drug, and Cosmetic Act replaced the 1906 Food and Drugs Act. Among other things, it required the label of every processed, packaged food to contain the name of the food, its net weight, and the name and address of the manufacturer or distributor.

1957—The Poultry Products Inspection Act authorized the USDA to regulate, among other things, the labeling of poultry products.

1969—The White House Conference on Food, Nutrition, and Health addressed deficiencies in the American diet. It recommended that the federal government consider developing a system to identify the nutritional qualities of food.

1973—The FDA issued regulations to require nutrition labeling on food containing one or more added nutrients or whose label or advertising includes claims about the food's nutritional properties.

1990—The FDA proposed extensive food-labeling changes, including required nutrition labeling for most foods, standardized serving sizes, and uniform use of health claims.

2003—Mandatory nutritional labeling of nearly all foods was required.

and safe to eat. Likewise, equipment advertised to be suitable for brewing coffee should do so in a way that does not endanger its operator or the consumers of the coffee.

You will learn later in this chapter and in others that the UCC governs many important aspects of buyer-seller relationships.

State and Local Legislation

There are many state and local laws, ordinances, codes, and rules related to the buying and selling of food and beverages and other hospitality services. Also, state and local governmental agencies often work cooperatively with federal agencies to influence the buying process. For example, the federal government develops food safety and consumer protection programs that require an inspection and testing program for food processing plants, food storage, and food distribution points. Generally, these businesses must first be **licensed** by the state in which they are located to demonstrate compliance with sanitation and related requirements.

These facilities are then regularly inspected to ensure continuing compliance with established standards.

Other consumer protection issues are often part of each state's inspection activity. For example, packaged foods are test-weighed to verify net contents; ground beef is tested for fat content and extenders; labels are reviewed for the

Buyer's Guide to Purchasing Term

License   A legal document that allows one to operate a business or provide a service.

PROFESSIONAL PURCHASING PREVENTS PROBLEMS (1.2)

Menus Must Be Labeled Accurately

A common problem: Nutrition-related information on menus is not accurate.

Foodservice operators must understand the highly technical use of words that are used to describe menu items. Examples are the terms *free, low,* and *light:*

- *Free.* This term means that a product contains no (or only a trivial or inconsequential) amount of the item such as fat, saturated fat, cholesterol, sodium, sugar, and/or calories that it is describing. For example, *calorie-free* means fewer than 5 calories per serving, and *sugar-free* and *fat-free* both mean less than 0.5 grams (g) per serving. Words meaning *free* include *without, no,* and *zero. Skim* means the same as fat-free milk.
- *Low.* This term can be used to describe foods that can be eaten frequently without exceeding dietary guidelines for fat, saturated fat, cholesterol, sodium, and/or calories. Descriptions of *low* include the following:

  Low-fat: 3 g or less per serving
  Low-saturated fat: 1 g or less per serving
  Low-sodium: 140 mg or less per serving
  Very low sodium: 35 mg or less per serving
  Low-cholesterol: 20 mg or less and 2 g or less of saturated fat per serving
  Low-calorie: 40 calories or less per serving

Words meaning *low* include *little, few, low source of,* and *contains a small amount of.*

- *Light.* This word has two meanings:

  That a nutritionally changed product contains one-third fewer calories or half the fat of the reference food. If 50 percent or more of a food's calories are from fat, the reduction must be 50 percent of the fat.

  That the sodium content of a low-calorie, low-fat food has been reduced by 50 percent. In addition, *light in sodium* may be used to describe a food in which the sodium content has been reduced by at least 50 percent.

Note: The term *light* still can be used to describe a food's texture and color, as long as the word explains the intent. Examples: "light brown sugar," "light and fluffy"

---

honesty of the statements that are made; and eggs, bottled water, and many other food products are inspected to ensure purity, grade, and the accuracy of informational labels. State agencies often work under contract with the FDA to manage these sanitation and production inspections.

The USDA also maintains cooperative grading agreements with the various state departments of agriculture and other state agencies. Federally licensed graders perform their work at product points of origin. For example, they work in the fields while a crop is being harvested and in wholesale terminal markets throughout the country.

Some states have passed laws that require state-specific inspection or grading programs. For example, the Florida Department of Citrus (FDOC) protects and enhances the quality and reputation of Florida citrus fruit and processed citrus products.

Hospitality buyers must keep up to date on state and local legislation affecting the buying process. Active membership in a state restaurant, lodging, or other industry trade association and ongoing review of the information they supply is a good way to learn about state rules and regulations.

PURCHASING CONTRACTS

The agreements made between buyers and sellers are called *contracts,* and professional buyers should have a good working knowledge about the basics of these documents, which specify the terms of their product orders with suppliers.

Not every agreement between two parties is a contract because legally enforceable contracts must have specific components. To help minimize disagreements about the specifics of a contract, key contract terms should be directly and clearly addressed. In this section of the chapter you will learn about the following:

- Types of contracts
- Elements in legal contracts
- Important contract terms and clauses
- Product warranties

Types of Contracts

Contracts and the laws that affect them have been established to ensure that all parties to an agreement understand exactly what they have agreed or promised to do. Contracts may be established either in writing or orally. Written contracts are usually preferred because it is easier to establish the responsibilities of each party. Time can cause memories to fade; representatives may leave their jobs and be replaced with new staff members; and honest recollections, even among the most well-intentioned parties, can differ.

Many hospitality agreements are, however, made orally and are enforceable by the courts. When the buyer for a night club telephones a beverage supplier and orders five cases of beer, an enforceable contract is established. The buyer agrees to pay for the beer when delivered, just as the vendor agrees to deliver the product. Similarly, if a restaurant manager is required by local law to have the fire-suppression system above the deep-fat fryers inspected twice a year, the agreement to do so may not be committed to writing each time an inspection is made. In fact, if the same company has performed the inspection for several years, the inspection company, rather than the restaurant manager, may decide on the exact date of the inspection to efficiently schedule its staff. In that case, the presence of the inspector, access to the facility, an invoice for services performed, and a written inspection report submitted after completion of the job are indications that an oral or written inspection agreement existed, even if there was no oral or written agreement for that specific inspection.

Buyers at Work (1.3)

Sam hired the area's most popular vocal and dance band to play at his hotel's New Year's Eve party. Tickets were $300.00 per couple and, due in part to the advertised entertainment, tickets quickly sold out.

One reason that the band was popular was the talented lead singer. Sam was stunned when, on the night of the party, the band's manager announced that the lead singer was ill and was being replaced by a singer unknown in the local area.

As Sam feared, many guests were disappointed because they could not hear the singer they had paid to see. Sam ended up refunding a large amount of money to satisfy the guests who had complained about the hotel's "false advertising."

At the end of the night, the band manager asked Sam for the band's full payment.

1. If you were Sam, would you want to pay the band the full amount you had agreed to when entering into the contract? Why or why not?
2. If this issue were heard by a court of law, which party (Sam or the band) do you think the judge would support? Why?
3. In the future, what can Sam do to avoid this type of problem?

Elements in Legal Contracts

Regardless of whether a contract is oral or written, it must include specific elements to be legally **enforceable.**

To be enforceable, a contract must be legally valid, and it must include an **offer, consideration,** and **acceptance.**

Not all agreements made between two or more parties are legally valid. If, for example, a restaurant buyer "agrees" to purchase an endangered species of animal for a menu item, the buyer would have no claim if the seller did not deliver the product. The reason is that courts will not enforce a contract that requires breaking a law to comply with it. Agreements to perform illegal acts are not enforceable. Therefore, to be enforceable, a contract must be made by parties who are legally old enough to make the contract, and the activities specified in the contract must not violate the law.

If a contract is valid, the first element in a legally enforceable contract is an offer. An offer precisely states what the offering party is willing to do and what he or she expects in return. The offer may include very specific instructions for how, where, when, and to whom the offer is made. The offer may include deadlines for acceptance. In addition, the offer will include the price or terms of the offer.

To illustrate, when a school foodservice director places a produce order, an offer is made. He or she offers to buy the products at the supplier's quoted price. The offer sets the terms and responsibilities of both parties. The offer states, "I will promise to do this, if you will promise to do that." Buyers should understand that the courts will enforce contracts that have clearly identifiable terms, even if those terms are heavily weighted in favor of one of the parties. Therefore, it is important to understand all terms of an offer before making or accepting it.

Consideration is the second essential element in an enforceable contract, and it is the part of the contract that identifies the value, payment, or cost. In a valid contract, each party must receive consideration. In the above example, the buyer's consideration is the produce and the seller's consideration is the price charged for the products.

Consideration does not need to be money. Assume that a hospitality buyer agrees to host an employee party for a newspaper in exchange for the newspaper providing free advertising. In this example, the restaurant's consideration is hosting the party, and the newspaper's consideration is the advertising. **Trade-outs** are relatively common in the hospitality industry.

Courts are concerned that consideration exists but not its size. A meat supplier may sell a steak for $1.00, $10.00, or even $100.00. The buyer can agree or not agree with the supplier's price. As long as both parties to a valid contract agree, the amount of consideration is not generally a concern of the court. Buyers who willingly agree to "pay too much" for something will not later find courts willing to side with their complaint if the seller delivers the agreed-upon product or service.

Buyer's Guide to Purchasing Terms

Enforceable (contract)   A contract recognized by the courts as valid and subject to the court's ability to require compliance with its terms.

Offer   A proposal to perform an act or to pay an amount that, if accepted, becomes a legally valid contract.

Consideration   The payment made in exchange for the promise(s) in a contract.

Acceptance   Agreement to the exact terms and conditions of a specific offer.

Trade-out   An agreement between two businesses in which the contract's consideration is not cash.

Did You Know? (1.4)

In the hospitality industry, legal *acceptance* of a contract may be established several ways:

- *Oral or nonverbal.* In its simplest form, the acceptance of an offer can be done orally, with a handshake, or even with a "yes" nod of one's head.
- *Acceptance of full or partial payment.* To replace a hot water heater in a restaurant, a supplier requires "one-half the price down upon acceptance." The offer of the buyer's deposit would indicate that the buyer accepted the price and the supplier's terms.
- *Agreement in writing.* The best way to indicate acceptance of an offer is usually by agreeing to the offer in writing. When the sum of money involved is substantial, contracts should normally be confirmed in writing.

A legal offer and its consideration made by one party must be clearly accepted (the third contract element) before the contract comes into existence. The acceptance must exactly duplicate the terms of the offer for the contract to be valid. Otherwise, it is a counteroffer (which will yield a new contract) rather than an acceptance. When acceptance mirrors the offer made, an **express contract** has been created.

An offer may be accepted orally or in writing; however, it must be clear that the offer's terms were accepted. For example, a contractor who offers to change the light bulbs on an outdoor hotel sign cannot merely quote a price then proceed to complete the job without a clear form of contract acceptance by the property's authorized purchaser.

Contract Terms and Clauses

Following are some important contractual terms and clauses that buyers should review carefully to help ensure that they understand the obligations they will assume:

- *Payment terms.* Required down payments, dates for partial payments, interest rates on remaining balances, payment due dates, and penalties for late payments are among the important terms that should be clearly specified in the contract and reviewed carefully by the buyer.
- *Delivery (or start) dates.* For some delivery dates, a range of times may be acceptable. For example, food and beverage deliveries might be accepted by a kitchen manager "between the hours of 8:00 a.m. and 4:00 p.m." Sometimes the delivery or start date may be unknown. For example, replacement parts for old equipment may no longer be available and must be custom-made when needed. Then the supplier may state that the repair will be made when the replacement parts become available.
- *Completion or end date.* This is needed to indicate when contract terms end. If a painter is hired to paint a dining room, this date identifies when the painter's work should be finished. If the contract is written to guarantee a price for a product purchased by a restaurant, the end date is the last day that price will be honored by the supplier.
- *Performance standards.* These refer to the quality of products or services received. This can be a complex area because quality can be difficult to measure. The thickness of asphalt paving concrete is easily specified. However, the quality of an advertising campaign is more difficult to evaluate.

Buyer's Guide to Purchasing Term

Express contract   A contract in which the elements of the agreement are clearly understood and stated, either orally or in writing.

- *Licenses and permits.*   These may be required for contracted work and should be the responsibility of the product or service supplier. Trade persons such as carpenters and electricians, who must be licensed or certified by state or local governments, should be prepared to prove they have required credentials. The buyer should require verification.
- *Timing of ownership transfer.*   Buyers normally assume ownership of goods when they are delivered in good condition and are accepted by the buyer's representative. Sometimes, however, transfer of title can take place at a different time. For example, international goods must pass through many parts of the distribution channel before being delivered to the buyer. If buyers assume ownership before product delivery, terms should be clearly spelled out and agreed upon.
- *Indemnification (if applicable).*   Accidents can happen while a contract is being fulfilled. For example, a supplier's vehicle may injure a person while making a delivery. Buyers should ensure, in writing, that their organization will be **indemnified** by the seller's organization.

    While it is important for all contract clauses to be reviewed by a competent adviser, an indemnification clause should be written (or reviewed) by a qualified attorney.
- *Nonperformance clauses.*   Buyers should decide what the two contracting parties will do if the contract terms are not fulfilled. In the case of purchasing products and services, the best solution may be for the buyer to buy from a different vendor.
- *Dispute resolution terms.*   It may be a good idea for contracting parties to agree in advance about how to settle any disputes that may arise. If a contract is between two parties from different states, contract language can specify the laws of the state in which the contract will be governed.

Product Warranties

The promises, or **warranties,** made by a seller can influence the buyer.

Purchasers must ensure that they understand the terms of all contracts into which they enter. If they do not, expensive and time-consuming lawsuits can result.

© Royalty-Free/CORBIS

Buyer's Guide to Purchasing Terms

Indemnify   To reimburse for a loss.

Warranty   A promise made by a seller about a product that is a legal part of a contract.

Before finalizing the purchase of products or services, wise buyers determine what warranties, if any, are included in the purchase. Because a warranty is part of the contract, it is important to ensure that any warranties offered orally are documented in writing.

Warranties can be either expressed or implied. An **expressed warranty** is created when a manufacturer, salesperson, or sales literature makes a statement of fact about the capabilities and/or qualities of a product or service. Example: "This dishwasher uses six gallons of water for each rinse cycle." Then that seller is legally required to deliver a product that does what has been expressed (use six gallons of water during the machine's rinse cycle).

You should recall that the Uniform Commercial Code requires that every product sold must be fit for its use and free of defects. Therefore, even if a seller does not specifically claim that products are to be free of defects, a buyer would expect that a product would be fit for consumption (if a food or beverage) or in good working order (if equipment or machinery). This unwritten expectation is called an **implied warranty.**

Products sold in the United States must generally conform to two implied warranties: the item is fit to be used for a particular purpose and the item will be in good working order and meet the purposes for which it was purchased.

Sellers can disclaim expressed or implied warranties by inserting applicable language into their sales contracts, but these statements must be in writing and must be agreed to by both parties.

PROFESSIONAL PURCHASING PREVENTS PROBLEMS (1.3)

Be Sure to Obtain the Best Warranty Coverage

A common problem: Many hospitality buyers fail to negotiate additional or extended warranties before making a purchase.

Purchasers should attempt to negotiate the longest, strongest, and most comprehensive warranty possible, and they should always insist that the warranty be in writing. Specific warranty-related questions that buyers should ask sellers include the following:

- How long is the warranty?
- When does the warranty begin?
- Will the warranty include the charges for any parts and/or labor required to make needed repairs?
- Are any parts of the purchase not covered by the warranty?
- Is the warranty in force if we do not follow the manufacturer's guidelines for routine service and maintenance?
- Who can perform routine service and maintenance requirements?
- Who pays the charges to deliver the defective product to the repair location and to return it to the hospitality operation?

Buyer's Guide to Purchasing Terms

Expressed warranty   A stated promise about a product or service that is a legal part of a contract.

Implied warranty   An unstated promise about a product that is always a legal part of the sales contract.

Buyer's Guide to Internet Resources: Legal

Web Site	Topic
www.fda.gov	U.S. Food and Drug Administration
www.usda.gov	U.S. Department of Agriculture
www.fsis.usda.gov	Food Safety and Inspection Service (U.S. Department of Agriculture)
www.osha.gov	U.S. Occupational Safety and Health Administration
www.atf.treas.gov	U.S. Bureau of Alcohol, Tobacco, and Firearms
www.law.cornell.edu/ucc/ucc.table.html	Uniform Commercial Code
www.smallbusiness.findlaw.com	Contract-related standard business forms
www.businessnation.com/library/forms	Free contract clause language
www.answers.com/topic/implied-warranty	Implied warranties

ETHICAL CONCERNS AFFECT PURCHASING

Some people believe that any activity that is not illegal is legal and, therefore, acceptable. However, professional buyers understand that an activity may be legal but still wrong. They know the difference between legality and **ethics.**

Ethical Actions Are Needed

Ethical behavior is that which society considers the "right thing to do." Purchasers who act ethically may avoid legal problems when they do not know exactly what the law requires. If their actions are ever questioned, a review about the ethics of their behavior will be likely.

While it is sometimes difficult to determine what behavior is (and is not) ethical, six guidelines (questions) can be of help. We'll illustrate them in the following story.

Susan is the purchasing director for a hotel planning a party for which a large amount of wine and champagne is needed, and she places the order with a single supplier. One week later, a case of expensive champagne is delivered to her home with a letter of thanks and a statement hoping for much future business. Before Susan decides to keep the gift, she should ask herself the following six questions:

1. *Is it legal?* It may not be an illegal act for Susan to accept the champagne. However, there could be state liquor laws that prohibit suppliers from giving gifts of alcoholic beverages. Also, her employer (the hotel) may have a gift-acceptance policy that limits the value of gifts that can be accepted, and a violation may lead to disciplinary action or termination. If so, accepting the gift might be considered "illegal" from her company's perspective.

   Assuming there is no law and/or hotel policy about the gift, the second question becomes important.

2. *Does it hurt anyone?* Susan can drink the champagne without personal harm. However, will she show favoritism to this supplier when she considers future suppliers' bids (Can she remain fair and objective?), or will she think about the free champagne she received? If she cannot be objective, her employer may be harmed if the prices are higher than those of other suppliers

Buyer's Guide to Purchasing Term

Ethics The proper conduct of individuals as they interact with others based on their own moral principles.

bidding on the same quality of products. If she does think she can make objective decisions, the third question should be considered.

3. *Is acceptance of the gift fair and honest?*   How might others feel about the gift of free champagne? Fairness dictates that Susan should consider whether the benefit helps the hotel or her. Does she really think she can remain objective and continue to search for the best quality of alcoholic beverages at the best price when she has been rewarded for her choice and may be again? If Susan believes she can, question four becomes important.

4. *Would I care if it happened to me?*   If Susan owned the hotel and knew that a manager had accepted this gift, would she question the manager? Would she like all managers to receive gifts? If she would not be concerned if she were the owner, Susan should consider question five.

5. *Would I publicize my action?*   In many cases this is the most important question. Would Susan keep the champagne if she knew that tomorrow morning the headlines of her city's or company's newspaper would read: *Purchasing Director Receives Free Case of Expensive Champagne After Placing Large Order with Supplier?* If Susan believes her action could be publicized without harm to her reputation, she should then think about the last question.

6. *What if everyone did it?*   Susan should next consider whether the process will ever stop. What if the executive housekeeper received a personal set of towels whenever she ordered new terry products for the hotel? Would (should) Susan receive a new television whenever she ordered them for the hotel?

After your consideration of the above questions, you probably agree that it is unethical (even if it is legal) for Susan to keep the champagne. Instead, she could do one of the following:

- Return it with a note stating her appreciation but indicating the hotel's (or her own) policy about accepting gifts.
- Ask her boss about the best action to take.
- Give the gift to the general manager to be placed into the normal beverage inventory (if allowed by local liquor laws).
- Donate the champagne for the hotel's employee holiday party.

Buyers at Work (1.4)

Ronald is the VP of operations for a multi-unit, quick-service restaurant chain and supervises three regional vice presidents, each of whom is responsible for approximately fifty stores. The organization has just implemented a supervisory training program built around several key principles that are emphasized in a training CD sold by a trade association. Ronald has requested that his regional vice presidents ask each of the unit managers to purchase a CD for the new training effort.

One of the regional VPs pointed out that the cost of buying all the CDs would be pretty significant. His suggestion: "Let's just buy one copy, and then we can duplicate it for each unit manager. We'll save thousands of dollars, and besides, we are a member of the association. In effect, they work for us, and the association certainly has more money than we do."

Assume you were Ronald:

1. Would you allow the CD to be purchased and duplicated for use at each unit? Defend your answer.

2. Assume that the action suggested were not illegal (although it probably is), and that the duplication was not likely to be detected by the association. Use the six-step questioning process introduced in this chapter. As a result of this process, do you think the proposed action is ethical? Why or why not?

3. Do you think Ronald should be concerned about the regional VP who made this suggestion? What might Ronald think about him or her?

Purchasing Code of Ethics

Objective:

The objective of this purchasing code of ethics is to ensure that purchasers do not use their position for personal gain and will, at all times, enhance the standing and reputation of the company.

To achieve this objective, purchasers will do the following:

1. Make all decisions based on the company's financial objectives and operating policies.
2. Attempt to obtain maximum value for the purchasing dollars that are spent.
3. Decline all personal gifts or gratuities.
4. Grant all competitive suppliers equal consideration based on their abilities and the company's benefits.
5. Conduct business with suppliers in an atmosphere of good faith, without intentional misrepresentation, and in keeping with all laws.
6. Demand honesty in suppliers' oral statements, advertisements, and product samples.
7. Make every reasonable effort to negotiate a mutually agreeable settlement for any supplier controversy.
8. When possible, provide a prompt and courteous reception for all salespersons who call on the company for legitimate business purposes.
9. Cooperate with trade and professional associations to promote and develop ethical business practices.
10. Counsel and guide the organization's buyers to uphold this purchasing code of ethics.

Presented By: *Read and Agreed to By:*

_____   _____

(Company official)   Purchaser

_____   _____

Date   Date

FIGURE 1.5   Sample Purchasing Code of Ethics

Purchasing Codes of Ethics

Some hospitality organizations have developed purchasing codes of ethics to provide guidelines for their buyers. Experienced purchasers know that the temptation to consider unethical acts can be immense. Sometimes, unethical actions lead to even more serious and illegal activities that can subject the buyer to imprisonment. To help purchasers avoid this temptation and to provide consistency in ethical decision making, some hospitality organizations develop and implement buyers' codes of ethics. Figure 1.5 is an example.

Sometimes a company's ethical philosophy and/or purchasing code of ethics is included in the employee handbook. While it is important to follow applicable laws (see Point 5 in the sample purchasing code of ethics), laws do not exist that address every situation that buyers will encounter. Ethical behavior, however, is consistent and is important to the long-term success of professional hospitality purchasers.

Professional purchasers ensure that their relationships with suppliers are consistently ethical and in line with their employer's purchasing code of ethics.

Photodisc/Getty Images

Buyer's Guide to Internet Resources: Ethical Concerns

Web Site	Topic
www.ethics.org/resources/decision making model.asp	Steps in ethical decision making
www.josephsoninstitute.org/MED/medtoc.htm	Ethical decision making
www.ism.ws/tools/guides/guides28	Articles relating to purchasing ethics

Purchasing Terms

Procurement *2*
Purchasing *2*
Value *3*
Call brand (liquor) *4*
Quality *4*
Make or buy analysis *4*
Cash flow *4*
Price quotation *5*
Contract *5*
Expedite *5*
Purchasing director *7*
Purchasing agent *7*
Purchasing system
 (centralized) *7*

Purchasing system
 (decentralized) *7*
Issue (product) *8*
Delivery invoice *8*
Staff position *8*
Line position *8*
Purchase order *9*
Job description *10*
Speculative
 purchasing *10*
Bartering *11*
Green purchasing *12*

Blood-borne
 pathogens *14*
Hepatitis *14*
Revenue *14*
Sales *14*
Producer *14*
Wholesaler *14*
Retailer *14*
Caveat emptor *14*
Uniform Commercial
 Code (UCC) *14*
License *15*

Enforceable
 (contract) *18*
Offer *18*
Consideration *18*
Acceptance *18*
Trade-out *18*
Express contract *19*
Indemnify *20*
Warranty *20*
Expressed warranty *21*
Implied warranty *21*
Ethics *22*

Make Your Own Purchasing Decisions

1. Assume that you are the manager of a small restaurant with three departments: food production, dining room service, and beverage operations. How might you organize the purchasing function for your restaurant? In other words, "Who would do what?"
2. Assume that you are the manager of a very large restaurant. What would be the advantages to use of a centralized purchasing system? A decentralized system? Which type of system would you use? Why?
3. What are three examples of times when a hospitality buyer might best use a verbal (oral) contract rather than a written contract?
4. Many owners and managers in the hospitality (and other) industry believe there is too much government regulation and that excessive legislation hinders their ability to make the best decisions for their organizations. What is your opinion about the regulation of purchasing aspects of hospitality operations based on what you read in this chapter?
5. Do you think that all buyers in every unit of a large, multiunit organization should follow the same purchasing code of ethics? Explain your answer.

2

Determining Quality Requirements

Purchase Specifications and Make-Buy Analysis

The first step in purchasing is to determine products that are needed. While obvious (you can't purchase something until you know what it is), this step can be a challenge: the process must be customer focused, and some products can be purchased or made on-site. For example, if hamburgers are on the menu, patties of the correct weight can be purchased, or cooks can portion and shape bulk ground beef patties. This chapter begins with a discussion of product need and introduces the concept of quality concerns and purchasing decisions.

The old saying "You get what you pay for" is generally true in the world of professional purchasing. In Chapter 1 you learned that value (the relationship between price and quality) is a most important concern and, in this chapter, you will study how quality is addressed as purchase decisions are made.

Purchase specifications identify and explain the operation's quality requirements. When used, suppliers will know the desired product quality, and they can quote prices accordingly. While there may be legitimate factors that affect differences between suppliers' prices, quality variations should not be among them when specifications are used.

To be most helpful, purchase specifications should contain basic information. Purchasing staff (or those with these responsibilities in smaller organizations), user department employees who will use the products, and potential suppliers can all help to ensure that necessary information is addressed in specifications.

Early drafts of specifications should be reviewed and revised, as necessary, and trial orders can be placed to ensure that product descriptions reflect property needs. When the "specs" are ready for use, they should be circulated to potential suppliers who should then quote prices on and deliver products that meet the specifications' quality requirements. Details about the development and use of specifications are presented in this chapter.

As already suggested, sometimes purchasers can buy products that reduce the amount of on-site labor that is needed. Should they do so? Like most other purchasing concerns, there is no easy answer other than *"It all depends."* Several factors must be identified and carefully considered as product purchase or production alternatives are studied. A formal process called make or buy analysis can help with these decisions, and you will learn about it in this chapter.

■ ■ ■

Outline

ALL ABOUT QUALITY

Figure 2.1 (originally shown as Figure 1.2) indicates that the first step in the purchasing process is to identify product need. The second step relates to determining quality requirements for needed products, and the third step reminds us about the use of make or buy analysis. This figure is shown again to provide the context within which these three steps are be discussed in this chapter.

Purchase Products That Are Needed

Is it a waste of time to mention that products should not be purchased unless they are needed? If you have ever walked through a food-service storeroom and noticed dusty cases of products that have been stored a long time, you would know that these items were purchased but not needed. Perhaps old food products remain in the storeroom because of menu changes. However, couldn't they have been used in daily specials or for other purposes? Also, consider food products in

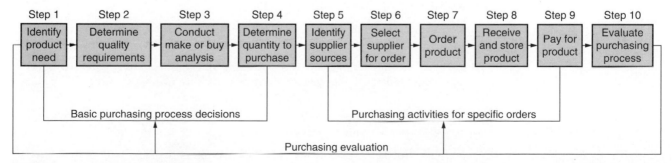

FIGURE 2.1   Steps in Procurement Process

storage areas that are discarded because of quality loss before use. Couldn't they have been purchased in smaller quantities based on actual usage levels?

Who determines what customers want? They (the customers) do, and in **chain** hospitality organizations, corporate-level marketing and other experts "translate" identified needs into the products offered to customers. Owners and managers of independently owned and operated properties use their best judgments and experience to determine customers' wants and needs, and these decisions drive menu planning and, as a result, purchase requirements. Those who purchase can help to determine product needs, assess quality requirements, and consider whether items should be prepared on-site or be purchased with some "built-in" labor. These are among the decisions to be made before product orders can be placed and are the topics discussed in this chapter.

Definition and Importance of Quality

For some hospitality buyers, the concept of quality is hard to define. They may make a decision about quality when they see products delivered by the supplier. Then it is often too late to take corrective actions other than to reject the items (which can disrupt production) or to negotiate a lower price with their sales representative (and a lower price for a product of inadequate quality is never a "deal"). In Chapter 6 you'll learn about ensuring that product quality standards *have been* met when they are delivered. However, one must also plan and effectively communicate with suppliers to best ensure that quality standards *will be* met when they are received.

Product quality relates to its intended use. The buyer must first define what a product will be used for; then the proper quality of product becomes the one that is closest to being suitable for its intended use.

Assume that a cook will prepare spaghetti sauce with a recipe requiring tomato products, fresh vegetables, ground beef, and several seasonings. What **market form** of tomato products should be used for the sauce: fresh whole tomatoes, tomato pieces of relatively uniform or irregular sizes, tomato sauce, and/or **puree?**

If the cook is employed by a **high-check average** restaurant where customers believe that "fresh is best" and where high selling prices help to offset high labor costs involved with processing fresh foods, there may be no canned tomato products used in the spaghetti sauce recipe. However, if the cook works in a **family-service restaurant** where **convenience foods** are frequently used, there may be no fresh tomato products in the sauce.

Buyer's Guide to Purchasing Terms

Chain   A multi-unit hospitality organization.

Market form   Alternative ways that food products can be purchased. For example, bread can be purchased in fresh baked and sliced or frozen, preweighed dough portions, among other alternatives.

Puree   A thick, souplike mixture made by blending or mashing food until it is smooth and without lumps.

High-check average (restaurant)   A restaurant offering relatively expensive meals required because of the higher costs of products, services, and other features of the dining experience.

Family service restaurant   A table service restaurant featuring a wide variety of reasonably priced meals with, typically, no alcoholic beverages available.

Convenience foods   A food item that has some or all of the labor built in to it, which otherwise would be provided on-site.

Buyers must constantly be aware of the guests' quality expectations as they develop standards for the food products they purchase.

Real Life/Getty Images Inc.-Image Bank

Purchasers must know the intended use of the product to understand required quality. In the above examples, fresh tomatoes may be used for numerous products in high-check average restaurants, and they may be used in only fresh salads and/or for plate garnishes in another type of property.

Customers increasingly demand value when they visit hospitality operations, and it is just as important for purchasers to search for value when they buy products for their employer. Customers and buyers both must ask, "Is the product I am considering really worth what it costs?" (*Note:* Many customers and purchasers really want to "get more than what they are paying for," and our definition of *value* is then expanded.)

To this point, we have discussed quality in the context of the products that are purchased. However, an organizational definition of **quality** is also important: the consistent delivery of products and services according to expected standards. This goal is always difficult to attain, but it is impossible to accomplish if the products required to produce quality meals are unavailable because of inadequate purchasing procedures. Buyers must purchase products meeting quality requirements to help their organization meet its total quality commitments.

Some hospitality managers use the term **quality assurance** to refer to all activities that an organization undertakes to attain quality. In the context of purchasing, these include the following:

- Considering the products that provide the best customer value
- Defining quality and developing purchase specifications that identify quality standards
- Evaluating suppliers to ensure that they consistently deliver the proper products at a fair price
- Emphasizing the importance of maintaining quality standards
- Training purchasing personnel to accomplish purchasing activities

Buyer's Guide to Purchasing Terms

Quality (organizational view)   The consistent delivery of a hospitality organization's products and services according to expected standards.

Quality assurance   All activities that help a hospitality organization to attain quality.

- Inspecting to ensure that quality standards are met when products are delivered
- Determining corrective actions that address purchasing defects
- Obtaining **feedback** to improve purchasing

Another quality concept, **"total quality management,"** relates to the pursuit of organization-wide quality by all staff members. The emphasis is placed on improving **processes** and **procedures** rather than on identifying **defects** that occur. Effective purchasers improve existing and discover new processes to help their organization meet quality requirements. Increasingly, this involves assistance from suppliers who provide value by using their knowledge, experience, and information to help the hospitality organization better serve its customers.

Economics of Quality

Because a purchaser's emphasis on providing customer value is a priority, perhaps the best tactic would be to reduce selling prices. For example, wouldn't a dinner with a "reasonable" menu selling price of $35 be a great value if it were priced at $25? Unfortunately, the organization offering such a low price would be unprofitable and would likely go out of business.

Concerns about customer value should consider competitive alternatives. Guests paying $35 for a meal will think it is a value if it is "worth" more than any other meal that they can purchase at that price. Hospitality operators must consistently provide better value for their customers and better value than their competitors.

Purchasing staff help customers to receive value. First, they assure that the products purchased benefit the customers' hospitality experience. For example, the quality of ingredients used to prepare an entrée is an important factor in a guest's dining experience. Managers must determine what their guests want, and purchasers must help to define these needs and ensure that products meeting these standards are purchased.

Purchasers also help to achieve quality by eliminating excessive costs as higher-than-necessary quality is removed from purchases, and by reducing unnecessary costs. (*Note:* This is not a suggestion to "buy cheap." Instead, it reinforces the quality definition cited earlier: proper quality relates to suitability for intended use.) This depends on many factors, including how the ingredient will be used and what the customers want. Savings made from effective purchasing yield reduced costs that can be passed on to the customer to encourage greater value perception, and/or they can be used to help the organization remain financially viable.

There are four different costs of quality:

1. *Prevention costs.* Example: The cost to develop a purchase specification that describes a product of proper quality for its intended use.

Buyer's Guide to Purchasing Terms

Feedback Information that allows managers to evaluate the effectiveness of processes or procedures.

Total quality management An organization-wide commitment that focuses on the encouragement and support of quality management in all activities to best meet the needs of employees and customers.

Process A series of actions (procedures) developed to achieve a result.

Procedure One step in a process.

Defect A variation from an expected standard for a product or performance of a service.

2. *Appraisal costs.* Example: The cost incurred to inspect incoming products to ensure they meet quality requirements.
3. *Internal failure costs.* Example: The cost of errors and rework created by use of inappropriate products.
4. *External failure costs.* Example: The cost incurred by using suppliers' products that were not noticed to be out of compliance with purchase specifications. These costs include dissatisfied customers and frustrated employees who must produce menu items with the improper ingredients.

Unfortunately, there is no simple or fast way for managers or purchasers to determine the financial effect of the four types of quality costs just noted. What is the relationship between prevention and appraisal costs to internal and external failure costs? Wise purchasers incur the former (prevention and appraisal costs), and their counterparts without effective purchasing systems incur the latter (internal and external failure costs). Wise purchasers understand that prevention and appraisal costs are typically less than internal and external failure costs.

PURCHASE SPECIFICATIONS DEFINE QUALITY

Purchase specifications describe the quality requirements of products that are purchased. They are an important communication tool to help ensure user department personnel, purchasers, and suppliers have the same understanding about quality needs.

Effective purchase specifications are

- as simple and short as possible while providing an accurate product description.
- capable of being met, whenever possible, by several suppliers to encourage **competitive bidding.**
- identifiable, when possible, with currently available products to minimize customization costs.

- capable of being verified to ensure proper quality is received.
- reasonable; compliance tolerances are practical. Example: A five-ounce pre-portioned meat item might have a **tare allowance** of one-quarter ounce. An item could, therefore, weigh between 4⅞ and 5⅛ ounces and be acceptable (meet the specification).

Uses of Specifications

Specifications are useful during purchasing and receiving.

PURCHASING   As you've learned, purchase specifications inform suppliers about the quality standards required for the products being purchased. They allow suppliers to quote applicable prices for the product when a specified volume and other order requirements are known. Specifications can be described in several ways, including the following:

- *Brand or trade name.*   Purchasers who specify a specific brand of ketchup (Heinz, for example) are indicating a quality preference. It is probably based on their experience with the product and/or the product's reputation. There is typically at least one advantage and one disadvantage to using a brand for a purchase specification. The specification is quick and easy to write because it simply involves specifying the brand. However, there are typically a limited number of (perhaps only one) suppliers in a local area who can provide the desired product (brand) and, as a result, competitive pricing is reduced or eliminated.
- *Certification with industry specification.*   The U.S. Department of Agriculture's Institutional Meat Purchasing Specifications (IMPS), the North American Meat Processors Association (NAMP), and its Meat Buyer's Guide (MBG) numbers are examples. When a purchaser specifies, for example, NAMP #1185, a bottom sirloin butt steak meeting specific quality standards is identified. U.S. grading standards are additional examples of widely circulated and recognized trade specifications and are available for many products.
- *Careful description of required product.*   Unfortunately, there are many products that cannot be quickly summarized by a brand name or a trade-recognized product number. Fresh seafood, dairy products, and bakery items are among the products for which written purchase specification statements are needed.
- *Use of samples.*   Samples of products currently used by a hospitality operation may serve as specifications. Consider a restaurant that produces specialized bakery products. The purchaser may investigate the possibility of buying these items ready-made, and samples may be given to possible suppliers to identify the quality standards required for purchased products.

Some, especially large, hospitality operations use specifications for **private label** product manufacturers. For example, canned goods containing high-use items used by a **casual-service restaurant** chain feature the company's name on

---

Buyer's Guide to Purchasing Terms

Tare allowance   The allowable variation in the weight of a product purchased by weight.

Private label   Products manufactured by one company and made available under the brand (label) of another company. Example: A quick-service restaurant chain may provide condiments labeled with its name that are manufactured by another company.

Casual-service restaurant   A table-service restaurant featuring a wide range of menu items at a reasonable price; typically alcoholic beverages are available.

Food purchase specifications are required to best ensure that purchasers consistently receive the desired quality of fresh produce.

Ricardo Arias, Latin Stock/Photo Researchers, Inc.

Did You Know? (2.2)

Purchase specifications may not be required for every product purchased. Purchasers should first develop specifications for the relatively few items that represent the largest purchasing costs. For example, expensive meat and seafood items are of greater concern to the purchasers than inexpensive condiments and lower-cost spices, herbs, and seasonings.

Purchasers working for hospitality organizations without specifications may develop a schedule (for example, develop one purchase specification every month) so over time the organization can benefit from their use.

---

the packets/cans. Typically, these items are made by manufacturers who may produce similar products for other companies and even sell the same product under their own brand label.

Purchase specifications must be updated when needs change because of evolving customer preferences and/or new marketplace alternatives. When specifications are used and when competitive bidding systems are in place, all suppliers can quote prices on the same quality of product. This helps to eliminate one reason (quality differences) supplier price quotations can differ.

RECEIVING It does little good for a hospitality operation to develop purchase specifications if they are not used at time of receiving to confirm that quality standards are met.

Experienced purchasers know they are likely to pay for the quality of products they order, even if that quality is not received. Suppliers must know an operation's specifications to deliver the proper quality of products. However, if receiving staff do not know specification requirements or do not check incoming products against them, quality variations can still occur. Receiving personnel have no more important task than to ensure that the products being received meet product standards. Then the property will receive what it paid for: an item that represents value for the organization and enables it to provide customer value.

Buyers at Work (2.1)

"Don't we have enough work to do already?" Dean asked Josie during a coffee break. Dean was a cook at the Columbia Grill, and Josie was the receiving and storeroom clerk.

"We've not had any problems with the quality of our food products," Dean continued. "Sometimes products we need aren't available, and then we just substitute something else. At other times we get deals on products we don't normally use, and we find ways to incorporate them in the menu."

"Yes, I agree," said Josie. "And sometimes products that are delivered don't really meet our quality requirements, but we're able to negotiate lower prices for them so nobody loses, do they?"

"I think we realize some things that the owners, the executive chef, and the accounting people don't understand," said Dean. "We don't need detailed purchase specifications because we can handle any situation that arises. I'm not concerned if we have purchase specifications if they don't affect me. However, it is going to be frustrating if the need to develop them affects my work."

1. What are some ways that purchase specifications can help the work of the cooks at the Columbia Grill? How, if at all, might their work tasks be negatively affected?
2. What can the manager do to address the negative feelings that these employees have about the implementation of purchase specifications at the restaurant?
3. How do you think the use of purchase specifications will improve the overall operation of the Columbia Grill?

Development of Specifications

Purchasing staff, user department personnel, and suppliers can assist as specifications are developed.

ROLE OF PURCHASING STAFF   Purchasers can do much to facilitate the development of purchase specifications. They can research, communicate about, and

---

PROFESSIONAL PURCHASING PREVENTS PROBLEMS (2.1)

Proper Product Receiving Practices Are Critical

A common problem: Specifications have been developed, but products of improper quality are received.

Less-than-ethical suppliers can quote a price for a product of lower quality than specified by the purchaser if they think the products will not be inspected during the receiving process.

Prices submitted by these suppliers will likely be lower than those of other suppliers who quote prices based on the desired (higher) product quality. In the event a quality problem is noted when items are received, the supplier can exchange the product, apologize for the "error," and deliver the correct quality product. In this instance, the low price will mean that the supplier loses money on the transaction, and in the future, the supplier will likely quote prices based on desired product quality. (The supplier has learned that this organization uses appropriate receiving practices.)

Over the long term, the unethical supplier could successfully quote a lower-than-reasonable price to other purchasers for a higher-quality product and substitute a lower-quality (and lower-cost) product for delivery. To guard against this tactic, incoming products should always be compared to written specifications to help ensure that buyers receive and pay for product quality they ordered.

Checking to ensure that a product meets purchase specifications at the time of receiving is easy when the item is purchased by brand.
Brian Haimer/PhotoEdit Inc.

develop these purchasing tools because busy user department personnel typically have less time for these tasks. Assistance can include the following:

- They can study the exact needs for items described in the specifications. Effective buyers keep current by reading industry trade publications, meeting with suppliers, and attending trade shows. They can make suggestions as product usage questions are addressed. Their input can help reduce product costs without compromising quality standards.
- They can research alternative products and suppliers. Discussions with existing suppliers, requests for referrals to other suppliers, and discussions with purchasing peers in other organizations may be helpful.
- After potential suppliers are identified, purchasers can obtain information and product samples, if necessary, and provide these resources to user department personnel for evaluation.
- They can facilitate in-house analysis of products currently used for which specifications are being developed or revised, and for new products for which specifications do not exist. Meetings, including **taste panels** with department staff, other property officials, and even guests can be conducted.
- They can develop specification drafts. General information from suppliers and trade organizations along with specific characteristics suggested by in-house personnel can be useful as they do so.
- They can share drafts of proposed purchase specifications with suppliers to obtain feedback and to assure that the resulting specifications do not limit the number of suppliers who can provide products.
- They can implement the use of specifications.

ROLE OF USER DEPARTMENT PERSONNEL   The employees who will use the product will know about its intended use. Additionally, they will likely have suggestions about "good" and "bad" features of existing products and can identify important quality characteristics.

Buyer's Guide to Purchasing Term

Taste panel   Persons involved in a formal process to sample (evaluate) products using factors such as taste, color, and smell.

Suppliers add value to their relationships with purchasers when they provide information helpful in developing purchase specifications.

Photolibrary.com

Staff members with extensive industry experience may be able to suggest potential supply sources and/or have a network of peers in other hospitality organizations who can make suggestions about product alternatives.

User department employees can evaluate alternative products, review early drafts of specifications, and raise issues to be addressed with purchasing staff and/or with potential suppliers.

ROLE OF SUPPLIERS   Purchasers will benefit from the technical information and support provided by suppliers during the specification development process. Also, as suppliers note the purchaser's sincere interests in using specifications, they are more likely to consistently ensure that the products they provide will meet the applicable specifications.

(*Note:* Some purchasers are cautious about using suppliers for specification development because they believe there is a risk that some confidential information such as advance notices of new menu item rollouts will be provided. Also, suppliers not involved in the specification development process may believe that the organization's relationship with other suppliers reduces their selling opportunity, and competitive pricing benefits will be lost.)

In the increasingly complex discipline of hospitality purchasing, the advice and counsel of specialists can be helpful. Suppliers are experts in the products/ services they provide, and their assistance as specifications are developed provides another example of value in the buyer-supplier relationship.

Buyers at Work (2.2)

"I'm from the 'old school' that thinks purchasers should have only a conservative business relationship with their suppliers," said Ajay as he spoke with Mindy, the food services director for a large school district. Ajay was responsible for all purchasing in the school district, including the needs of the foodservice program.

"You're right about our need to be transparent and to have a very conservative fiscal management policy because we are spending the public's money. I would have many of the concerns even if we operated a restaurant that was not funded by tax dollars," replied Mindy.

"However, we also must use our budget wisely, and we are not experts in everything required to serve meals to thousands of students," she continued. "We must know when we need expert advice, and I think the development of purchase specifications for new food items is an example.

(Continued)

"Ajay, I know you purchase thousands of items to meet our district's needs, including educational resources, school maintenance and repair items, and safety supplies. Add food products to the list, and you must be overwhelmed. Shouldn't we obtain advice from food suppliers who can help us make these important decisions, if we do not become obligated to them? Won't this help to make better use of the taxpayers' money to benefit our students?"

"You're right, Mindy. I'll admit that we've made many purchases on a trial-and-error basis and have probably lost money in the process. I'm just concerned about the public's perception of our involvement with suppliers and that some unethical suppliers might try to take advantage of us."

1. How might the role of suppliers in establishing specifications differ for hospitality organizations operated by government agencies and those owned by private investors?
2. Assume that Mindy can convince Ajay to receive input from suppliers as purchase specifications are developed. What are examples of "conservative" assistance that might be useful at the beginning stages of supplier involvement?
3. What other types of external assistance besides that from suppliers is probably available to Ajay and Mindy as they develop specifications?

Specification Information

What information should be included in a purchase specification? This question will be addressed in this section.

CONTENT OF SPECIFICATIONS   Many hospitality organizations use a template of basic information for the products for which specifications are developed. An example is shown in Figure 2.2.

Product Name: _____ Specification No.: _____
Menu Item Name (if applicable): _____
Product Use: _____
_____
_____

General Product Description: _____
_____
_____

Specific Information (as applicable)
• Count/portion size: _____
• Tare allowance (if applicable): _____
• Processing requirements: _____
• Drained weight (canned items): _____
• Trade number or grade: _____
• Weight: _____
• Variety, style, type: _____
• Packaging requirements: _____
• Geographic origin: _____
• Yield percent:_____
• Other special information: _____
_____
_____

Quality Inspection Procedures: _____
_____

Other Requirements and General Information: _____
_____

Specification Implementation Date: _____

FIGURE 2.2 Sample Purchase Specification Format

Menu Item	Sirloin steak on a bun
Product	Bottom sirloin butt steak; 6-ounce boneless portion
NAMP Number*	1185
Grade	USDA Choice
Weight range	6 ounce with a .25 ounce tolerance
Trim level	Zero trim
Packaging	Individual vacuum packaged; 12 portions per box
Special considerations	Aged at least 10 days
State of refrigeration	Fresh product; temperature not to exceed 40°F (4°C)

Note: The "NAMP Number" refers to a reference number for the desired product that has been established (assigned) by the North American Meat Processors Association (NAMP).

FIGURE 2.3   Specification Based on Industry Standard

Figure 2.2 notes many details normally addressed in a purchase specification. However, it also includes two features less commonly included: information about product use and quality inspection procedures.

When purchasers provide product use information (recall this chapter's definition of quality that considers a product's intended use), suppliers will better understand the purpose for which the product is needed. Then they might suggest other products that were not considered or were not available when the specification was developed.

Including product inspection procedures on the specification emphasizes that the operation is serious about assuring that quality requirements are met. Also, another opportunity for input becomes possible if the supplier suggests additional methods for product inspection. Why would suppliers be concerned that the purchaser receives the proper quality of products from their counterparts? They know that unethical competitors may substitute products of lower quality to enable them to quote low prices.

SAMPLE SPECIFICATION   Figure 2.3 and Figure 2.4 show two purchase specification formats that address some of the factors identified in Figure 2.2. They also illustrate the concern that a hospitality organization should use a specification that is "best" for its own purposes.

Implementation Procedures

After purchase specifications have been developed, they must be implemented. Figure 2.5 notes steps useful in implementing specifications for products already being purchased for which no specifications exist and for new products not currently used by the organization.

Let's review the steps in Figure 2.5:

- *Step 1: Review Specification.*   The purchaser should be able to develop a draft of the purchase specification after receiving input from user department personnel, suppliers, and his or her own research. Alternatively, the organization may have an existing specification that is being evaluated.
- *Step 2: Conduct Value Analysis.*   **Value analysis** relates to efforts to increase the value for the money spent and/or to increase the satisfaction that results

Buyer's Guide to Purchasing Term

Value analysis   Techniques used to increase value for the money spent for a product and/or to increase the satisfaction that the product provides.

Name: TOMATO SAUCE

Description: Tomato sauce is a lightly concentrated version of tomato juice in which other seasonings besides salt are added to the product. The additional seasonings in this product are normally sweeteners such as sugar or corn syrup, vinegar, onion, and garlic. Generally the product is of medium texture and practically free from defects.

REQUIRED FANCY

Quality Factors	Max Points	Minimum	USDA Grade A
Color	25	23	21
Consistency	25	23	22
Defects	25	22	21
Flavor	25	23	21
Total Score	100	91	85

USDA EXPLANATION OF QUALITY FACTORS USED IN GRADING CANNED TOMATO SAUCE

COLOR	Color in tomato sauce is currently determined by the Munsell Color/Disc method. The color should be typical of tomato sauce made from well-ripened tomatoes that have been properly prepared and processed.
CONSISTENCY	Refers to the viscosity of the product and its tendency to hold its liquid portion in suspension. Consistency is determined using the Bostwick Consistometer Method. To meet U.S. Grade A, there should be no more than a slight separation of free liquid when the product is poured on a flat grading tray.

Maximum Bostwick Value

Required Fancy	11 cm
USDA Grade A	14 cm

Note: Lower value is best.

ABSENCE FROM DEFECTS	Refers to the degree of freedom from defects such as dark specks or scale-like particles, seeds, particles of seed, tomato peel, core material, or other similar substances. This factor is evaluated by observing a layer of the product on a smooth, white, flat surface.
FLAVOR	The product should possess a good, distinctive flavor characteristic of good-quality ingredients. Such flavor should be free from scorching or any other objectionable flavor of any kind.

Purchase unit is case (6–#10 cans; 106 ounces net weight per can).

Note: This specification provides details for Fancy tomato sauce (the highest grade) and Grade A products (the second-highest grade), both of which may be purchased based on intended product use by the buyer.

FIGURE 2.4 Specification Based on Quality Factors

from product use. Results of value analysis can yield reduced costs, increase cooperation between departments, and improve supplier relationships.

To illustrate the value analysis process, consider that a **cross-functional team** composed of purchasing and user department personnel and others can provide diverse viewpoints to address questions such as the

Buyer's Guide to Purchasing Term

Cross-functional team   A group of employees from several different departments who work together to resolve a problem.

FIGURE 2.5   Implementing Purchase Specifications

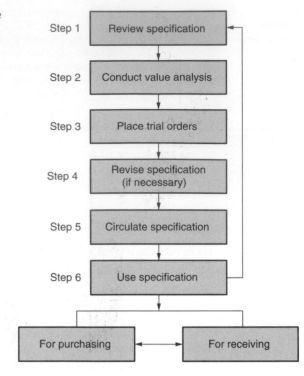

following: "What is this product?" "What is it for?" "What does it cost?" "Is there anything else that would fulfill this product's purpose as well or better than this product and, if so, what would it cost?" The team's efforts can evolve through several phases:

- Reviewing the present specification.
- Speculating about and considering alternative products and uses for products being examined.
- Recommending proposals, ideas, and suggestions to improve the specification.

Did You Know? (2.3)

There are often advantages to using one food product for several purposes when doing so will not sacrifice quality standards. This process is called "**menu rationalization**", and when used, fewer products must be purchased, received, stored, issued, and placed into production. Product knowledge and skills relating to handling procedures can also be reduced.

Must a restaurant use different sizes of shrimp for shrimp cocktail appetizers, shrimp plates, shrimp casserole dishes, and shrimp salads? If so, the reason should relate to the need to define required quality in terms of intended use. However, if the number of required shrimp sizes can be reduced, the above-noted benefits may result.

Wise purchasers consider the relationship between products, their purchase specifications, and other similar products when they develop specifications.

Buyer's Guide to Purchasing Term

Menu rationalization   Analysis of existing menu items and the ingredients used to produce them with the goal of reducing the number of different items to be purchased.

- *Step 3: Place Trial Orders.*   Ideally the specification allows several suppliers to provide products of acceptable quality. Trial orders from several suppliers can help confirm that the written specification yields products meeting quality standards.
- *Step 4: Revise Specification (if necessary).*   Significant research and analysis have, we hope, yielded a specification that accurately reflects the organization's quality standards for the product being described. However, changes, if any, noted as a result of studying products received from trial orders should be considered.
- *Step 5: Circulate Specification.*   Suppliers who will be asked for price quotations should receive a copy of specifications. These may be sent to the suppliers electronically, hard copies can be given to a supplier's representative, and/or copies can be included in a handbook given to all suppliers.
- *Step 6: Use Specification.*   As noted earlier, current and accurate specifications identify quality standards required for products being purchased, and they help receiving personnel to confirm that incoming products meet quality requirements. Figure 2.5 also reminds us that the process of implementing purchase specifications is ongoing. The availability of new products, changing customer preferences, and results from future value analysis teams may yield revised specifications.

Buyer's Guide to Internet Resources: Purchase Specifications

Web Site	Topic
www.foodproductdesign.com	Commonly purchased food products and overview of quality issues
www.foodproductiondaily.com	Food processing news that affects food quality
www.findarticles.com	Taste panels (Type "taste panels" into the site's search box)
www.sysco.com	A quality assurance program developed by one large food distributor (Click on "Customers" on the site's home page then click "Quality assurance")
www.usfoodservice.com	Procedures used by one distributor to maximize food safety before product shipment (Hover mouse over "Brands, Food & More" and click on "Food Safety & Quality Assurance" at the site)

MAKE OR BUY ANALYSIS

To this point in the chapter, you've learned about the first two steps in the purchasing process presented in Figure 2.1: Identifying product need (step 1) and determining quality requirements (step 2). It's now time to discuss the make or buy analysis process (step 3).

Make or buy analysis decisions consider whether food items should be produced by hospitality employees or purchased with some or all of the labor "built in" that otherwise would need to be provided on site. These decisions have significant marketing, financial, human resources, and other implications.

Responsibilities for Make or Buy Analysis

In large hospitality organizations, make or buy analyses are often undertaken by purchasing personnel. Concerns that prompt the analyses can originate with user department personnel confronted by production challenges and/or with purchasers desiring to resolve operating problems. In small properties without specialized purchasing assistance, make or buy decisions are typically made by managers, supervisors, or others in the **chain of command.**

Factors Affecting Make or Buy Analysis

Hospitality managers frequently are confronted by problems that must be resolved, others that would be "nice" to address, and still others causing challenges of which they are unaware. An overriding concern is always to increase value for the customer while reducing costs. However, none of these concerns would ever be addressed if managers decided to consider alternatives "when they got around to it." Instead, they must be alert to better ways to do things, and make or buy analysis provides a tactic to review product quality concerns of the customers and property cost concerns.

Numerous issues should be considered as make or buy decisions are made. Figure 2.6 identifies some questions that might prompt an interest in make or buy analysis when products are currently being produced by the organization's employees.

Now let's consider the opposite of the above discussion. Assume that the hospitality organization is purchasing a product from an external supplier. Should it continue to do so? Questions to address as this decision is made include those in Figure 2.7.

The list of factors in Figures 2.6 and 2.7 suggest two very important concerns that are part of every make or buy decision:

- Which alternative consistently yields the product of appropriate quality from the customers' point of view?

- Are changes in production volumes causing staff difficulties?
- Are prices for necessary products or ingredients increasing?
- Is there an interest in increasing the variety of menu items without increasing labor costs?
- Is new (expensive) equipment necessary to continue on-site production?
- Is there interest in allowing staff to focus on their **core competencies?**
- Is it difficult to maintain a consistent source of supplies?
- Is there a limited number of suppliers available?
- Are alternative products in the marketplace?
- Does purchase from an external supplier impact other items? Example: Does a menu item require a sauce that is an ingredient in other menu items?
- Is equipment/space available to store products purchased in other market forms?
- Are there special concerns about returning to on-site production if there are unanticipated **outsourcing** problems?
- Will purchase quantities be of interest to suppliers?
- Will future costs of on-site product production change? If so, why and how much?

FIGURE 2.6   Questions that Prompt Make or Buy Analysis: Products Produced On-Site

---

Buyer's Guide to Purchasing Terms

Chain of command   The path by which authority (power) flows from one management level to the next within the organization.

Core competencies   The base of employees' knowledge and skills required to attain the organization's mission.

Outsourcing (product)   The activity of purchasing a product from a supplier that otherwise could be produced by the organization's employees.

- Have product quality requirements changed?
- Have volume requirements changed?
- Are there problems with the consistency of products that are purchased?
- Are purchase costs higher than anticipated?
- Has our need for the product changed?
- Are there supplier relationship difficulties?
- Are there special concerns about returning to product purchase if there are unanticipated problems with on-site production?

FIGURE 2.7 Questions That Prompt Make or Buy Analysis: Products Purchased from Suppliers

Did You Know? (2.4)

Which type of automobile is "better": a Ford or a Chevrolet? Fans of both makes of cars will be able to defend their answer to this question, and it is unlikely that anything can be said or done to change their opinion.

Which is better: beef stew **"made from scratch"** at a restaurant or a frozen market form of the product? Responses are often based on the same factors used to determine auto preferences, including experiences and subjective judgment. However, the best answer to both of the questions just posed may be "One cannot generalize." Many factors must be addressed to answer the make or buy question for the specific hospitality operation. The purpose of the analysis is not to "confirm" what those conducting the study already think or know. Instead, it is to assess the best alternative for the specific organization by considering the factors judged most important to it.

- Assuming equivalent (acceptable) quality, which product alternative is least expensive?

The make or buy analysis process discussed in the next section addresses these two questions. Experienced purchasing professionals know that thoughtful study is needed, and the more the decision affects customer value and costs, the more carefully decisions must be made.

Steps in Make or Buy Analysis

Several steps are involved in the make or buy analysis process, and they are introduced in Figure 2.8.

Before discussing Figure 2.8, note that the quality of alternative products must be assessed before their costs are determined. In fact, the first six steps in the figure relate to quality aspects of the decision, and only two steps (Steps 7 and 8) concern costs of the decision. This reinforces a point made earlier: make or buy analysis is not a decision about cost alone. Instead, it is a decision about quality and costs. It does little good to determine the costs of product alternatives if the product cannot be used because of unacceptable quality.

Now that we've emphasized the need for quality, let's review Figure 2.8:

- *Step 1: Determine Need.* You've learned that need relates to intended use. If a product is not needed, it should not be purchased or produced on site.

Buyer's Guide to Purchasing Term

Scratch (made from) The use of individual ingredients to make items available for sale; for example, a stew may be made on-site with vegetables, meat, and other ingredients required by the standard recipe.

FIGURE 2.8   Steps in Make or
Buy Analysis

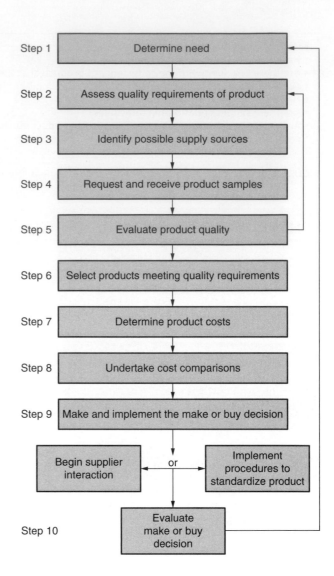

Step 1 — Determine need

Step 2 — Assess quality requirements of product

Step 3 — Identify possible supply sources

Step 4 — Request and receive product samples

Step 5 — Evaluate product quality

Step 6 — Select products meeting quality requirements

Step 7 — Determine product costs

Step 8 — Undertake cost comparisons

Step 9 — Make and implement the make or buy decision

Begin supplier interaction   or   Implement procedures to standardize product

Step 10 — Evaluate make or buy decision

- *Step 2: Assess Quality Requirements of Product.*   How is the quality of the product produced by the employees described? What type, quality, and amount of ingredients are used? What is the portion size? What are the most important factors suggesting the need for a make or buy analysis?

  This step is critical because the result should be a product definition or description that provides a standard against which to evaluate alternative products. If an acceptable product cannot be produced, either it will have to be purchased or it cannot be offered. If desired quality cannot be described, it cannot be measured, and it will be difficult to evaluate as alternative products are evaluated (see Step 5).

- *Step 3: Identify Possible Supply Sources.*   User department employees may know about external suppliers, and purchasers may have collected information about alternative supply sources. Department managers and others may learn about potential suppliers as they visit trade shows, review trade magazines, and discuss challenges with current suppliers of similar products and services. The numerous electronic buying guides available are another easy way to identify potential sources of supply.

- *Step 4: Request and Receive Product Samples.*   Potential suppliers of the product being considered for outsourcing should be informed that the organization is considering the purchase of their products. When detailed information about the desired product or services is provided (Steps 1 and 2),

---

PROFESSIONAL PURCHASING PREVENTS PROBLEMS (2.2)

There Are Many Possible Supply Sources for Commonly Used Menu Items

A common problem: Purchasers conducting make or buy analysis are frequently not aware of numerous manufacturers who can provide needed convenience foods.

Assume you were considering the alternative of purchasing several desserts currently being produced by your production personnel. Historically, alternative suppliers of these items would be identified by personal contact with existing suppliers ("Do you sell these items, or do you know someone who does?") and/or by looking in the yellow pages of a local telephone book. Today, however, an electronic search of the marketplace involves just a few clicks on one's computer mouse. A fast search may reveal numerous manufacturers and suppliers and even product alternatives of which a buyer may be unaware.

To view the power of one search site, go to www.business.com. Then enter a menu item such as frozen beef stew or a dessert item such as fresh cheesecake into the site's search box.

Purchasers using this search technique will likely discover numerous alternative products that would otherwise be unknown. In the process, a greater variety of alternatives may yield a product that provides acceptable quality and costs that make it a reasonable alternative to on-site production

---

it is easier for potential suppliers to assess whether their products might be useful.

Purchasers should know their organization's policies about product samples. If a product sample is desired, the request is fairly straightforward. However, the process depends on whether the product will replace one currently being produced (the applicable specification should be provided) or the item will be new to the menu. Then the purchaser may request samples of alternative products that meet general quality requirements.

- *Step 5: Evaluate Product Quality.* Product samples should be evaluated using the product currently produced on-site as a **benchmark.** Historically the evaluation of alternative product samples has been called **"can-cutting."** This is a reference to cans of food products that were cut open to enable contents such as corn or string beans from alternative suppliers to be compared relative to factors such as size consistency, proper color and shape, and **drained weight** (amount of the contents that is food product versus canning **liquor**). This term is still used in some organizations to describe the comparison of any food products even if they are not canned goods.

Who participates in these product evaluations? A cross-functional team of food production and purchasing personnel, food and beverage managers, service staff, and individuals from other departments (if in a hotel) might participate in taste comparisons. Guests may be given samples and asked their

---

Buyer's Guide to Purchasing Terms

Benchmark   A standard used for comparison.

Can-cutting   The act of comparing alternative food products against each other and against desirable purchase characteristics.

Drained weight   The quantity (weight) of food in a container after the liquid in which it is packed is removed; also called servable weight.

Liquor (canning)   The liquid in which canned vegetables is packed.

opinions. Formal taste panels may be used within a controlled environment in large organizations considering large-volume purchases. When alternative products are being evaluated, **"blind testing"** helps to ensure the brand and/or the supplier is unknown during the evaluation to avoid favoritism.

- *Step 6: Select Products Meeting Quality Requirements.* A formal evaluation of product alternatives (Step 5) will identify those that meet the property's quality requirements (Step 2). It is then necessary to determine the costs of acceptable products and to compare them with products produced on-site.

- *Step 7: Determine Product Costs.* All significant costs incurred as the product is produced should be identified. What is "significant"? The utility costs incurred by an oven used to bake bread may be easy (or difficult) to determine and may (or may not) be considered "significant." A good rule of thumb is to determine the estimated cost for all expenses incurred to produce a product if it is considered practical (cost effective and reasonable) to do so.

- *Step 8: Undertake Cost Comparisons.* The costs for purchasing and preparing a required product should be compared. If the steps in Figure 2.8 are followed, it will be an apples-to-apples comparison based on products of equal quality rather than an apples-to-oranges comparison in which products of different quality are compared.

- *Step 9: Make and Implement the Make or Buy Decision.* At this point the planning team will know the quality and cost differences of the products being evaluated. While these are important, others must also be considered. For example, it is unwise to select a product of acceptable quality and at a very favorable price from an undependable supplier. (One would hope they were eliminated in Step 3.) However, service factors are among those that should be considered as part of the "big picture" evaluation during the make or buy decision.

  Further interaction with the selected supplier will be necessary if a "buy" decision is made. Alternatively, if external supply sources will not be used, procedures must be implemented to assure that products purchased for on-site production are standardized (consistent).

- *Step 10: Evaluate Make or Buy Decision.* Was the decision to produce or buy the product a good one? The phrase "only time will tell" may be relevant to answering this question. Situations that can affect the decision do change. As suggested in Figure 2.8, the make or buy process may need to be repeated in the future.

Did You Know? (2.5)

The ten-step process just described to make product purchase or on-site product production decisions can also be useful for determining whether services such as window cleaning or landscape maintenance should be done by employees or **external service providers.** When service alternatives are being considered, the decision-making process is often referred to as **do or buy analysis.**

Buyer's Guide to Purchasing Terms

Blind testing The act of evaluating product samples without knowledge about the brand of or supplier from whom the product is available.

External service provider A person or organization that provides (sells) a service.

Do or buy analysis A process to determine whether services should be provided by the organization's employees or obtained from an external service provider.

Buyers at Work (2.3)

"Why are we even considering this?" asked Juan as he and Claudia walked to the back of the kitchen. "We've both been cooking here a long time, and there's no need to make a change now—or ever."

Juan and Claudia were about one hundred feet from the food prep table where a representative of a local meat supply company was standing and about to make a presentation on the purchase of fresh bulk ground beef. At her side was a representative of a kitchen supply company who had brought an automatic patty-making machine for demonstration.

Over the past few weeks, the restaurant manager, cooks including Juan and Claudia, and others including service staff had been working on an "upscale" menu for their popular casual-service restaurant. A suggestion had been made to replace the present frozen hamburger patties with a "fresh ground" product that would be portioned and shaped on-site and would be flavored with a variety of "secret seasonings" that could be ordered by the guests. Cooks would portion and shape the patties before service and add requested seasonings as the burgers were grilled to order.

While Juan and Claudia were viewing the demonstration and listening to the sales pitches of the suppliers, they both were thinking that the concept of an "upscale" burger could be accomplished just as well with the currently used frozen patty and that the desired product could just as easily and less expensively be accomplished with a different bun (baked off-site), serving plate, and a "fancy" garnish.

1. Why might Juan and Claudia oppose the suggestion about the new market form of ground beef being considered?
2. What might the restaurant manager have done from the first time the "upscale" burger concept was suggested until now to reduce possible employee resistance to the concept?
3. What role should suppliers, including the two making the current presentation, play in the make or buy decision?
4. What tactics from this point might the restaurant manager use to encourage the cooks' active and genuine participation in the make or buy analysis process?

Was this hamburger "made from scratch" (portioned and pattied manually from bulk ground beef), or was it made with the use of a patty-making machine to save labor costs?

Getty Images, Inc.-PhotoDisc

Example of Make or Buy Analysis

You have just learned about a ten-step make or buy process, and you have learned details about quality, how to describe it, and how to ensure that quality standards are addressed when products are purchased. Most of these principles also apply to quality aspects of the make or buy decision. However, there is more to be said about costing concerns, and we'll consider them using an example of a potential purchase of a food product.

The Sea Coast Restaurant does a great lunch and dinner business during the six days it is open each week. The luncheon buffet offers a modest variety of items during the week along with its menu of salads, soups, sandwiches, and some "lunch specials." During the evenings, a salad bar is offered as a complement to the entrées on the dinner menu. Each Sunday a buffet line with a wide variety of items, including several fresh salads is offered.

A tossed salad is available for **à la carte** purchase or as an accompaniment during each meal period, and it is popular. Because salads are selected by the guests visiting the buffet/salad bar, they serve themselves the amount and type of salad ingredients desired. The buffet offers a large and frequently replenished bowl of fresh, chopped lettuce and numerous items, including shredded carrots, sliced radishes, and spinach leaves. Other ingredients, toppings, and dressings are also available.

Since the restaurant opened, iceberg lettuce has been purchased several times weekly to ensure a fresh product. The outside leaves and core are removed, and the product is carefully washed, quartered, and chopped. The amount of lettuce judged sufficient based on the meal forecast (number of guests) is prepared in advance, placed into plastic transport tubs covered with damp (and clean) foodservice towels, and stored in the walk-in refrigerator. Tubs of chopped lettuce are transported to the buffet as needed. Lettuce remaining on the buffet at the end of the meal period is placed back in plastic tubs, covered with a damp cloth, and held in refrigerated storage until the next meal period, when it is used on the salad bar.

The restaurant's managers have worked with the cooks to reduce costs without sacrificing quality. However, rising produce costs, increased labor rates, and the difficulty in finding qualified production personnel is creating challenges.

The restaurant's produce supplier has made a suggestion: "Perhaps you should purchase fresh, chopped lettuce in a plastic bag that is ready for service without any required preparation."

The manager wants to learn more about the pros and cons of this idea, and she undertakes a make or buy analysis. First, she obtained product samples and, after carefully evaluating them with production staff, confirmed that the quality of the two alternatives (on-site processed and off-site processed and pre-chopped lettuce) was acceptable.

Because there were no quality differences, the manager next assesses the cost differences. Figure 2.9 shows the estimated costs associated with on-site processing of the lettuce, which are based on several assumptions:

- 70% **yield**
- Purchase unit = case (24 heads)

Buyer's Guide to Purchasing Terms

À la carte   Individually priced; not included in the price of a meal.

Yield (%)   The amount (%) of the as-purchased weight of a food item that is edible after it is processed; see as-purchased (weight).

- Case weight (**as-purchased** weight) = 26 pounds
- Case cost = $32.96
- Portion size = 1 cup (2 ounces **edible portion**)
- Cook's hourly rate – $9.75
- Cook's benefits = 15% of hourly rate
- Preparation time = 40 minutes per case (24 heads)

Note: Cost estimates are used in this example for illustrative purposes only, and they are not meant to suggest that one alternative or the other is least expensive or the best alternative. Ounces (edible portion) per cup (head lettuce) information is from Lynch, F. "Table of Food Yields & Equivalents: A Food-Costing Aid for Chefs." Chef Desk (www.chefdesk.com), 1997.

When reviewing the information in Figure 2.9, note that the manager first determined the number of edible portions (EP) contained in one head of lettuce and

---

Calculate Food Cost for One Portion (2 Ounces)

STEP A. DETERMINE NUMBER OF EDIBLE PORTIONS (EP) IN ONE HEAD OF LETTUCE

1 head = 1.08 pounds (AP): 26 pounds per case ÷ 24 heads (number of heads per case)

1 head = 12 oz. (EP): 1.08 pounds (AP weight per head) × 70% (yield)* = .75 pounds or 12 ounces (16 ounces per pound × .75 pounds)

Number of 2-oz. servings per head of lettuce = 6 (12 ounces per head ÷ 2 oz. per serving)

STEP B. DETERMINE FOOD COST PER PORTION

1 head of lettuce = $1.37 ($32.96 ÷ 24 heads)

1 portion of lettuce – $0.228 ($1.37 ÷ 6 portions)

STEP C. DETERMINE LABOR COST PER PORTION

Labor cost (1 case) = $7.47	$9.75 (hourly rate) + $1.46 (fringe benefits; 9.75 × 15%) × ⅔ hour (40 minutes = ⅔ of 60 minutes [one hour])
Labor cost (1 head) = $0.311	$7.47 (labor cost per case) ÷ 24 (number of heads in case)
Labor cost per portion = $0.052	$0.311 (labor cost per head) ÷ 6 (number servings per head)

STEP D. DETERMINE TOTAL FOOD AND LABOR COST PER PORTION OF LETTUCE

Food cost	$0.228
Labor cost	0.052
	$0.280

*If there is 70% yield, then there is 30% waste (100% − 70% = 30%). Waste represents lettuce not used (outer leaves and core).

FIGURE 2.9 Alternative 1: Prepare Fresh Lettuce On-Site

Buyer's Guide to Purchasing Terms

As-purchased (weight) The weight of a product before it is processed, prepared, or cooked; also called "AP weight."

Edible portion (weight) The weight of a product after it is processed, prepared, or cooked; in other words, the amount that is available for service to guests; also called "EP weight."

the food cost for one portion of lettuce (see, respectively, Steps A and B). Then the labor cost per portion was calculated (in Step C), and a total food and labor cost per portion ($0.280) of on-site processed lettuce was then calculated (in Step D).

Now the manager must determine the cost of a 2-ounce portion of pre-processed chopped lettuce, and several assumptions are used:

- 100% yield
- Purchase unit = 5 pound bag
- Cost per purchase unit = $18.47
- Portion size = 1 cup (2 ounces edible portion)

Figure 2.10 reviews the manager's cost estimates for the processed lettuce.

Note first that it is much easier (fewer calculations needed) to determine the per-portion cost of the bag of processed chopped lettuce and second that the cost per portion was $0.462. Figure 2.11 reviews the cost comparison of the two alternatives (process chopped lettuce on-site or purchase processed chopped lettuce).

Figure 2.11 indicates an estimated savings of $0.182 per portion and $263.90 per week if the manager continues to purchase lettuce for on-site processing.

Implementing Make or Buy Decisions

Completing a make or buy analysis is not difficult. Because, as you've just learned, "paper savings" do not necessarily equal "real world" savings, managers must

STEP A.	DETERMINE NUMBER OF EDIBLE OUNCES (EP) IN ONE BAG OF PROCESSED LETTUCE
	1 bag = 80 oz. (#5 × 16 ounces per pound)
STEP B.	DETERMINE NUMBER OF PORTIONS PER BAG
	1 bag = 40 portions (80 ounces per bag ÷ 2 oz. [portion size])
STEP C.	DETERMINE FOOD COST (ONE PORTION)
	One portion = 0.462 $18.47 (cost for one bag) ÷ 40 (number of portions per bag)

FIGURE 2.10   Alternative 2: Purchase Processed Chopped Lettuce

Did You Know? (2.6)

Purchasing pros know that you "can't bank a paper savings!" In the example illustrated in Figure 2.11, the manager estimated a savings of approximately $0.182 per portion when head lettuce was processed by the restaurant's employees. However, consider the assumptions that were made in the calculations yielding this estimate:

- The as-purchased cost of a case of lettuce (twenty-four heads).
- The yield (servable portion of the head lettuce).
- The purchase cost of bagged lettuce.
- The portion size of the salad.
- The labor costs, including fringe benefits for the processing employee(s).
- The length of time required to process a case of lettuce.

If any of the above assumptions are wrong and/or change, the numbers leading to the make decision will also change. Among numerous factors, costs may vary, processing procedures may yield more or less edible portion sizes, and the time required for different staff members to process head lettuce may not be the same.

Careful study is required as make or buy cost comparisons are planned and undertaken, and on-going review of changing conditions that affect the study's results is also required.

	Bagged lettuce	$0.462
(On-site processed; includes labor)		0.280
	Cost difference	$0.182

Weekly Cost Difference

Assume:	100 guests/day (lunch)	×	5 = 500
	125 guests/day (dinner)	×	6 = 750
	200 guests (Sunday brunch)		200
			1,450 guests/week

Weekly cost savings (on-site preparation) = $263.90 (1,450 guests × $0.182)

FIGURE 2.11   Per-Portion Cost Comparison of Chopped Lettuce Alternatives

"work their assumptions" and implement the tactics assumed when the make or buy analysis was developed. There is frequently a significant difference between what the make or buy analysis assumes and the actual practices that are used after decisions are implemented.

Consider, for example, a make or buy analysis that determines labor costs will be saved if preportioned hamburger patties are purchased because it will no longer be necessary to spend on-site labor hours for this task. Preportioned hamburger patties of the same quality as their bulk-purchased counterparts will likely be more expensive. Will labor hours be reduced to compensate for the higher per-unit cost? If so, the savings suggested by the make or buy analysis may be realized, and costs can be reduced. However, if the cooks' schedules are not revised to reduce labor hours, food costs will be higher (because a more expensive market form of ground beef will be purchased), and labor costs will remain the same. The result: higher operating costs using the preportioned patties even though the analysis suggested lower costs.

As a second example, assume that specialized hamburger patty–forming equipment is purchased to reduce the labor hours needed to portion patties purchased in bulk. Because equipment costs will increase, this cost must be more than offset by the reduced labor cost (fewer labor hours) if the decision is to be a good one. However, if labor hours are not reduced, equipment costs will be higher, labor costs will remain the same, and the financial effect of the make or buy analysis will be harmful rather than helpful.

The results of a make or buy analysis may take time to implement when production staff require a learning period to develop the skills required to produce new menu items.

Mira.com/Artist Name

Experienced buyers ensure that all practical details are addressed when a make or buy analysis is performed. Then there is a lesser chance that surprises will arise when the decision is implemented. Changes in "how we have done things in the past" and the need to defend the **status quo** represent aspects of make or buy decisions that are difficult to consider during the analysis. However, they can cause significant challenges when decisions are implemented. The best approach: ask for input from affected personnel, including those who will be working with revised products and/or work methods. First, their input can be helpful, and second, their "buy-in" may reduce the resistance to change that is otherwise possible.

Evaluating Make or Buy Decisions

As noted in Step 10 in Figure 2.8, make or buy decisions should be evaluated. This can be done more objectively if the information used for the analysis such as the number of labor hours or dollars of anticipated costs provide a benchmark against which to compare actual numbers.

Unfortunately, systems to track make or buy analysis information are frequently not in place. In the above examples, a restaurant would not typically track the number of hours of preparation labor required to process a case of lettuce, nor would the managers identify the number of hours required to portion bulk ground beef into patties. Instead, the times required for both of these tasks would probably have to be tracked several times just to develop the information needed for the make or buy analysis.

It is difficult to monitor (evaluate) the effectiveness of make or buy decisions when special procedures are needed to do so. Should a cook be asked to "keep track" of the time needed to chop lettuce for a make or buy analysis? Should the purchasing agent or the chef assume this responsibility?

Managers and others evaluating make or buy results are less likely to give a priority to reviewing the effect of a study that has already been implemented. This is especially true if changes implemented from the study were originally suggested or agreed to by those who are now asked to perform the evaluation.

It is important to evaluate the results of make or buy analysis when there are cost changes such as wage or food cost increases. New equipment, revised work processes, and the availability of new market forms of food are other examples of factors that can make an analysis out of date.

Did You Know? (2.7)

Purchasing pros know about the **Hawthorne effect,** which relates to the tendency of persons being observed to act differently than if they were not observed. For example, a cook being timed as he or she chopped lettuce might work more productively than normal. Then the production time noted during the make or buy study might be less than the time really required, and the time spent on the task after the study might be longer than actually needed.

Buyer's Guide to Purchasing Terms

Status quo   The way things are currently done.

Hawthorne effect   The tendency of people to act differently when they are being observed than when they are not being observed.

Busy hospitality managers may, at least subjectively, evaluate changes resulting from a make or buy analysis immediately and for a short time after changes are made. After a relatively short time, however, the new product or process will replace its earlier alternative and become the accepted way that things are done.

Wise hospitality professionals recognize the need to use make or buy analysis as one tool in their efforts to ensure that they please their guests while minimizing costs.

Buyer's Guide to Internet Resources: Make or Buy Analysis

Web Site	Topic
www.outsourcing.com	Outsourcing (use of external suppliers) (Click on "Buyers" when you reach the site)
www.saraleefoodservice.com	Convenience products (bakery and meats) for volume food purchasers
www.affi.com	History of frozen foods
www.findarticles.com	Processed produce in restaurants (Enter "processed produce in restaurants" into the site's search box)
www.soupbase.com	Prepared soup bases sold through distributors
www.windsorfoods.com	Frozen foods
www.tyson.com	Convenience food products manufactured by the world's largest poultry company
www.chefdesk.com	Purchasing ideas for chefs
www.preparedfoods.com	Prepared foods (Enter the item of interest (examples: "frozen desserts" or "beef stew") into the site's search box)
www.chow.com	Sous vide (a cooking method that expands alternatives in make or buy analysis) (Enter "sous vide" into the site's search box)
www.hollymatic.com	On-site food processing equipment

Purchasing Terms

Chain *28*
Market form *28*
Puree *28*
High-check average (restaurant) *28*
Family service restaurant *28*
Convenience foods *28*
Quality (organizational view) *29*
Quality assurance *29*
Feedback *30*

Total quality management *30*
Process *30*
Procedure *30*
Defect *30*
Purchase specification *31*
Competitive bidding *31*
Tare allowance *32*
Private label *32*
Casual-service restaurant *32*

Taste panel *35*
Value analysis *38*
Cross-functional team *39*
Menu rationalization *40*
Chain of command *42*
Core competencies *42*
Outsourcing (product) *42*
Scratch (made from) *43*
Benchmark *45*
Can-cutting *45*
Drained weight *45*
Liquor (canning) *45*

Blind testing *46*
External service provider *46*
Do or buy analysis *46*
À la carte *48*
Yield (%) *48*
As-purchased (weight) *49*
Edible portion (weight) *49*
Status quo *52*
Hawthorne effect *52*

Make Your Own Purchasing Decisions

1. Some hospitality operations develop purchasing specifications (or, alternatively, receive them from headquarters in the case of chain organizations) but use them only when price quotations are solicited. They do not use them during receiving to ensure that quality standards are met. Do you agree or disagree with this approach? Defend your response. What would you do or what would you say to receiving personnel if you were the new general manager at a property and noticed that the receiving process excluded the use of these tools?

2. The chapter suggests that the primary responsibility for developing purchase specifications in large organizations should rest with the purchasing department. What are the advantages and disadvantages to this suggestion and to an alternative plan in which specification development is the responsibility of the user department? Which alternative is best? Why?

3. The process described for developing purchase specifications involves input from several sources, including suppliers, and it will require some time and effort. Is the process practical in a large organization? A smaller organization? What, if any, shortcuts can you suggest to simplify the process?

4. Assume that a make or buy analysis indicated that a desired service of the proper quality could be obtained from several service providers at approximately the same cost. How should the service provider selection decision then be made?

5. You are the food and beverage director of a mid-sized hotel that has a very temperamental chef. His personal decisions represent the only way he thinks food production activities should be managed. You want to begin serving appetizers in the lounge during late afternoon and early evening to build that business. The chef has no interest in considering convenience food alternatives because he "knows" these products are of inferior quality and will hurt his reputation. He is also concerned about the time needed to prepare these new items because he is busy with other ongoing food production activities. How should you proceed if you want to implement your lounge/appetizer concept?

3

Determining Purchase Quantities

Purchasing Pros Need to Know!

Purchasers must ensure that the employees who require products and services will have them available when needed. This concern, by itself, does not seem difficult. However, taken in the context of quality assessment, pricing concerns, supplier selection, and the other challenges you are learning about in this book, the task becomes more difficult.

Many food and beverage products are perishable, and quality deterioration is likely if they are held in storage for excessive periods. Storage space is expensive, and some products are prone to theft. It is clear, then, that purchasing in larger-than-necessary quantities is not appropriate. Inventory shortages because of insufficient purchase volume are equally unacceptable. As a result, purchasers must be concerned about the balance of "too much" and "too little" as they make purchase quantity decisions. Numerous factors affect the quantity of products to be ordered. Production volumes, quantity discounts, and available storage space are just a few of the special concerns to be considered.

There are two basic approaches to purchasing based on whether products are intended for immediate use or for longer-term availability. Both methods will be discussed, and their pros and cons will be presented. Product yields can affect purchase quantities when on-site processing occurs, and these important considerations are addressed in the chapter. Purchasing decisions require forecasts of production requirements, so the relationships among forecasting, production schedules, and purchasing needs will be discussed.

Not surprisingly, technology can help purchasers predict needs so quantity requirements will be better known. These modules are typically part of a complete purchasing system, but we will focus on production forecasting concerns in this chapter. As we do, you'll learn that basic procedures for manual forecasting are incorporated into production and purchase quantity decisions driven by modern technology.

Two nontraditional purchasing systems help to reduce purchase quantity concerns as inventory-related decisions are made. Just-in-time purchasing and supplier-managed purchasing systems allow purchasers to make long-term purchase commitments without assuming responsibility for on-site storage of the products that are purchased. These systems may be used more frequently in the future by, at least, larger hospitality operations, and we will present a brief overview of them in a concluding section of the chapter.

■ ■ ■

Outline

Correct Purchase Quantities Are Important
    Purchase Needs Can Be Forecasted
    Improper Product Quantities Create Problems
        Excessive Quantities
        Inadequate Quantities
    Basic Inventory Concerns

CORRECT PURCHASE QUANTITIES ARE IMPORTANT

Figure 3.1 (originally shown as Figure 1.2) reviews the basic steps in the purchasing process. We discussed Steps 1 through 3 in Chapter 2, and this current chapter is devoted entirely to Step 4: determine quantity to purchase.

Purchase Needs Can Be Forecasted

Most hospitality operations have recurring purchase needs. Examples include restaurant and hotel food and beverage operations with preplanned menus, noncommercial foodservice operations that use **cyclical menus,** and lodging operations that routinely order specific bed linens, guest room amenities, cleaning supplies, and other items. One possible exception may be a catering business whose only revenue source is special catered events. However, even these operations typically offer preplanned menu suggestions to event sponsors that feature entrées, salads, desserts, and other items that have been used in the past.

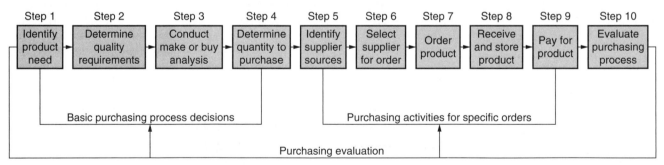

FIGURE 3.1 Steps in Effective Purchasing

Buyer's Guide to Purchasing Term

Cyclical menu   A menu that is repeated on a recurring basis (example: every twenty-one days); cyclical menus are most frequently used in noncommercial foodservice operations. Also known as a "cycle" menu.

The previous examples emphasize the relationship among forecasted customer volumes, production requirements, inventory levels, and the quantities of items to be purchased. Purchasers typically use different procedures to determine necessary quantities for different products. Highly perishable items such as dairy products and fresh produce, for example, cannot typically be purchased in quantities greater than those that will be used over a several-day period. Frozen and canned foods can, if one desires, be purchased for several months (or longer) usage, and other products such as cleaning supplies and paper goods could be purchased in quantities sufficient for even longer time periods.

Improper Product Quantities Create Problems

Problems can occur when products are purchased in greater or lesser quantities than necessary.

EXCESSIVE QUANTITIES   Problems can arise when an excessive quantity is purchased:

- It ties up **capital** that otherwise could be used for another purpose.
- It affects **cash flow.** Products in inventory for excessive times must be paid for before they are used, and that money could be used for other purposes.
- It can affect flexibility. Purchasers may be less interested in taking advantage of special buys at significant discounts when excessive quantities are already on hand. Also, the adoption of new products may be slowed.
- More space must be available to store products.
- There is an increased risk of **theft** and **pilferage.**
- Quality deterioration may occur with perishable products.
- There is an increased risk of product damage or destruction.
- Handling costs increase. Example: Additional time is required to conduct inventories and to perform storeroom cleaning duties.

Are excessive inventory quantities ever acceptable? Ideally, the answer is "no." However, excessive products may be purchased to compensate for poor or inadequate forecasting ("We need to have some products available in case our customer counts are wrong") and to allow for inconsistent supplier performance. This may occur when deliveries are frequently late and/or when shortages occur. (*Note:* Effective management planning and supplier selection decisions can help purchasers maintain proper inventory levels.)

INADEQUATE QUANTITIES   Inadequate purchase quantities can create **stock outs** with the following problems:

- Inability to meet production requirements
- Need to revise production plans to compensate for stock outs
- Possibility of disappointed customers who may visit a property to enjoy a favorite item that is unavailable

Buyer's Guide to Purchasing Terms

Capital   The amount invested in a hospitality operation by its owners (stockholders) and the amount, if any, of invested income retained by the organization that is invested in it.

Theft   The act of unlawfully taking another's property.

Pilferage   The act of stealing small quantities over a relatively long time period.

Stock out   The condition that arises when a product is no longer available in inventory.

The possibility of delivery delays must be considered because they affect the quantity of products that are ordered.

John W. Warden/Stock Connection

• The (probably) unknown effect on consumer choices that affect sales data used for future purchase forecasts; example: Customers who would have ordered the stock-out item must select other menu items, which overstates the popularity of that item and understates the popularity of the stock-out item.

As you've seen, problems arise when there is an excessive or an inadequate supply of products on hand. Many of these problems relate to the exact quantity of products that are ordered.

Basic Inventory Concerns

Products that are purchased and received can be moved into storage areas or enter production immediately. Examples of the latter occur when special steaks required for a catered event are received today for production this evening and when a specific liquor has been out of stock at the bar or on **back order** from the supplier and is now delivered. There are numerous inventory control procedures that become important when products enter storage areas, and these are discussed in Chapter 6.

For reasons including convenience, cost, and practicality, most hospitality buyers do not purchase individual products when the quantities on hand reach an ideal order point for each item. Instead, items are typically divided into several categories, and all (or most) products within that type are ordered at the same time. For example, all fresh produce, fresh meats, and dairy products may be grouped into their specific categories. Then orders are placed for all items within these categories at the same time (and often from the same supplier for that order). This process means that the quantity of each product ordered may be different (more or less) than would be purchased if the order were being placed for just that product.

FACTORS AFFECTING PURCHASE QUANTITIES

Traditionally, the primary factors related to purchase quantity decisions involved the estimated sales forecast (production needs) of an operation; consideration of volume purchase discounts, if any; available storage space; and cash flow. These remain important considerations, but purchasing systems that involve more significant buyer-supplier relationships can affect decisions about the quantity of

---

Buyer's Guide to Purchasing Term

Back order The situation in which a product normally available in a supplier's inventory is out of stock and has been ordered from the supplier's own product source.

Did You Know? (3.1)

The quantities of products ordered must consider **safety levels:** the amount of stock to be available in on-site inventory at all times. Reasons to maintain a safety level include the following:

- To ensure that products are available if supplier delivery schedules are not maintained
- To guard against production forecasting errors when production volumes might be greater than planned
- To allow for planning errors
- To replace products that may be found to be unusable
- To consider miscounts in the quantities of products actually available
- To compensate for product theft or pilferage

The above concerns are important and should be considered. However, managers should not have safety levels that are excessively large because of cost, space needs, and quality deterioration, among other reasons.

All purchasers should attempt to attain the goal of having the right amount of inventory of each product available, and the balance between too little and too much is an ongoing challenge.

Buyers at Work (3.1)

"I know they're expensive, but we're careful, aren't we?" questioned Katie as she talked to Chef Natava. "Besides, we can always use them, so they won't go to waste." Katie was Natava's assistant at the Sandy Waters Inn & Spa, and Natava had just met with the property's purchasing director and food and beverage director about unplanned rising food costs.

"I share your concerns and what we might do about them, Katie," said Natava. "It does make sense to pay close attention to our most expensive items, and beef tenderloins are certainly in that category. They are a regular on our menu, and I wonder if they should be because of price fluctuations. In the past I always tried to have more than we needed available so we wouldn't run out. I wasn't concerned about having too much because we could always process extra loins into tenderloin tip casseroles we could sell for daily specials."

"Well, Natava, that sounds like a great idea to me. So what's the problem now?" asked Katie.

"Well, the problem is that now is different than before," replied Natava. "Our manager asked the food and beverage director to identify ways to lower food costs without reducing quality. She, in turn, asked the purchaser and me for ideas. The purchaser has less to do than me, and he reviewed past purchase orders. Now he says that there isn't always a direct correlation between what we need, what we get, and what we sell, and he used beef tenderloin as an example."

"Well," said Katie, "what are you going to do now?"

"I guess I don't know. The food cost is high, and I need to accept some responsibility for that. I must do something to show good results on next month's food and beverage departmental income statement."

1. What problems can arise with Chef Natava's current tactics for using beef tenderloin? How can his excessive use of this item increase food costs?
2. Assume you are the food and beverage director. What specific assignments to analyze food cost would you give to the purchaser? To Chef Natava?
3. What problems might arise if tenderloins were purchased in excessive quantities? In inadequate quantities?

Buyer's Guide to Purchasing Term

Safety level   The minimum quantity of a specific product that must always be available in inventory.

products to be shipped to a property for a single delivery on a single purchase order. Newer alternatives consider the total quantity of products for which the purchaser will commit to buy over longer time periods. Products may be delivered over many months (or longer) or can be delivered very frequently (even daily) to minimize storage space and other problems related to inventory management. These newer systems require purchasers to think about purchase quantities in a new way, and the amount of product for which a commitment will be made and delivery frequency become separate negotiation concerns. Purchase quantities, then, do not necessarily refer to the amount of product to be delivered at one time for (relatively) immediate use or to replenish inventory levels for a specific order period.

Several other concerns may be important when purchase quantities are determined:

- Many suppliers specify that a minimum dollar value of products be delivered to help compensate for delivery costs.
- When product prices are increasing, purchasers may receive permission to buy in larger-than-normal quantities. Conversely, when market prices are decreasing, buyers may purchase in smaller quantities than normal to increase the turnover of these items and to take advantage of lower prices when future purchases are made.
- Larger quantities may be purchased when, for example, suppliers or manufacturers offer **closeouts** such as short-term promotional discounts to introduce new products and/or to quickly sell products with outdated packaging.
- Trial orders, samples, or other unusually small quantities of products may be ordered at times when new menu items are being considered. A proposed item might, for example, be offered as a "daily special" on several occasions to assess customers' interests.
- Machine parts and supplies for equipment being discontinued by the manufacturer may be purchased in a large quantity to expand the property's useful life of the equipment and/or to gain cost savings because these items will, in the future, need to be purchased from other sources if they will be available at all.

PROFESSIONAL PURCHASING PREVENTS PROBLEMS (3.1)

Suppliers Can Provide Input to Product Purchase Decisions

A common problem: Buyers do not seek purchase advice from their suppliers.

Suppliers can offer service and information that affects a purchaser's decision about the quantity of products to be ordered. As this occurs, purchasers gain value in their relationships with their suppliers. For example, purchasers will not know about closeout specials unless they are informed about them. They cannot take advantage of trial orders or obtain samples unless the suppliers are willing to consent to these typically costly concessions. Rigid definitions of minimum orders for delivery may be "bent" in some instances. Advance information about changes in future market prices may be known by purchasers who keep up with changing market conditions. However, suppliers may have even more current and insightful perspectives about marketplace changes that can be shared. Here is a suggestion: Purchasers should ask suppliers about how they (purchasers) can save purchase dollars without reducing quality. The answers they receive may be surprising and very useful.

Buyer's Guide to Purchasing Term

Closeout   A tactic used by suppliers or manufacturers to quickly move (sell) unwanted inventory by reducing selling prices.

Some cities limit times when trucks can make deliveries to properties in downtown areas. Buyers must consider nontraditional delivery schedules and their effect on the quantities of products to order if these restrictions apply.

Peter Byron/PhotoEdit Inc.

TRADITIONAL PURCHASING METHODS

Traditional hospitality purchasing methods are designed to obtain items for immediate use and for longer-term requirements. We'll look at both of these systems.

Quantities for Immediate Use

Perishable food products such as fresh produce, bakery, and dairy items must be purchased in small quantities that can be used within a short period. Less perishable items such as frozen foods, grocery items, and materials and supplies used by personnel in other departments can be purchased for immediate use or can be stored for longer-term use.

The quantities of perishable products to be purchased require knowledge about the amount of products on hand and an estimate of the quantity needed for the order period. Assume the purchaser determines that eight cases (twenty-four heads each) of lettuce will be needed during the three days for which an order is being placed and that there are one and a half cases available in storage:

8.00 cases	(−)	1.50 cases	(=)	6.50 cases
Quantity Needed for Order Period (3 days)	(−)	Quantity Currently Available	(=)	Quantity to Purchase

Number of cases to order = 7.0

In the example above, the purchaser, working in cooperation with the chef and/or other food and beverage personnel, determines that eight cases of lettuce are needed for the next order period (three days). However, he also notes that there are 1.50 cases (approximately thirty-six heads) currently available. Therefore, 6.50 cases must be purchased (8.00 cases − 1.50 case = 6.50 cases). The purchaser knows that there is typically an increase in product cost when a supplier is asked to **split cases,**

Buyer's Guide to Purchasing Term

Split case A case of less than full purchase unit size sold by a supplier. Example: A supplier sells five #10 cans of peaches rather than a full case containing six #10 cans. Also called broken case.

so it is an easy decision to round up and order seven full cases to meet the property's needs for 6.50 cases. (*Note:* Some suppliers selling to wholesale accounts will not even ship split cases.) Higher charges for broken case quantities are one reason that many small-volume hospitality organizations buy from retail outlets such as buyer clubs. These businesses may sell commercial-sized containers (for example, one #10 can containing approximately twelve cups) at a price lower than a wholesale supplier who would prefer to sell by case lot (six #10 cans per case) only.

The process used to determine the quantity of lettuce to purchase can also be used to calculate the quantities of other perishable items needed for the order period. (*Note:* After the purchaser knows the required items and quantities of each item needed for the order period, he or she can request price quotations from eligible suppliers using a price quotation system detailed in Chapter 5.)

The process just described works well when purchasers can accurately estimate the quantity of items needed for the order period. Typically, the general usage rates of these products are known. Assume business is relatively slow during the first several days of the week (Monday through Thursday) and much busier for the weekend (Friday through Sunday). Purchasers may know the normal usage rates for perishable products during the slower first part of the week and use the process just described to determine purchase quantities for orders to be placed on Friday or Saturday for Monday delivery. (*Note:* Because the quantity of products available at the end of the weekend will not be known when the order for the first part of the week is placed, a conservative estimate (perhaps no on-hand inventory) may be factored into the quantity-to-purchase decision.)

Continuing with our example, the purchaser will then also place an order for perishable goods on Thursday for delivery on Friday. The estimate of higher weekend usage will be known, and the quantity of product currently available when the order is placed can be determined, so it is factored into the purchase quantity decision.

The quantities of products routinely needed must be adjusted as business volume varies. Additional quantities will be needed when business volume is expected to increase because of celebrations, holidays, and other activities. Conversely, business volume estimates will be reduced at other times because of, for example, periods of poor weather and when business is normally slower.

Professional purchasers are always alert to the need to revise the normal quantities of products ordered. They consider situations such as excessive spoilage or waste (which suggests quantities should be reduced) and when stock outs and "emergency" orders consistently occur (which suggest that purchase quantities should be increased).

Generally, purchasers with experience in a specific hospitality organization can establish a foundation of normal (routine) purchase quantities for perishable products and can adjust these for changes in estimated business volumes.

Quantities for Long-Term Use

Hospitality organizations require nonperishable products that purchasers often buy in quantities to last more than several days. However, the factors affecting purchase quantities already noted apply to these items, and purchasing and inventory options are available for each product. When nonperishable products are received, they are typically physically placed into storage areas and purchase information may be entered into the property's perpetual inventory system. (*Note:* Receiving and inventory procedures are discussed in Chapter 6.)

Several systems can be used to determine purchase quantities for nonperishable items when the products are to be delivered to the property at the same time. Procedures used to determine purchase quantities can also differ for different products. As expected, more attention should be paid to managing inventory levels of the most expensive products.

MINIMUM-MAXIMUM INVENTORY SYSTEM   The **minimum-maximum inventory system** requires the purchaser to determine for each product in the system the minimum and the maximum quantity below which and above which, respectively, inventory levels should not fall or rise.

Minimum-maximum inventory system procedures involve determining the quantity of each product that should be ordered to bring the existing inventory level back to the maximum point allowable when the order is received.

The minimum-maximum inventory system is best used when:

- there are standard quality specifications for the products being purchased and these quality requirements do not change.
- product prices are relatively constant.
- products are used in relatively consistent quantities.
- products are expensive (and, therefore, require more extensive purchasing and inventory controls).
- the same type of products will be used in the future.
- products are not perishable. (*Note:* In the hospitality industry, few products, if any, are purchased with the intention that they will remain in inventory for extensive time periods. Exceptions may include some wines, items such as kitchen utensils, and supplies used by maintenance personnel.)
- reasonable maximum quantities do not present storage space problems.
- inventory and storage procedures help ensure that stock is rotated and that theft and pilferage are minimized.

The minimum-maximum inventory system is best used to control the relatively few and most expensive **"A" items.** It is not typically applicable to inexpensive, low-volume, and nonperishable products without a long storage life. Instead, the par inventory system discussed in the following section is often used for these items.

Several concepts (terms) must be understood as the minimum-maximum inventory system is discussed:

- *Purchase unit.*   The standard size of the package or container in which the product is typically purchased. For example, many canned fruit and vegetable products are purchased by the case (six #10 cans per case), and frozen shrimp may be purchased by the case (ten five-pound boxes or bags per case).
- *Product usage rate.*   The number of purchase units (see above) used during a typical order period.
- *Order period.*   The time (number of days or weeks) for which an order is normally placed. For example, canned goods may be purchased once monthly, and frozen shrimp may be purchased once every two weeks.
- *Lead time.*   The number of purchase units typically used during the time between placement and delivery. For example, if three cases (fifty pounds

Buyer's Guide to Purchasing Terms

Minimum-maximum inventory system   A system to calculate product purchase quantities that considers the minimum quantity below which inventory levels should not fall and the maximum quantity above which inventory levels should not rise.

"A" items   The relatively few items that cost the majority of purchase dollars. Examples typically include meats, seafood, and alcoholic beverages.

Usage rate (minimum-maximum system)   The number of purchase units used during a typical order period.

Lead time (minimum-maximum system)   The number of purchase units typically used during the time between order placement and delivery.

each) of frozen shrimp are normally used during the several days separating product order and receipt, the lead time for this product is three cases.
- *Safety level.*   The minimum number of purchase units that must always remain in inventory in case of late deliveries and unexpected increases in product usage rates.
- *Order point.*   The number of purchase units to be available in inventory when an order is placed.

Assume that a seafood restaurant uses a large quantity of frozen shrimp of a specified size. It is an expensive "A" item included in the property's minimum-maximum inventory system. Let's further assume the following:

- Purchase unit (frozen shrimp): Case = 10 boxes (5 lb. each; 50 lb. total)
- Product usage rate = 42 cases per order period
- Order period = 2 weeks (14 days)
    Note: Daily usage rate = 3 cases (42 cases per order period ÷ 14 days)
- Product lead time = 4 days
    Note: Number of cases used during lead time = 12 cases (3 cases per day × 4 days)
- Product safety level = 12 cases

The purchaser now can address several questions about the purchase quantities for frozen shrimp.

Question #1   What is the maximum number of cases of shrimp that should ever be available in inventory?

42 cases	(+)	12 cases	(=)	54
Usage rate cases	(+)	Safety level	(=)	Maximum cases

Question #2   What is the order point for the shrimp?

12 cases	(+)	12 cases	=	24 cases
Lead time	(+)	Safety level	=	Cases at order point

The order point (24 cases) can be verified:

No. of cases available when shrimp is ordered	24 cases
(−) No. of cases used until shrimp is delivered (product lead time)	(12 cases)
Number of cases available when shrimp is delivered (safety level)	12 cases

Question #3   How many cases of shrimp should be ordered at the order point (when there are 12 cases in storage)?

42 cases	(+)	24 cases	(=)	66 cases
Usage rate	(+)	Order point	(=)	Cases to order

The number of cases to order at the order point can be verified:

Cases available = 66 (24 cases [order point] (+) 42 cases [usage rate])

(−) Lead time cases = 12

54 cases (maximum inventory level)

Buyer's Guide to Purchasing Term

Order point (minimum-maximum system)   The number of purchase units that should be available in inventory when an order is placed.

Question #4   How many cases of shrimp should be ordered if an order is placed when there are 30 cases in inventory? The order point for shrimp has not been reached, but the order is placed with other frozen seafood products, and all products will be purchased from the seafood supplier at the same time.

Step A: Calculate the number of cases of shrimp that exceed the order point:

30 cases	(−)	24 cases	(=)	6
Cases in storage	(−)	Order point	(=)	Excess cases

Step B: Calculate the number of cases to order:

42 cases	(−)	6	(=)	36 cases
Order point	(−)	Excess cases	(=)	Cases to order

The 36 cases of shrimp to order when there are 6 cases in excess of the order point can be verified:

36	(+)	30	(=)	66
Cases ordered	(+)	Cases in inventory	(=)	Total cases available when order is placed

66 cases	(−)	12 cases	(=)	54 cases
Cases available	(−)	Lead time cases	(=)	Maximum number of cases

When reviewing the questions above, note that information relating to product usage rate, order period, lead time, and safety level can be used to determine the following:

- The minimum number of cases to be in inventory
- The maximum number of cases allowable in inventory
- The order point (number of cases)
- The number of cases that should purchased if an order will be placed before that product's order point is reached

The safety level for the product represents the minimum number of purchased units below which product quantities cannot decrease. Factors to consider when establishing the safety level include the following:

- *The lead time required for reorders.*   As the frequency of deliveries decreases, the number of lead-time units should increase. When delivery timing and schedules are not predictable, minimum inventory levels must be increased to consider this uncertainty and to reduce the possibility of stock outs.
- *The product's usage rate.*   As the volume of product usage increases, safety levels may need to be increased accordingly. It is more likely to expect greater volumes of unexpected purchases for higher-sales-volume items than from lower-sales-volume items. Likewise, more customers are likely to be dissatisfied with stock outs of popular items. (*Note:* The goal is to reduce/eliminate stock outs so no customer or user department employee will be dissatisfied or frustrated.)

An ideal safety level will minimize the possibility of stock outs without the need to maintain excessive quantities of products in inventory.

Several factors also influence the decision about the lead times established for products. They can be established by considering the amount of time generally required for an order. If usage and safety levels incorporate a margin ("cushion") for unanticipated problems, a small variance in the length of lead time is not critical. However, as these usage and safety level quantities are minimized, greater concerns about lead-time problems are warranted, and it is more likely that time-consuming expediting will be required to obtain needed items.

Conditions that could increase the length of product delivery lead times include the following:

- When suppliers are not dependable (and this should be an important factor in deciding whether to continue to do business with them)
- When the hospitality operation is in a remote location and long delivery delays are more common
- When market situations cause unpredictable conditions that affect the availability of products and the potential need for back orders of some items

Potential advantages to use of the minimum-maximum inventory system include the following:

- Excessive stock buildup is less likely if a reasonable maximum inventory level has been established.
- The minimum level provides a cushion against stock outs.
- The system is easy to understand, explain, and use.
- Actual purchasing performance can be monitored against expected performance. Reasons for inventory levels that exceed and are less than those established for the system can be investigated, and corrective actions can be taken as necessary.
- Analysis of inventory levels may yield changes in product order quantities that might not otherwise have been noticed.

Potential disadvantages to the system are the following:

- It may not be the optimal way to calculate required quantities. There are, for example, computer-assisted systems that provide more detailed and accurate forecasts of quantity purchase needs and the timing for purchases. These systems are increasingly used by larger and even relatively small hospitality organizations. (*Note:* This topic is discussed later in this chapter.)
- The assumptions used to establish the system's safety and lead-time calculations may decrease its accuracy, which can yield excessive inventory or stock outs.
- Quantity discounts may not be possible when maximum inventory quantities cannot be exceeded and when these levels are below supplier-specified quantities for which discounts are applied.
- Some staff time is required to initially consider and calculate accurate safety and lead-time estimates.

The quantity of a specific product that is ordered can affect the price per purchase unit, and amounts based on minimum-maximum calculations may be adjusted accordingly.

Photolibrary.com

PAR INVENTORY SYSTEM   A **par inventory system** is similar to the minimum-maximum inventory system just discussed because the quantity of products purchased brings inventory levels to an allowable maximum (par). The system is commonly used for alcoholic beverages (beer, wines, and spirits), dishwashing and other chemicals, linen supplies, and other nonperishable products.

The quantity of product used for the par is determined on the basis of experience, "trial and error," and other factors discussed above relative to safety stock levels and usage rates for the minimum-maximum system.

Let's see how the par system works. The manager (who is also the purchaser) of the Desert Oasis Bar and Grill has established a par level of ten cases (twenty-four bottles per case) of Desert Waters beer. She orders the item on Tuesday for delivery on Thursday to maintain this par level. Before ordering, the manager counts the number of cases available and "rounds down" to the nearest full case. Example: This week she has four full cases and an opened case with seven bottles. Because only full cases are included in the par calculations, she notes four cases in inventory.

The manager also knows that she normally uses about one case each on Tuesdays and Wednesdays (the two days between order and delivery), and she also recalls the seven bottles in an open case. Therefore, she believes her estimate of a two-case usage for Tuesday and Wednesday will not yield a stock out.

Next she determines the need to order eight cases from the local supplier:

$$
\begin{array}{ccccccc}
(10\ \text{cases}) & (-) & 4 & (-) & (2) & (=) & 8 \\
\text{Par level} & (-) & \begin{array}{c}\text{Number of cases}\\\text{available}\end{array} & (-) & \begin{array}{c}\text{Number of cases}\\\text{used before}\\\text{delivery}\end{array} & (=) & \begin{array}{c}\text{Number of}\\\text{cases to order}\end{array}
\end{array}
$$

If her usage estimate is correct, the par inventory level will be maintained when the delivery arrives:

$$
\begin{array}{ccccc}
4 & (-) & 2 & (=) & 2 \\
\begin{array}{c}\text{Number of cases}\\\text{available}\end{array} & (-) & \begin{array}{c}\text{Number of cases}\\\text{used}\end{array} & (=) & \begin{array}{c}\text{Number of cases}\\\text{available at delivery}\end{array}
\end{array}
$$

$$
\begin{array}{ccccc}
(2) & (+) & 8 & (=) & 10 \\
\begin{array}{c}\text{Number of cases}\\\text{available at}\\\text{delivery}\end{array} & (+) & \begin{array}{c}\text{Number of cases}\\\text{delivered}\end{array} & (=) & \begin{array}{c}\text{Par inventory}\\\text{level}\end{array}
\end{array}
$$

Buyer's Guide to Purchasing Term

Par inventory system   A system in which purchase quantities are calculated on the basis of the number of purchase units required to return inventory quantities to a predetermined level.

You'll notice that the manager was able to make an easy and fast determination about the number of cases of Desert Waters beer to order by considering the following:

- The established par level
- The number of cases currently available
- The number of cases likely to be used between when the product was ordered and delivered

The par inventory system has advantages (it is fast and simple) that must be countered with the potential disadvantages of stock outs. These can occur, for example, if the par level is too low, the usage rate is higher than expected, and/or the purchaser is unable to expedite another delivery if unforeseen problems occur. (Examples include higher-than-expected usage during the delivery time or an unanticipated special event.)

Par inventories do not typically create problems with excessive quantities on hand because wise buyers decrease par levels if they notice that quantities on hand are increasing. Conversely, decreased quantities available immediately before deliveries are made will likely be noticed, and anticipated usage rates are considered so par levels can be adjusted. The process just described is a trial-and-error method that over time works well in many hospitality operations.

OTHER SYSTEMS TO DETERMINE PURCHASE QUANTITIES   The widely diverse situations within which purchasers work enable the use of other systems to determine purchase quantities:

- *Exact requirements system.*   This involves the purchase of products in exact quantities needed. For example, a special banquet function may be planned with an entrée item not generally used for other purposes. The exact quantity required for that special event would be ordered on a one-time basis, and no permanent inventory of that product would be desired.
- *Cyclical ordering system.*   This method involves a periodic assessment of inventory quantities with a decision then made about the need for additional quantities. For example, consider a large quantity of light bulbs purchased some time ago and a decreasing inventory level as they are used. At some point, a decision will be made to purchase additional quantities of the light bulbs.

  This process is used to determine the quantity of many items purchased by hospitality operations. While not a useful method for expensive and frequently used "A" items, it can be used for other items, especially when suppliers can provide short delivery lead times.
- *Cooperative (pool) buying.*   This method involves several organizations that combine orders for a similar quality of products who submit one rather than separate orders to a supplier. This method may not have a direct effect

---

Buyer's Guide to Purchasing Terms

Exact requirements system   A purchasing system in which specific products in specific quantities are purchased for a specific function or for a nonrecurring purpose.

Cyclical ordering system   An ordering method that involves a periodic assessment of quantities of products available in inventory with a decision made at that time about whether additional quantities should be purchased.

Cooperative (pool) buying   An ordering method that involves several organizations that combine orders for a similar quality of products and who submit one rather than separate orders to a supplier.

on the quantity of products purchased by a specific organization. However, participants may need to agree to purchase a minimum quantity when they place an order for a specific item, and/or to remain members of the cooperative buying system.

- *Economic order quantity (EOQ) method.* This typically computerized method involves using mathematical calculations to analyze costs related to factors such as product price, usage rates, and internal handling costs to determine an order quantity with the lowest total variable costs. The method can yield lower inventory levels and fewer orders with minimal chance of stock outs.

- *Definite quantity contract.* Large-quantity buyers may enter into an agreement with a supplier to purchase a definite quantity of products over a specified number of deliveries. Purchasers estimate the total quantity of product required for the contract period by considering anticipated business volumes during the order period. Delivery charges, if any, imposed by the supplier and available storage space are also considered as delivery frequency is determined.

    This method may have merits when significant quantity discounts (a likely incentive for the purchaser to make a long-term commitment) are involved and a consistent supply source is assured. It is also most useful when potential inventory excesses can be utilized and when purchasers desire to minimize the time and effort required to select suppliers for more frequent orders.

- *Requirements contracts.* This method is similar to the definite quantity contract just discussed, except that the purchase quantity is not fixed. For example, a purchaser may have an agreement with a dairy to deliver varying quantities of milk based on sales volume needs at the same per-gallon price for a specific time period. (*Note:* There may be an agreed-on minimum quantity.) The advantages to this system are similar to those discussed for a definite quantity contract. One further advantage to the purchaser (with, possibly, a higher per-unit cost attached) is that the purchaser can be more flexible; only a range of quantity needs rather than a fixed quantity must be estimated and negotiated.

- *Open market purchasing.* For products purchased in small quantities and at minimum value, the calculation of exact quantity needs is less important. A workable procedure may be that items such as office supplies in a small organization will be purchased at a local retail business in a quantity roughly equal to consumption using a petty cash system. (Petty cash systems are discussed in Chapter 6.)

Buyer's Guide to Purchasing Terms

Economic order quantity (EOQ) method   This involves use of mathematical calculations that allow purchasers to determine product order quantities that yield the lowest total variable costs.

Definite quantity contract   A commitment made by a purchaser to a supplier that a specified (definite) quantity of products will be purchased and delivered to the organization in a specified number of deliveries.

Requirement contracts   Commitments made by a purchaser to a supplier to purchase a minimum quantity of a specified product during a specific time period.

Open market purchasing   A purchasing method involving the use of petty cash systems to purchase small quantities of items.

Product Yields Affect Purchase Quantities

The purchasing task would be very easy if all products purchased have a 100 percent yield, and some products do. For example, frozen preportioned eight-ounce hamburger patties have an approximate eight-ounce (100 percent) yield. (*Note:* The menu should indicate that the patty has a **portion size** weight of eight ounces as purchased (AP) because there will be some cooking loss resulting in an edible portion (EP) weight of slightly less than eight ounces.)

The quantity to purchase is relatively easy to determine when there is a 100 percent yield. Consider the eight-ounce frozen portions of hamburger steak noted above:

$$
\begin{array}{ccccc}
\text{Estimated} & & \text{Number of} & & \text{Quantity of} \\
\text{portions} & & \text{portions} & & \text{eight ounce} \\
\text{required for} & (-) & \text{in} & (=) & \text{portions} \\
\text{order period} & & \text{inventory} & & \text{required}
\end{array}
$$

Purchasers typically buy preportioned meat products by the pound (1 lb. = 16 oz.), and there are two 8-ounce portions per pound (16 oz. ÷ 8 oz. = 2 portions). Standard packaging containers may be ten-pound boxes or bags (10 pounds × 2 8-oz. portions per pound = 20 8-oz. portions per container) or 25-pound packaging units (25 lb. × 2 8-oz. portions per pound = 50 8-oz. portions per container).

Many products, however, do not have a 100 percent yield, and it is more difficult to determine the quantity of these items to purchase even when the number of portions required is known.

Example: Assume that a manager for an upscale restaurant is planning a banquet for 100 guests, and the host has requested that six-ounce tenderloin fillets be served. The restaurant purchases whole tenderloins weighing about ten pounds that have an AP cost of $14.75 per pound. This entrée is a popular choice, and the restaurant's buyer, working with the chef, has performed **yield tests** that reveal there is an approximate 60 percent yield for the desired product.

The buyer can use yield test information for numerous purposes. For example, he or she can calculate the following:

- *Production loss.* This is the amount (weight and/or percent) of a product's AP weight, which is not servable because of, for example, trim loss from fat and bones and shrinkage from cooking (roasting).

  In our whole tenderloin example, a ten-pound (AP) loin will have a 40 percent production loss:

$$
\begin{array}{ccccc}
100\% & (-) & 60\% & (=) & 40\% \\
\text{AP weight} & (-) & \text{yield} & (=) & \text{production loss}
\end{array}
$$

- *Weight after processing and cooking.* The loin will weigh only six pounds after on-site trimming and roasting:

$$
\begin{array}{ccccc}
10 \text{ lb.} & (\times) & [100\% - 40\%] & (=) & 6 \text{ lb.} \\
\text{AP weight} & (\times) & [\text{AP yield} - \text{production loss}] & (=) & \text{weight after processing}
\end{array}
$$

Buyer's Guide to Purchasing Terms

Portion size   The quantity (weight, count, or volume) of a menu item to be served to a guest.

Yield test   A carefully controlled process to determine the amount (weight and/or percent) of the as-purchased quantity of a product remaining after production loss has occurred.

Production loss   The amount (weight and/or percent) of a product's as-purchased weight that is not servable.

- *Amount of product to purchase (no inventory).*   The purchaser knows that only 60 percent of the quantity of whole tenderloins purchased will be servable for the banquet. The amount needed for the event, assuming no product is currently available on-site, can be easily calculated:

$$\frac{100 \text{ portions needed } \times 6 \text{ oz. per portion}}{60\% \text{ yield}} = \frac{600 \text{ oz.}}{.60} = 1,000 \text{ oz.}$$

$$\frac{1,000 \text{ oz.}}{16 \text{ oz.}} = 62.5 \text{ pounds}$$

Because each tenderloin weighs approximately ten pounds, the purchaser will need to buy seven loins (62.5 lb. ÷ 10-lb. loin = 6.25 rounded to 7 loins).

- *Amount of product to purchase if some product is available in inventory.*   Assume the purchaser has three whole ten-pound loins in storage that are not needed for another purpose. He or she must then purchase four additional loins to meet banquet production requirements:

$$7 \text{ loins needed} - 3 \text{ loins available} = 4 \text{ loins to purchase}$$

- *Cost per servable pound.*   The cost per servable pound is the cost of one pound of product that can be readily served to guests. In our example, the whole tenderloin costs $14.75 (AP) per pound and has a 60 percent yield. The cost per servable pound is $24.58:

$$\text{Cost per servable pound } = \frac{\text{AP price/\#}}{\text{yield \%}} = \frac{\$14.75}{.60} = \$24.58$$

- *Food cost for one portion.*   The restaurant manager will likely establish the selling price for the banquet based, at least in part, on the food cost incurred. Food costs for all items to be served must be determined and, for the tenderloin, it is as follows:

$$\frac{\text{Food cost}}{\text{(one portion)}} = \frac{\$24.58 \text{ (cost per servable \#)}}{16 \text{ oz.}} = \$1.54 \text{ (cost per ounce)}$$

$$\$1.54 \text{ (cost per ounce)} \times 6 \text{ oz. (portion size)} = \$9.24 \text{ (portion cost)}$$

Note: The tenderloin cost would increase if, for example, it were served bacon wrapped and/or with a sauce.

- *Selling price information.*   Some of the most popular menu pricing methods use markups based on food cost. We know only the entrée cost in this example ($9.24). Assume that the salad, **accompaniment costs** (the cost of all other food items served on the entrée plate), bread and butter, and dessert are $6.75 when prepared according to applicable standard recipes that have

---

Buyer's Guide to Purchasing Terms

Cost per servable pound   The cost of one pound of a product in a form that can be served to guests.

Food cost (portion)   The cost of one portion of a food item when it is prepared and portioned according to its standard recipe.

Accompaniment costs   Items such as salads, potatoes, and/or other choices that are offered with and included within the price charged for an entrée.

been **precosted** with current market costs. The manager can use this information to calculate the banquet's **base selling price** (assume the meal should be priced at a 35 percent food cost) based on its total **plate cost:**

Step 1—Determine total plate cost

$15.99	(=)	$9.24	(+)	$6.75
Total food cost	(=)	Entrée cost	(+)	Accompaniment cost

Step 2—Calculate the base selling price

$45.69		$15.99		.35
Base selling price	(=)	Total food cost	(÷)	Desired food cost percent

---

Did You Know? (3.3)

You've learned that buyers must know about product yields and production losses as they determine purchase quantities. What can they do to help ensure that the yield of an item is the same (or at least very similar) each time it is purchased so production quantities, costs, and selling price calculations can be reasonably accurate?

The following operating tactics are helpful. Each involves a management (not purchaser) responsibility, but each becomes especially important as the buyer's input about "real" product costs is shared with production managers:

- *Conduct yield tests.* Yield depends on a product's grade, AP weight, prepreparation and preparation methods, and cooking times and temperatures. Purchasers working with managers and food production personnel can obtain product samples, conduct yield tests, and make decisions about products that should be purchased.
- Incorporate yield test results into purchase specifications, share them with potential suppliers, and require that price quotations be based on the quality described in the purchase specification.
- Assume that all operating controls are consistently used. For example, when incoming products are received, they must be checked against applicable purchase specifications (see Chapter 6), ovens must be **calibrated** to ensure that desired temperatures are maintained, and cooking times and temperatures must be closely monitored.
- Consider use of industry standards such as the U.S. Department of Agriculture's Institutional Meat Purchase Specifications (IMPS) and standards developed by the North American Meat Processors Association (NAMP). (*Note:* See Chapter 7 regarding meat purchasing.)

Buyer's Guide to Purchasing Terms

Precost (recipe) The process of establishing the cost to produce all (or one) serving of a recipe by considering the recipe's ingredients, current ingredient costs, and the number of portions the recipe yields.

Base selling price The benchmark selling price of a menu item calculated by the use of a markup or other objective pricing method. After its calculation, managers may determine the actual selling price based on marketing issues, competitive pricing structures, and the "psychology" of menu pricing.

Plate cost The sum of all product costs included in a single meal (or "plate").

Calibrate (oven) To verify, check, or adjust the heating control of an oven against the actual internal temperature of the equipment.

In this example, the manager may price the banquet meal at $45.50, $45.75, or another amount that includes the base selling price as a pricing factor.*

Buyer's Guide to Internet Resources: Determining Purchase Quantities

Web Site	Topic
www.chefdesk.com	Food cost (yield information) for commonly used food products
www.purchasing.com	Minimum-maximum system (or numerous other purchasing-related topics). Type topic name in the site's search box.
www.inventoryops.com	Inventory safety levels; under "inventory management," click on "optimizing safety stock."
www.logistics.about.com	Inventory management practices. Type "Inventory Management" and "Purchasing" into the site's "Search" box.
www.scmr.com	Inventory management. Enter "inventory management" in the search box for this site.
www.businessknowhow.com	Inventory planning (or other purchasing-related topics). Type topic name in the site's search box.
www.adacoservices.com	Food and beverage product control, including inventory quantities.
www.comtrex.com	Food and beverage product control, including inventory quantities.
www.culinarysoftware.com	Information about software for food and beverage product control, including inventory quantities.

FORECASTING AND PRODUCTION SCHEDULES

Most methods used to determine purchase quantities consider production needs. As more products are used, inventory levels are depleted, and additional quantities must be purchased. The purchasing methods described in this chapter have, directly or indirectly, been driven by estimates (forecasts) of business volumes.

There are, however, exceptions to this relationship. Consider the routine practice of lodging properties to stock bed linens and guest room amenities on the basis of the number of rooms available at the property rather than on the number of guests who will occupy the rooms during a specific time period. Managers and their purchasing staff know (hope) that all of the rooms will be occupied sometime, and the products and supplies required to serve the highest occupancy needs must be available even though fewer items will actually be needed for lower occupancy periods.

Other examples include custodial supplies used to clean public spaces that are required in large amounts because these areas must be cleaned frequently without regard to the number of guests. Exterior window cleaning and parking lot maintenance supplies are additional examples of purchases that typically depend on factors other than guest counts.

---

*For details about menu pricing, see J. Ninemeier and D. Hayes. *Restaurant Operations Management: Principles and Practices.* Upper Saddle River, NJ. Pearson/Prentice-Hall. 2006. (See Chapter 6.)

Wise purchasers understand that these types of products should not be purchased without considering reasonable inventory levels. However, because these products are not perishable, judgment errors will not result in the waste that occurs when perishable products must be discarded. Careful attention to production needs based on forecasted sales volumes is, however, absolutely critical for perishable items.

The method used to make an accurate production forecast is relatively straightforward. Food and beverage managers track historic sales, make adjustments for anticipated events, and use this information to establish customer counts for future periods. This data, in turn, drives the quantities of products required for the planning period.

Manual Systems

Traditionally and even in many food and beverage operations today, forecasting calculations are done manually. Managers might record the number of total guests served for each meal period and use this data to develop future sales estimates. The average total number of customers served on Friday for the past five weeks might be used as a base for estimating consumer counts for next Friday. This process can then be repeated to generate customer count estimates for all days in the planning horizon. Manual systems can also be more specific. For example, managers might consider the percentage of customers likely to order specific menu items, and this detailed information is even more helpful to determine purchase quantities.

Consider the following example:

- The anticipated total number of customers to be served during the evening meal periods next week based on forecasts made from customer counts for evening meal periods for the previous 5 weeks = 670.
- The percentage of customers who ordered the steak entrée based on actual sales records for the past 5 weeks = 9%.
- Estimated number of steak entrées to be purchased by customers next week = 60 (670 estimated customers × 0.09 steak purchase percentage = 60 steaks sales estimate).

In this example, the estimate of customers served next week (the order period for frozen steaks) is 670 and is based on the average served during the evening meal period for the past five weeks. Because no out-of-the-ordinary events are anticipated that will affect customer counts, this base (670 customers) is used.

Historical records also reveal that approximately 9 percent of evening meal customers order this entrée. Therefore, the estimated number of steak entrée portions (60) can be easily determined. This process can be repeated to calculate the number of other entrée portions to be ordered, and managers can use spreadsheet programs such as Microsoft's Excel to quickly make the calculations.

With estimates of production needs for menu items known, purchasing personnel can then consider existing inventory levels and other information needed to make effective purchase quantity decisions for the coming week.

Ingredients required for other items, including entrée accompaniments, salads, desserts, and beverages, might be ordered on the basis of one or more of the inventory management systems discussed earlier in this chapter.

Manual systems are made easier with the use of **point-of-sale (POS) systems** that automatically generate customer counts, menu item sales, and

Buyer's Guide to Purchasing Term

Point-of-sale (POS) system   A computerized device that records sales and payment information, among numerous other functions.

The proper quantity of products must be ordered to ensure that production personnel have the ingredients necessary to prevent stock outs and customer disappointment.

Mira.com/Artist Name

(seemingly) innumerable other types of information as a result of tallying transaction data.

Most POS systems routinely generate this predictive information to forecast the quantities of items that should be purchased. Because these calculations are made electronically, they are probably not considered manual systems. However, manual effort may still be required to determine quantity needs for all nonentrée products required for the order period.

Computerized systems that provide more detailed quantity-to-purchase information are also available and are discussed next.

Computerized Systems

Up to this point, we have discussed a system used to forecast the quantity of products needed that uses information generated by a basic POS system. However, systems that assist purchasers with more electronically generated information helpful in purchasing tasks are also available.

Advanced POS systems can track the sale of every menu item to determine the quantity of ingredients that should have been used to produce them. This information can be used for food cost control purposes to answer the following question: To what extent does actual product usage match theoretical usage based on actual sales? The data can also be used to assist in determining product purchase quantities for subsequent order periods.

In an oversimplified example, assume that **standard recipes** have been interfaced with the POS system. The number of customers ordering each menu item is easily determined, and this information is used to determine the quantities of ingredients that should have been used.

Assume that standard recipes indicate that two ounces of tomato sauce are used in each chili portion and one ounce of tomato sauce is used in each meat loaf portion at the Home Town Restaurant. Assume also that tomato sauce is not an

Buyer's Guide to Purchasing Term

Standard recipe   Instructions to produce a food or beverage item that will help ensure that quality and quantity standards are attained.

ingredient in any other dinner product served at the property. Because the number of persons ordering chili and meat loaf are known, the quantity of tomato sauce used as an ingredient in these items can also be calculated. The total quantity of tomato sauce used to serve customers during the evening meal period can be combined with the total amount of this product used to produce menu items for other meal periods (for example, tomato sauce is used in the sauce for breakfast omelets and for casserole dishes used for lunch). The total amount of tomato sauce used can be "converted" into purchase units (for example, the number of cases of six #10 cans). For example, if approximately one-eighth cup of tomato paste is, on average, used for each customer, this estimate (one-eighth cup) can be multiplied by the estimated number of customers to be served to determine the quantity of tomato sauce likely needed.

Computerized systems do not replace the need for managers and purchasing staff to use their judgment as purchase quantity decisions are made. However, these systems do provide a benchmark of information to help determine the actual quantity of product that should be purchased.

NONTRADITIONAL PURCHASING SYSTEMS

This chapter concludes with a brief discussion of two nontraditional purchasing systems that have application to the hospitality industry. Both systems involve a "partnership" between buyer and seller, and they provide examples of how value-added information and services from a supplier can be more cost effective than traditional methods that emphasize only lowest cost.

PROFESSIONAL PURCHASING PREVENTS PROBLEMS (3.2)

Technology Provides Useful and Easy-to-Use Information

A common problem: Many managers and purchasers do not take advantage of their POS system's capabilities.

This chapter has previewed the role that technology increasingly plays in helping purchasers to determine the quantity of products that are needed. Basic information provided by most point-of-sale systems can be used to estimate the quantity of each menu item that has been sold. Because many are "A" items, these electronic systems help purchasers to control their most expensive items. POS systems can also use information from standard recipes to provide usage information about their ingredients that can provide assistance in determining product quantities needed for future purchases.

Both of these technology advancements can be compared to traditional (manual) methods of tallying hard copy guest checks to yield calculations about sales forecasts. Modern systems are more accurate, and as important, they allow managers and purchasers to use their time for creative decision making rather than spending it to generate information. Few managers tally guest checks manually today. Many, however, do not use the capabilities of their POS systems to provide very important purchasing information. (*Note:* Detailed information about technology will be presented in Chapter 12.)

Buyers at Work (3.2)

"There is never a good time to run out of a product, but today is absolutely the worst time!" shouted Harry as he grabbed the telephone.

Flora, a cook at the Calvin Avenue Retirement Center had seldom seen Harry, the head cook, so angry.

"I fixed the problem this time, but I'm going to lose bargaining power the next time this happens," said Harry as he put down the phone. "The salesperson is dropping off the two cases we need this morning, and we can then do the preprep later this afternoon.

"This started when our facility administrator centralized purchasing to coordinate our purchase needs with the other three retirement centers our company operates. I see the advantage—volume discounts—but we don't receive the quantity of product we order. Before this change, I could determine the number of cases needed, contact the supplier, and simply place an order. What could be easier?"

"Well, I'm glad you noticed that we didn't have what was needed to prepare our holiday dinner for tomorrow," said Flora. "It's a shame the suppliers didn't deliver the quantity of items we need."

"There's got to be something wrong with our purchasing system," replied Harry, "and I hope they fix it soon!"

1. What procedures should Harry be using to determine the quantities of products he is requesting the company's purchasing agent to obtain for him?
2. Assuming that Harry is specifying the appropriate quantity of items, what problems could create the present situation in which the desired product quantities are not being delivered?
3. What concerns would you have about a centralized purchasing system that allows an individual in a specific unit (the retirement center) to contact suppliers directly? Is this a good or bad idea? Defend your response.

Just-in-Time Purchasing

Most purchasing methods discussed in this chapter involve ordering a specified quantity of product for a specific order period with one delivery for all products in the order. (*Note:* Two systems (definite quantity contracts and requirements contracts) did incorporate the concept of deliveries being negotiated separately. **Just-in-time (JIT) purchasing** is a variation of these two methods.)

The goal of a JIT system is for the necessary quantity of required products to arrive when they are needed for production. For example, products required for the next day's production might be delivered the previous afternoon. Some additional storage space would be available to store small quantities of products for "emergency" use.

Potential advantages to JIT systems include the following:

- Reduced on-site storage space
- An improved "partnership" with suppliers
- Lessened time and problems caused as interactions with numerous suppliers occur
- Reduced waste from spoilage

Buyer's Guide to Purchasing Term

Just-in-time (JIT) purchasing   A purchasing system in which a long-term commitment is made with a supplier to make frequent product deliveries to enable the hospitality organization to minimize on-site product storage; also called "lean purchasing."

Traditional Purchasing	JIT Purchasing
• Purchase in relatively small quantities.	• Purchase commitment for greater quantities of products.
• Fewer deliveries of greater quantities.	• Frequent deliveries of smaller quantities.
• Products rejected at time of delivery are reordered.	• Items rejected are redelivered without an additional order.
• Lowest price is the primary purchasing objective.	• Total acquisition cost is the primary purchasing objective.
• Supplier determines delivery schedule.	• Purchaser determines delivery schedule.
• Formal communication (e.g., purchase orders).	• Less formal communication.
• Innovations are discouraged.	• Innovations are encouraged (required).
• Significant time spent on purchasing functions.	• Less time spent on direct purchasing activities.
• Purchaser-supplier "partnership" is not a consideration.	• Purchaser-supplier "partnership" is critical.

FIGURE 3.2   Traditional and JIT Purchasing Systems

- Fewer opportunities for theft and pilferage
- Reduced amount of money tied up in inventory

Purchasers using a JIT system must "qualify" a supplier to make the process most beneficial, so concerns about **single sourcing** can be overcome: "What do we do if we can't get necessary supplies from our single supplier?"

Potential concerns about JIT include the following:

- Production issues and delays if products are not delivered
- Apprehension about making significant changes in existing purchasing systems
- The need for significant planning to ensure that a system is cost effective and to develop procedures for its implementation and operation

Figure 3.2 Reviews major differences between traditional and JIT purchasing systems.

How might a JIT system actually work in a hospitality organization? Let's consider the food and beverage operation in a large hotel in an area with a strong base of tourist business yielding a high occupancy rate (e.g., a branded hotel in Waikiki, Honolulu, Hawaii). Top-level managers and their purchasing staff meet with suppliers to explain their potential interest in a JIT system with a six-month commitment to a single supplier to provide specific products. The hotel will require deliveries six days each week, and the supplier must provide an agreed-on quantity of on-site "backup" products. Numerous other details must also be considered and agreed on.

Suppliers are asked to quote an amount above an agreed-on standard such as the published market price available from several available sources that he or she will charge. For example, an egg supplier may agree to supply whole eggs meeting the buyer's specification for three cents per dozen above the published market price. The supplier chosen will be the one submitting the lowest markup price above the current market price for each delivery.

Buyer's Guide to Purchasing Term

Single sourcing   The concept of relying on only a single supplier as the source of one or more specific products.

Perishable produce may be received daily when a just-in-time purchasing system is used. However, it still must be checked when delivered to confirm that quality requirements are met.
Vincent P. Walter/Pearson Education/PH College

There are two basic types of quantity purchases involved in this system. Some grocery goods (e.g., canned tomato paste and paper goods) are used on a fairly consistent basis, and a **standing order** is established for these items. Unless adjustments are made, the same quantity of these products will be delivered daily.

Other products, including produce, required in significantly larger quantities than the standing order because of large banquets and specialty items required for catered events are electronically ordered each day.

Products required for the next day's production are delivered in the afternoon of the previous day with the hotel's receiving personnel performing normal receiving tasks (see Chapter 6), and items are moved into applicable storage areas. They remain on the transport carts used to move them from the loading dock or receiving area to the store room. The next morning products are transported to applicable production areas, and carts are returned to the receiving area for that afternoon's delivery.

While the above case study is oversimplified, it illustrates the mutual commitment between purchaser and supplier and suggests the type of value-added services that are important for a successful partnership.

Supplier-Managed Inventory

With traditional purchasing systems, products are ordered and received, and the hospitality organization takes ownership of and responsibility for products when receiving is completed. Another approach involves the supplier maintaining the inventory at the hospitality organization with ownership (cost) transferred to the organization when products are issued.

A **supplier-managed inventory** has potential advantages for the hospitality organization and the supplier. The former incurs no financial responsibility for care of or carrying costs for product inventory until products are issued. The supplier

---

Buyer's Guide to Purchasing Terms

Standing order   An agreement made between a purchaser and a supplier that the same quantity of specified product is required for each delivery.

Supplier-managed inventory   A purchasing system in which the supplier retains ownership of products until they are issued to a production area.

will likely generate a larger dollar value of product sales to the hospitality organization as the single-source supplier than he or she might otherwise. The hospitality organization should receive higher levels of service and improved cash flow, and suppliers should obtain significant **customer loyalty** from the hospitality organization.

The supplier-managed inventory system and the JIT system reviewed previously have several characteristics in common:

- They encourage (require) collaboration between purchaser and the supplier.
- The emphasis moves away from minimizing cost (perhaps at the expense of the other party) to minimal costs for both companies.
- The foundation for an ongoing agreement means that both the purchaser and seller will understand their responsibilities and have a shared goal: to assist each other.
- There is an emphasis on continuous improvement for both the purchaser and the supplier to enhance quality and reduce waste.

Buyer's Guide to Internet Resources: Computerized Forecasting and Nontraditional Purchasing

Web Site	Topic
www.adacoservices.com	Food and beverage product control, including inventory quantities.
www.comtrex.com	Food and beverage product control, including inventory quantities.
www.culinarysoftware.com	Food and beverage product control, including inventory quantities.
www.foodtrak.com	Food and beverage product control, including inventory quantities.
www.menulink.com	Food and beverage product control, including inventory quantities.
www.strategosinc.com	Just-in-time purchasing. Click on "search site," and type "Just in time" into the search box.
www.effectiveinventory.com.	Supplier (vendor)-managed inventory. Click on "Article Archives" then "Achieving Success with Vendor-Managed Inventory."

Buyer's Guide to Purchasing Term

Customer loyalty   The concept that the purchaser gives a priority to a specific supplier because of past positive experiences the purchaser has with that supplier.

Purchasing Terms

Make Your Own Purchasing Decisions

1. The text included the statement that hospitality purchasers do not typically purchase products for inventory. What do you think that statement means? Do you agree or disagree? Defend your response.
2. What are examples of ways in which purchasers should closely interact with user department personnel to determine the quantities of products to be purchased?
3. What, if any, special purchasing-related concerns are important when determining the quantity of "A" items that should be purchased that may not be applicable to the purchase of lower cost products?
4. What are some pros and cons of just-in-time purchasing? Of supplier managed inventory systems?
5. What are practical ways that small hospitality operations might utilize technology to help determine the quantities of products that are needed?

4

Identifying and Maintaining Supply Sources

Purchasing Pros Need to Know!

To this point, you've learned about the importance of effective purchasing, how to identify product needs and quality requirements, and procedures to analyze whether products should be prepared on-site or purchased as a convenience food. You've also learned about the many factors to consider and several basic methods that can be used to determine purchase quantities. It is now time to consider this chapter's topic: procedures to select potential suppliers and how to manage and evaluate the ongoing professional purchaser-supplier relationship.

How are supply sources determined? One all-too-frequently-used tactic, "Purchase from whomever offers the least expensive items," is not reasonable. Instead, the time and effort that is devoted to the supplier sourcing decision should reflect its importance. The best suppliers assist the buyer's organization to attain its other purchasing goals: to purchase the right products at the right time in the right quantities and at the right price. Customer-driven goals cannot be attained unless all of these concerns are met, and each is affected by the suppliers who provide products to the organization.

What are desirable characteristics that define good suppliers? Not surprisingly, there is a wide range of factors that influence the desired relationship between suppliers and the hospitality organization. You'll learn about each of them in this chapter.

With these important characteristics in mind, how should the few among the (frequently) many alternative suppliers be determined? There are numerous sources of information to help purchasers make these decisions, and a preselection assessment process can be used for this purpose. Both of these topics will be discussed.

There are two basic ways to order products from suppliers: relatively long-term purchase commitments (for example, for three or more months) can be made, or supplier selection decisions can be made each time more products are needed (sometimes two or more times weekly). The second alternative is used most frequently, but you'll learn about factors to consider for both of these alternatives.

Throughout the chapter, you'll learn about several other important supplier sourcing issues. They include the use of broad-line suppliers carrying many different products and specialty suppliers offering narrow product lines, wholesale buying clubs, and cooperative (pool) buying alternatives. Two other issues, purchasing for multi-unit operations and supplier tiering (the use of primary and secondary suppliers) will also be briefly addressed.

There are numerous benefits to long-term relationships with selected suppliers. The best partnership results when there are policies in place to define, from the purchaser's perspective, the most important "dos and don'ts" of the relationship. These policies can be included in a supplier handbook that addresses a wider range of concerns, and both of these topics are discussed in this chapter.

Finally, you'll learn how to evaluate the suppliers with whom you do business. Should your organization continue its relationship with each current supplier? If "yes," what can be done to maximize the benefits of this partnership?

Supplier selection and relations are very important to the success of a hospitality organization's purchasing program. Your study of this chapter helps to ensure that you understand policies and procedures that wise purchasers use to benefit their organizations.

■ ■ ■

Outline

SUPPLIER SOURCING DECISIONS ARE IMPORTANT

Figure 4.1 (originally shown as Figure 1.2) shows where supply source decisions fit in to the purchasing process being discussed in this book. To this point, we have discussed Steps 1 through 3 (in Chapter 2) and Step 4 (in Chapter 3). In this chapter we will explain Step 5: identify supplier sources.

Hospitality managers know that their organizations benefit from carefully selected suppliers who provide significant value for the purchasing dollars that

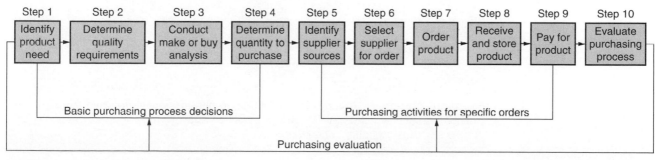

FIGURE 4.1 Steps in Effective Purchasing

are spent. You've learned that the information and services provided by the best suppliers are well worth the (typically) **incremental costs** that are incurred as the organization does business with them.

What is a **supplier?** We'll use the term to mean any business (large or small, located within or away from the community) that sells products to a hospitality organization. While not discussed extensively in this book, the term **service provider** is also used in the hospitality industry in reference to suppliers who sell services rather than products to hospitality buyers.

Many hospitality observers would not likely use the term *partnership* to describe an ideal relationship between the hospitality organization and its suppliers. They know that the concept implies that "partners" share in the financial rewards of the business, and this benefit must be reserved for the organization's owners and employees, not for its suppliers. However, a partnership can also involve persons with joint interests who are on the "same side" as they maximize efforts to mutually benefit from their interactions. This use of the term can relate to the hospitality organization–supplier relationship, and the task of selecting suppliers who will become "partners" with the organization is very important.

Supplier sourcing decisions affect the organization's ability to attain its objectives. Therefore, much more attention is required than a strategy expressed by "Let's purchase from our usual suppliers" or "Let's buy at the best price we can get." Both of these approaches may be part of the supplier sourcing decision, but they should not be the only or even the most important concerns. Customers cannot be satisfied unless the organization consistently has the products required to meet (or exceed) their expectations. Effective suppliers enable hospitality organizations to best serve their customers, and this makes it easy to defend the importance of the supplier sourcing decision.

Large organizations with centralized purchasing systems enjoy another benefit from making the right supplier sourcing decisions: there is a reduced chance that supply problems will occur that would hinder the team relationship between purchasing staff who select the products and other staff members in the organization who use them.

Supplier sourcing involves decisions about which suppliers will be asked to submit prices for the products that are needed. However, the task also involves developing relationships with other potential supply sources that may be useful in the future. Supplier alternatives may become important as the organization's product needs change, and/or if the best efforts of those with purchasing responsibilities do not yield the desired partnership with current suppliers.

Buyer's Guide to Purchasing Terms

Cost (incremental)   The additional cost, if any, incurred by purchasing products from a supplier providing excellent information and service compared to another supplier who does not.

Supplier   Any business (large or small, located within or away from the community) that sells products to a hospitality organization.

Service provider   Any business that sells services to a hospitality organization.

Sourcing (supplier)   Activities undertaken to determine which, often from among many, suppliers will be requested to quote prices for the products and services to be purchased by the hospitality organization.

devote less time to identifying suppliers of other products and **capital equipment** items. However, it is also interesting that some purchasers spend more time and effort selecting and evaluating suppliers for relatively infrequent purchases than they do for commonly used items that, over time, represent larger financial commitments.

There are many sources of information about potential suppliers, and a purchaser's previous experience, if any, with them is likely to be among the most useful. In fact, some purchasers consider this to be the most important factor, and after identifying a good supply source, they continue to use the supplier unless problems arise. (*Note:* many of us use this approach as we make our own personal buying decisions. We are loyal to specific merchants, and we exclude others who provide products and services of equal (or even greater) value, in large measure because of the comfortable relationships we have developed with our favored businesses.)

The concept of identifying and entering into long-term, mutually beneficial relationships with suppliers will be noted throughout this book. However, because new suppliers start their businesses and other suppliers go out of business, buyers will benefit from

- confirming that the suppliers currently being used remain the most beneficial.
- determining whether any changes in purchasing procedures or relationships can be helpful.
- allowing suppliers to address concerns that will improve the relationship from their (the suppliers') perspectives.

Procedures for supplier sourcing range from using detailed tactics to learn about or screen unfamiliar suppliers to others that confirm an existing supplier should continue to be the primary supply source. (*Note:* Some purchasers use one or more suppliers for each product as their primary source(s) for a specified time period (e.g., six months), and they reevaluate the suppliers to determine which will be used as the supply source for the next purchasing cycle (six months).)

There are numerous sources of information about potential suppliers other than the purchaser's experience with them. It is hoped the identification of possible supply sources is one of the purchaser's ongoing research and information responsibilities, and this activity should not be undertaken just when there is an immediate and specific need for a supply source. Supplier information sources include the following:

- *Reputation of supplier.* The purchaser's knowledge of the marketplace in general and those providing products and services to the local area more specifically will assist in the supply source selection decision.
- *Trade publications.* Effective purchasers keep up with industry-related information. For example, they keep current with electronic and print magazines, newsletters, and bulletins to learn about manufacturers, suppliers, and others in **distribution channels** that may be supply sources.
- *Electronic marketing information.* There are numerous buyers' guides made available by industry publications, trade associations, chambers of

---

Buyer's Guide to Purchasing Terms

Equipment (capital)   Assets valued at a predetermined amount with a useful life of more than one year that are used by the hospitality operation to produce products and/or provide services.

Distribution channel   The organizations and/or individuals that are involved in the process of making a product or service available to a hospitality organization.

PROFESSIONAL PURCHASING PREVENTS PROBLEMS (4.1)

What Are Potential Services of Supply?

A common problem: Buyers cannot identify product supply sources.

Modern technology makes it easy to identify potential supply sources for current and new products required by a hospitality operation. Assume you are a restaurant purchaser who wants to buy new dinnerware. One tactic is to contact a local restaurant supply company (perhaps the one with whom you normally do business) to obtain information and prices.

However, an additional useful technique involves use of an electronic buying guide. This can help you obtain a significant amount of information about the product that can influence your purchasing needs, identify one or more specific manufacturers, and even locate local supply sources for the product.

To learn how this process works, use the buying source for *Restaurants and Institutions Magazine,* www.foodservice411.com.

When you reach the site, click on "Foodservice Equipment & Supplies." When you reach this page, click on "Suppliers" then type "dinnerware" in the "Search for" box. Click on "China Tableware," and numerous manufacturers will be identified. You may, for example, click on "Oneida Foodservice," and you will be linked to that company's Web site, where you can learn about available products and related information.

---

commerce, and other sources that allow purchasers to search on the basis of, for example, a needed product to identify numerous possible sources.

- *Supplier representatives.* You've learned that good suppliers provide information to their **accounts.** Purchasers asking their suppliers about companies selling noncompetitive products may learn about useful supply sources.
- *Trade shows and other professional meetings.* Many **trade shows** offer opportunities for **qualified buyers** to learn about suppliers and their products. These professional meetings typically include time for attendees to visit exhibits and to meet with and sample, if applicable, the exhibitor's (supplier's) products.
- *Other employees of the organization.* Staff members working at the purchaser's property and purchasing peers at other properties (especially if the property is part of a multi-unit organization) may have knowledge about potential products and suppliers. Cooks, for example, who have worked in other foodservice operations may be asked about supply sources used by their previous employers.
- *Other information sources.* Supplier catalogs, the yellow pages of the local telephone directory, and files of mailing brochures and other information collected and cataloged by the buyer are examples of additional and potentially helpful supplier information sources.

Buyer's Guide to Purchasing Terms

Accounts   A term used by suppliers for the hospitality organizations to whom they sell products.

Trade show   An industry-specific event which allows suppliers to interact with, educate, and sell to individuals and businesses that are part of the industry; also called exhibition.

Buyers (qualified)   Persons with the authority to make purchase decisions for their organization.

Trade shows can help hospitality buyers to learn about what's new in the marketplace, and that can benefit their operations.

David Young-Wolff/ PhotoEdit Inc.

Supplier Preselection Concerns

You'll learn about the basic factors used to evaluate the performance of existing suppliers later in this chapter, but the same factors are also important when you consider the potential suppliers whom you ask to submit price quotations for the products you need. As already noted, a purchaser's experience with existing suppliers will be important when considering whether that relationship should continue. However, suppliers with whom the purchaser has no experience are generally evaluated only by subjectively considering their capabilities and the potential for a mutually beneficial relationship.

The time and effort spent on assessing potential suppliers relates, at least in part, to the financial importance of the relationship. Most of an organization's purchase dollars are spent with relatively few suppliers, and relatively few of the products and services purchased require the largest percentage of dollars spent for all product purchases. Not surprisingly, then, a priority effort to identify suppliers for these important purchases is required. Also, purchasers of products for which the buyer has relatively little experience will also require more extensive supplier assessment.

Efforts to consider the quality of service likely to be provided by potential suppliers are very useful. Unfortunately, service cannot be evaluated until after it is delivered. That is why a supplier's reputation is so important: purchasers can normally assume that a supplier who has provided excellent service will continue to do so. High-quality service occurs as the supplier provides timely and accurate price quotations, meets delivery schedules, makes it easy for purchasers to contact one's **distributor sales representative,** and willingly assists in problem solving. These are all examples of desired and expected services that are important in a preferred purchaser-supplier relationship.

You've learned that the quality of information provided by suppliers is another special concern as purchasers interact with suppliers. This factor is, therefore, very important when supplier sourcing decisions are made. Will high-quality technical advice be provided, and to what extent will a potential supplier be interested

Buyer's Guide to Purchasing Term

Distributor sales representative   The person who is the purchaser's most immediate contact with the supplier; often abbreviated "DSR"; commonly called "salesperson" or "account executive."

It does little good to purchase a product at a good price if it is not delivered when the hospitality operation requires it.

Michael Newman/PhotoEdit Inc.

in providing information to help the purchaser's organization address its ongoing challenges? Answers to these and related questions should help purchasers in their decision-making process, especially when a supplier enjoys that reputation with a large number of other purchasers.

The financial stability of your own hospitality organization is of concern because your suppliers want assurance that they will be paid on a timely basis for the products and services they provide. However, the reverse is also true: purchasers must be concerned that suppliers pay their own bills on time so they (the suppliers) will obtain the products that they will sell to the organization. Purchasers want to develop a relationship with suppliers whose financial stability results from the same practices used by the hospitality organization. Benefits of improved work methods, reduced costs, and better products with fewer defects can then be shared with the buyer's organization.

Some purchasers conduct on-site inspections of a potential supplier's facilities to observe factors such as work methods, cleanliness, and the general organization of the facility. The condition of transport equipment is also important when, for example, highly **perishable** fresh produce, meats and seafood, and dairy products must be delivered during warm weather.

Increasingly, the potential supplier's e-commerce capabilities must be evaluated. Electronic communication including **requests for price quotations,** the resulting supplier-provided prices in response to the price quotation request, and payment statements are examples of **business-to-business** capabilities of potential suppliers that are important to many hospitality purchasers.

Determining Preferred Suppliers

It is hoped the supplier's reputation and communication with potential suppliers and with others who can comment on the suppliers' capabilities, the purchaser's

---

Buyer's Guide to Purchasing Terms

Perishable   The condition in which quality is reduced, and spoilage occurs quickly when applicable products are not properly handled and stored.

Request for price quotations   A request made by a purchaser to a potential supplier asking for the price that will be charged for products of a specified quality and quantity.

Business-to-business   E-commerce interactions between businesses (e.g., business transactions between hospitality organizations and their suppliers).

own research, and visits to suppliers' facilities will help the buyer to make supplier selection decisions. Figure 4.2 shows a sample supplier preselection form that a purchaser can use to assess the potential benefits of using specific suppliers. It presents an overview of the information useful to make this important decision. (*Note:* This form is not the same as the form used to evaluate suppliers already providing products and services to the hospitality organization. The supplier evaluation process, including this form (Figure 4.4), is discussed later in this chapter.)

Approved suppliers who have not previously been used by the organization may initially be used as a secondary supply source if a tiering system is in use. (This topic is discussed later in the chapter.) Small orders placed over time will then provide purchasers with additional insights about their preselection decision. Unfortunately, supplier selection decisions for one-time and/or infrequent purchases, such as a new dish-washing machine for the kitchen, do not provide opportunities for trial-and-error selection. These decisions are typically made on

---

Supplier Name: _____

Contact Information: _____

Products Provided: _____

Representative: _____
Telephone: _____
E-mail: _____
Address: _____
_____
_____

Sources of Information about Supplier (check all that apply)

☐ Interviews with supplier references
☐ Distributor's sales representative
☐ Sales manager
☐ Other interviews: _____
  _____

☐ On-site visit
☐ Trade publications
☐ Electronic marketing information
☐ Other: _____

Evaluation Factors	Unacceptable	Acceptable	Comments
Quality (Follows Standards)	☐	☐	_____
Service Procedures	☐	☐	_____
Service Philosophy	☐	☐	_____
Management Systems	☐	☐	_____
Facilities/Delivery Equipment	☐	☐	_____
E-Commerce Applications	☐	☐	_____
Financial Stability	☐	☐	_____
Reputation	☐	☐	_____
Information (Technical Support)	☐	☐	_____
Input from Others	☐	☐	_____
Sanitation/Food Safety (if applicable)	☐	☐	_____
Current Customer Recommendations	☐	☐	_____
Experience (years in business: _____)	☐	☐	_____

Total

Other Information: _____
_____
_____

Supplier Selection Decision: _____
_____
_____

Purchasing Director: _____   Date: _____

FIGURE 4.2 Supplier Preselection Form

the basis of the buyer's experience with equipment manufacturers and the local distributors who sell and service the equipment, along with their reputation.

Alternative Ordering Methods

In Chapter 3, you learned that usage rates; perishability issues, if any; and volume purchase discounts are among the factors that have traditionally been important as purchasers determined the length of time for which orders were placed. For example, a restaurant buyer requiring fresh ground beef might order and receive products from a supplier several times weekly. If frozen ground beef products were used, orders of these less perishable products could be placed less frequently but in larger quantities. In both instances, however, a supplier selection decision (even if it were to continue to use the same supplier) was made each time an order was placed.

Today, however, buyers increasingly have numerous other purchasing alternatives that affect their supplier sourcing decisions.

BROAD-LINE SUPPLIERS **Broad-line suppliers** sell a wide (broad) range of products, in contrast to **specialty-line suppliers** that provide a narrow (focused) product line. The former offer a wide variety of items (but often with few alternative items within each item category) in contrast to the latter, who offer few items but a deep selection with the product lines that are available.

A purchaser might, for example, purchase frozen bread dough from a full broad-line supplier who has just a few variations of this product, but who also offers hundreds or even thousands of additional products. The frozen bread varieties offered are those that would be acceptable to the majority of product users. By contrast, specialty frozen food suppliers may offer buyers the choice of many additional varieties of frozen bread dough and, if purchase quantities warranted it, could even produce (or obtain) special products to meet a hospitality organization's exact requirements. This frozen food supplier would, however, likely offer few, if any, items outside of its specialty lines.

Advantages of broad-line suppliers are those related to reducing the number of suppliers who must be selected and with whom purchasers must interact. These include the following:

- Reduced per-unit costs that are often available with increased purchase volumes
- Decreased costs associated with the purchasing and accounting aspects of order placement
- Less time required for purchasing tasks
- Less time required for product receiving activities
- Reduced time needed to evaluate, select, and interact with specialty-line suppliers

Many hospitality purchasers use broad-line suppliers, and these organizations are becoming more popular as distribution channels evolve. Some of these companies are also becoming still larger as they merge with other distributors, including those with specialty lines. As this occurs, the large get larger in much the same way that hotel and restaurant chains purchase other hotel and restaurant chains as a growth strategy.

Buyer's Guide to Purchasing Terms

Broad-line supplier A supplier who provides a wide variety (hundreds or even thousands) of products; also called one-stop shopping supplier.

Specialty-line supplier A supplier who offers a deep selection of relatively few products.

There are potential disadvantages to relying on one-stop shopping suppliers, and these may include the lack of detailed product knowledge and information that can be provided by the supplier's representatives and a lack of variety if very specialized products are required.

WHOLESALE BUYING CLUBS   One-stop shopping sources also include **wholesale buying clubs,** such as Sam's Club and Costco, in which hospitality purchasers buy products as a result of personal visits to the supplier's (store) location. As decisions are made to purchase from these buying clubs, buyers are, in fact, making supply source decisions.

Wholesale buying clubs offer alternative supply sources for some, especially small, hospitality organizations. Buyers may find many of the products they commonly use, and purchases can be made frequently (even daily) if there are cash flow or other concerns. Buyers may be able to call in their orders, which can then be ready for pickup when they arrive at the store, and charge accounts for delayed payment plans may also be available. Some buying clubs will even deliver products to the purchaser's property if delivery quantity requirements are met. As these services evolve and increase, buying clubs become more similar to traditional distributors. As they do so, the clubs become more attractive supply sources to hospitality buyers representing organizations of all sizes.

Increasingly, as well, grocery stores offer a variety of products in large purchase unit sizes, and they provide another alternative to hospitality buyers. Local merchants may become the supplier of choice for some, especially small-volume buyers who use **cash-and-carry** supplier sources.

COOPERATIVE (POOL) BUYING   Some hospitality purchasers use another product source that affects their supplier sourcing decision: a cooperative (pool) purchasing system. This method was introduced in Chapter 3, where you learned that it involves several (or more) organizations combining orders for products of the same quality. One combined order is then submitted to the supplier who has quoted the lowest price for them, and products are then delivered to each participant's location.

State hospitality associations and for-profit co-ops may offer these services. Participants often note an advantage of lower prices resulting from the higher volume of products being ordered when purchase quantities are combined.

To learn about one food buying co-op, go to www.hsgpurchasing.com. This is the Web site for Hospitality Services Group, a consulting and purchasing organization that assists independent restaurants.

The purchasing methods discussed to this point in the chapter have involved developing a supply source composed of suppliers who provide product requirements for an order period of a short duration (usually just several days or weeks) with one delivery (pickup) for all products in the order. However, in Chapter 3 you learned about two methods—just-in-time and supplier-managed inventory— which expanded the order period and quantity of products to be delivered within it. These methods require specialized services from the supplier who provides these services and, therefore, may be applicable to only the largest foodservice organizations. In that chapter you also learned about definite quantity contracts and

---

Buyer's Guide to Purchasing Terms

Wholesale buying clubs   Businesses that, for a membership fee, allow buyers to purchase products in large quantities and often in large purchase unit sizes at prices less than their retail competitors.

Cash and carry   A purchasing alternative in which the buyer travels to the supplier's site (e.g., grocery store), selects desired products, and pays for them at the time of purchase.

Information discovered from the Internet may help to identify suppliers interested in nontraditional purchasing systems.
ANDREAS POLLOK/Getty Images, Inc.-Taxi

Did You Know? (4.2)

In the real world of hospitality purchasing, many approaches to supplier selection and subsequent ordering typically are used at the same time. For example, a purchaser for a large restaurant may

- make supplier selections for fresh seafood purchases from one or more specialty suppliers based on current prices for required quality each time an order is placed.
- participate in a long-term agreement for the purchase of some products from a broadline distributor, and purchase other products from this distributor when price quotation responses warrant doing so.
- purchase select paper goods from a local wholesale club.
- use a nearby grocery store for emergency purchases.

requirements contracts in which buyers and suppliers make commitments for product purchases over extended time periods. You can see, then, that the type of ordering system desired (e.g., a traditional system of ordering for a few days, daily orders because of little or no on-site storage, and very long-term purchase commitments) affects the type and number of suppliers in the sourcing decision.

OTHER SUPPLIER SOURCING ISSUES

Several special supplier sourcing concerns may be important to hospitality purchasers in selected situations. They include those relating to multi-unit organizations and the use of supplier tiering.

Suppliers for Multi-Unit Organizations

Multi-unit hospitality organizations can be composed of company- and/or **franchisee** operated units. Managers and purchasers in these organizations typically have less opportunity to select suppliers than their counterparts in independently

Buyer's Guide to Purchasing Term

Franchisee   One who owns (or leases) the property and building and who purchases the right to use a franchisor's brand name and operating procedures for a fixed period of time in return for agreed-on sales royalties and other fees; see *franchisor*.

operated single-unit properties because they may be required to use specific suppliers, including **subsidiaries** owned and/or operated by the company. Also, purchasers in franchised operations frequently use **franchisor** approved suppliers, or at least they must use suppliers whose products meet franchisor-required quality standards. Within these broad limitations, purchasers in some multi-unit organizations do (or do not) use local supply sources, do (or do not) use the chain organization's approved vendors, and do (or do not) participate in buying cooperatives operated at national, regional, or state levels. It is difficult to generalize further about supply sources for multi-unit organizations. However, within this context, one can note that whatever the process used to select suppliers, product consistency between properties is typically necessary, and this occurs by using purchase specifications developed for use within the entire organization.

Supplier Tiering

Most hospitality organizations limit the number of suppliers of a specific product with whom they will request price quotations and place orders during a specific time period. As noted earlier, however, suppliers with whom the organization does not have previous experience might initially be given occasional and/or small-volume (trial) orders to help evaluate that supplier's products and business practices.

Hospitality purchasers may have concerns that, for whatever reason, a **primary supplier** could become less dependable or even go out of business. To address the concern about a continuing source of supply, additional suppliers may be used to provide some products as backup to their primary supplier counterparts. The purchaser's reasoning for doing this is that he or she is managing for the future and preparing for contingencies that he or she hopes will never happen but for which one should be prepared.

Purchasers using this approach use two tiers (categories) of suppliers:

1. Primary suppliers who are the preferred sources from whom most product needs are obtained
2. Secondary suppliers who provide a relatively small amount of a specific product

---

Did You Know? (4.3)

Many hospitality organizations want to invest in their communities. One way to do so is to buy locally. Food and beverage operations, including multi-unit organizations, may have few, if any, nonlocal sources for highly perishable fresh products such as fresh breads, pastries, and dairy products. For many other products, however, most hospitality buyers do have choices. Purchasers should realize that they should not make local purchases if quality standards will be compromised or if significant financial disadvantages result. However, with these restraints in mind, many organizations buy from local sources when equal or better products can be purchased at the same or lower prices than elsewhere.

Buyer's Guide to Purchasing Terms

Subsidiary   A company that is owned by a larger company. Example: A large multi-unit chain organization may own a company that produces meat items used by the organization.

Franchisor   One who owns and manages a brand and sells the rights to use it to franchisees; see *franchisee*.

Primary supplier   The supplier who receives all or most orders from a buyer for a specific product or line of products; also called "primary vendor."

PROFESSIONAL PURCHASING PREVENTS PROBLEMS (4.2)

Don't Become Too Comfortable with Suppliers

A common problem: Consistently buying a product from the same supplier saves time but may be an unwise business practice.

Purchasers know that there may be several potential advantages to a single supply source for specific products. These include the following:

- Reduced purchase unit costs applicable to larger volume purchases
- Incentives for the supplier to provide maximum service and information
- Better assurance that the purchaser will receive products if there are shortages because the buyer's organization will likely be favored if it is a large-volume buyer.

    There are, however, two other potential concerns to a single supply source: (1) unplanned supplier interruptions caused by, for example, a serious weather problem (e.g., hurricane) or labor dispute, and (2) a concern about the supplier becoming dependent on the hospitality organization. Very-large-volume purchasers may want to limit the amount of a supplier's business that they (the purchasers) represent so the supplier does not become dependent on the purchaser. Severe problems for a supplier partner can occur if, for example, the hospitality organization changes purchasing requirements and no longer needs products that represent a significant segment of a supplier's business.

    Changing conditions may warrant a review of ongoing relationships with and changes in the suppliers used by the hospitality operation. Many buyers reconsider their arrangements with primary suppliers on a recurring basis, and the evaluation tactics discussed later in this chapter may lead to a decision to continue the business relationship. Alternatively, other primary suppliers may be selected for the next cycle of product purchasers.

Buyers at Work (4.1)

"They're just doing it to save a few dollars, and the savings are just not worth it!" Chef Joey was talking about the decision to revise the supplier selection process at the Chatterville Bistro. Joey was talking to Pedro, the head bartender at the restaurant.

    "You're right, Joey," said Pedro. "We've done well doing what we do: you buy the food products, and I buy the wine, beer, and liquor. I know you have a tougher job because you have more supplier choices than I do because there are only a few beverage distributors. However, we help the owner because of our excellent relationships with the suppliers. Just a week or so ago, you told me about a delayed shipment, and then the salesperson helped us by making a special delivery on Saturday afternoon. I also remember the time that we received some decorator mirrors for our bar area from one of the distributors."

    "Well, that's all changing now," said Joey. "This place has been successful because of us, and now the boss is building another property across town. In the future, we've got to determine what we need and send her the information. Then she will combine the orders from our restaurant and the new operation, send them out to bid, and accept the order from the least expensive supplier. Do you think it will work?"

    "No," said Pedro. "I don't think it will work like she thinks it will. First of all, we're in the hospitality business, and we ought to be hospitable to our suppliers as well as to our customers. Basing every purchase decision on who's the cheapest doesn't seem to fit that philosophy. Also, I'm not even sure if the menu or the customers will be the same at both places. How will she get around these problems?"

(Continued)

"I don't know, Pedro," replied Joey, "but I do know about one thing: the first time that I don't have a product that I need, I'm going to complain. The second time it happens, I'm out of here!"

1. What must the owner do to best ensure that the new centralized purchasing system will work well?
2. What, if anything, should the owner say to Chef Joey and Pedro about their concerns? How will she manage the morale problems that could occur when the new purchasing system is implemented?
3. How should the suppliers for the centralized purchasing system be selected? What, if any, priorities should be given to the existing suppliers?

Buyer's Guide to Internet Resources: Supplier Sourcing Concerns

Web Site	Topic
www.purchasing.com	Supplier selection factors (Enter "supplier selection" in the site's search box).
www.avendra.com	The largest procurement services company serving the hospitality industry.
www.gfs.com	The marketplace store of Gordon Food Services, a very large regional foodservice distribution.
www.sysco.com	Sysco Corporation, a foodservice distributor with 170 locations throughout the United States, and areas of Canada. (While at the site, review the information and services provided by this supplier.)
www.rimag.com	Foodservice suppliers (enter this term into the site's search box).
www.foodservice.com	Weekly food *Market Reports* (click on this term on the site's banner).
www.usfoodservice.com	General foodservice supplier information.

SUPPLIER RELATIONS

The concept of **supplier relations** relates to how buyers interact with their suppliers. A professional relationship is important, and the purchasing policies expressed in a purchasing handbook can help to enhance and maintain this relationship. These topics are discussed in this section.

Purchaser-Supplier Relationships

How should purchasers interact with their suppliers? Figure 4.3 shows the range of possibilities.

Buyer's Guide to Purchasing Term

Supplier relations   How purchasers interact with their suppliers.

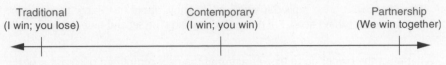

FIGURE 4.3 The Purchaser-Supplier Relationship

As you review Figure 4.3, note that the traditional (I win; you lose) philosophy is at one end of the range, and at the other end, you'll note a partnership relationship (We win together). A middle point along the range is labeled "Contemporary (I win; you win)."

Purchasers and their hospitality organizations typically have differing relationships with each of their suppliers that may be noted at each of the points along the range of possibilities noted in Figure 4.3. Supplier-specific relationships are based on numerous factors, including many already described in this chapter. This is to be expected because purchasers do not (cannot) attempt to develop a "one size fits all" relationship with each supplier.

It is important that potential relationships between the hospitality organization and its suppliers be considered as sourcing decisions are made. Purchasers will not interact with suppliers with whom they do not want to do business, and it is just as true that suppliers will not want to provide products to organizations that do not share their basic business philosophies. Also, the efforts expended to evaluate and include specific suppliers in sourcing decisions will be lost if a compatible ongoing relationship cannot be maintained.

There are several general factors that often influence the relationship between the purchaser's organization and its suppliers:

- *Relative size (business volume) of both organizations.* A large hospitality organization is not likely to consider the development of a partnership with a supplier providing a tiny fraction of the purchaser's needs for a product or service. The reverse is also true: a very large supplier is not likely to devote significant time and effort to develop an extensive relationship with a small-volume restaurant or hotel. (*Note:* This is one reason that multi-unit organizations develop centralized and coordinated purchasing systems that command the attention of potential suppliers.)
- *Reliance on a supplier.* This can occur if, for example, a supplier is the only source of a unique specialty item and when a supplier has exclusive distribution rights to specific products sold in the purchaser's location.
- *Compatibility.* The extent to which the purchaser and supplier share cultural, moral, and ethical (among other) beliefs that help shape their businesses affects their relationship with each other. If there is not a good fit, one or both of the parties may wish to limit the purchaser-supplier relationship to a position on the more traditional end of the range noted in Figure 4.3 if the supplier is included in the buyer's sourcing decision.
- *Extent of asset commitment.* Manufacturers who work with suppliers to commit research and development efforts to extend product lines and/or increase production capacities to better serve large-volume hospitality organizations help their supplier representatives to maintain a long-term relationship with purchasers. Their ability and willingness to do so will likely have a positive influence on the purchaser's desire to potentially order products from the supplier.

Importance of Professional Relationships

Buyers want their suppliers to treat them fairly and should recognize that they (the buyers) should treat suppliers in the same manner. Long-term relationships thrive when cooperative efforts that emphasize trust, flexibility, and innovation as

Independent restaurant owners can receive excellent information from suppliers about ways to resolve operating problems, and access to this information benefits the relationship between the buyer and seller.

Michael Newman/PhotoEdit Inc.

total acquisition costs (not just product purchase costs) are addressed. Both parties benefit from the improved communication and increased levels of trust that result.

The best supplier relations occur when the purchaser has undertaken effective supplier preselection evaluation (recall this chapter's earlier discussion of this topic).

What factors are typically among those that will affect the relationship between the purchaser and supplier from the former's viewpoint? It is hoped these are the same concerns that were considered as the decision to select the supplier is made. The purchaser's experience with suppliers will be based on factors including the following:

- Consistency of product quality
- On-time delivery schedules
- Effectiveness of communication
- Value pricing
- Interest in addressing the purchaser's concerns
- Level of service provided
- Quality of information supplied
- Payment processing procedures

How the above and related factors are addressed by the supplier directly affects the purchaser's perception of the relationship with the supplier. Also, the relationship is likely to become stronger when few, if any, problems related to these concerns arise over time. Then buyers have a greater incentive to continue and expand their business relationships with these suppliers.

Supplier-Related Policies

Purchasers working with top-level managers typically develop numerous **policies** to guide them as they make decisions about important purchasing issues.

Buyer's Guide to Purchasing Terms

Total acquisition cost   The sum of all costs required to use a product or make equipment operable. Example: After a dish-washing machine is purchased, it must be installed (plumbing, electrical, and ventilation), and operators must be trained (in addition to other required costs).

Policy   A (usually) written statement of principles or guiding actions that indicates what should be done in specific, recurring situations.

These policies provide guidance about appropriate actions to be taken when buyers are confronted with a specific situation. Purchasing policies help to provide consistency because issues will always be addressed the same way, and problems will be resolved in the manner required by the applicable policy.

Hospitality organizations typically implement policies that address many different concerns. Some that affect the potential relationship between purchasers and suppliers consider topics such as the following:

- Accepting gifts
- No favoritism shown to any supplier
- **Reciprocal purchases**
- Use of local suppliers
- **Conflicts of interest**
- **Competitive bids**
- **Backdoor selling**
- Trial orders
- Samples
- Free meals/Entertainment
- **Sharp practices**
- Taking advantage of suppliers (e.g., when one supplier's price is provided to a second supplier with the hope that the latter will reduce his or her selling price)

For a review of ethical concerns relating to purchasing policies, including those relating to relationships between purchasers and suppliers, review the information in Chapter 1.

Purchasing Handbooks

Purchasers in many, especially large, hospitality organizations develop **purchasing handbooks.** These become excellent communication tools to help inform new and to remind longer-term suppliers about the property's purchasing policies and procedures.

Buyer's Guide to Purchasing Terms

Reciprocal purchases   A transaction in which a supplier agrees to purchase something from the purchaser if the purchaser agrees to purchase something from the supplier. Example: The purchaser makes an advertising commitment with a local newspaper, and in return, newspaper managers agree to spend a specified amount of money on food and beverage purchases at the property; also called "bartering" or "counter-purchasing."

Conflict of interest (purchasing policy)   A business situation in which a hospitality employee has an interest in another organization that could (or does) compromise his or her loyalty to the hospitality organization.

Competitive bids   A tactic to compare suppliers' prices for products of acceptable quality to determine the least expensive price; sometimes called "competitive pricing."

Backdoor selling (purchasing policy)   The act of a supplier attempting to contact or influence a user department employee without approval of purchasing personnel.

Sharp practice (purchasing policy)   Bargaining between the purchaser and potential seller in such a way that the purchaser unethically takes advantage of the seller.

Purchasing handbook   A document developed by the hospitality organization to inform suppliers about purchasing policies and procedures that must be followed at all times.

Buyers at Work (4.2)

"I guess the 'good old days' are just about gone!" said Riley, the buyer for Handy's Chicken House, a chain of six restaurants in the suburbs of a very large metropolitan area. He was speaking to Rondo, the general manager of one of the units. Both men were leaving a meeting of corporate-level and general management staff for the organization.

The purpose of the meeting was to roll out a new purchasing system that represented a significant amount of change for everyone. Up until now, the unit managers had placed all of their product orders with Riley, who then combined them for all units and requested bids from several suppliers in the area. The system worked well, in part because each unit offered the same menu and because Riley had established long-term relationships with the suppliers who were used.

Beginning now, however, unit managers were encouraged to offer several **signature items** that could be unique to their specific property. This decision was made at the managers' request in efforts to give them additional decision-making opportunities in the management of their units. Managers were also allowed to select their own suppliers for the ingredients required for these menu items. During the meeting, the organization's owner stressed that, while some centralized purchasing control would be lost, it was worth it because of the increase in the morale of unit managers and its effect on expanded success of the units.

In addition to losing centralized control over purchasing, Riley was affected in another way: competitive bids for all products purchased would be required, requests for price quotations would need to be issued to new suppliers in addition to the ones traditionally used, and a conflict-of-interest policy was implemented. (This directly affected Riley because his brother-in-law owned a poultry company from whom the organization purchased much of its products.)

"This has been a good meeting for us general managers," said Rondo, "but I don't think you would agree."

"You're right, Rondo," said Riley. "There are likely to be duplicate orders for products purchased by the units. Also, I think the same type of problems that now occur with our centralized buying system will still occur, and the emphasis will be on cost savings rather than on service and information."

1. What do you think about the plan to give unit managers the opportunity to offer specific menu items and to purchase the products for them in efforts to increase their decision-making opportunities?
2. How would you respond if you were the organization's owner if Riley indicated his preference to continue purchasing poultry from his brother-in-law's organization because "prices might be a little higher, but so is the quality of service and the amount of useful information we receive"?
3. Assume that you were the organization's owner. How would you work with Riley to implement the new centralized purchasing requirements? What, if any, resistance do you think Riley might offer to the new policies?

The topics that can be addressed in purchasing handbooks are broad, and they include the following:

• General information about the hospitality organization, including a brief overview of its history, an organizational chart showing key positions, customer market descriptions, and its mission statement

---

Buyer's Guide to Purchasing Term

Signature item   A unique menu item that attracts customers to a specific foodservice operation.

- Basic purchasing procedures with an emphasis on contracts and communication between the organization and its suppliers (may include statements about the need for competitive bidding, alternate supply sources, and procedures used to select suppliers)
- Procedures for product receipt, including inspection
- Payment policies and procedures
- Purchasing policies
- Details about electronic purchasing procedures
- Copies of (or references to) purchasing forms
- Information about preferences for "green" (environmentally preferable) products
- General information about the purchase of services, construction and remodeling, equipment, and supplies

Once developed, the organization's purchasing handbook should be provided to all suppliers with whom the organization does business. Hard or e-copies should be provided to representatives of suppliers who make unannounced visits (**cold calls**) to purchasing staff, and they should be provided with **requests for proposals (RFPs)** sent to prospective suppliers of one-time purchases.

As with all other materials developed by the organization, purchasing handbooks must be maintained (kept current), and most important, they must be used as a foundation for how the purchasing department operates.

SUPPLIER EVALUATION PROCEDURES

The quality of each supplier's products, services, and information must be regularly evaluated to ensure that the hospitality organization is receiving the anticipated value for its purchase dollars. Some evaluation is ongoing and occurs in the routine day-to-day interactions that purchasers have with the supplier. While it is not reasonable that a supplier must always be only as good as its last interaction with the purchaser's organization, it is also true these routine interactions affect longer-term relationships.

You've learned that several factors are important when initially determining the suppliers to be used and that these same factors affect the relationship between the two parties. (Examples of these factors were noted in Figure 4.2). However, in addition to these informal and ongoing evaluations, purchasers in many hospitality organizations also conduct more formal assessments. This is especially important for suppliers of high-cost and/or high-volume products, for new suppliers, and for those in which an expanded (partnership) relationship is desired.

In large organizations the process can begin as purchasing staff meet with user department personnel to discuss supplier performance, and the rating form used to initially select suppliers can be a helpful benchmark for this evaluation. Information from other persons in the organization, including the accounting and

---

Buyer's Guide to Purchasing Terms

Cold calls   A term relating to unannounced (unscheduled) visits by supplier representatives to hospitality purchasers.

Request for proposals (RFP)   A notice sent by a purchaser to suppliers providing general information about a one-time need such as for construction, remodeling, or a new service. Suppliers are requested to provide suggestions and associated costs for meeting the purchaser's needs.

Effective purchasers assemble numerous kinds of information that can help them objectively evaluate supplier performance.

Tomas del Amo/PacificStock.com

Did You Know? (4.4)

Hospitality purchasers should recognize that suppliers may have suggestions about how, from their own perspectives, the relationship between the buyer and seller can be improved.

If they thought about it objectively, many purchasers would likely recognize that they create awkward situations for their suppliers in much the same way that customers of the hospitality organization create problems for it. For example, every hotel and restaurant manager has customers who try (sometimes successfully) to take advantage of them. Examples range from restaurant guests who do not "enjoy" their meal and request a refund after the meal is almost completely consumed to hotel guests wanting a free room because of an alleged problem that, even if true, was relatively minor, such as discovering a clean but water-spotted decanter in the complimentary in-room coffeemaker.

Purchasers also sometimes place suppliers in positions that create challenges. Consider, for example, the common (and reasonable!) supplier policy that incoming deliveries should be carefully checked to verify accuracy and that the responsibility for and ownership of products transfers to the purchaser when delivery invoices are signed. Every supplier has stories about minor requests for "policy exceptions" when after-delivery quality concerns are noted for products of relatively low value. Most suppliers will allow a purchase credit for these items so their relationship with the purchaser is not affected. However, suppliers may also have experience with purchasers who later allege that many cases of products signed for at time of delivery were never received or that a large equipment item that was received was later found to be damaged in a way that would have been easily noticed at time of delivery.

What is the proper response to these credit requests? While the answer probably, in part, relates to the volume of business the purchaser gives to the supplier, purchasers in these examples should be alert to the need to improve their receiving practices, and their supplier partners should urge that this be done. (*Note:* Some suppliers add a slight up-charge in product prices for some organizations in which these problems routinely occur to compensate for the "give backs" that will likely be necessary.)

---

purchasing staff themselves, is also useful, as are discussions with supplier representatives, including sales managers. In smaller organizations, the manager may perform all of these assessment tasks.

The timing of formal supplier evaluation activities is important. Assessment should be done as sourcing decisions about primary suppliers for future purchasing cycles are made. If, for example, the purchaser desires to award a contract for disposable paper supplies for a six-month period, an assessment of performance of existing suppliers is important when determining to whom RFPs for this purchase should be sent.

Supplier evaluation is a critical component of the evaluation of the entire procurement process (see Chapter 6), and Figure 4.4 shows a sample supplier rating form.

Part 1: About Supplier

Supplier Name: _____

Contact Information: _____

Representative: _____

Telephone: _____

E-mail: _____

Part 2: General Rating Factors

	Rating			
	Unacceptable	Acceptable	Excellent	No Opinion
Rating Factors	0 1	2	3	
Consistent Quality (Follows Standards)	☐ ☐	☐	☐	☐
Service Procedures	☐ ☐	☐	☐	☐
Service Philosophy (Cooperation)	☐ ☐	☐	☐	☐
Management Systems	☐ ☐	☐	☐	☐
Facilities/Delivery Equipment	☐ ☐	☐	☐	☐
E-Commerce Applications	☐ ☐	☐	☐	☐
Financial Stability	☐ ☐	☐	☐	☐
Reputation	☐ ☐	☐	☐	☐
Information (Technical Support)	☐ ☐	☐	☐	☐
Input from Others	☐ ☐	☐	☐	☐
Sanitation/Food Safety (if applicable)	☐ ☐	☐	☐	☐
Current Customer Recommendations	☐ ☐	☐	☐	☐
Experience (years in business: _____)	☐ ☐	☐	☐	☐
Total Points	___ ___	___	___	___

Part 3: Specific Information

	Unacceptable	Acceptable	Excellent	No Opinion
Accurate Orders	☐ ☐	☐	☐	☐
On-time Deliveries	☐ ☐	☐	☐	☐
Emergency Requests	☐ ☐	☐	☐	☐
Purchase Costs	☐ ☐	☐	☐	☐
Total Acquisition Costs	☐ ☐	☐	☐	☐
Payment Policies/Procedures	☐ ☐	☐	☐	☐
Discounts	☐ ☐	☐	☐	☐
Total Points	___ ___	___	___	___

Part 4: Other Information

_____

_____

_____

Part 5: General Recommendations

☐ Continue Use of Supplier   ☐ Discontinue Use of Supplier

Comments: _____

_____

Director of Purchasing: _____ Date: _____

FIGURE 4.4 Sample Supplier Rating Form

Buyer's Guide to Internet Resources: Supplier Relations and Evaluation

Web Site	Topic
www.darden.com	Supplier relations information for Darden Restaurants (Olive Garden, Red Lobster, and others). When you reach the site, click on "Search" then enter "supplier relations."
www.mcdonalds.com	Corporate responsibility concerns applicable to suppliers. (Click on "Corporate Responsibility Report" then "Responsible Purchasing.")
www.pprc.org	Evaluation and certification of suppliers for organizations that are concerned about the environment.
www.cvmsolutions.com	Supplier diversity programs. (Click "Supplier Diversity" on the site's home page.)
www.ism.ws	Supplier evaluation. (Enter "supplier evaluation" into the site's search box.)
support.dialog.com/searchaids/dialog/dnbser.shtml	Dun and Bradstreet supplier evaluation report used to learn financial and operational information about a supplier's business. (Enter "supplier evaluation report" into the site's search box.)
hbswk.hbs.edu/item3551.html	Tactics that purchasers can use to convert short-term supplier relationships into longer-term partnerships.

Purchasing Terms

Cost (incremental) *84*
Supplier *84*
Service provider *84*
Sourcing (supplier) *84*
DNA certificates *86*
Equipment (capital) *87*
Distribution channel *87*
Accounts *88*
Trade show *88*
Buyers (qualified) *88*
Distributor sales representative *89*

Perishable *90*
Request for price quotations *90*
Business-to-business *90*
Broad-line supplier *92*
Specialty-line supplier *92*
Wholesale buying clubs *93*
Cash and carry *93*
Franchisee *94*
Subsidiary *95*

Franchisor *95*
Primary supplier *95*
Supplier relations *97*
Total acquisition cost *99*
Policy *99*
Reciprocal purchases *100*
Conflict of interest (purchasing policy) *100*

Competitive bids *100*
Backdoor selling (purchasing policy) *100*
Sharp practice (purchasing policy) *100*
Purchasing handbook *100*
Signature item *101*
Cold calls *102*
Request for proposals (RFP) *102*

Make Your Own Purchasing Decisions

1. What is your definition of a good supplier that would help you evaluate the performance of a potential supplier when you were making a sourcing decision? An existing supplier?

2. How would you, as the director of purchasing for a large hotel with a large-volume banquet operation, decide whether to maximize the use of broad-line suppliers who can provide, in effect, a "one-stop shopping" service or, alternatively, use several specialty suppliers with a large variety of fewer categories of items?

3. Assume you are the manager of a large-volume restaurant and have used the same supplier for most of your products for many years. After reading this chapter, you have learned about procedures for supplier preselection and about supplier evaluation to best ensure that you are receiving maximum benefits from your relationship with suppliers. How would you begin to imple-ment supplier preselection and evaluation pro-grams in your restaurant?

4. Assume you are the owner of three very large-volume restaurants in the same city. What basic procedures would you use to reduce your prod-uct purchase costs because all three units offer the same menu and use the basic products?

5. What are the pros and cons of developing and using a purchasing handbook if you were a direc-tor of purchasing for an organization. Would you use one? Why or why not?

5

Selecting Suppliers and Ordering Products

Purchasing Pros Need to Know!

You're learning that purchasing is an important and complex activity involving much more than just "calling in an order" or inputting information at a supplier's Web site. In this chapter we'll focus on the steps that occur after supplier sourcing decisions (see Chapter 4) determine the suppliers from whom specific purchases will be made.

Pricing is an important aspect of the purchasing process, and it is important to move beyond an oversimplified idea of price ("cheapest is best") to appreciate how pricing should affect purchasing. Buyers should understand how different viewpoints affect pricing perceptions, and these will be explored in the chapter.

How should you choose suppliers from among those who are prequalified? Since all suppliers should use the property's purchase specifications, each should quote prices for the same quality of product and level of service. Then a request for price quotation process can be used, and the supplier quoting the lowest price will receive the order. At other times, however, especially for seldom-ordered and/or high-cost purchases, negotiation is needed.

A successful long-term relationship requires that both parties "win" at the negotiation table. Negotiation topics are often much broader than "What will you sell it for?" and "How much will you pay?" A wide range of knowledge and abilities is useful as negotiators plan and conduct negotiation sessions, and significant time and effort may be needed to prepare for negotiation. After determining its objectives, facts can be assembled, and the negotiator can consider the most crucial concerns and others that are less important that can be conceded.

The actual negotiation session begins with an introduction, which is followed by discussion (the actual negotiation process), and the conclusion allows both parties to review and summarize negotiation outcomes. Negotiation agreements must be implemented, and several follow-up activities are required to ensure this occurs.

Product ordering procedures tend to become more formalized as the volume of business increases. In this chapter you'll learn about procedures used by small, decentralized operations and in their larger, centralized counterparts.

Special ordering concerns, including the use of competitive bids and analysis of proposal responses, must be understood, as should details about the use of purchase orders. Information about order placement and the management of delivery delays is also important, and these topics will be discussed.

We'll conclude the chapter by reviewing how buyers increasingly use technology to yield practical and cost-effective advantages to the ordering process.

■ ■ ■

Outline

OVERVIEW OF ORDERING PROCESS

The **ordering** process occurs when a buyer makes specific commitments to a seller for a specific purchase.

Figure 5.1 (originally shown as Figure 1.2) reviews purchasing steps being discussed in this book.

Buyer's Guide to Purchasing Term

Order (product)   The process by which a buyer makes specific commitments to a seller for a specific purchase.

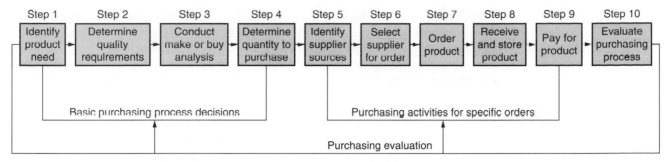

FIGURE 5.1   Steps in Purchasing Process

When reviewing Figure 5.1, note that we have already addressed Steps 1 through 3 (in Chapter 2 and Steps 4 and 5 (in Chapters 3 and 4, respectively). In this chapter you will learn about Step 6 (select supplier for order) and Step 7 (order product). Each step in the purchasing process is very important, and the creative efforts expended in earlier steps are wasted if thoughtful follow-through does not occur during subsequent steps.

The first four purchasing steps involve significant interaction between the purchaser and other hospitality personnel. When supplier sources are determined (Step 5), suppliers are selected for specific orders (Step 6), and actual orders are placed (Step 7), the buyer has significant interactions with suppliers.

Communication Affects Ordering

Managers in small-volume hospitality organizations undertake purchasing activities as one among many responsibilities. Large-volume organizations typically employ one or more persons with full-time purchasing responsibilities. Regardless of organizational structure, internal communication is required to

- determine exactly what products must be purchased.
- assess proper product quality requirements.
- determine which products should be produced on-site and which should be purchased from suppliers.
- identify the quantity of products needed and length of time for which products should be purchased.

Managers in small operations may make these decisions by themselves or in cooperation with their staff members. Managers in larger operations may make these decisions with assistance from purchasing personnel. In both instances, buyers require information for sourcing decisions and to determine those with whom specific orders should be placed.

Supplier sourcing and selection and order placement activities may only involve conversations between buyers and sellers in small properties, while extensive written communication is typically used in larger organizations. Examples include purchase specifications (discussed in Chapter 2) and purchase orders (discussed in this chapter). You're learning that the basic principles required for effective purchasing are similar regardless of an operation's size. Buyers must always tell suppliers exactly what is required, and this cannot be done unless exact product needs have been determined.

Unfortunately, communication difficulties or other problems can occur when orders are placed. If this happens infrequently, the buyer and the seller will likely cooperate to resolve the issue. Then their relationship will improve, and the satisfaction that results encourages a continuing partnership. However, if there are frequent problems that (from the buyer's viewpoint) are caused by the supplier, this works against the purchaser's ongoing interest in placing additional orders. Also, suppliers are less likely to provide value-added services for their problem accounts.

Common Ordering Challenges

There is an old saying, "You can't solve a problem until you are aware of it." Unfortunately, receiving and user personnel may be aware of problems with incoming products that are not shared with purchasing personnel, and buyers cannot address these concerns. Examples include the following:

- *Product shortages.* If a supplier experiences difficulty obtaining items for resale, purchasers will need to obtain them elsewhere. One would hope that delivery invoices (see Chapter 6) are routed through the buyer so he or she will note the problems.
- *Problems with quantities or purchase unit sizes.* Different packaging sizes may be substituted for those ordered. Example: An order for one fifty-pound bag of flour is met with five ten-pound bags of flour. While fifty pounds of flour are still received, the price per pound is often less when ordered in a fifty-pound bag. Even if a price adjustment is made (and it should be), production employees must still spend excessive time opening numerous bags of flour when filling flour bins.
- *Problems with on-site shortages.* Purchasers must always be careful when determining the quantities of product to order. Numerous examples of potential problems were noted in Chapter 3. However, product theft, pilferage, and spoilage, among other factors, can create unexplained (surprise) decreases in inventories, which create the need for ordering before purchasers may normally expect to do so.
- *On-site storage capacities.* Storage equipment and space is always expensive, and kitchen designers work hard to plan ideal storage requirements. Unfortunately, the ideal capacities for an operation being planned may be significantly over- or understated for foodservice operations that may follow that which was initially planned. Purchasers for high-volume operations with inadequate storage space have ongoing ordering challenges (often involving more frequent and expensive deliveries) and/or the need to create additional storage space when, most often, there is none available without converting (repurposing) other space.
- *Coordination between receiving and user personnel and purchasers.* Purchasers should manage by walking around and be physically present on random occasions when products are received. They can observe products in storage and production areas and participate in conversations and meetings to receive input from receiving and production personnel about the products being ordered.

Did You Know? (5.1)

There are times when market-related problems affect the sources of suppliers who normally carry an item. A recurring example is fresh produce. Poor weather conditions can destroy or damage crops for an entire growing season. Limited availability then creates significant shortages and high prices, and purchasers must pay more for products that are typically of lower quality. Wise buyers consider how they might substitute other products and/or discontinue offering some items until the market recovers.

PRICING CONSIDERATIONS

Price is the amount of money needed to purchase a product, and it is an obvious purchasing concern. However, obtaining the lowest price is *not* an objective of effective buyers. It is the right price, not the lowest price, that is important. Few restaurateurs think that the best meals are the cheapest meals, and hoteliers would agree that the best hotels are not always those with the lowest per-night guest room charges. A focus on lowest price usually indicates a buyer's misunderstanding about how prices are determined.

What Determines Sellers' Prices?

Four primary factors influence the prices buyers pay for their products:

1. *Prices reflect product costs.*   Assume you were selling a product for which you paid $10.00. To recover your costs, make a profit, and maintain your business, you must sell your product for more than $10.00. If the $10.00 you paid for the item was fair and if your own customers do not value the product enough to pay more than $10.00 for it, you will go out of business.

   (*Key point:* With few potential suppliers, competition is reduced, and the buyer risks paying higher future prices. A buyer and seller partnership is ideal, and the buyer should expect to provide a fair (reasonable) profit to the supplier in return for the products, services, and information the buyer receives.)

2. *Prices reflect consumer demand.*   Prices are generally influenced by consumer **demand.** When products are scarce and many buyers want them, the prices charged will generally be high. Sometimes the price reflects a limited supply (e.g., rare wines of limited quantity). In other cases it is the consumers' willingness to pay (not scarcity) that most influences price (e.g., expensive bottled waters).

   (*Key point:* Buyers should know when they are paying for scarcity and when they are paying a premium price for a consumer **fad.** This is important because consumer willingness to pay for fads can vary or quickly cease based on factors beyond the buyer's control.)

3. *Prices reflect service features and enhancements.*   Consider two buyers: one pays $100.00 for a case of fresh chicken but must pick it up at the supplier's location, and the other pays $101.00 for the case, but it is delivered to the buyer's restaurant. Who received the best price? Despite the one-dollar additional cost, the second buyer received a service (delivery) that would justify the price increase.

   (*Key point:* Foodservice operators know that guests ordering food and beverage items also benefit from the restaurant's location, furnishings, **ambiance,** and service levels. Likewise, hospitality buyers experience sellers' enhancements. Timely delivery, knowledge of the supplier's personnel, accurate invoicing, and ease of order placement are examples of service enhancements reflected in a supplier's pricing structure.)

Buyer's Guide to Purchasing Terms

Price   The amount of money needed to purchase a product or service.

Demand   The total amount of a product that buyers want to purchase at a specific price.

Fad   A heightened interest in something by many consumers that lasts for a short time.

Ambiance   The atmosphere (character or mood) projected by a restaurant.

Did You Know? (5.2)

As recently as the mid-1990s, significant sales of bottled water in restaurants were virtually unheard of. The 2000s, however, saw an explosion in the sale of bottled waters in foodservice operations. Selling prices were high relative to the purchase price, and profits were good.

Beginning in the late 2000s, however, environmental concerns caused many consumers, including foodservice buyers, to reconsider these purchases. Increasingly, customers began to ask, "What is the real source of this water? Does it come in plastic or glass? How much energy is spent to bottle and ship it? Is it really superior to water from our local water supply?" The consumers' view of value (and, therefore, what they were willing to pay) was changing. The value of products (what they can be sold for) can change, and these changes should be carefully monitored.

---

4. *Prices reflect supplier quality.* Foodservice operators with a reputation for quality food and outstanding service can charge more for their products, as can suppliers who consistently provide excellent products and high-quality services.

(*Key point:* Buyers who focus on only purchase price without considering the supplier's reputation may receive neither quality nor value. Unethical suppliers who do not stand behind their products and services often cost buyers much more than what the buyers originally paid.)

Buyers' Views about Price

There are numerous traditional and nontraditional views about pricing that can affect a buyer's perceptions about the topic.

TRADITIONAL VIEWS Buyers with a traditional view of pricing assume that suppliers evaluate cost structures and arrive at a price that is low enough to attract customers and high enough to generate a reasonable profit. Then they make one or more assumptions:

- *Increased price = increased quality.* A twenty-year-old scotch whiskey will likely taste better and cost more than a five-year-old product produced by the same distillery. However, buyers making this assumption must ensure they are comparing similar products: prices for twenty-year-old scotch should not be compared to those of five-year-old products.
- *Increased price = scarcity and value.* Buyers may think that rarity justifies higher pricing. Buyers purchasing rare French wines understand the importance of this belief. However, recall our earlier definition of *demand:* the total amount of a product buyers want to purchase at a *specific price.* When demand is strong, it will be reflected in price. However, scarcity alone is not a reason to justify increased prices. If it were, your one-of-a-kind childhood drawings would be valuable as art. Unfortunately, product scarcity frequently reflects widespread lack of consumer interest and justifies a lower (not higher) price.
- *Increased price = increased image.* Hospitality buyers may be subject to peer pressure and self-image like other consumers. Guests dining at a restaurant will likely perceive the restaurant more favorably if a well-known Heinz or Hunts condiment is used rather than an unknown brand. Wise buyers know that paying for image makes sense only when the image is appreciated or demanded by guests. If not, the price paid for the image is wasted.

LESS TRADITIONAL VIEWS   There are also less traditional views of pricing that reveal important aspects of it:

- *Price and cost are unrelated.*   This view of pricing recognizes that a seller's cost and selling price may not correlate. When true, significant savings can result. Assume a ban on smoking tobacco occurs. The price of tobacco would likely fall significantly, even though tobacco production costs would not change. Instead, what changed would be the consumers' interest in buying tobacco. It is not the cost of tobacco production that justifies its (or any other product's) price but, instead, the price that results from consumer demand. Buyers who encounter situations in which sellers must sell below their costs can obtain lower prices.
- *Cost + value = price.*   Most cost accounting books suggest a common and traditional view about establishing prices:

  Cost + Desired profit = Selling price

  A less traditional view restates the approach:

  Cost + Buyer value = Selling price

  The second viewpoint suggests the buyer, not the seller, determines price, and the buyer's value arises from his or her needs and not from the product itself. In this view, value relates to the buyer's perception and buyers (not growers, manufacturers, distributors, or brokers) determine selling prices.

  Buyers are not interested in a seller's cost. If owners simply needed to compute their costs and add desired profits to yield a fair selling price, anyone could remain in business. However, customers making restaurant visit decisions do not care about the restaurant's operating costs nor its desired profits. They care about only whether the restaurant provides value to them. If it does, they will pay the posted prices. If it does not, they will not pay the price.
- *Differential pricing is normal.*   Is it fair to price identical products differently for different customers? The concept of **differential pricing** states that it is fair and often essential for long-term profitability.

No business should charge higher or lower prices based on a buyer's ethnicity. However, many hospitality organizations have historically practiced differential pricing based on sex, age, and other factors. Ladies' nights at dance clubs, senior citizen meal discounts, and reduced children prices are examples of differential pricing for different customers that may not be based on the seller's cost of providing the product.

Hospitality buyers who receive preferred prices for high-volume purchases or less frequent deliveries typically pay lower prices than buyers who do not. Effective purchasers ask about requirements necessary to receive favorable supplier prices.

Factors Affecting Pricing

Several factors directly affect the prices hospitality buyers pay for products. Prices charged for utilities, including electricity, gas, water, and sewage, and for alcoholic beverages are, to some degree, governmentally controlled and/or regulated, and are not subject to normal price negotiation.

Buyer's Guide to Purchasing Term

Differential pricing   The act of charging different customers different prices for the same product.

Many restaurants offer differential pricing as they provide children's menus, smaller portions, and reduced charges for meals consumed by their younger guests.

Janeanne Gilchrist © Dorling Kindersley

PROFESSIONAL PURCHASING PREVENTS PROBLEMS (5.1)

Save Money without Reducing Quality

A common problem: Buyers do not know how to reduce costs.

Can two restaurant buyers purchase the same products from the same supplier and pay different prices? Yes, and for several reasons, none of which relate to unreasonable pricing structures. For example, it costs the supplier money for each delivery that is made. Fewer deliveries mean reduced costs, which can be passed on to the applicable buyer.

Prompt payments also reduce suppliers' costs, and these savings can, in part, be passed on to the buyer's organization. Higher-volume purchasers can receive discounts offered to purchasers who place the majority of orders with the same supplier. There are sensible opportunities to reduce purchase costs without sacrificing product quality, and professional buyers take advantage of them.

In a **free market,** what one pays for products is determined by the buyer and seller. When you voluntarily enter into a purchase contract, its terms dictate the prices you will pay.

Contract pricing is common in the hospitality industry for many products and especially for services such as exhaust hood cleaning, carpet cleaning, and snow removal. For example, the buyer may agree to a service provider's offer to clean all front windows of the restaurant for a stated fee paid each time the windows are cleaned. Frequently, however, prices may change each time products are ordered or services are desired, and a system to determine prices from alternative suppliers is required.

You've learned that buyers must decide whether to buy products or services from one or more suppliers. Generally, using more suppliers requires additional time for ordering, receiving, and invoice processing. However, a single-source supplier may charge higher prices if he or she believes there is no competition. Therefore, on

---

Buyer's Guide to Purchasing Terms

Free market An economic system in which businesses operate without government control in matters including pricing.

Contract pricing A pricing alternative in which buyer and seller agree to a specific price for a defined product or service for a stated time period or until one party terminates the agreement; also called "fixed-price contract."

The cost to purchase the ingredients to prepare the food on this plate will differ for two purchasers based on numerous factors, including volume of products purchased and the buyer's payment history.

© Dorling Kindersley

principle, buyers often split their business among several suppliers. (*Note:* The likelihood of a single-source supplier increasing the prices for higher-volume customers is small. Offering favorable pricing makes good business sense for suppliers, and it is in their interest to offer better pricing to retain a high-volume buyer's business.)

A supplier's cost for delivering a $1,000 order is not much different from delivering a $100 order: each of these deliveries likely requires one truck and one driver. When the supplier's cost of delivery can be spread across more items, the result is a decrease in the per-unit price charged to the buyer.

Purchasing all applicable products from one supplier can be costly if the items vary widely in quality and price or if they are difficult to obtain. Some buyers **split orders** for items such as meats, produce, and some bakery products among several suppliers, most often with a primary and a secondary source for each category. (*Note:* The use of primary suppliers was discussed in Chapter 4.)

The logic of using multiple suppliers appears sound, but sometimes it is not. Buyers who continually compare prices among competing suppliers and select, when quality is the same, the supplier offering the lowest price appear to be minimizing their costs. However, **cherry pickers** will likely be serviced last.

If a buyer purchases only a supplier's low-priced items, limited service results because the buyer has not considered service level, long-term relationships, dependability, or other nonprice factors in the purchase decision. The result is likely to be minimal per-unit price and minimal quality and service levels.

Buyers who do not pay their bills in a timely manner will likely pay more than their competitors for similar products. Suppliers often add the extra cost of carrying "slow-pay" accounts to the prices charged these buyers because, in effect, the supplier's funds are used to pay for the purchases.

Discounts

Many suppliers offer buyer **discounts** after normal prices are established.

There is a difference between a lowered price and a discount. Discounts are price reductions offered to selected buyers based on some specific characteristic or action. If instead the reduction is offered to all potential buyers, it is a simple price reduction.

Buyer's Guide to Purchasing Terms

Split orders   The purchasing tactic of using more than one supplier for a specific type of product for the purposes of ensuring competitive pricing and better product availability.

Cherry picker   A slang term for a buyer who purchases only a seller's lowest-priced products.

Discount   A deduction from the price buyers normally pay for products.

Suppliers are creative and there are reasons for devising discounts. Buyers should ask about all discounts offered by their suppliers because doing so allows them to pay a low **net price.**

There are several types of discounts.

PROMPT PAYMENT DISCOUNT   The buyer's payment history is a factor in a supplier's price. Discounts for prompt payment are common because suppliers want to reward accounts who pay their bills on time. Discounts typically apply when the entire amount owed is paid within a predetermined number of days or, in some cases, when **cash on delivery (COD)** is used. (*Note:* Purchasers with an unacceptable credit history will likely be placed on a COD basis without receiving a prompt payment discount. In addition, they may pay a premium to compensate for the financial risk the seller incurs.)

QUANTITY DISCOUNT   Many suppliers offer quantity discounts to encourage customers to increase their purchases. Buyers like them because they yield lower net prices. Sellers benefit because the cost of producing or delivering additional products is generally marginal after the **fixed costs** associated with producing the initial number of items have been recovered.

Sometimes quantity discounts are offered for the total amount purchased (order amount) rather than for an increased purchase of one item. In other cases, total order amounts and increased quantities may be combined over a given time to yield the total discount.

While quantity discounts can be significant, buyers must be cautious. Purchasing more product than needed can create product waste, especially for perishable products. Also, there may be additional costs to finance and store excess products needed to qualify for the quantity discount.

CUSTOMER STATUS DISCOUNT   Preferred customer status is another reason discounts may be offered. Unlike restaurants, which generally charge the same price to all customers, suppliers may offer status-based discounts depending on their (the suppliers') objectives.

Customer status discounts may result from factors including length of customer relationship; nonprofit business status; annual purchase volume; membership in a specific company, brand, or chain; and/or a supplier's desire to expand sales in a new industry segment or location.

SPECIAL DISCOUNTS (PROMOTIONS)   Special discounts are often associated with holidays, seasons, or exclusive events and are usually motivated by a desire to increase brand or product awareness. Discounts may be offered when a seller is interested in clearing inventories of older or discontinued products. Knowledgeable buyers learn about the reasons for special discounts, and they never accept defective or lower-than-desired-quality products simply because they are discounted.

Buyer's Guide to Purchasing Terms

Net price   The total or per-unit amount paid for products after all discounts have been applied to the purchase price.

Cash on delivery (COD)   A transaction in which a buyer pays the full amount owed at the time products are delivered.

Fixed cost   A business expense that does not vary based on the revenues generated by the business. In the restaurant business, examples include mortgage and insurance payments.

	Case Price (6 #10 cans)
Normal Case Price	$42.00
Less Seller's "2% Prompt Payment" Discount	($0.84)
Less Manufacturer's After-Purchase Rebate	($3.00)
Less Total Discounts and Rebates	$3.84
Net price	**$38.16**

FIGURE 5.2 Net Price Computation for One Case of Peaches

Rebates are similar to discounts and are often promotional. As you've learned, discounts are deductions from normal selling prices. Rebates are a discount offered *after* a purchase has been made at the normal selling price.

Manufacturers often use special rebate offers to introduce new products or to increase awareness and sales volumes of existing products.

Effect of Price Reductions

Figure 5.2 illustrates the effect of discounts and rebates on the net price of one case of sliced peaches purchased in cases containing six #10 cans.

If six cans are purchased for $38.16, the cost of one can is $6.36 ($38.16 per case ÷ 6 cans). This per-can price can be compared among different suppliers when the buyer evaluates competitive costs.

Restaurant guests do not buy their peaches by the can. A price calculation challenge results because buyers must know what they paid for the product in the portion size to be served to guests. Example: A portion size of four ounces (EP) of peaches is served at Sally's Restaurant, and the drained weight of one can in the case of peaches is 76 ounces. Sally will obtain 19 portions of peaches

Buyers at Work (5.1)

Did you say "Two fer?" asked Inga, the food and beverage manager and buyer for the Bayshore Country Club.

"No," replied Phyllis, her sales representative from the Green Grower's Produce company. I said, "Two *per*, and it's a special discount program we're running all summer. Two deliveries per week. So it's a called a Two Per!"

"Explain it again," said Inga.

"Well," replied Phyllis, "with all the fresh produce available during the summer, we are extra busy processing it, and we can't add staff because, after summer ends, things return to normal. Instead of delivering produce to you three times a week like normal, if you accept two weekly deliveries during the summer, we offer a 10 percent discount on all produce purchases. That can save you lots of money."

If you were Inga:

1. What are three changes that would immediately occur if you reduced the number of weekly produce deliveries from three to two?
2. What additional costs might be incurred if you participated in this discount program?
3. Should Inga participate in this discount program? Why or why not?

Buyer's Guide to Purchasing Term

Rebate　An after-purchase discount offered by the product maker (or seller); sometimes called a "cash back offer."

Purchasers, managers, and food preparation personnel must be aware of the production loss that occurs as heads of lettuce are processed into the edible portions that will be served to the guests.

Richard Embery/Pearson Education/PH College

per can (76 ounces ÷ 4 ounces) and 114 servings per case (19 portions per can × 6 cans per case).

Knowledge of portion size is important because it affects plate cost, which in turn is used to establish selling prices. (*Note:* The effect of portion size, portion cost, and plate cost on menu item selling prices was detailed in Chapter 3.) Portion costs also allow buyers to compare supplier's prices, even if there is variation in the package size, purchase unit, and/or market form of the products purchased.

Buyer's Guide to Internet Resources: Overview and Pricing

Web Site	Topic
www.ishp.org	Hospitality purchasing association
www.purchasingsolutions.co.uk	International purchasing association
www.bcg.com/publications/files/Procurement_Mar_01.pdf	Managing purchasing costs
www.about.com	Articles regarding reducing costs by effective management (Enter "reducing procurement costs" into the site's search box)
www.markitek.com	Information from seller's perspective about product pricing and interactions with buyers (Click on "Archives" when you reach the site)

NEGOTIATION BASICS

Effective purchasers are effective negotiators. Sometimes a single issue, such as price, is the only concern, but several issues, including price, service, and payment terms, may also be considered. Negotiation can involve one representative of the hospitality organization (the purchaser) and the supplier, or they can involve several persons with both organizations. Negotiations can be face-to-face and/or undertaken electronically, and the time required can be a few minutes or several months (or longer).

Definition

Negotiation is a process in which parties reach agreement about disputes, determine courses of action, and bargain for their individual and mutual advantages. Compromise and agreement with an incentive to overcome each other's concerns are part of most successful negotiations.

There are three possible outcomes from any negotiation process:

1. Reach a mutually acceptable agreement
2. "Agree to disagree"
3. Determine that additional negotiation is needed

Win-Win Negotiation Is Best

Some negotiators believe that one party must win and the other party must lose. This might occur when a buyer negotiates with a specialty foods supplier for a one-time purchase. If both parties believe that a future business relationship is unlikely, the issue of price is likely to be very important. The seller wins as the price goes up, and the purchaser wins as the price comes down.

More commonly, successful negotiation allows both parties to win, and this is the desired outcome for a long-term relationship. A supplier granting a price concession might desire a long-term relationship with the purchaser, and a buyer may pay more if a special delivery time can be arranged.

The concern that suppliers provide value has already been emphasized and is important in win-win negotiating. The term *mutual gains bargaining* describes negotiating with the purpose of win-win results.

Negotiation and Value

While the cost of a product is important, its value (the relationship between price and quality) is more important. Good suppliers provide more than just products. Their service and information is part of a product's cost, and is included in the deliverable to the buyer. Therefore, since information and service is bundled with the purchase price, they, like price, can be negotiated.

How much is it worth to a hospitality organization to consistently receive the correct quality of products in the right quantities at the agreed-on price?

Did You Know? (5.3)

The best supplier relationships are generally win-win. Just as restaurant managers have no long-term interest in selling meals at a loss, a supplier wants to earn a fair profit. Purchasers must look for value as purchase decisions are made, and they recognize that the long-term success of their suppliers requires a reasonable (but not excessive) profit. They know the price of items they buy includes a profit markup. However, because it is part of the cost, the supplier's profit is factored into the purchaser's value decision.

Buyer's Guide to Purchasing Terms

Negotiation   A process in which parties reach agreement about disputes, determine courses of action, and bargain for their individual and mutual advantages.

Mutual gains bargaining   Negotiation with the objective that both parties gain a lasting (ongoing) benefit.

Alternatively, how much does it cost if these purchasing goals are not consistently attained? How important is product information and specialized expertise to help the organization address problems? Those who negotiate on price to the exclusion of these and other concerns are often shortsighted. Unfortunately, many purchasers learn this when they pay a low price for products they do not receive (or do not receive them when they are needed). Wouldn't it be better to pay a slightly higher price and purchase from a more dependable supplier?

Let's consider price negotiation from the supplier's view. Would a supplier want to do business with a purchaser who paid a low price if the chances for payment are low and **accounts receivable** payments will be slow? Do suppliers want to sell to organizations who consistently allege product defects or who have all-too-frequent stock outs with the need for expedited supplier deliveries?

Hospitality purchasers want to purchase from good suppliers who, in turn, want to sell to good hospitality organizations. Tactics used during and the results of negotiation are influenced by the relationship between both parties.

Successful Negotiation Traits

The success or failure of negotiation is typically affected by the negotiators'

- personalities and skill levels.
- compatibility.
- expectations about the other's strengths and weaknesses, intentions and goals, and commitments to positions.
- tactics to address the other party's bargaining position and to move both sides toward a mutual outcome.

Many skills used by effective negotiators are the same as those necessary for success in any management position. Effective negotiators are excellent communicators. Persons who are creative thinkers and who are dedicated to their organization and able to understand the other party's interests will likely be more effective negotiators than others without these traits. These characteristics can be learned or at least can be improved. People skills, especially listening ability, are important as is the ability to solve problems and make decisions critically.

Effective negotiators can spot problems with the other party's logic, and they can identify errors, untruthful information, and deception. It is not always easy to analyze statements objectively and quickly discover what questions should be asked and what statements should be questioned. Also, the need for negotiators to be polite and courteous, to be respectful, to show concern, and to recognize the other party as a person (not as an adversary) should be obvious.

Steps in Negotiation

Figure 5.3 shows steps in negotiation.
Let's review each of the negotiation steps identified above.

NEGOTIATION PREPARATION Preparation for negotiation is sometimes deemphasized, and there is not a rule of thumb about how much time is needed. However, the importance of the outcome will likely influence the preparation efforts needed.

Buyer's Guide to Purchasing Term

Accounts receivable Money that is owned to but has not been received by an organization.

Buyers at Work (5.2)

"The price of seafood is increasing. This is partially a seasonal thing, and we're coming into the wrong season! However, I think we're still paying more for seafood than we should, and I want to find other seafood sources."

Joe, the manager of Jack's Restaurant, was speaking to Michael, the executive chef, who replied, "I like our suppliers because they sell good products and give good service. They help us with our menu changes, and their ideas and product samples allow us to make some good decisions. You're the boss, but I would like to express our price concerns to the salespersons and then see what happens to our prices."

"OK, Michael, let's try it," said Joe, "but if prices keep increasing, I'm going to find some new suppliers."

Assume you were Joe:

1. Would negotiation help now? Why or why not?
2. What, if anything, could you do to reduce your seafood costs?
3. What would you think about Michael's idea to speak with the salespersons as a tactic to reduce cost?

Purchasers must know exactly what that they want. Answers to the following questions can help drive negotiation objectives:

- If the negotiation process is ideally effective, what will happen?
- How will we know?
- How will we benefit?
- What will be our relationship with this supplier?
- How will our customers benefit?

It is also necessary to define responsibilities of those on the negotiation team and to arrange details, including time and location.

Some negotiation results, including a lower price, larger discount, and faster or different delivery times, may be easy to quantify. However, other issues such as service quality and ways to improve product value may be more difficult to objectively assess.

Wise negotiators establish **going-in** positions that prioritize desired outcomes from the negotiation. For example, desired quality changes may be very

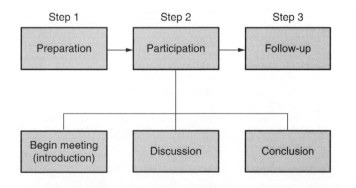

FIGURE 5.3 Steps in Negotiation

Buyer's Guide to Purchasing Term

Going-in (negotiation position)   The first offer made on a negotiating point by one party.

important, and different delivery times might be a lesser concern. If a negotiator desires twice-a-week delivery instead of the current, once-weekly delivery (the going-in position) but knows that delivery on another day is acceptable, this can become the **fallback** position.

Careful preparation can yield going-in and fallback positions for a negotiator's most important concerns. However, one party may change a fallback position if the other makes a concession on an issue that encourages a revised fallback position on another concern.

In the example above, the supplier is concerned about delivery costs and will not want to provide twice-weekly delivery unless compensated for it. The supplier also recognizes the purchaser's perspective: Friday deliveries are best (most of the organization's business is on the weekends), and no additional delivery costs are incurred. Then the buyer will benefit and receive greater value. Also, the supplier has probably gained an edge when the next negotiation point is discussed.

You've learned that purchasers and suppliers desire a mutually beneficial relationship, and it affects their negotiation interests. Wouldn't you rather pay $4.21 per pound for ground beef patties if you were confident that you would receive the right amount and quality of a product rather than pay $4.19 per pound to another supplier if quality control and reputation suggests the possibility of inconsistency? One would hope poor-performing suppliers would be eliminated during supplier sourcing decisions (see Chapter 4).

Purchasers planning negotiation sessions should consider common-ground agreements to use as a foundation for the process. For example, both parties should agree about the importance of proper quality and that they share an interest in better serving customers.

Figure 5.4 shows factors that affect the negotiation success of purchasers and suppliers.

Figure 5.5 reviews possible negotiation planning issues when the session will involve an existing supplier.

NEGOTIATION PARTICIPATION All of the purchaser's negotiation preplanning work should benefit the organization as the participation step occurs. Figure 5.3 shows three parts to the actual participation (negotiation) activity:

1. *Meeting introduction.* Being on time and ready for negotiation is important and can help yield a positive environment. Emphasizing the benefits of

Purchasers Improve Negotiating Position When	Suppliers Improve Negotiating Position When
• they pay their bills on time. • large quantities are purchased. • quality standards are reasonable. • there is a long-term relationship with the supplier. • commonly available products are purchased. • they practice ethical purchasing procedures. • their organization is a good community citizen. • they desire a win-win relationship with the supplier.	• product quality meets the purchaser's standards. • the purchaser's service expectations are met. • there are few product delivery errors. • there are few payment processing problems. • company representatives act professionally. • they provide useful information. • they help the purchaser solve problems. • they provide value. • they desire a win-win relationship with the purchaser.

FIGURE 5.4 Negotiation Success Factors

Buyer's Guide to Purchasing Term

Fallback (negotiation position) The point beyond which a negotiator will not compromise on an issue.

Purchase Agreement Issues	**Quality Specification Issues**
• Are current product costs reasonable? • What is our experience with the supplier? • To what extent have quality requirements been met? • Have there been serious problems? If so, what? • When must a supplier decision be made?	• Has the supplier maintained quality? • What specific quality problems have occurred? • Are changes needed in how quality is measured? • Can we replace the product with another item for which quality problems are less likely?
Delivery Issues	**Financial Issues**
• What is the desired frequency of delivery? • What quantities of products will be purchased? • What is the supplier's preferred delivery time? Can it be altered? • Have there been delivery problems? If so, how were they resolved? (What are the supplier's suggestions?)	• What credit terms, if any, are appropriate? • What, if any, changes in payment policies and procedures are desired?

FIGURE 5.5   Negotiation Planning Issues

the relationship, indicating an interest in reaching mutually successful conclusions, and reviewing basic agreements are useful actions.

2. *Meeting discussion.*   The situation will determine helpful negotiation procedures. Negotiators should never argue. (If problems are encountered, a helpful solution is better than pointing blame!) They should provide summaries of important points to minimize communication problems. They also know that **body language** can help one understand what the other party thinks.

  Successful negotiators realize that, in one way or another, everything is negotiable. They quickly ensure that they are negotiating with someone who has the authority to make decisions. They can read between the lines, listen more than they speak, and ask open-ended questions that can't be answered with a "yes" or "no." Effective negotiators are patient, and they don't accept the first offer. Also, they don't make one-sided concessions; if a purchaser receives something (e.g., frequent deliveries), he or she gives up something (e.g., less frequent payments). They also

- learn the other's position before stating their own.
- know one cannot negotiate without options, and one option is always walking away."
- ask questions, make simple points, and don't get involved with technical details.
- know the limits of their authority.
- have applicable data, information, and notes available and remain focused on the issues.

3. *Meeting conclusion.*   Always end the meeting by congratulating the other party because, one would hope, the negotiation session provided a win-win outcome.

Buyer's Guide to Purchasing Term

Body language   Nonverbal actions such as gestures, poses, movements, and expressions that a person uses to communicate.

Significant planning and great interpersonal skills are required to successfully negotiate with hospitality suppliers.

Stockbyte/Jupiter Images Picturequest-Royalty Free

NEGOTIATION FOLLOW-UP   Negotiation agreements must be implemented. After the meeting, both parties should know who will do what and when because it will affect their future relationship. Clarifications and summaries can help ensure effective communication, consistent opinion, and the mutual understanding necessary to implement the agreement.

Final steps in negotiation follow-up include the following:

- Ensuring that persons follow the negotiated agreement
- Preparing written contracts that address agreement provisions

Buyer's Guide to Internet Resources: Negotiation

Web Site	Topic
www.negotiatormagazine.com	General negotiation topics
www.changingminds.org	Wide variety of negotiation topics (Enter "negotiation" into the site's search box)
www.smithfam.com	Negotiating tips and strategies (Enter "negotiation" into the site's search box)
www.freeworldacademy.com	Business negotiation advice (Click on "negotiation" on the site's home page)
www.negotiationskills.com	Negotiation questions and answers (Click on "advice" then "interest-based negotiation")

PRODUCT ORDERING BASICS

Small hospitality organizations using decentralized purchasing and larger operations with more centralized purchasing use different ordering procedures.

Small Properties

You've learned that small hospitality organizations do not employ full-time purchasing staff. Instead, a decentralized purchasing process using some or all of the following steps is often implemented:

- Persons responsible for purchasing are identified. In a very small operation, the owner/manager may purchase everything. If department heads are employed, they may purchase the products required by their department. In a small restaurant, the chef, beverage manager, and dining room manager may, respectively, purchase food, beverage, and dining service–related products and supplies.

- Department heads have purchasing authority to spend to a preestablished limit (for example, $1,000) after which owner or unit manager approval is required.
- Department buyers make basic purchasing decisions, including the quantities of products needed (often to increase inventory levels to a predetermined **par level**) and quality requirements. They may also make supplier selection decisions, which frequently involve purchasing products from the suppliers who have always been used.
- Purchasers complete purchase documents determined by property policy. In some organizations they retain documentation until orders are delivered. Then they or a representative sign delivery invoices for incoming orders, and the original purchase documents and delivery order are routed to those with accounting responsibilities. In other properties purchase documents are immediately sent to accounting staff who retain them until signed delivery invoices are received.

Large Properties

The purchasing process is more formal in a large hospitality organization. Figure 5.6 reviews the basic steps that might be used. (*Note:* All of these steps can be

---

Did You Know? (5.4)

Many symbols and abbreviations are commonly used in request for price quotations, purchase orders, delivery invoices, and other purchasing documents. Hospitality purchasers must know what they mean, and they must use and interpret them correctly. Some examples include the following:

Symbol/Abbreviation	What It Means
# or lb	pound (# can also means "number")
oz	ounce
ea	each
bu	bushel or bunch
pu	purchase unit
tsp or t	teaspoon
Tbsp, T, or Tbs	tablespoon
pt	pint
qt	quart
gal	gallon
doz	dozen
c	cup
%	percent
AP	as purchased
°F	degrees Fahrenheit
°C	degrees Celsius

Buyer's Guide to Purchasing Term

Par level   A predetermined level at which quantities of products in inventory should be maintained.

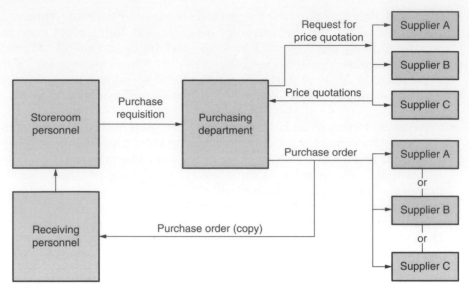

FIGURE 5.6   Ordering in Large Hospitality Organization

automated, and information about automated systems will be discussed later in this chapter.)

Let's review Figure 5.6.

- Purchasing personnel order additional quantities of products when they receive a **purchase requisition** from storeroom personnel indicating that additional products are required.

Figure 5.7 shows a sample purchase requisition.

- After receiving the purchase requisition, purchasing personnel issue a request for price quotation (RFP) to suppliers prequalified in earlier sourcing decisions (see Chapter 4).
- Suppliers interested in providing the products return a price quotation indicating their current selling prices for items meeting the property's quality requirements as explained in purchase specifications (see Chapter 2).
- After analyzing the price quotations, purchasing personnel issue a purchase order to the chosen supplier. A copy is also routed to receiving personnel so they will know details about incoming deliveries. (*Note:* When manual purchasing systems are used, the RFP and the purchase order are frequently the same document. Prices are requested, the RFP is returned, and a copy is then used (returned to the supplier) as a purchase order confirming acceptance of the seller's prices.

Purchasing personnel may also route a copy of the purchase order to accounting staff who retain and compare it to the delivery invoice provided by receiving personnel after product delivery.

Special Ordering Concerns

Concerns about competitive bids and the analysis of price quotation responses are an important part of the ordering process in large hospitality operations.

Buyer's Guide to Purchasing Term

Purchase requisition   A hard copy or electronic form used by storeroom personnel to inform purchasing employees that additional quantities of products are needed.

Requesting Department: _____   Requisition Number: _____

Date Needed: _____

ITEM	PURCHASE UNIT	NUMBER OF UNITS NEEDED	SPECIFICATION NUMBER

Authorized by: _____   Current Date: _____

FIGURE 5.7   Purchase Requisition

COMPETITIVE BIDS   Many hospitality organizations use **competitive bids** to determine the supplier offering the lowest costs for products of the required quality.

Is a requirement for competitive bids with its emphasis on lowest cost contrary to an emphasis on value (the relationship between price and quality) because bidding stresses cost differences? Buyers using competitive bids will *not* be emphasizing only the lowest cost when they have completed other activities described in earlier chapters, including the following:

- Determining quality requirements for desired products and expressing them in purchase specifications distributed to prequalified suppliers
- Considering the proper quantity of products needed and clearly communicating this information
- Prequalifying suppliers using, when possible, the purchaser's experience and objective factors that assess the supplier's commitment to quality, value-added services, and provision of information

---

Buyer's Guide to Purchasing Terms

Bid (competitive)   A supplier's response to a purchaser's request for price quotation.

Award (to supplier)   The act of selecting and notifying a supplier that its response to a request for price quotation was accepted.

Buyers at Work (5.3)

Ralph and Lorraine have been friends since college. Now Ralph is the purchasing director for the Provincial Golf Club. Lorraine has also done well and is the sales manager of the largest broad-line distributor in Ralph's region.

Their professional relationship was mutually beneficial; Lorraine received occasional complimentary golfing, and Ralph frequently received helpful information about his purchasing challenges.

One day Lorraine called Ralph with some good news. "Our company is changing some supply sources, and we must move some products quickly. I can e-mail you a list of these items so you can have a first choice of anything you want."

"Thanks, Lorraine," replied Ralph. "We always want to reduce our purchasing costs; maybe there're some deals that we can use."

"Sure thing, Ralph," said Lorraine. "You're one of our best accounts, and alerting you about this is the right thing to do."

1. Assume there are products on Lorraine's list that Ralph uses. Assume, however, that they are of a different quality and/or are available in purchase unit sizes not currently used. Should Ralph purchase the items if there are significant savings? Defend your response.
2. Assume there are products on Lorraine's list that Ralph is currently using, and they are exactly what the club needs. How should Ralph determine the quantity of these items to purchase?
3. Assume the club's general manager is aware of Lorraine's long-term personal and professional relationship with Ralph. What, if any, special procedures are needed to ensure that the club's interests are safeguarded?

When the above activities are completed, buyers can be reasonably assured that suppliers' prices will be for products of the same quality and quantity and that services provided will be acceptable. Then the only reason for price differences will relate to a supplier's interest in doing business with the purchaser (in other words, the extent to which the supplier will accept a lower profit markup).

Wise buyers know that suppliers operate their businesses in the same way as hospitality organizations: they work hard to reduce costs without sacrificing quality. They innovate, use technology when applicable, and ensure that their labor force is fairly treated and productive. Then they can operate more efficiently and can pass savings on to the customers while still generating a fair financial return.

ANALYSIS OF PRICE QUOTATION (RFP) RESPONSES   What are the buyer's concerns when reviewing price quotation responses submitted by suppliers? They should first verify that the supplier is submitting a bid for the same products in the same quantity specified in the RFP. If there are no variations, the buyer's next concern relates to the quoted costs. If the supplier did not submit a price for one or more specific items in the RFP, the buyer may exclude that supplier's price quotation response from further consideration. Whether this is done depends on how the buyer will select the supplier:

- *On the basis of the lowest total price for all items noted on the price quotation responses.*   In this case a supplier quoting a price for only some products would be excluded. Advantages include the ability to purchase all items from one supplier and avoid the paperwork required when multiple suppliers are used. (*Note:* While costs associated with issuing purchase orders and completing follow-up documentation processing is difficult to quantify, many organizations believe the cost to be $25.00 or more.) A likely disadvantage to this supplier selection method is that the buyer may be paying a higher price for some products.

Product	Purchase Unit	Supplier A	Supplier B	Supplier C
Ground beef	Pound	3.29	3.24	3.31
Tenderloin steak	Pound	9.87	9.59	10.03
Chicken	2½# bird	5.29	5.47	5.54

FIGURE 5.8   Sample Supplier Competitive Bid Analysis

- *On the basis of the prices quoted for each product in the price quotation response.*   Supplier A may have submitted the lowest price for several products and would receive a purchase order for them. Supplier B may have submitted the lowest prices for other products, which will be purchased from it. Here is the advantage: the lowest price will be paid for every item. However, there is a disadvantage: the time and expense required to interact with more than one supplier as orders for all products are placed.

Figure 5.8 shows a supplier competitive bid analysis for three items. Note that Supplier A submitted the lowest price for chicken, and Supplier B will be awarded the ground beef and tenderloin steak purchases. Buyers may reserve the right to accept only specific products requested on an RFP. Also, many organizations reserve the right to not award a bid to any supplier submitting a price quotation in response to a specific RFP.

Close Look at Purchase Orders

Purchase orders are used primarily by buyers in larger organizations to authorize (approve) the purchase of products of a required quality in a specified quantity at an agreed-on price from a specific supplier. Figure 5.9 illustrates a purchase order that might be in a hard-copy or electronic form.

When reviewing Figure 5.9, assume that the Summerville Restaurant buyer sent RFPs to several suppliers, including Acme Grocers, and the buyer selected Acme Grocers to provide the order. Specifications were previously sent to Acme Grocers, and both the buyer and seller are aware that RFP prices quoted must be based on products meeting these quality requirements.

Note that in the upper right-hand corner, the purchase order (PO) number and date are included as is the preferred delivery date and property contact information

---

Did You Know? (5.5)

Suppliers know that some organizations may purchase only some of many products based on their (the supplier's) price quotations. They may, then, increase their prices for specific items out of concern that they will only be awarded a relatively small portion of the entire purchase order. Experienced buyers may request that suppliers indicate the percentage discount, if any, offered on the total order if the buyer purchases all products on the RFP from the supplier. Some purchasers also request that suppliers provide price quotations two ways: (1) the price including delivery to buyer's location and (2) a second price for buyer pickup at the supplier's location. The latter might be useful in some situations, including when specialty products are purchased in small quantities and for purchases when the supplier's location is close to that of the buyer.

Purchase order

From/ship to	Purchase from	PO No.	34X135
Summerville Restaurant 1710 W. Summer Street Summerville, NV 00000 Telephone: 000-000-0000	Acme Grocers 2451 Elm Rd. Center Place, NV 00000	PO Date:	7/16/xx
		Delivery Date:	7/20/xx
		Contact:	John Davis
		Terms:	Net 30

Item	Quantity	Purchase	Purchase Unit Price	Total Price	RFP #
Green beans	4	Case (#10 cans)	34.50	138.00	1715700
Flour, all purpose	3	Bag (#50)	22.17	66.51	1715700
			Total	783.17	

Terms and Conditions:	Buyer:	John Davis	Date:	7/16/xx
This purchase order expressly limits acceptance to the terms and conditions stated above and included on the following page. Any additional terms and conditions are rejected.				

FIGURE 5.9 Sample Purchase Order

if the supplier has questions. The purchase order also indicates that the terms are "Net 30." This means that the buyer will pay the total amount of the invoice ($783.17) within thirty days of the delivery date. (*Note:* Sometimes buyers negotiate a discounted price for faster payment. For example, payment terms might be: "2/10; net 30." Then the buyer will receive a 2 percent discount if the total invoice is paid within ten days; otherwise the total invoice amount is due within thirty days of the invoice date.)

PURCHASE ORDER PROCEDURES Procedures for issuing purchase orders typically include sending copies to the supplier and the property's receiving personnel. Additional copies may also be retained by the purchasing department and may be forwarded to accounting personnel. In most large properties, all orders except small purchases for which **petty cash** is used are authorized with a purchase

Buyer's Guide to Purchasing Term

Petty cash   A cash fund used to make relatively infrequent and low-cost product purchases.

order. In small organizations with a decentralized system, purchasers may use a standardized purchasing form (preferred) or another form approved by the person(s) with accounting responsibilities.

TERMS AND CONDITIONS Suppliers and purchasers typically require **terms and conditions** that apply to their transactions. For example, suppliers typically identify minimum purchase values that must be met before deliveries are made, and they may deliver on only specified days.

Purchasers may have general concerns to be addressed in their supplier agreements. Often these are included in **boilerplate** language that is part of all purchase orders.

Examples of boilerplate language include the following:

- *Purchase order to be exclusive agreement.* The purchase order specifically identifies all buyer's and seller's responsibilities.
- *Services and deliverables.* Seller agrees to provide the products described in the purchase order, including compliance with all terms and conditions.
- *Delivery schedules.* Deliveries will be made within a reasonable time to the location specified by the buyer.
- *Risk of loss.* The seller assumes the risk of loss to products until they are received (i.e., the delivery invoice is signed) by the buyer.
- *Packaging and crating charges.* All packaging and crating charges are included in the product price or stated clearly as a separate charge in the purchase order.
- *Payment of invoices.* Buyer will pay the seller the amount agreed on in the purchase order.
- *Guarantees and warrantees.* Sellers warrant that products will be free from defects and conform to specifications.
- *Sellers are independent contractors.* Sellers cannot commit the buyer for obligations under another contract.
- *Sellers are responsible.* Sellers must pay taxes and maintain records required by governmental authorities relating to the products they sell.
- *Insurance.* Sellers must maintain insurance required by law.
- *Indemnification.* Seller will hold the buyer and his or her organization harmless from claims, liabilities, damages, and other costs related to the products being sold.
- *Disposition of rejected products.* Seller will pick up any items refused at time of delivery.
- *Confidentiality.* Information related to the product sale will not be shared with anyone.
- *Termination.* Buyer can terminate the purchase order if the seller fails to comply with it. Also, the seller can terminate the agreement if the buyer does not pay the seller for products delivered within a specified time period.

Buyer's Guide to Purchasing Terms

Terms and conditions General provisions that apply to a supplier's price quotations and a buyer's purchase orders regardless of the specific products being purchased or sold.

Boilerplate (language) Contract clauses addressing concerns that do not change in different applications.

Indemnification A contractual clause in which one party agrees to assume specific legal responsibilities without the right to claim any compensation from the other party for any problem that results.

PROFESSIONAL PURCHASING PREVENTS PROBLEMS (5.2)

Protect Yourself from the "Lowball" Prices

A common problem: Products offered for sale at low prices are not delivered.

Some unethical suppliers may submit a bid for one product on an RFP at a very low price or for a product not in stock. If the buyer awards the purchase based on the total price for all products in the price quotation response, the **lowballed** product will not be delivered.

Wise hospitality buyers recognize that this can occur, and they address it with a boilerplate remedy: "The buyer reserves the right to purchase, at current market prices, any missing products in the quantity specified in the purchase order with the difference between the quoted and actual product cost subtracted from the amount that the buyer owes the supplier."

- *Legal remedies.*   The buyer specifies how it will recover damages incurred if the seller fails to perform.
- *Failure to perform.*   Neither the buyer nor the seller will be penalized for failing to perform for reasons beyond their control (e.g., fire or flood).
- *Limitations on subcontracting.*   Sellers must indicate the extent to which part of the purchase order will be subcontracted.
- *Invoice information.*   Invoices should be sent to a specified location. Separate invoices are required for each specific purchase order, and invoices should indicate applicable purchase number orders.
- *Quantities.*   Shipments must be in the quantities ordered.
- *Provisions for packaging.*   Requirements relating to construction of shipping containers, packing materials, and bar or other coding can be specified.

Timing and Product Orders

You've learned that when traditional purchasing systems are used, orders are placed when inventory levels must be increased to meet future production requirements. The timing of order placement typically also considers factors such as the following:

- Supplier delivery schedules
- Minimum inventory levels and order lead times
- Out of stock, emergency, and other unexpected purchases may need to be made with little or no lead time. Use of effective purchasing practices should minimize these last-minute purchase requirements, but they may still occasionally occur.

Standing orders typically involve minimal, if any, ordering time. A restaurant may have an agreement with a coffee or dishwashing chemical supplier to provide coffee-related products and dishwashing chemicals, respectively. A route person may visit the property on a predetermined basis (e.g., every Tuesday

---

Buyer's Guide to Purchasing Terms

Lowball (selling price)   A selling price significantly below current market price that a supplier quotes for a product that he or she does not intend to deliver to the buyer.

Subcontract   A contract that is part of another contract; someone may enter into a contract with someone else who contracts with a third party to perform part of the original contract obligation.

The buyer knows that the quantity of products in storage affects the time when additional quantities of products should be ordered.

Vincent P. Walter/Pearson Education/PH College

morning) and replenish applicable products to a predetermined par level. A delivery invoice signed by and left with an authorized person at the property is used as the basis for payment.

Expediting Procedures

Purchasers may sometimes expedite deliveries because, in spite of the best planning, within-property problems can occur that affect orders. The needs of user departments can be misunderstood (purchase requisition problems can arise), and inventory management issues may misstate inventory quantities. Weather conditions, strikes, and problems creating errors as delivery vehicles are loaded are examples of supplier-related reasons for product shortages.

Useful tactics to obtain products in emergency situations vary according to the situation, and several alternatives are noted in Figure 5.10.

Purchasers should consider the need to expedite purchases as an opportunity to correct problems. They should work with suppliers to anticipate and resolve supplier-related causes of product shortages and quality issues. More than very infrequent problems caused by the purchaser's organization must be corrected, and those caused by the supplier may create the need for an examination of a continued relationship.

Technology and the Ordering Process

Purchasers can use technology in numerous ways at every step in the process to order products from suppliers. In this section we'll review automated ordering alternatives.

Challenge	Possible Expediting Tactic
1. Inadequate quantity at time of delivery.	1. Purchase product from another supply source.*
2. Improper product quality.	2. Purchase the product from retail source.
3. Purchaser error; product needed quickly.	3. Pick up product at supplier's location; buy product from retail source.
4. Product shortage (multi-unit property).	4. "Borrow" product (complete proper interproperty transfer form).
5. Product on back order (but available at the supplier's location before time of need).	5. Request that supplier make special delivery or that the product be delivered by a sales representative.

*A purchase order clause (terms and conditions) allowing the buyer to purchase the missing product in the marketplace with a credit to the amount owed the supplier for the difference between the quoted and actual price paid is useful.

FIGURE 5.10 Examples of Expediting Tactics

Buyers at Work (5.4)

Flora, the kitchen manager at the Pine Hill Retirement Center, had ordered some boneless turkey rolls for a special luncheon to be served to her senior citizen residents and their families. The frozen products were ordered five days ago for delivery two days ago. Her salesperson had called to advise that they were on back order but would be delivered today. She had just tried (the third time) to reach the supplier and her salesperson without success. Knowing that she needed the turkey rolls, she purchased them from a local food warehouse that was open to the public and placed them in her walk-in refrigerator to thaw.

Flora arrived at her office at about seven o'clock the next morning and had two messages. The supplier had called to explain that the delivery truck had broken down, and the product would definitely be delivered tomorrow (which was now today). The message also noted that there had been a temporary telephone interruption due to the installation of a new telephone system.

The second message was from her salesperson, who explained that a personal emergency had kept him away from the telephone throughout the previous day and night.

"Well," she said to herself, "they had reasonably good excuses for delivery problems, but what should I do now that I've spent several hundred dollars at the local warehouse store to purchase the product that I knew required thawing and preparation today?"

Assume you are Flora:

1. Would you have purchased the turkey rolls even though you had an outstanding purchase order for the product with this supplier? Explain your response.
2. What, if anything, would you have expected your supplier and sales representative to have done to contact you?
3. What should you do now?

Many software developers offer systems that merge the purchasing functions so, for example, buyers can (1) determine menu item sales and resulting decreases in product inventory based on the sales, (2) calculate remaining product inventory levels based on ideal usage required to generate the sales, and (3) alert purchasers and others when product order points are reached. These subsystems, taken together, allow technology to assist managers and purchasers with control to make effective decisions.

Details about the use of technology to manage nonpurchasing-related aspects of hospitality operations are beyond the purpose of this book.[i] However, we will now review procedures to determine inventory levels and communicate with suppliers. (*Note:* Additional information about technology and purchasing is presented in Chapter 12.)

DETERMINING INVENTORY LEVELS   Traditional ordering systems consider existing inventory levels and may be implemented when order points are reached. Alternatively, purchases can be made on a regularly scheduled basis by considering the quantity in inventory when specific orders are placed. Automated systems can maintain an ongoing count of products in inventory. Systems can track the quantities of products entering inventory (which increase inventory balances) and record the quantities of products leaving inventory (which reduce inventory levels). This data can be accessed at any time and provides an instant answer to the question "How much product do we have, and how much should we order?"

Automated systems can do much more than simply track products into and out of storage areas. Point-of-sale (POS) systems track customer counts, revenues, and other information so restaurant managers can tally counts of menu items sold. If standard recipes are used, managers can track the quantities of ingredients used to produce each menu item and adjust remaining inventory balances accordingly.

Assume that POS data indicates that 325 hamburger steaks were sold during a specified time period. If the standard recipe for this menu item requires 5 ounces (as purchased weight) of ground beef for each entrée, approximately 101.6 pounds of ground beef should have been used for this purpose: 325 hamburger patties $\times$ 5 oz. (AP) = 1,625 oz. $\div$ 16 (number of oz. in pound) = 101.6 pounds.

Similar tallies can be made of the number of pounds of ground beef of similar quality that should have been used to produce other products that have been sold, and the total quantity of ground beef that should have been used will be known. If inventory management software is interfaced with POS software (or if software containing both sales and inventory applications is used), one can calculate the approximate quantity of ground beef that should remain in inventory as follows:

Beginning inventory of ground beef

plus	Incoming shipments of ground beef
equals	Total available ground beef
minus	Amount of ground beef used (from POS data)
equals	Amount of ground beef in inventory.

As seen above, technology provides at least two methods to determine the quantities of products on hand to help purchasers with ordering decisions: (1) track product movements in and out of storage areas and (2) track quantities of specific ingredients based on sales. In practice, both methods may be used. After verifying sales quantities with physical count information from accounting personnel, purchasers have inventory quantity information necessary for ordering. At the same time, managers can consider reasons, if any, for differences between theoretical (sales) counts from inventory movement and ingredient usage and the actual physical count of product on hand. (*Note:* While some variation may be expected for reasons including overportioning and leftovers, significant variation will require analysis and corrective action.)

COMMUNICATING WITH SUPPLIERS Communication between buyers and sellers is necessary at several times during the ordering process. Examples were discussed earlier and include when the following happens:

- Purchaser requests prices for specific products with a request for price quotation (RFP)
- Supplier provides a price quotation (bid) in response to the RFP
- Purchaser awards an order to the supplier with a formal purchase order

Each of the above steps is increasingly automated. Some organizations post terms and conditions related to their purchase orders on the Internet. The use of technology streamlines the ordering process, reduces time-consuming paperwork, and allows for a much less complicated information tracking and storing processes.

Many suppliers allow (encourage) purchasers to place their orders online rather than use salespersons to take orders physically (in person) or by telephone, facsimile, or even with e-mail messages.

A commonly used online ordering system uses several steps. Purchasers do the following:

- Enter the supplier's Web site and use a protected identification code to reach their accounts
- Enter products desired into an order template on the screen (*Note:* Buyers can review previous orders and note current prices for desired and/or alternative products as ordering information is entered.)
- Provide other information and complete the ordering process

While purchasing technology applications such as those just described apply to the ordering process, they will increasingly be useful for numerous other purchasing-related responsibilities as well.

Buyer's Guide to Internet Resources: Ordering

Web Site	Topic
www.sysco.com	Large foodservice distributor (Click on "Order Entry" when you reach the site)
www.adacoservices.com	Automated procurement management system
www.costguard.com	Automated procurement management system
www.htmagazine.com	Automated procurement (Enter "automated procurement" into the site's search box)
www.formdocs.com	Design of purchase orders
www.hospitalitynet.org	Requests for proposals information (Type "request for proposals" into the site's search box.)

Purchasing Terms

Order (product) 108
Price 111
Demand 111
Fad 111
Ambiance 111
Differential pricing 113
Free market 114
Contract pricing 114
Split orders 115
Cherry picker 115
Discount 115

Net price 116
Cash on delivery (COD) 116
Fixed cost 116
Rebate 117
Negotiation 119
Mutual gains bargaining 119
Accounts receivable 120

Going-in (negotiation position) 121
Fallback (negotiation position) 122
Body language 123
Par level 125
Purchase requisition 126
Bid (competitive) 127
Award (to supplier) 127

Petty cash 130
Terms and conditions 131
Boilerplate (language) 131
Indemnification 131
Lowball (selling price) 132
Subcontract 132

Make Your Own Purchasing Decisions

1. What are five specific actions that buyers can take to determine a seller's reputation for providing quality products and services?
2. All suppliers value prompt payment and offer some discounts for buyers who pay cash on delivery. In other cases a buyer's payment history can be so poor that vendors will sell on nothing less than a cash-only basis. What are some disadvantages associated with cash-only deliveries? What can buyers do to minimize those disadvantages if they must operate in a cash-only situation?
3. Bacon is one example of an item that is typically portioned not by weight, but by slices. What are some other items that are not portioned by weight? How could a dishonest supplier suggest low EP prices when selling such items? What can wise buyers do to guard against such actions?
4. Assume you are a purchaser negotiating with a long-time supplier with whom you have had an excellent working relationship. How, if at all, would this past experience affect the style and tactics you would use while negotiating? How does your response change if you are negotiating with a supplier with whom you have had a marginal relationship?
5. How would you determine the types of terms and conditions that you as a buyer for a hospitality organization would use for purchase orders? What, if any, assistance would you request from your organization's attorney?

Endnote

1. Interested readers are referred to Michael Kasavana and John Calhill, *Managing Technology in the Hospitality Industry*, 5th ed. (East Lansing, MI: Educational Institute of the American Hotel & Lodging Association, 2007).

6

Purchasing Follow-Up: Receiving, Storage, Payment, and Evaluation

Purchasing Pros Need to Know!

It does little good to use the purchasing principles discussed in earlier chapters unless effective management continues as products are received and stored. Additionally, payment procedures desire special attention as does the evaluation of purchasing with the goal of continuous improvement. Each of these activities is addressed in this chapter.

Purchasers must receive the quality and quantity of products that were ordered, and this requires that properly trained staff members confirm that the quality of incoming products meets purchase specification requirements. A properly designed receiving area with necessary tools and equipment also affects how well receiving activities will be implemented. Policies and procedures addressing how receiving should be done must be consistently used to best ensure that purchasers receive what they have ordered and will pay for. Two additional concerns, the use of technology and security precautions, are also important and will complete our discussion of product receiving practices.

Trained personnel, appropriate spaces, and the right tools and equipment are important product storage concerns too. Also, the appropriate policies and procedures are necessary to ensure that quality, cost, and record-keeping requirements are addressed, and to minimize quality losses and excessive costs during storage. Technology is increasingly used to generate and analyze storage-related information and to manage security concerns, and these topics will be discussed in detail.

Paying suppliers involves more than just writing a check. Communication, including documentation among accounting, purchasing, and receiving personnel, is needed to process, verify, and approve supplier payments. Important payment policies and procedures will also be reviewed.

Most hospitality organizations pay for purchases with traditional checks. Security concerns important in reducing opportunities as they are used will be noted as will the use of petty-cash systems for low-cost purchases.

The significant commitment of time, financial, and other resources required mandate that purchasing activities be evaluated. However, this process is challenging because there may not be a direct relationship between a property's financial success and an effective purchasing operation. For example, a restaurant might meet its financial goals but still be able to reduce costs without compromising quality standards if purchasing improvements were made. Alternatively, purchasing activities might be performed very well, but the operation may not meet financial goals due to factors unrelated to purchasing. Unfortunately, purchasing evaluation is often overlooked because it cannot be accomplished unless goals indicating specific purchasing-related expectations are established. Then success can be evaluated by determining the extent to which the goals were attained. Some financial, operational, and other factors to be considered as purchasing goals are developed will be explored in this chapter.

■ ■ ■

Outline

OVERVIEW OF RECEIVING AND STORAGE

Figure 6.1 (shown earlier as Figure 1.2) reviews basic purchasing steps and sets the context for this chapter's discussion about receiving, storage, payment, and evaluation. Products ordered (in Step 7) must be properly received and stored (in Step 8), and they must be paid for (in Step 9). Evaluation (Step 10) to improve the purchasing system completes the purchasing process.

Let's begin our study of product **receiving** and **storage** with definitions.

Buyer's Guide to Purchasing Terms

Receiving   The transfer of ownership from a supplier to a hospitality operation when products are delivered.

Storage   Holding products under optimal storage conditions until they are needed for production or use.

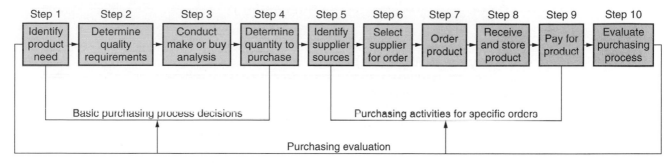

FIGURE 6.1   Steps in Effective Purchasing

FIGURE 6.2   Range in Control of Receiving and Storage Practices

Who is responsible for receiving and storage tasks? Property size is important, and Figure 6.2 indicates that responsibilities typically become more defined as property size increases.

Let's look at Figure 6.2. In a small operation (Box A), the manager or the person responsible for food production or beverage service may receive and move incoming products to storage areas. Then everyone may be responsible for storage and issuing (sometimes meaning that, perhaps, no one is directly responsible). Products are simply placed in storage areas and are removed when needed. Beverage storage areas, however, may be locked because of security (theft) concerns.

Mid-sized properties (Box B in Figure 6.2) include many franchised restaurant units and hotels. These operations tend to have designated persons who, while not occupying full-time purchasing positions, have received specific training for receiving and storage and who can address quantity, quality, security, and record-keeping concerns.

Large properties (Box C in Figure 6.2) typically employ full-time purchasing staff whose primary responsibilities relate to receiving and storage. In the largest properties, especially hotels, these duties are split, and one or more persons with specialized receiving duties and others with storage tasks are employed.

Procedures for receiving and storing fresh fruits and vegetables must ensure that products available for production are just as fresh as they were when harvested.

Veiga, Luis/Getty Images Inc. -Image Bank

Buyers at Work (6.1)

"I've been working here five years, and now I can't be trusted!" exclaimed Craig as he spoke with Lacko. Both had attended a meeting called by the new owner of the Avery Bay Restaurant. The new owner used most of the meeting to talk about his plans.

"I feel like you," said Lacko. "Our new boss has some good ideas. However, his cost-management concerns are radical. The present owner had this place for many years, and it was successful. What's wrong with doing what we've done? Does the new guy really think he will make more money by weighing every single item that comes in here, by locking the storeroom doors when we are here, and by challenging us to find a way to steal?"

"You know, Lacko," said Craig, "I don't want to steal, and our futures are tied to the success of this place. I wish he recognized that we're honest, treat us like we are, and keep things the way they've been until he has a reason to change."

Assume you are the new restaurant owner:

1. Should you recognize that there will be resistance to change when you implement new procedures? Why or why not? If so, what can you do to address the employees' concerns?
2. Is it good idea to learn how existing systems work before making any significant changes? Defend your response.
3. What are potential advantages and disadvantages to implementing strict receiving and storage procedures in a small restaurant when you don't know about problems, if any, that create a need for them?

RECEIVING ESSENTIALS

Effective receiving requires attention to personnel, the receiving area, and the tools and equipment needed for receiving activities.

Personnel

Qualified and trained personnel are needed to perform receiving tasks. The (unfortunately all-too-common) practice that "whoever is closest to the back door when the delivery person arrives should sign the delivery invoice and put the items in storage" is not defensible.

Many receiving procedures are clerical or physical in nature; however, the ability to recognize the quality of incoming items and to confirm that they meet the property's standards requires training and experience. This is especially important for products such as fresh produce, meats, and seafood that are not typically purchased by a brand name. In these cases observation and inspection are essential to ensure that purchase specification requirements are met. One would hope the persons being trained for receiving positions can work shoulder to shoulder with experienced buyers or food production personnel to learn about products meeting quality requirements.

Successful receiving personnel use the following guidelines:

- *Maintain sanitation standards.* Food safety/sanitation concerns are incorporated in the property's purchase specifications, and these are important aspects of quality. Sanitation concerns also apply to the receiving area, to the tools and equipment used, and to the procedures implemented to handle products being received.
- *Have knowledge of appropriate technology.* Technology can expedite receiving and storage procedures and provide accurate information if used properly.
- *Have the necessary physical strength.* Incoming cases of products can weigh thirty pounds or more. Flour and sugar are routinely packaged in

fifty- or even hundred-pound bags, and packages of these sizes are often purchased because of lower purchase unit prices. (*Note:* The Americans with Disabilities Act prohibits discrimination against persons with disabilities. The ability to lift heavy or bulky containers may (or may not) be a **bona fide occupational qualification (BFOQ).** Hospitality managers must know about and consider ways to modify receiving tasks to accommodate otherwise qualified persons.)

- *Be able to resolve problems.*   What should be done if incoming products do not meet quality requirements? What if incorrect quantities are delivered? These and other challenges make a receiving clerk's job responsibilities anything but routine.
- *Maintain a concerned attitude.*   The best staff members want to assist their organization. Concerned receiving personnel are committed to helping the hospitality organization move toward attaining its mission, and they recognize their role in helping to serve the customers.

Space, Tools, and Equipment

Ideally the receiving area was considered when product flow concerns were initially planned. Receiving areas are often close to the kitchen's back door but, in large organizations such as hotels and many restaurants, they are often part of or adjacent to the loading dock. Small properties may use little more than a relatively large space close to a back door. Adequate space to assemble all incoming products is necessary for counting and/or weighing products, and a receiving scale is needed. Space for transport equipment is likely required, and this can be significant if **pallet** loads of products are received.

Receiving areas may require space for a desk, file cabinet, or other equipment, and often computer access is required because of the increasing use of technology during receiving. Useful tools include pocket thermometers (to determine temperatures of perishable products) and plastic tote boxes or other containers to transport ice for products such as fresh poultry and to store cleaning tools and equipment used in the area. Increasingly, personal digital assistants (PDAs), notebook or laptop computers, and/or other wireless devices are used to access purchasing and inventory records required while receiving.

RECEIVING PROCEDURES

Figure 6.3 reviews the steps required for effective receiving.[1]

As you review Figure 6.3, note that the delivery invoice should be compared to the copy of the purchase order to ensure that the quantity and price of products agreed on when purchased are correct when delivered. Some items, such as cases of canned goods, can be counted, but other items, such as fresh meats, ordered by the pound must be weighed.

Figure 6.4 shows a delivery invoice.

When reviewing Figure 6.4, note that it summarizes a delivery made by XYZ Provisions to the Oakville Family Diner on 7/16/xx. The invoice number

---

Buyer's Guide to Purchasing Terms

Bona fide occupational qualification (BFOQ)   Qualifications legally judged reasonably necessary to safely or adequately perform all job tasks in a position.

Pallet   A platform (rack) typically constructed of wooden slats and used to store and/or move cases of products stacked on it.

FIGURE 6.3 Steps for Effective Receiving

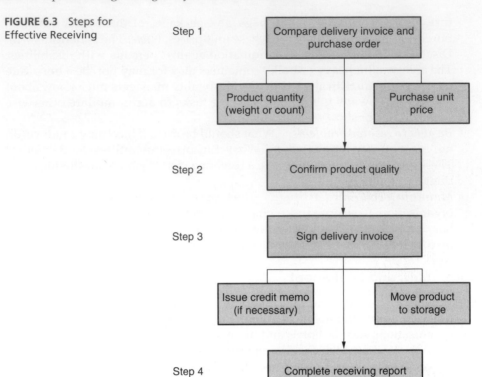

Step 1 — Compare delivery invoice and purchase order
- Product quantity (weight or count)
- Purchase unit price

Step 2 — Confirm product quality

Step 3 — Sign delivery invoice
- Issue credit memo (if necessary)
- Move product to storage

Step 4 — Complete receiving report

FIGURE 6.4 Sample Delivery Invoice

Delivery Invoice	Invoice No. 100001	Invoice Date: 7/15/xx

Sold by:	Sold to:	Ship to:
XYZ Provisions	Oakville Family Diner	Oakville Family Diner
236 Spruce Street	132 N. 10th Street	132 N. 10th Street
Campusville, NY 00000	Anyville, NJ 00001	Anyville, NJ 00001
Telephone: 111-111-1111	Account No. 7891011	
Fax: 111-111-1112		

Buyer's Purchase Order No. 6800105	Delivery No. X314YZ	Delivery Date: 7/16/xx

Item	Product No.	Quantity	Purchase Unit	Price/Unit	Total Price
Ground beef	170	4	#10 poly bag	34.70	138.80
Pork links	321	2	Case (#20)	49.80	99.60

Terms Net due in 14 days	Total Amount Due	$785.41

Received by: _____   Date: _____

Distribution: Retain original copy; second copy to buyer.

and date along with other information, including the restaurant's account and purchase order numbers and XYZ Provisions' delivery number and delivery date are included.

The delivery invoice lists each item that was ordered and delivered. Note the provision for the receiving clerk's signature ("Received by") and a second copy to be sent with the payment for the delivery.

Figure 6.3 indicates that the second step in the receiving process involves confirming that the quality of the incoming products meets the property's purchase specifications. This step is important and probably the most challenging. Standards incorporated into purchase specifications must be easily observable so incoming products can be compared with the specifications. If receiving personnel have concerns about product quality, the restaurant manager and/or chef should be asked for assistance.

If no variation from product standards or other quality-related problems are observed, the delivery invoice can be signed (Step 3 in Figure 6.3). However, if there are product shortages or other problems, a **credit memo** should be signed by both the foodservice employee and the supplier's delivery person to confirm that adjustments to the delivery invoice will be necessary.

After the delivery invoice has been signed, Step 3 in Figure 6.3 indicates that receiving personnel must quickly move products to their storage areas. Reasons include the following:

- To help prevent quality deterioration of refrigerated or frozen products
- To reduce the possibility of product theft

Figure 6.3 suggests a final step in product receiving: complete a **receiving report**. This is used in foodservice operations that calculate food costs on a daily basis because it helps separate information on delivery invoices into the components required for daily food costing.[2]

Did You Know? (6.1)

In small owner-operated restaurants, the owner/manager will likely perform some or all receiving tasks. In larger operations the manager may delegate this task to the chef or kitchen manager, and in still larger properties, a receiving and/or storeroom clerk may be employed. Regardless of organizational structure, the manager has some receiving responsibilities that cannot be delegated:

- Develop and implement policies requiring the consistent use of effective receiving procedures
- Ensure that persons responsible for receiving are properly trained and can identify the quality standards addressed in purchase specifications
- Provide the proper receiving equipment and ensure that it works (e.g., a receiving scale must be available and routinely adjusted to ensure accuracy)
- Inform suppliers about the need for delivery persons to spend the time necessary for receiving procedures to be implemented.

Buyer's Guide to Purchasing Terms

Credit memo   An accounting document used to revise (correct) information about product quantities and/or costs initially recorded on a delivery invoice.

Receiving report   A document that separates incoming food costs into components required for daily food cost calculations.

FIGURE 6.5 Receiving Report

Date:_____

Supplier	Invoice	Product	Purchase Unit	No. of Units	Unit Price	Cost	Directs (Food)	Stores (Food)	Beverages
A	10735	Eggs	Case[a]	2	$34.50	$69.00	$69.00		
B	221	Sirloin Steaks	Pound	55	$14.70	$808.50		$808.50	
							410.50	1,254.00	

[a]There are 30 dozen eggs in a commercially packed case of eggs.

Figure 6.5 shows a sample receiving report.

SPECIAL RECEIVING CONCERNS

Receiving procedures are affected by numerous concerns, including those relating to quality, technology, and security.

Ensuring Quality

It does little good to develop purchase specifications unless they are used during receiving to confirm that incoming products meet quality standards. Experienced purchasing professionals know they will likely pay for the quality of products identified in the specification even if this quality is not received.

An exhaustive list of ways to identify quality is difficult (impossible?) to develop and depends on the items being purchased. For example, Chapters 7 and 8 in this text, relating to, respectively, entrées (meat, poultry, seafood) and produce, dairy, and egg products, note special quality requirements for these items. The chapters also list numerous Web site sources for additional information that can help buyers develop applicable purchase specifications.

Recall that a property's purchase specifications may include a description of procedures to be used during receiving to help ensure that quality requirements are met.

Effective receiving personnel can determine whether incoming products meet quality requirements. Sometimes this involves noticing that **slack-out seafood** is

Buyer's Guide to Purchasing Term

Slack-out seafood   Seafood that has been frozen then thawed and presented as a fresh item that can be sold at a higher price than if it were purchased frozen.

PROFESSIONAL PURCHASING PREVENTS PROBLEMS (6.1)

Problems Are Not Detected at Time of Delivery

A common problem: Delivery problems are discovered after delivery invoices are signed.

Receiving personnel should check incoming products before they sign the delivery invoice. However, shouldn't suppliers wanting to improve their relationship with purchasers also make concessions if problems are noted after the document is signed? Can't suppliers just absorb the cost or pass them back to their sources in the distribution channel?

Suppliers know that human error can result in products being accepted that should have been refused. Reputable suppliers are not likely to create difficulties about the details of the contract that typically apply when the buyer assumes ownership.

However, this problem can become significant when expensive capital equipment is received. Assume a dishwashing machine valued at thousands of dollars is delivered by a freight company that transported it directly from the manufacturer. An employee signs for the equipment without knowing how to properly receive the item or even realizing the need to alert a manager about the delivery. The equipment supplier is later notified that the equipment is damaged, and a replacement request is made. The supplier does not know who is responsible: Was the equipment shipped in damaged condition? Did the problem occur during cross-country transport and/or after it arrived at the property? Neither the manufacturer nor the freight company will likely assume responsibility because the delivery invoice is signed, and the supplier will not be reimbursed by anyone for a several-thousand-dollar refund or repurchase. What would a reasonable businessperson expect the supplier to do?

Purchasers must ensure that effective receiving practices are consistently used. They might ask suppliers about recommended general receiving practices and detailed factors to address as specific products are received. The best suppliers want to provide products meeting specifications at reasonable prices. It is to their (the suppliers') benefit to educate hospitality buyers about how reputable suppliers can offer lower prices and provide proper product quality. Buyers can use this information to detect problems caused by other suppliers without these good intentions.

---

being represented as a fresh product. At other times they can determine that the lengthy and sometimes confusing names of imported wines do not match those on the purchase order. They check expiration dates on applicable containers and understand that produce products in the center of a shipping container may not be of the same quality as those on the visible top levels.

Implementing Technology

How can technology assist receiving personnel? First, paperwork can be eliminated and resulting communication problems can be reduced. Traditional hard-copy purchase orders identifying purchase commitments can be electronically routed to receiving personnel. Wireless technology allows receiving personnel to check incoming products without the need to print a copy of the purchase order. Those purchasing in large volumes can specify **bar code** labels on incoming containers so quantity and cost information can be scanned and automatically entered into the property's inventory management system. Properties of all sizes with bar-code readers and accompanying software programs can use bar-code technology to assist with purchasing and inventory management.

Buyer's Guide to Purchasing Term

Bar code   Numerous machine-readable rectangular bars and spaces arranged in a specific way to represent the letters, numbers, and other symbols used to identify a product.

Bar-code technology can be used to determine quickly and accurately the quantity and cost of products in storage areas.

Spike Mafford/Getty Images, Inc. -Photodisc.

Radio frequency identification (RFID) technology uses wireless transponders affixed to the products in inventory. These systems enable wireless tracking of inventory in real time throughout the property.

Technology enables electronic versions of purchase specifications, delivery schedules, and communication between user department, purchasing, accounting, and receiving personnel to be more conveniently routed. Also, information from daily invoices can be electronically summarized on daily receiving reports that generate information used for daily food costing calculations or other purposes.

Security

Security concerns at the time of receiving relate to any reasons the property may pay for products it does not receive. Problems can include the following:

- *Short weights.* A carton containing, for example, forty-five pounds of fresh steaks should be weighed. Ideally, steaks are removed from cardboard cartons for weighing. Container weight becomes more significant when fresh seafood or fresh poultry is packed in heavy, waxed cardboard containers containing the product packed in shaved ice. In these cases product removal is necessary.
- *Assorted contents.* A carton containing thirty pounds of ground beef and twenty pounds of preportioned steaks will weigh the same (fifty pounds) as a carton containing twenty pounds of ground beef and thirty pounds of fresh-cut steaks. However, the value of the first container is much less than that of the second container, so different items must be weighed separately.
- *Missing items.* A suggestion from the delivery person to, "Just sign the delivery invoice; I'll deliver additional products without putting it on the invoice next time," cannot be followed. First, the same receiving person may not be on duty or forget the missing item at the next delivery. Second, a delivery person is unlikely to have the authority to request products not listed on delivery invoices be placed on the truck.

Buyer's Guide to Purchasing Term

Radio frequency identification (RFID) An electronic wireless tracking system that uses a transmitter to provide noncontact and automatic location of stock throughout the hospitality property.

Did You Know? (6.2)

Special receiving procedures may be useful for multi-unit organizations:

- A copy of the delivery invoice may be routed to the centralized purchasing office where it can be matched with the delivery invoice that accompanied the order to the property.
- A **blind receiving** method might be used. Purchase orders indicating the products but not the quantities being received may be sent to receiving personnel by those in the centralized purchasing department. Then staff in each property record the quantities of incoming products by count or weight. This information is routed to the central purchasing office to be matched with the delivery invoice containing purchase quantities sent by the supplier to the central purchasing office. Since they know this information will be verified, receiving personnel are more likely to carefully count and record the number of purchase units of products delivered, and delivery shortages are more likely to be identified and reported.

Delivery personnel should not have access to nonpublic areas of the hospitality operation. Consider the possibility of theft when they are in storage areas (especially where liquor is stored) or, even worse, if they gain access to back-of-house corridors and employee-only elevators in hotels. Then access to other storage areas and even guest rooms may be possible, and employees or guests can be harmed by persons who are **trespassing.**

Buyer's Guide to Internet Resources: Receiving

Web Site	Topic
www.barcoding.com	Barcoding, Inc.
www.intellitrack.net	IntelliTrack
www.ebarcode.com	eBarcode (Catalog of bar-coding hardware)
us.mt.com	Storeroom receiving scales (Enter "receiving scales" into the site's search box)

STORAGE ESSENTIALS

Product storage concerns involve personnel, storage areas, and tools and equipment involved in the activity.

Personnel

In small properties storeroom personnel are likely those who receive products. Large organizations may use persons with specialized storeroom responsibilities

Buyer's Guide to Purchasing Terms

Blind receiving A receiving method in which receiving personnel are aware of the products but not the quantities to be delivered. Receiving personnel forward product count and/or weight information to a centralized purchasing office where delivery information is matched with the supplier's invoice.

Trespass Unlawful (without the owner's permission) entry of a person onto the property of another person.

who must be able to maintain sanitation standards and use appropriate technology. They must be able to perform required physical tasks and resolve storage-related challenges, including those related to inventory control discussed later in this section. Their interest in performing as a committed member of the hospitality team is also very important.

Storage Areas

The ideal location of storage space is close to the receiving area and between the receiving and food/beverage production areas. However, this **work flow** emphasis has at least one potential disadvantage: it may be easier for employees to steal items from unlocked storage areas when they leave the property through the back door. Also, storage areas are frequently affected by restaurant remodeling, which can occur several times during the building's life. Sometimes frozen storage is relocated to an outside location to convert interior space for other uses. Storage space may also be moved to distant areas, including building levels different from those used for food preparation/service. Storage space is an important part of work-flow patterns, and ideally it should not be assigned to any leftover space that is available.

Small foodservice operations may have one dry storage area consisting of a few shelves to a small room and one or more small (several door) refrigerators and freezers. Large-volume operations may have separate dry storage areas for foods and alcoholic beverages and several (or more) **walk-in** freezers and refrigerators. Large hotels and other high-volume operations may have several dry, refrigerated, and frozen storage areas in different locations The need for storage space in any property relates to production volumes and the frequency of product deliveries.

Tools and Equipment

Shelving is a major item of storage equipment.[3] It is typically removable and adjustable in small refrigerators and freezers, but mobile units are often used in walk-ins and dry storage areas. Metal shelving is easy to clean and contributes to proper air circulation. Local sanitation codes often require that shelving units keep stored food or beverage products at least six inches off the floor and several inches away from the walls to allow for air circulation and to reduce the possibility of rodent infestation.

Pallet storage is often used in large operations to allow products to be stored in shipping containers. This practice avoids the "double-handling" that would occur if products were removed from their cases, placed on shelving units, and later placed on mobile transport carts when issued. Transport equipment including carts, dollies, and rolling bins (for flour and sugar in properties with on-site baking operations) may be needed. Also, computer hardware, even in a wireless environment may be available in storage areas.

While necessary receiving tools and equipment vary by type and size of operation, some items are standard in any receiving operation, including the following:

- *Scales.* These should be of two types: those accurate to the fraction of a pound (for large items) and those accurate to the fraction of an ounce (for

---

Buyer's Guide to Purchasing Terms

Work flow   The movement of people, products, and supplies; the placement of equipment; and the design of work areas in ways to encourage productivity.

Walk-in   A term relating to large refrigeration and freezer spaces ("rooms") that typically require physical entry for product access.

smaller items and preportioned meats). Scales should be calibrated regularly to ensure accuracy.

- *Wheeled equipment.*   Hand trucks, carts, and/or dollies, should be available to move incoming products quickly and efficiently to their proper storage areas.
- *Box cutters.*   These must be properly maintained and used to allow receiving personnel to quickly remove excess packaging and accurately verify the quality of delivered products. Care must be taken when using this tool, so proper training is essential.
- *Thermometers.*   Foods must be delivered at their proper storage temperatures. For many operators, these temperatures are as follows:

Item	Acceptable Temperature Range	
	°F	°C
Frozen foods	10°F or less	−12°C or less
Refrigerated foods	30°F–45°F	1°C–7°C

- *Calculator/adding machine.*   Vendor calculations should always be checked, especially if the invoice has been prepared by hand. This may be done by receiving staff in some operations and by accounting personnel in others. A printing calculator is best and will be used when the original delivery invoice is changed because of incorrect vendor pricing or because items listed on the invoice were not delivered. In addition, invoice totals will change when all or a portion of the delivery was rejected because items were of substandard quality.

Records Area

This area should ideally include a desk, telephone, computer, fax/copy machine, file cabinet, and ample office supplies such as pens, pencils, and a stapler. While larger operations are more likely to have such an area, small-volume operations still have a need for basic equipment. In all cases the records area should include copies of all purchase specifications to avoid confusion about whether a delivered food or supply item meets quality requirements.

STORAGE PROCEDURES

Ensuring Quality

There are three basic types of storage in foodservice operations:

1. *Dry storage (50°F–70°F; 10°C–21.1°C).*   This is for grocery items such as canned goods, cereal products such as flour, and alcoholic beverage products.
2. *Refrigerated storage (less than 41°F; 5°C).*   This is for items including fresh meat, produce, and dairy products.
3. *Frozen storage (less than 0°F; −17.8°C).*   This is for items such as frozen meats, seafood, and French fries.

(*Note:* Some foodservice operations provide for relatively extensive storage in workstations, including food preparation and serving areas.)

Quality problems can arise even under the best environmental conditions if appropriate storage times are exceeded. Product quality is also affected when the environment is not properly maintained. Raw food products should be stored beneath cooked/ready-to-eat foods. Items should not be stored under water/sewer lines located overhead that can be a source of contamination. Foods should never be stored near sanitizing, cleaning, or other chemicals. (*Note:* Chapter 11 provides more details about cleaning, sanitizing, and other chemicals.)

Here are Storage Guidelines for Selected Food Items		
	STORAGE PERIOD	
PRODUCT	**In Refrigerator** **40°F (4°C)**	**In Freezer** **0°F (−18°C)**
Fresh meat		
Beef		
Ground	1–2 days	3–4 months
Steaks and roasts	3–5 days	6–12 months
Pork		
Chops	3–5 days	4–6 months
Ground	1–2 days	3–4 months
Roasts	3–5 days	4–6 months
Cured meats		
Lunch meat	3–5 days	1–2 months
Sausage	1–2 days	1–2 months
Gravy	1–2 days	2–3 months
Fish		
Lean (e.g., cod, flounder, haddock)	1–2 days	up to 6 months
Fatty (e.g., blue, perch, salmon)	1–2 days	2–3 months
Chicken		
Whole	1–2 days	12 months
Parts	1–2 days	9 months
Giblets	1–2 days	3–4 months
Dairy products		
Swiss, brick, processed cheese	3–4 weeks	*
Milk	5 days	1 month
Ice cream, ice milk	—	2–4 months
Eggs		
Fresh in shell	3 weeks	—
Hard-boiled	1 week	—

*Cheese can be frozen, but freezing will affect the texture and taste.

FIGURE 6.6   How Long Will It Keep?

(Sources: Food Marketing Institute for fish and dairy products; USDA for all other foods.)

Figure 6.6 reviews recommended storage times for some commonly purchased products.

Record Keeping

Managers must know about the quantity and cost of products in storage. Inventory level affects product costs because it is used to calculate **cost of goods sold** (often called "food cost" or "beverage cost"), which is an important component of the **income statement** for a food and beverage operation.

Buyer's Guide to Purchasing Terms

Cost of goods sold   The cost of the food or beverage incurred during a specific period to generate food or beverage revenue during that same period; simplified to "food cost" or "beverage cost"; sometimes referred to as "COGS."

Income statement   A summary of a business's profitability that details revenues generated, expenses incurred, and profits or losses realized during a specific accounting period (such as a month); also known as the "statement of income and expense" or "profit and loss (P&L) statement."

Item	Purchase Unit	No. of Units[a]	Purchase Price	Total Price
Green Beans	Case	3	$26.50	$79.50
Rice	#50 bag	2	$12.10	$24.20

[a]Ideally items are stored in their purchase containers to reduce double-handling and to make it easier to mark information about receipt date and costs. It is also, for example, easier to count one case of six #10 cans of a product than it is to count six individual cans of the product when they have been removed from the case.

FIGURE 6.7   Physical Inventory Form

Assume that Shandra takes an inventory of food products in her restaurant's storage areas on September 30 (the last day of the month) and determines its value to be $7,475.[4] (*Note:* This amount will also reflect the inventory value on October 1, the next day.) An inventory taken on October 31 (the last day of that month) shows the value of food on hand to be $8,740.

Shandra's restaurant paid $20,555 for food and generated food *revenues* of $58,500 during October. Her cost of goods sold (food) for October is:

$7,475	(+)	$20,555	(−)	$8,740	(=)	$19,290
Value of	(+)	Purchases	(−)	Value	(=)	Cost of
Beginning		During		of Ending		Goods Sold
Inventory		October		Inventory		(Food)
(Oct 1)				(Oct 31)		in October

The cost of goods sold (food) is often expressed as a percentage of food revenue. Using Shandra's data above:

$19,290	(÷)	$58,500	(=)	33.0% (rounded)
Cost of Goods	(÷)	Food Revenue	(=)	Monthly Food
Sold (Food)				Cost %
				(October)

The above calculations show that Shandra's restaurant incurred an actual food cost of $19,290, which is 33.0 percent of food revenue. She can compare this information to her expected food cost (e.g., from her October operating budget and/or from food cost and revenue data generated by her point-of-sale system).

Many foodservice operators make manual calculations using forms similar to that illustrated in Figure 6.7 to conduct a **physical inventory.**

When reviewing Figure 6.7, note there are three cases of green beans with a purchase price of $26.50, yielding a total cost (inventory cost) of $79.50 (3 cases × $26.50 = $79.50). One would hope the count of this and all other items in storage is undertaken by two persons. This reduces the opportunity for one dishonest person working alone to modify inventory data to avoid the detection of theft. One could be a manager who counts inventory units, and the second should be an employee not involved with storage responsibilities who can complete the form.

Buyer's Guide to Purchasing Term

Inventory (physical)   A process used to determine the quantity and cost of inventory on hand at a specific point in time (typically the end of the month). Information is used to develop financial sheet statements and for product control purposes.

Alcoholic beverages, including these bottles of wine, are valuable and prone to employee theft. They must be carefully controlled while in storage.

Getty Images-Stockbyte.

Did You Know? (6.3)

A perpetual inventory system works just like a personal checkbook. When money (food and beverage products) is deposited in the bank (brought into the storeroom), the balance in the checking account (food/beverage products in the storeroom) is increased. When money is withdrawn from the bank (food/beverage products are issued to production areas), the balance of money (food and beverage products) in the bank (storeroom) decreases. Therefore, just as individuals can always know the amount of money in their checkbooks, a manager or purchaser will be aware of the quantity of products in inventory when a perpetual inventory system is used.

Inventory counts are also needed to determine actual beverage costs. However, the cost of this inventory often includes the value of products in central and behind-bar storage areas, so a more extensive inventory assessment process is necessary.

A second record-keeping issue concerns maintaining **perpetual inventory** information for selected products to allow managers and purchasers to track the quantity of products in inventory.

While it is often not practical or even useful for many operations to maintain all products under perpetual inventory, it can be helpful for the relatively few and expensive "A" items (see Chapter 3). Because alcoholic beverages are expensive and prone to theft, they are prime candidates for control under a perpetual inventory system.

Figure 6.8 shows a perpetual inventory form.

Note that there were 37 individual (six-ounce) portions of steak available on 9/7, and 25 steaks were issued. None were returned to the storage area, so there was a balance of only 12 steaks (37 steaks − 25 steaks) in inventory. On 9/8 35 steaks were received and brought into the storage area, and 20 steaks were issued. This left a net balance of 15 steaks, which increased the inventory balance to 27 portions. The calculation is as follows:

For 9/8:
12 steaks (beginning balance) + 35 (in) − 20 (out) = 27 steaks (ending balance)

On a random basis, the general manager, chef, and/or purchasing agent should spot-check the number of strip steaks to ensure that the number of portions actually available in inventory equals the perpetual inventory balance.

Buyer's Guide to Purchasing Term

Perpetual inventory   A system to track products entering and issued from storage areas so managers know the quantity of products that should be in inventory.

Item: Sirloin Steaks (6 oz.)   **FIGURE 6.8** Perpetual Inventory Form

| Date | No. of Purchase Units | | Balance |
	In	Out	
Start			37
9/7/xx	—	25	12
9/8/xx	35	20	27

Security Concerns

If food and beverage products are purchased then stolen, operating expenses will be increased, but there will be no revenue. Then costs will be greater than necessary, and profitability will be lower than expected.

Storage areas can be thought of as bank vaults, and storage procedures can be driven by the question, "How should money be managed in a bank vault?" Keeping products in lockable areas with walls extending to the ceiling and limiting access to storage areas to authorized persons can help reduce employee theft. Differences between quantities of "A" items noted in perpetual inventory records and the quantities actually available in storage should be investigated. Some properties use employee package inspection programs to reduce the possibility of unauthorized carryouts.

There are alternatives to full-time storeroom personnel to limit access to storage areas. Keeping storage areas locked with scheduled times when a manager issues items is one possibility. It is also possible to keep "A" items locked and under perpetual inventory while allowing general access to those storage areas used for items that are less expensive and less prone to theft.

TECHNOLOGY AND STORAGE

Computerized applications have also changed how inventory can be controlled. Bar coding and RFID are examples. When items are received and entered in inventory, quantity and cost balances automatically increase. When products are issued, inventory quantities and values are automatically decreased. The resulting usage rates help to control food and beverage costs, plan purchase quantities, and allow perpetual inventory balance information to be maintained with almost no effort.

Physical inventories undertaken to verify the accuracy of perpetual inventory balances can be automated with optical scanning. Manual counts can be taken with entries into a PDA that is wirelessly connected to the computer system, or data can be electronically transferred after the unit is connected to the computer. Records of items nearing expiration dates, information about items discarded because of spoilage, and listings of items that have attained order points provide additional examples of how technology can affect storeroom management.

Computerized locking systems similar to those used for hotel guest room doors are also helping managers control and monitor storage area access. They indicate whose key was used to enter the storage area (the person to whom the key card was issued), and the date, time of entry, and length of stay in the storage area.

Surveillance equipment is now relatively inexpensive and is increasingly used to note entry into storage areas in real time or on a recorded motion-activated basis.

Buyer's Guide to Purchasing Term

Surveillance equipment   Video cameras and other devices that allow managers to monitor access to areas where security is of concern.

Buyer's Guide to Internet Resources: Storage

Web Site	Topic
www.traulsen.com	Commercial refrigeration equipment
www.metro.com	Commercial shelving
www.ag.ndsu.edu/pubs/yf/foods/fn5791.htm	Storage and handling suggestions for frozen, dry, and refrigerated foods
www.food-management.com/article/12418	Prevention of storeroom theft
www.culinarysoftware.com	Computerized inventory management system
www.barvision.com	Beverage inventory management system
www.hiendsecurity.com	Numerous types of security concerns

PURCHASING AND THE ACCOUNTING PROCESS

Accounting requires special attention because all products ordered must be paid for. In small hospitality organizations, the owner may be the manager, purchaser, and bill payer. In larger organizations purchasing and accounting tasks may be split into two support departments: purchasing and accounting. **Separation of duties** helps to reduce the chance for theft and/or fraud, which can occur when one manager (or department) is responsible for combined functions.

The responsibilities of accountants in hospitality organizations extend far beyond their role in purchasing. However, because a large percentage of a hotel, restaurant, or noncommercial foodservice operation's revenues is used to purchase required products, accounting personnel must give this responsibility a high priority.

The task of paying the bills when products are purchased involves more than assembling some paperwork and writing a check. The saying "Every penny counts" has never been more true than it is today. It is critical that all suppliers be paid what and when they are owed. However, it is equally important to ensure that they are not paid more than they are owed or paid for the same item more than once.

Documentation Is Critical

Accounting personnel prepare bills for payment, and to do so requires communication, information, and coordination among purchasing, receiving, and accounting personnel. The basic process is the same regardless of whether a manual and/or computerized system that eliminates paperwork is used.

Let's consider documentation that is forwarded to accounting personnel in preparation for payment in varying sizes of hospitality operations:

- *Small restaurant or hotel; owner/manager present.* Products are ordered and may be received by the manager. A copy of the purchase order (or perhaps just a copy of the applicable delivery invoice) is used by the

---

Buyer's Guide to Purchasing Terms

Accounting   The process of summarizing and reporting financial information used by the hospitality organization.

Duties, separation of   The management control principle that emphasizes that no single person should control all steps in a process.

Documentation for accounting begins with information from the point-of-sale (POS) system because production requirements based on sales reduce inventories and create the need for purchase requisitions.

David Young-Wolff/PhotoEdit Inc.

owner/manager for payment purposes. (*Note:* The owner may pay the bill or transfer documentation to an off-site bookkeeper for payment.)

- *Small restaurant or hotel; absentee owner.* In this situation, the manager of the property is employed by the owner. Procedures for purchasing and receiving may be undertaken by the manager and/or staff with documentation routed to the bookkeeper for payment. However, the supplier may send a separate copy of each delivery invoice directly to the absentee owner or bookkeeper so both copies of the delivery invoice can be matched.
- *Large hospitality operation; separate purchasing and accounting departments.* A copy of the purchase order is sent from purchasing to receiving personnel who check incoming orders against it. The purchase order and signed delivery invoice are then routed to the purchasing department to be matched before being sent to the accounting department as payment authorization. (*Note:* Sometimes receiving personnel send purchase orders and delivery invoices to the chef or foodservice director, who then routes them to purchasing personnel. The reason for doing this is to review the documentation. "Do we normally purchase all of these items and in these quantities?" "Do prices seem reasonable and in line with other recent purchases?")

Communication Between Accounting Personnel and Suppliers

Accounting personnel have reduced need to interact with suppliers about pricing and related concerns when they have proper documentation. However, one problem that arises as bills are prepared for payment relates to credit memos that identify problems noticed during delivery, such as the following:

- *Incorrect price charged.* Example: The purchase order price for ground beef is $3.17 per pound, but the delivery invoice states $3.27 per pound.
- *Back order.* Example: The product is not available and cannot be delivered but was included on the original delivery invoice.
- *Short weight or count.* Example: Ten cases of lettuce were ordered and are included on the delivery invoice, but only five cases were received.
- *Items rejected because of unacceptable quality.* Example: Items do not meet purchase specification requirements and are rejected on attempted delivery.

Credit memos are typically issued by the supplier at the time of delivery. They should be treated like cash because they represent a credit (reduction) of the

---

Did You Know? (6.4)

Purchasers know that their organization's relationship with suppliers is based on the interactions of all personnel, including accounting staff. The need for more-than-occasional credit memos issued by a specific supplier typically suggests that the continued relationship between the two parties should be evaluated.

Differences between agreed-on and delivery prices and quality and quantity concerns should be investigated. If problems are caused by hospitality employees, reasons should be discovered and procedures should be revised to minimize their future occurrence. If problems are caused by suppliers, they should be directed to take necessary corrective actions.

Because purchasers (not accounting personnel) typically make supplier selection decisions, input from accounting staff should be requested and used as input to supplier evaluation and selection decisions.

---

amount otherwise owed to the supplier based on the delivery invoice. Most frequently, they are attached to the applicable delivery invoice for routing to purchasing and on to accounting personnel.

Payment Policies and Procedures

Because delivery invoices indicate the products and quantities of items for which suppliers expect payment, they must be carefully studied to ensure that there are no quantity and/or price differences between items on the purchase order and those listed in the delivery invoice. Accounting personnel must verify that all arithmetic **extensions** are correct, file the invoice with the applicable documentation, and pay it at the appropriate time.

Two basic methods can be used to pay suppliers:

1. *By invoice.* Delivery invoices and supportive information are manually or electronically filed for payment on a specific date, and these bills are paid when due. If an approved invoice must be paid by July 16, it may be pulled

---

Did You Know? (6.5)

The need to confirm arithmetic extensions applies to machine-processed delivery invoices just as it does to manual tallies. Some purchasers, however, believe that machines don't make mistakes, and they don't verify the accuracy of computer-generated information. However, the data used by machines is most often entered by humans, so data-entry errors can occur, and all delivery documentation should be reviewed.

It is also important to confirm there are no hidden charges such as order processing fees, delivery charges, or other costs not agreed to at the time of the order. Also, rounding calculations can be programmed to increase charges from, for example, $189.95 to $190.00. Over time, these excessive charges can become significant, so experienced buyers are careful to detect them.

Buyer's Guide to Purchasing Terms

Extension   Arithmetic calculations such as the item quantity multiplied by the unit price to determine the total item cost.

Invoice (payment method)   A method of paying supplier bills on a by-delivery basis; the amount specified by the delivery invoice is paid at or before the time specified on the invoice.

Statement 107643

Bayside Produce
117 Bayside Street
Anytown, Any State 00000
Telephone: xxx-xxx-xxxx
Fax: 111-111-1111

Account No. ____ 1735210 _____
Delivered to: Garden Inn Restaurant
                  300 Garden Lane
                  Anytown, Any State 00000
                  Attention: Jack David, Director of Purchasing
                  Telephone: 222-222-2222

Invoice No.	Delivery Date	Amount Due	Adjustment	Net Amount Due
10711	2/10/xx	$173.59		$173.59
10928	2/13/xx	$310.80	($21.55) Credit memo #2138	$289.25
12541	2/18/xx	$190.51		$190.51
13401	2/23/xx	$290.18		$290.18
			Total	$943.53

Payment due on receipt. Please send payment to the above address.

Duplicate: Please return top copy with payment and retain second copy.

Thank you.

FIGURE 6.9   Sample Supplier Statement

on July 10 for final review, signature, and mailing on July 11 to allow time for mail delivery.
  2. *By statement.*   Processed documentation, including delivery invoices, is filed by the supplier awaiting receipt of a statement of account. A produce supplier may request payment every two weeks and does so by submitting a statement listing delivery invoices applicable to the two-week period for which payment is requested. Then all invoices covered by the statement, less adjustments if any, are paid at the same time.

Figure 6.9 shows a sample supplier statement.
When invoices are to be paid (either individually or along with several others in a statement), a check covering the correct amount of the supplier's bill should be prepared for signing.
Procedures for control of payments by check include the following:

• Check protectors that mechanically imprint the amount of checks should be used.
• The person who signs the checks should mail them.
• More than one signature might be required for all checks or for those written in excess of a specified amount.
• Invoices and vouchers should be identified as paid when checks are written.

Buyer's Guide to Purchasing Term

Statement (payment method)   A method of paying supplier bills for a specific time period; payment is based on the sum of delivery invoices for each delivery during the period.

- Invoices are filed, along with authorizing documents, by the supplier's name.
- Blank checks for emergency or other use are never signed.
- A system to control spoiled, voided, or other unused checks is used.

All checks should be imprinted with the name of the business and should be marked *Void after 60 days*.

- Supplies of blank checks should be kept in a secure place. When check-signing machines are used, signature plates must be securely controlled when not in use.
- All checks written are made payable to a person or company; no checks should be made payable to "cash" or "bearer."
- Unless checks are signed by the owner/manager, others who sign checks should not have access to petty cash funds, and they should not be authorized to approve cash disbursements and record cash receipts.
- **Outstanding** checks that are not returned or cashed promptly are followed up on.
- Bank records should be carefully examined to confirm that all checks issued have been processed. No checks should be missing.
- The name of the payee must be the same on the check, check record, and invoice.

Buyers at Work (6.2)

Patty is the controller for the High Town Hotel. She and Alice, the property's purchasing agent, have worked together for several years, and they also enjoy bowling on the same team.

Patty knew about a current scandal in her community: the business manager of the local public school was recently indicted for theft of public funds that occurred when he submitted invoices for services performed by a fictitious company. After his approval, the invoices were routed to someone else in the business office for payment.

"The school district's business manager was caught by the district's accountant, and he should have known better because the school district separated the duties of the persons responsible for managing expenses and for paying them," Patty said to herself. "However, Alice and I are good friends. I wonder if we could also be teammates in a venture that would help both of us to make a little extra money?"

1. What procedures should be implemented to separate the duties of the purchaser and those of the accounting manager in this (and all other) hotels to reduce opportunities for collusion?
2. What, if any, tactics can the general manager and other officials use to routinely determine whether collusion between the purchaser and accounting personnel may be occurring?
3. Assume that the general manager determines that collusion between Patty and Alice may be occurring. What should he or she do?

Buyer's Guide to Purchasing Term

Outstanding (check)   Checks written by a person or business that have not been cashed or returned.

Petty Cash Purchases

Normally, hospitality organizations minimize the use of cash payments for purchases. Checks allow for better control of expenses, and **audit trails** can be developed and more easily traced. However, some minor expenses, such as office supplies and even emergency food purchases from grocery stores, are best paid from a **petty cash fund** because it is more practical and less expensive to do so.

Petty cash funds must be maintained in secure locations and be administered by responsible managers. A restaurant's petty cash bank might be kept in the property manager's office. A large hotel may have a petty cash fund at the front desk administered by the front office manager, another in the chef's office for food and beverage use, and one or more for use by other departments as well.

Petty cash funds should be established on an **imprest** (cash advance) system:

- The amount of money in the petty cash fund should be based on the normal value of petty cash purchases for a specific time period (e.g., two weeks).
- A check charged to "petty cash" is written and used to establish the petty cash fund.
- When purchases are needed, cash is removed from the cash bank. The change from the purchase transaction and the purchase receipt is returned and, after confirming that the amount (cash change plus receipt) equals the amount removed, both the cash (change) and receipt are placed in the cash bank. A petty cash voucher is attached to the receipt.
- When the petty cash fund must be replenished, a check is written to "petty cash" for the value of paid receipts in the fund. This check, converted to cash, replenishes the fund to its original value.
- At any point in time, the actual value of the petty cash fund should equal the original amount of money allocated to petty cash: cash in the bank plus paid receipts for all purchases.

Buyer's Guide to Internet Resources: Accounting Procedures

Web Site	Topic
www.ganson.com	Check-writing software (Click on "Check Software" when you reach the site)
www.medlin.com/medlin_index.html	Accounts payable software (Click on "Accounts Payable" when you reach the site)
www.microsoft.com	Accounts payable processing procedures for small businesses (Type "Accounts Payable" into the site's search box)
www.checkfree.com	Paying bills at the bank. (Click on "Pay Bills Online" then "Learn About Paying Bills At Your Bank.")
www.ezysoft-dev.com	Automated development of credit memos
www.irislink.com	Scanning, archiving, and encoding supplier invoices for processing and payment (Click on "Invoice Reading" when you reach the site)

Buyer's Guide to Purchasing Terms

Audit trail   A step-by-step record that allows financial data to be traced to its source.

Petty cash fund   A small amount of cash on hand used for relatively low-cost purchases.

Many aspects of purchasing can be evaluated informally in day-to-day conversations among managers, production personnel, and purchasing staff.

Bruce Ayres/Getty Images Inc. - Stone Allstock

EVALUATION OF PURCHASING

Purchasing professionals know that the evaluation of purchasing is important. They want to understand the extent to which purchasing goals have been attained. They also understand the importance of assessing how purchasing activities might be improved to enable future goals to be attained even more effectively.

They are also aware that evaluation may be overlooked, done quickly ("just get it over with"), and/or undertaken incorrectly because, for example, "We know we can't do any better." They also recognize that purchasing cannot evolve from simply buying things to becoming an important component of the organization's success unless an ongoing method of improvement activities is in place.

Reasons to Evaluate Purchasing

There are several reasons the purchasing process should be evaluated:

- *To recognize the function.* Busy managers are concerned about the most important things. If managers cannot (or do not) measure the overall performance of purchasing, their actions suggest that it is unimportant (at least relative to other activities that are evaluated).
- *To determine improvement benchmarks.* If measurable factors are used to evaluate purchasing, they provide standards against which to assess improvement. For example, if the number of stock outs is known for a previous period, a goal to reduce them can be established. Then process improvement activities can be measured to assess whether stock outs are reduced.
- *To manage costs.* Money saved through effective purchasing increases profitability. Money must be wisely spent, and purchasers can be challenged to work with user department personnel to determine how to reduce costs without sacrificing quality.
- *To establish procedures for measuring and rewarding the performance of purchasers.* Their work outputs should meet expectations.
- *To improve.* Purchasing evaluation can help purchasers and managers learn how the process can be improved.

Evaluation and Purchasing Improvement

Figure 6.10 illustrates how purchasing performance can be assessed.

Let's use product costs to illustrate how the evaluation process noted in Figure 6.10 can be implemented.

- *Step 1: Develop purchasing goals.* Efforts to reduce product costs without sacrificing quality should be a primary concern. However, it is difficult to

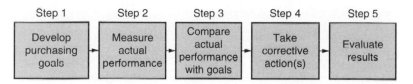

FIGURE 6.10   Overview of Purchasing Evaluation Process

determine the causes of higher-than-desired costs. If product cost evaluations are based on total dollar purchases, high costs could be due to ineffective purchasing, ineffective handling and control procedures, or simply increased sales. However, if product costs are based on **purchase unit costs,** they can be linked to purchasers. However, buyers have no control over the marketplace, which significantly influences purchase unit costs. One compromise is expressed in the following goal: Purchasing personnel shall maintain per-unit purchase costs for "A" products at no more than 2 percent above the adjusted market costs for the time period covered by the evaluation. Market prices for these products are publicly available, and they can be used as a benchmark against which to compare purchase prices.

- *Step 2: Measure actual performance.*   Delivery invoices available for "A" items can be summed to yield actual per-unit costs. The average purchase unit cost can be calculated for the evaluation period (beginning purchase unit cost + ending purchase unit cost ÷ 2) to yield the average purchase unit cost for "A" products.

- *Step 3: Compare actual performance with goals.*   The actual purchase unit cost for the "A" products is known (from Step 2), and it can be compared with the average purchase unit cost for products of the same quality available from market sources. If the actual purchase unit cost is not above the planned purchase unit cost, the stated goal was attained. However, if the

---

PROFESSIONAL PURCHASING PREVENTS PROBLEMS (6.2)

You Can't Measure the Attainment of Unmeasurable Goals

A common problem: Goals used for evaluation are not objective.

Purchasing goals must be measurable to permit evaluation. Consider the following goal: Purchasers will minimize product purchase costs during the next six months. This objective is not measurable because there is no way to assure that products were purchased at the lowest possible cost.

A better-stated goal might assign purchasers the responsibility to maintain product purchase costs at a level of no more than 103 percent of product costs for the previous period. This goal is measurable. If product purchases were $100,000 for the previous six months, they can be no more than $103,000 for the period of evaluation given the same production volumes. (*Note:* This goal assumes that $100,000 was a reasonable product cost based on usage and sales during the previous period. If this cost were excessive, the revised purchasing goal improperly approves and extends this excessive cost.)

The best approach is to use a goal such as the one stated earlier: Per-unit purchase costs for "A" products should be no more than 2 percent above the adjusted market cost for the time period covered by the evaluation. This goal is measurable, it isolates the role of purchasing staff in the expenditure, and it allows for cost changes beyond the purchaser's control.

Buyer's Guide to Purchasing Term

Purchase unit cost   The cost for a specified unit such as pound, case of specified size, or other container.

Buyers at Work (6.3)

"We've done well for many years, so why must we change?" asked Chason as he spoke to Hubert, the general manager of the Sea Coast Hotel.

"Chason, you're a great purchasing manager, and I'm not complaining about your performance, which is exceptional. Our reason for the evaluation of purchasing has nothing to do with you. We want to ensure we are using our resources as wisely as possible."

"Hubert, I know about evaluation. I think it's important for departments that generate revenues. However, a support department such as purchasing has a tough time defining measurable performance indicators. You can't go by cost because we have no control over the products after they enter storage areas. All I do is select suppliers and order products. Suppliers here are competitive, and they want our business. Things like untimely deliveries, quality problems, and stock outs don't occur. I don't know how you can evaluate purchasing. We're doing the best job that we can, and I wish you would just take my word for that. I'm always trying to reduce costs while recognizing quality concerns."

Assume you are Hubert:

1. How would you respond to Chason about his concern that revenue-producing but not support departments should be evaluated?
2. What types of evaluation factors would be applicable to and within Chason's control?
3. Chason said his primary job is to select suppliers and order products. What else can he do to help the Sea Coast Hotel with its longer-term concerns?

actual purchase unit cost was greater than the expected (planned) cost, investigation may help to assess reasons for the variation. Was the goal attained in previous periods? If so, there may be a special problem to be investigated. If the purchase unit goal was not previously met, purchasers must reassess whether the goal is reasonable and, if it is, to undertake more concerted efforts to move toward achieving it.

- *Step 4: Take corrective action.* When the comparison between expected and actual performance (Step 3) suggests a problem, corrective action is required. If multiple problems are observed, buyers typically address those that are most significant first unless "quick and easy" successes of minor problems are possible.
- *Step 5: Evaluate results.* Did corrective action (Step 4) adequately address problems discovered during the evaluation? Purchasers should also confirm that no spin-off problems were created. They may determine that high costs can be reduced by use of different suppliers, and while costs might decrease, other problems such as late deliveries may occur.

If purchasers determine that corrective actions were successful, the evaluation process was effective: problems were identified and were corrected as a result of the evaluation. However, if a problem is not satisfactorily addressed and/or if additional problems now occur, it is necessary to plan additional corrective actions (Step 4) to further improve the purchasing process.

Purchasing Goals and Evaluation Factors

Purchasing goals relate to its purpose within the hospitality organization. If the property is most concerned about prices, the emphasis will likely be on purchasing products at the lowest possible price. If price and quality are important, there will be an increasing emphasis on value (the relationship between price and quality).

Figure 6.11 indicates how the focus of evaluation changes as the purchasing function becomes more important.

Function of Purchasing	Focus of Evaluation
Price-Conscious Purchasing Price and Quality Purchasing	• Cost per purchase unit • Total purchase costs • Maintain budget • Development of specifications • Supplier performance (selection) • Make–buy analyses • Suppliers' assistance to the organization

FIGURE 6.11   Evaluation of Purchasing Based on Its Function

When price-conscious purchasing is most important, the tasks are essentially reactive and mostly clerical; "Get products into the organization when they are needed at a low cost." The importance of purchasing increases as price and quality concerns (value) become important. Price will still be important, but it may be evaluated along with other factors, including the number of specifications developed, problems with suppliers, the number of make-buy analyses completed, and instances of supplier-added assistance.

Purchasing evaluation factors can also consider operational concerns, financial issues, and other evaluation concerns.

OPERATIONAL CONCERNS   Basic operational concerns relate to product or service quality, quantity, timing, and price. Examples of how some of these factors can be measured are listed in Figure 6.12.

Note that most of the evaluation factors in Figure 6.12 are relatively easy to measure because the applicable data is often collected and used for other purposes.

FINANCIAL ISSUES   Numerous purchasing evaluation factors address financial concerns. These include relationships (ratios) such as the following:

- Purchases as percent of revenue: $\dfrac{\text{Total purchases (\$)}}{\text{Total revenues (\$)}}$

- Purchasing department operating expenses as percent of revenue:

$$\dfrac{\text{Purchasing department operating expenses (\$)}}{\text{Total revenues(\$)}}$$

- Purchasing department operating expenses as percent of total purchases:

$$\dfrac{\text{Purchasing department operating expenses (\$)}}{\text{Total purchases (\$)}}$$

Operational Concern	Evaluation Factor
Quality	Percentage of shipment rejects Number of production problems related to product quality
Quantity	Number of stock outs Inventory turnover rates compared to goals Number of expedited orders
Timing	Suppliers' delivery performance Time for requisition processing Time required for corrective action
Price	Prices paid against expected prices Prices paid for key items compared with market indexes Prices paid against budget

FIGURE 6.12   Operational Concerns and Evaluation Factors

Evaluation involves determining whether operating goals related to purchasing are attained. Existing information can typically be used for this evaluation.

Getty Images, Inc. -Photodisc.

(*Note:* Purchasing ratios are suggested by the Center for Advanced Purchasing Studies. Purchasing Performance Benchmarking for the U.S. Foodservice Industry. Tempe, Arizona.)

OTHER EVALUATION FACTORS Purchasing activities can be evaluated relative to other concerns, including the following:

- *Relationships with other departments.* How many purchasing-related complaints were logged by personnel in other departments? Are complaints made by purchasing staff regarding other department personnel? How many purchase orders must be expedited?
- *Creative assistance.* Have purchasing personnel discovered more than one useful supplier for difficult-to-locate products? Has the department helped to improve the productivity of user department personnel?
- *Effective purchasing policies.* Purchasing personnel can advise about policies for specification development, make or buy analysis, and single or multiple supply sources. What policies are needed? Are existing policies clearly stated? Are they understood and applied equitably by applicable personnel?
- *Supplier performance.* Many challenges within the purchasing function concern the failure of suppliers to meet purchasers' expectations. Are expectations reasonable? Why, if at all, do purchasers continue to interact with "problem" suppliers?

Evaluation of the purchasing department should also address the personnel who work within it. Are they qualified for and consistently able to perform effectively in their positions? Do purchasing staff participate in organizational activities?

Purchasing evaluation should be an ongoing process rather than being undertaken only when there is a problem. Effective purchasers and managers know that the most successful hospitality operations emphasize continuous improvement, and this concern relates to all departments and functions, including purchasing.

Buyer's Guide to Internet Resources: Purchasing Evaluation

Web Site	Topic
www.marketnews.usda.gov	Current market prices of numerous commodities
www.beefretail.org	Prices of beef sub-primal cuts
www.benchnet.com	Benchmarking practices and procedures
www.findarticles.com	Auditing purchasing activities (Enter "purchasing audits" into the site's search box)
www.about-goal-setting.com	Goal setting for businesses
www.capsresearch.org	Benchmarking information for purchasing evaluation
www.q2000.com.au	Goal setting (Click on "search" and type "goal setting" in the site's search box)

Purchasing Terms

Receiving *138*
Storage *138*
Bona fide occupational
   qualification
   (BFOQ) *141*
Pallet *141*
Credit memo *143*
Receiving report *143*
Slack-out seafood *144*

Bar code *145*
Radio frequency identifi-
   cation (RFID) *146*
Blind receiving *147*
Trespass *147*
Work flow *148*
Walk-in *148*
Cost of goods sold *150*
Income statement *150*

Inventory
   (physical) *151*
Perpetual
   inventory *152*
Surveillance
   equipment *153*
Accounting *154*
Duties, separation
   of *154*

Extensions *156*
Invoice (payment
   method) *156*
Statement (payment
   method) *157*
Outstanding (check) *158*
Audit trail *159*
Petty cash fund *159*
Purchase unit cost *161*

Make Your Own Purchasing Decisions

1. The chapter indicates that experienced purchasing professionals know their property will likely pay for the quality of products identified in the specification even if this quality is not received. What does this statement mean? Do you agree or disagree? Why?

2. Assume you supervise full-time receiving and storeroom clerks in a large hotel. A recent physical inventory count shows a one-case (twelve-bottle) difference in the inventory balance of a specific alcoholic beverage. The receiving clerk said the case was brought to the storeroom. However, the storeroom clerk said he did not receive it, so it was not entered into inventory records. What is the problem? How can it be resolved? What can be done to separate the duties and responsibilities of these two persons? How, if at all, can technology help to reduce this problem?

3. What are ways that purchasing and accounting managers can collude to defraud a hospitality

organization? What are basic controls that property managers should implement to help address these theft methods?

4. Assume that several financial, operational, and other goals were established for your purchasing department and that evaluation indicated the goals were not attained. How would you as the director of purchasing determine priorities for departmental improvements? Would you also consider additional goals beyond those that have yet to be addressed? Why or why not?

5. Assume you were responsible for purchasing in a hospitality organization that is implementing electronic systems for inventory management, ordering, and interfacing purchasing information with the property's accounting system. How might you interact with department staff members who are very much in support of applying the new technology? With those who are resisting changes?

Endnotes

1. This section is adapted from J. Ninemeier and D. Hayes, *Restaurant Operations Management: Principles and Practices* (Upper Saddle River, NJ: Pearson Prentice-Hall, 2006), chap. 10.

2. Details about daily food costing are found in J. Ninemeier and D. Hayes, *Restaurant Operations Management: Principles and Practices* (Upper Saddle River, NJ: Pearson Prentice-Hall, 2006), chap. 16.

3. This section is adapted from J. Ninemeier and D. Hayes, *Restaurant Operations Management: Principles and Practices* (Upper Saddle River, NJ: Pearson Prentice-Hall, 2006), chap. 10.

4. Detailed procedures to calculate cost of goods sold and to value inventory are beyond the scope of this discussion. Interested readers are referred to J. Ninemeier and D. Hayes, *Restaurant Operations Management: Principles and Practices* (Upper Saddle River, NJ: Pearson Prentice-Hall, 2006), chap. 16.

7

Meats, Poultry, and Seafood

Purchasing Pros Need to Know!

If you are like most foodservice buyers, meats, poultry products, and seafood will be some of the most expensive items you will purchase. It is also true that your guests' evaluation of these items will play a large part in how they view your business's overall performance. Inferior quality meat, poultry, and seafood items will result in a poor perception of your operation.

The word *meat* generally refers to edible beef, veal, pork, and lamb products, but poultry products are sometimes called meats. In the United States, the most popular poultry products are chickens, turkeys (a bird native to North America), and ducks. Other animals eaten for meat include game animals of various types. Some of these are considered meats (e.g., bison, deer, and rabbits), and others are considered by many to be poultry (e.g., quail and pheasants). In this chapter you will learn about both types of game because, in many operations, these are increasingly popular with guests.

Seafood, for many good reasons, is widely perceived as healthy food and is included on most restaurant menus. Like poultry, seafood is sometimes referred to as meat. In this chapter, however, seafood will be identified as being either fish or shellfish. Both types are popular with guests, so it is important that you know how to buy both types.

Today's meat, poultry, and seafood buyers choose from products sold in a variety of ready-to-use cuts and different market forms. In some ways this makes the job of buying easier, but it also means your knowledge of available market forms must be extensive. Because of the importance of these items, purchasing pros need to know a great deal when they buy meats, poultry, or seafood. In this chapter you will learn the basics necessary to effectively purchase these expensive, highly perishable, and very popular items.

■ ■ ■

Outline

MEATS

Meat is the term most often used to describe the muscled flesh of animals eaten for food. Typically, a distinction is made between muscle meats and organ meats (livers, hearts, kidneys, and the like). In the United States, the term *meat* is used even more specifically to describe the flesh of livestock animals (commonly beef, veal, pork, and lamb).

Meat is important because it typically serves as the main course, or **center of the plate** item for most foodservice operations.

Meat can be a very complex item to buy because each animal raised for food varies somewhat from other animals, and even from other animals in the same species. In addition, meat muscle can be cut in hundreds of ways, and it can be processed and sold in even hundreds more. The result is that meat sellers now offer virtually thousands of fresh and processed products to foodservice buyers.

While it can be complex, you can better understand the meat-buying process by remembering a few key principles. The first of these is that all meat sold in the United States must be federally inspected for wholesomeness. When inspected, each animal is stamped with a round purple vegetable dye mark that reads, *U.S. INSP'D & P'S'D*, as shown in Figure 7.1.

The mark is put on animal carcasses and large meat cuts, so it might not appear on smaller cuts such as roasts and steaks. However, meat that is packaged in

> ### Buyer's Guide to Purchasing Terms
>
> **Meat**   The body tissues of animals eaten for food.
>
> **Center of the plate**   The main course (entrée) in a multi-item meal. So named because the item most often is placed in the center of the plate when it is served.

FIGURE 7.1 U.S. Meat Inspection Stamp

an inspected facility will always have an inspection legend, which identifies the plant on the label. While voluntary in many cases, the U.S. government also assigns **quality grades** to meats (and other foods) and, in the case of some animals, **yield grades,** so you can know more about the various qualities and yield levels you are purchasing.

Understanding meat grades is important to you because, for example, the beef you will purchase might have been graded for quality or yield or both. (Recall that all meat must be inspected for wholesomeness.) Because meat grading is voluntary, many meat processors use their own labeling systems to provide quality assurance. These private systems do not necessarily use the USDA's meat evaluation factors. If you do buy these products, you must always inquire carefully about the quality level of the privately labeled items.

The second major principle for you to know about meat buying is that there are highly established standards for meat products. When these standards are known, you can more easily develop detailed specifications for the meat items you want to buy. To eliminate the confusing names given to meat cuts in different regions of the country, and by different product sellers, a uniform system of designating meat cuts has been developed. Each beef, pork, and lamb cut is identifiable by a number assigned by the **IMPS/NAMP** numbering system.

IMPS refers to the USDA-approved Institutional Meat Purchase Specifications for fresh beef, veal, pork, and lamb. Under IMPS, meats are classified using a numerical system (e.g., specific beef cuts are numbered in the 100 series, lamb in the 200 series, veal in the 300 series, and pork in the 400 series).

NAMP refers to the North American Meat Processors Association. Foodservice meat buyers, however, best know NAMP for *The Meat Buyer's Guide*, a publication that even more fully explains to buyers the IMPS numbered items. *The Meat Buyer's Guide* is intended for meat cutters and commercial meat purchasers and is the recognized reference for meat cuts. It is published annually to allow NAMP to maintain and illustrate the standard numbering system for NAMP-recognized cuts of meat. NAMP has issued its *Meat Buyer's Guide* periodically since 1963 (and now issues a *Poultry Buyer's Guide*).

A third important principle you must know regarding meat buying relates to the age of the meat you purchase. When an animal is killed for food, its muscle composition will continue to change as time passes. Some meats (such as beef, veal, and lamb) will improve in flavor as they continue to age for longer periods,

---

Buyer's Guide to Purchasing Terms

Quality grade   Designation of an item's quality rank relative to established standards of excellence (e.g., Grade A, Grade B, and the like).

Yield grade   An evaluation of the usable (edible) meat on an animal's carcass.

IMPS   USDA-approved Institutional Meat Purchase Specifications standardizing specifications for fresh beef, veal, pork, and lamb.

NAMP   The North American Meat Processors Association is the publisher of the popular book *The Meat Buyer's Guide*.

Did You Know? (7.1)

The NAMP offers its *Meat Buyer's Guide* for sale in hard-copy form. The USDA-approved IMPS for fresh beef, veal, pork, and lamb, however, is free and may be downloaded at www.ams.usda.gov. Just enter "IMPS" in the search window.

Large-volume purchasers such as government agencies, schools, restaurants, hotels, and other foodservice users reference the IMPS when buying meat products. The IMPS describes in great detail each cut of meat, with illustrations and photographs.

When you have downloaded the information, click on Fresh Beef (series 100) to see the type of detail provided by these published standards. In addition, you can click on one of the processed meats PDF files (e.g., Series 500 or 600) to review the specification details provided for these types of processed meat products.

while others (such as pork, poultry, and most seafood) do not improve. Those meats that are purposely aged may be either **wet aged** or **dry aged.**

Wet aging in vacuum-sealed plastic bags allows natural chemicals, enzymes, and microorganisms present in the meat to break down the meat muscle's connective tissue, which tenderizes and flavors it. As this chemical process occurs, the meat will develop an unpleasant odor that is released when the package is opened. This odor goes away in minutes, however, and has no long-term negative effect on the wet-aged item.

Dry aging also allows enzymes and microorganisms to break down connective tissue. Dry-aged meats, however, also lose 5 percent to 20 percent of their total weight during the aging process because meats are composed of large amounts of water, and it is this loss of water that results in the item's weight loss. Meats can also easily develop external molds, which add great flavor, but which must be removed before the meat is consumed. Dry-aged meats are usually of very high quality, costly, and obtained only through specialty distributors and butchers. These meats are especially popular with the guests who value the very best quality meats, even when the price they must be charged for these items is high.

Because you now understand meat quality, yield, standards, and aging principles, you know much of the information you need to effectively buy fresh meat products. It is important for you to understand, however, that increasingly, you will purchase your meats in a variety of processed forms. These include those packaged as ready to eat, those sold in single-serving microwaveable containers, and those using **boil-in-bag** cooking systems as well as those sold in more traditional canned, refrigerated, and frozen forms.

Beef

Beef is the meat of domesticated cattle and is one of the most popular types of meats served. While it is widely consumed in European, Asian, and American cuisines, you should know that, for religious reasons, beef is taboo to Hindus (and its consumption is discouraged among some Buddhists).

Buyer's Guide to Purchasing Terms

Wet aged (meats)   The storing of vacuum-packed meats under refrigeration for up to six weeks to improve their flavor.

Dry aged (meats)   The storing of fresh meats in an environment of controlled temperature, humidity, and airflow for up to six seeks to improve the flavor of the aged item.

Boil-in-bag   A cooking technique in which food is heated or cooked in the same bag in which it has been packaged.

FIGURE 7.2 Beef Cattle Parts

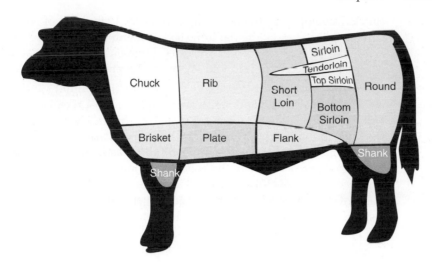

Most of the beef purchased in the United States comes from **steers,** the castrated male cattle specifically raised for beef. Beef is easily the most popular meat in the United States and is increasingly sold to foodservice operators in processed forms and cuts designed to reduce labor costs and increase product quality and consistency.

BEEF CUTS When cattle are slaughtered, the carcasses are cut into four pieces (called quarters). There are two front (fore) quarters and two rear (hind) quarters. Each quarter is then separated (*broken* is the word used by meat cutters) into **primal cuts** and, in most cases, subprimal (smaller) cuts. These primal and subprimal parts are then sold to meat wholesalers, retailers, and some foodservice operators, who then produce **fabricated cuts.**

Because meat preferences vary by culture and geographic location, it should not surprise you to know that primal cuts produced in, for example, Canada, Mexico, and the United States, are not identical. For U.S. buyers, however, primal cuts are carefully defined by the IMPS/NAMP numbering systems. While those in the meat industry use virtually every part of each animal they process, Figure 7.2 shows the common names of the cattle parts and primal cuts that will be important to you as a foodservice buyer.

It is good for you to have a solid understanding about the major parts of cattle that result in the meats you will buy. These parts include the following:

Chuck Chuck meat is taken from the animal's front shoulders (fore quarters) and mainly consists of very large muscles. These muscles are heavily used by the animal and, as a result, are somewhat tougher than other muscles. Counted from front to back, it includes the first five ribs of the animal. This area of the animal also contains a great deal of connective tissue, including **collagen.** Collagen melts during cooking, making the meat intensely flavorful. Cuts from this area benefit from slow, wet cooking methods such as stewing, braising, or pot-roasting. Cuts from this area are rarely broiled with the exception of the flat iron steak. The flat iron steak is derived from the most tender portion of the

---

Buyer's Guide to Purchasing Terms

Steer Male cattle raised specifically for food.

Primal cuts The large meat cuts taken from front and rear beef quarters. Subprimal cuts are products resulting from further breaking down of primal cuts.

Fabricated cuts The individual portions of meat cut from subprimal cuts.

Collagen A fibrous protein found in skin, bone, and other connective muscle tissues.

chuck. Developed by the research teams at the University of Nebraska and the University of Florida, the flat iron steak is gaining popularity with restaurants across the United States. The National Cattlemen's Beef Association funded the research required to develop this tasty, tender, and economical steak.

Rib   This tender and very flavorful part of the animal can be cooked any number of ways. It includes ribs six to twelve. Most recipes call for these ribs to be roasted, sautéed, panfried, broiled, or grilled. The most popular foodservice cut from this part of the animal is rib roast, also known as a standing rib roast (bone left in) or even more commonly as prime rib. Prime ribs can be purchased precooked with the bone in or boneless. This part of the animal also produces the rib eye steak (also called a Delmonico). These steaks are noted for their intense flavor. However, they are not as lean as some other cuts, and thus a significant number of consumers do prefer other types of steaks.

Short loin   The short loin includes only one rib (number thirteen). Fabricated cuts from this portion include porterhouse steaks (which include a sizable portion of the tenderloin), T-bone steaks (which include smaller portions of tenderloin), and club steaks (which contain no tenderloin). When the backbone is removed, this primal cut also produces the New York strip steak. This area also produces the tenderloin. The tenderloin taken from the short loin area is often sold separately. This muscle is located near the spine of a cow and is very tender. Normally, a steer will produce between four and six pounds of tenderloin, which when cut into steaks, is referred to as filet mignon. Known for its tenderness, filet mignon is the most expensive of all the steak cuts. Tenderloin fillets can be cut thin or thick and can be grilled, broiled, or fried with excellent results. All cuts from the short loin, however, can be sautéed, panfried, broiled, pan broiled, or grilled. As a buyer, you will pay the most per pound for cuts taken from this part of the beef carcass.

Sirloin   This cut produces the sirloin steak as well as sirloin tip roasts and other flavorful fabricated cuts. Top sirloin steak is a commonly sold item. The word *top* in this case, however, refers to the location of the cut, not the quality of the steak relative to other areas of the sirloin.

Flank   The meat from this portion of cattle is lean, muscular, and very flavorful. Flank is used primarily to produce flank steaks. Flank steaks have great flavor but must, when served, be carefully sliced thin and against the grain. You will likely buy flank steak if your operation wishes to make the classic dish London broil.

Short plate   This section is most often used for stew meat, where its rich, beefy flavor can be appreciated. It also produces the skirt steak (used by many foodservice operators in the popular Mexican dish fajitas) as well as short ribs.

Round   The round consists of lean meat well suited to long, moist cooking methods. Steamship rounds are very large roasts produced from this cut. Round may also be used as pot roast or cut into thick steaks for braising in dishes such as Swiss steak.

Shank/brisket   Traditionally used for **corned beef,** or Southwest-style barbecue, brisket is best prepared with moist heat or very low dry heat. Suitable preparation methods for shank/brisket include stewing, braising, and pot-roasting.

With all the possible products made from the primal beef cuts just described, it should come as no surprise that there are virtually hundreds of beef

---

Buyer's Guide to Purchasing Term

Corned beef   The process of preserving meat with salt. Corned beef (preserving beef with corns, or large grains of salt) is an ancient form of meat preservation.

forms available to buy. When selling to foodservice operators, most packers and distributors sell their larger cuts of beef as **box beef.**

Fresh beef sold in the United States takes many forms; however, overwhelmingly, the majority of beef selected for use in foodservice is purchased as either ground beef or as steaks. Because that is so, it is important that you know as much as possible about these two staple beef items.

Ground Beef The incredibly popular ground beef is sold in a variety of forms and sizes and under a variety of names. This is so because, year after year, hamburgers are the single most popular menu item in America. Buyers should know, however, that in the United States "ground beef" is not the same as "hamburger." Beef fat may be added to hamburger but not ground beef if the meat is ground and packaged at a USDA-inspected plant. However, a maximum of 30 percent fat by weight is allowed in either hamburger or ground beef. Both hamburger and ground beef must be labeled in accordance with federal law and marked with a USDA-inspected label, but these products are not typically graded. When it comes to buying ground beef, you should carefully do your research and understand exactly what you are buying.

Generally, most ground beef products are made from the less tender and less popular cuts of beef, but trimmings from more tender cuts may also be used. Some restaurants even specialize in steak burgers that are indeed made from ground beef produced from steaks.

The fat content of ground beef can range from 5 percent to 30 percent. While grinding tenderizes the beef and the fat reduces its dryness and improves its flavor, the process also creates problems. It is dangerous to eat raw or undercooked ground beef because it may contain harmful bacteria introduced during the grinding process. The USDA currently recommends that people not eat raw or undercooked ground beef. To ensure that all bacteria are destroyed in meat loaf, meatballs, casseroles, and hamburgers, the USDA recommends ground beef be cooked to a minimum internal temperature of 160°F (71°C).

Steaks As you learned, steaks come from selected primal and subprimal beef cuts. Steaks served as individual portions vary in quality and will vary even further based on how they are handled prior to cooking, the amount of time they are cooked, and the internal temperatures at which they are served. As a professional buyer, you should particularly understand the cooked-steak terms culinarians use when preparing beef steaks and ground meat products. These are listed in Figure 7.3.

Regardless of the preparation method that will be used to cook them, steaks served in foodservice operations may be cut from boxed beef (fabricated) on-site, purchased freshly cut, or purchased in a variety of **IQF** sizes.

FIGURE 7.3 Steak Internal Temperatures

Cooked	Traditional Temperature (USA)	Description
Blue	115°F–125°F	Blood-red meat, soft, very juicy
Rare	125°F–130°F	Red center, gray surface, soft, juicy
Medium rare	130°F–140°F	Pink center, gray-brown surface
Medium	140°F–150°F	Slightly pink center, becomes gray-brown towards surface
Medium well	150°F–160°F	Mostly gray center, firm texture
Well done	160+°F	Gray-brown throughout

Buyer's Guide to Purchasing Terms

Box beef The industry term for primal and some subprimal cuts of beef that are vacuum-sealed and shipped to the buyer in cardboard boxes.

IQF Short for individually quick frozen, this is a popular market form for many types of meats, poultry, and seafood.

Buyers at Work (7.1)

"I'm not going to cook it rare. It isn't safe," said Hendric, the head cook at the Gaslight Pub. "Tell the guests they have to have it well done."

"I tried that," replied Sandy, the server who had taken the order from one of the pub's best customers (an older man who ate at the restaurant at least twice a week). "He normally doesn't buy the burger, but today he wants a 'rare' hamburger. He is quite serious about it. Says he's been eating his hamburgers rare since the days of J. Wellington Wimpy, whoever that is."

"Well, I don't think we are supposed to serve rare burgers. I think it's illegal," replied Hendric.

"I don't want to lose a good customer," Sandy said. "Let's ask the manager what we should do."

Assume you are the buyer/manager at the pub, which is located in your own area:

1. Is serving rare burgers illegal?
2. What would you say to Hendric?
3. What would you say to Sandy?

Increasingly, foodservice operators can buy beef in a multitude of partially or fully precooked forms. In many cases the quality of these products can be good. They are especially useful when a shortage of talented back-of-house production staff make consistency of product a difficult goal to achieve. Beef is also a key ingredient in many canned or frozen convenience foods. Examples of such items include chili, stews, soups, and casserole dishes.

PURCHASING BEEF   As you have learned in this chapter, beef processors may choose to have their beef graded before selling it. While there are actually eight designated beef grades, commercial foodservice buyers such as you will typically choose from only those three detailed in Figure 7.4.

FIGURE 7.4   Three Highest USDA Beef Quality Grades

Product	USDA Seal

First
USDA Prime:
Prime-grade beef is the ultimate in tenderness, juiciness, and flavor. It is highly marbled, with large flecks of fat within the lean, which enhances both flavor and juiciness.

Second
USDA Choice:
Choice-grade beef has less marbling than Prime, but is of very high quality. Choice roasts and steaks from the loin and rib are very tender, juicy, and flavorful.

Third
USDA Select:
Select-grade beef is very uniform in quality and somewhat leaner than the higher grades. It is fairly tender, but because it has less marbling, it lacks some of the juiciness and flavor of the higher grades.

> ## PROFESSIONAL PURCHASING PREVENTS PROBLEMS (7.1)
> ### Meat Purchasing Doesn't Stop with Meat Delivery
>
> *A common problem:* Guests complain about meat quality, even when the meat products purchased are of high quality.
>
> The best buyer who purchases the best meats cannot prevent guest complaints if the meats purchased are poorly or improperly prepared. In the case of beef and other meats, this means using a cooking procedure appropriate for the cut of meat purchased. As a buyer, you should understand the two most common meat cooking procedures because a quality piece of meat cooked improperly will be of poor quality. When you are buying meats, it is best to match the cut of meat purchased with the cooking method that will be used to prepare it. Food buyers need not be expert chefs, however, when it comes to meat, especially beef. As a professional buyer, you need to fully understand the intended use for a meat item before you can effectively create a purchase specification for it. The two basic meat cooking methods are as follows:
>
> ***Dry-heat cooking methods*** Tender cuts of beef from the loin and rib are best cooked with dry-cooking methods, such as grilling, broiling, roasting, and sautéing. Grilling is characterized by cooking the beef over a high heat source, generally in excess of 650°F. This leads to searing of the surface of the beef, which due to the **Maillard reaction,** creates a flavorful crust. Broiling is similar to grilling, except that grilling is usually performed with the heat source *under* the beef, and broiling is usually performed with the heat source *above* the beef. Roasting is a method of cooking that uses hot air to cook the meat all the way around the product at the same time. Panfrying and deep-frying are also considered dry heat cooking methods.
>
> ***Moist-heat cooking methods*** Tougher cuts of beef from the round, brisket, flank, plate, shank, and chuck are generally best cooked by a moist-heat cooking method such as simmering or a combination of dry and moist cooking such as braising, pot-roasting, and stewing. Stewing involves immersing the entire cut of meat in a liquid. Braising involves cooking meats, covered, with small amounts of liquids (usually seasoned or flavored).

Beef carcasses (as well as lamb) are also graded on a scale of 1 to 5 for yield. Yield Grade 1 is given to those animals with the greatest yield (the most usable meat) and number 5 to those with the least usable meat.

Veal

Veal is the meat of young, usually male, beef cattle, called calves. Historically, veal has been very popular. Veal calves are actually a by-product of the dairy industry. Dairy cows must calve (give birth) before they begin to give milk. Thus, calves born but not used in the dairy herds were traditionally killed for food at an early age.

Some well-intentioned animal activists oppose the sale of veal, feeling that these animals are raised in poor conditions and are killed at too early an age. No hospitality professional would condone the raising of animals in morally wrong

Buyer's Guide to Purchasing Term

Maillard reaction Named after the French scientist Louis Camille Maillard, the Maillard reaction describes the browning process that takes place when food components such as sugars and proteins are heated. It occurs in most foods when they are cooked and results in the food's color change; also called the "Maillard effect."

Properly cooked steaks such as these are among the most popular of all entrée items.

James McConnachie © Rough Guides

conditions. Those who oppose the taking of these animals for food, however, typically make the mistake of comparing veal directly to beef.

Veal is commonly compared to beef because both come from cows. Veal and beef, however, have little in common. Veal meat is much lighter in color and finer in texture than beef. Additionally, veal usually comes from a (male) dairy calf. Commercially, veal is the best use for this animal as it maximizes the value of a calf that, if used to produce beef, would be difficult to grow and of very poor quality. Recall that these animals are born into dairy herds, not animals typically raised for their meat.

Prior to the commercialization of the veal industry, most dairy bull calves did not survive after the day they were born. They were killed because a dairy herd needed very few male bulls to continue the herd. In fact, as dairy farmers knew, an excess number of bulls would be detrimental to the herd. Thus, today's veal market uses the surplus from dairy herds, creating greater value for the dairy farmer and, as a result, helps hold down dairy costs while producing a highly desired and marketable meat product. The veal industry is tied to the dairy industry in other ways. Veal producers buy large amounts of milk by-products to create milk-fed veal products. Almost 70 percent of veal feeds (by weight) are milk products.

Although veal can come from any animal under the age of nine months, most are slaughtered at eight to sixteen weeks old. Veal is lighter in color than beef, is lower in fat, and has a milder flavor. It is used in a variety of dishes and cuisines.

Veal carcasses are cut into a foresaddle (front portion) and a hindsaddle (rear portion). A veal carcass yields five primal cuts: three from the foresaddle (the shoulder, the foreshank and breast, and the rib), and two from the hindsaddle (the loin and the leg). These cuts may be cooked whole or further fabricated.

PURCHASING VEAL   There are five USDA grades for veal and meat of calves. These are Prime, Choice, Good, Standard, and Utility. The last three grades are rarely sold to foodservice buyers. Prime veal is the most juicy and flavorful. Choice cuts are somewhat less juicy and flavorful than Prime cuts. When choosing veal, color is the best guide. The flesh should be creamy white, barely tinged with grayish pink, and the fat should be white. Meat that is pink or turning red means the veal is older than it should be. Veal's texture should be firm, finely grained, and smooth.

Dry heat may be used to cook the most tender veal cuts such as loin roasts, rib roasts, rump roasts, loin chops, rib chops, cutlets, and ground veal. Moist-cooking methods should be used for cuts such as shank cross cuts, shoulder roasts, breasts, and round steaks.

Pork

Pork is the edible meat from pigs (hogs) or domestic swine. The domestication of pigs for food dates back to about 7000 BC in the Middle East. However, evidence shows that Stone Age–man ate wild boar, the hog's ancestor. The earliest surviving written pork recipe is from China and is estimated to be at least two thousand years old.

Hogs were introduced to Florida by European explorers in the early 1500s and soon were raised in all parts of the United States. Today, with the exception of beef, Americans consume more pork than any other meat. The United States is one of the world's leading pork-producing countries. In fact, the United States is the third largest pork exporter, trailing only long-time world leaders Denmark and Canada.

U.S. pork production accounts for about 10 percent of total world supply. Interestingly, during the war of 1812, the U.S. government shipped pork to American soldiers packed in barrels stamped with the letters *US* as well as with the name of the meat packer, Sam Wilson. The soldiers referred to the meat as "Uncle Sam's," thus giving rise to the government's still-popular nickname "Uncle Sam."

As a professional buyer, you must understand that despite its extensive popularity, pork is also the meat most often avoided by large numbers of people worldwide. Throughout the Islamic world, many countries severely restrict the importation and/or consumption of pork products because Muslims are forbidden from consuming pork or any of its derivatives. Pork is also one of the best known of a category of foods forbidden under traditional Jewish dietary law. Today the pork sold in the United States is as safe and disease-free a product as is either beef or chicken. As a result, the avoidance of today's pork products is based solely on religious or other beliefs, rather than fears about the safety of the product.

The color of pork is interesting to buyers. Because of its high **myoglobin** content, fresh pork is red before cooking and becomes lighter as it is cooked.

According to the USDA, pork is considered a red meat because it contains more myoglobin than white meat such as chicken or fish. Despite this traditional definition of pork as a red meat, in 1987 the National Pork Board in the United States began an advertising campaign to position pork as "the other white meat" due to a public perception of chicken and turkey (white meats) as more healthful than red meats. The campaign was highly successful and resulted in 87 percent of consumers identifying pork with the slogan and, as a result, as a healthful meat item. Given the historical caution related to eating pork, the positive marketing benefits were significant, and the slogan is still in use today.

Pork used in foodservice operations is generally produced from young animals (six to seven months old) that weigh from 175 to 240 pounds. Much of a slaughtered hog is **cured** and made into ham, bacon, and sausage. The uncured meat is called "fresh pork" and comes from one of the animal's primal or subprimal cuts.

Buyer's Guide to Purchasing Terms

Myoglobin   The oxygen-transporting protein found in animal muscle.

Cured   Meat that has been treated to improve taste and extend the period of time it can be safely eaten.

FIGURE 7.5 Eight Primal Pork Cuts

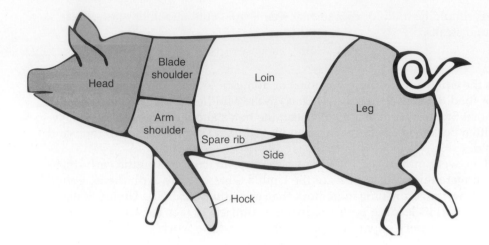

While the terminology used to describe fresh pork products varies somewhat by region of the United States and by country, foodservice buyers should understand the eight basic parts of a pig. Starting at the animal's head and moving clockwise (Figure 7.5), the major pork cuts and the foodservice products they produce are as follows:

Pork Cuts	Foodservice Use and Cuts
Head	This section is used for processed meat products (souse, pâtés, terrines)
Blade shoulder	This section includes the Boston butt, a square cut located just above the shoulder. The Boston butt is very lean and when smoked is called a cottage ham. Roasts and steaks cut from this section may be called blade roasts, boneless blade roasts, and blade steaks (pork steaks).
Loin	This section of the animal produces the chops, pork tenderloin, and pork back ribs that are so popular in foodservice operations. Boneless loin is used to make Canadian bacon. Other common cuts used in foodservice include rib roasts, sirloin chops, crown roasts, butterfly chops, and boneless center-cut loin roasts.
Leg	The leg of a pig includes the leg muscle and shank of the animal. The most popular use of this cut is the production of hams. These include boneless, bone-in, shank-in, and shankless varieties. This portion also includes the rear hock, used primarily in seasoning a variety of stocks, soups, and foods.
Side	Noted mainly for bacon production, this cut has a very high fat content. It is nearly always separated from the spare ribs prior to processing.
Spare Rib	Spare ribs are removed from the side of the animal for processing. They can be purchased smoked but are most often sold to foodservice operators in their fresh or frozen state. Increasingly, spare ribs are seasoned, soaked in flavored salt water **(brined)** or marinated prior to their sale to foodservice operators.
Hock	Used in the same manner as the hock from the rear leg, this product is most often stewed or braised.
Arm Shoulder	The arm shoulder is also known as the picnic or picnic ham portion. Picnics may be smoked but are also sold as fresh products for roasting. They are especially popular for barbecuing.

Buyer's Guide to Purchasing Term

Brined Soaked in flavored salt water.

Pork items, including those shown in this photo, are the most popular types of meats served at breakfast.

James Jackson/Getty Images Inc. -Stone Allstock

Pork is a unique form of livestock because the ribs and loin are not separated into two different primal cuts, as are the ribs and loin of beef, veal, and lamb. As with all meats, it is important to know the location of bones when cutting or working with pork. This makes meat fabrication and carving easier and aids in identifying cuts for purchase.

PURCHASING PORK USDA grades for pork reflect only two levels of quality: Acceptable and Unacceptable. Acceptable-quality pork is also graded for yield (the amount of usable meat). Unacceptable-quality pork, which is safe to eat but consists of meat that is soft and watery, is graded U.S. Utility and is not generally available for foodservice usage.

While the USDA does not grade pork, there are quality differences in fresh pork products. The marbling in pork (as in beef) is an indicator of quality. The more streaks of fat you see, the more tender and flavorful the pork will be. Pork that comes from certain breeds, such as certified Berkshire pork (known in Japan as kurobuta or black hog), has dark red meat and heavy marbling and is among the best pork you can buy.

Pork, on a per-pound basis, can be considered very expensive or very economical because of the large difference in cost between its various cuts. Demand for the various highly desired products (spare ribs and pork chops) dictates the prices charged for these cuts. It is also true that, when pork is highly processed (as for bacon and hams), its cost per pound also increases significantly.

When buying pork, you need to recognize that it can be labeled as *natural* if it complies with the USDA standards for natural processing. The standards require that the product not contain artificial ingredients, artificial coloring, or chemical preservatives, and can have only minimal meat processing done. It can be processed using traditional methods to preserve it and to make it safe to eat. Methods such as freezing, smoking, roasting, drying, and fermenting can be used.

For most foodservice operators, a large amount of the pork they will purchase has been processed. Figure 7.6 shows the inspection mark used on processed pork (as well as other meat) products. This mark should be on all processed pork items purchased.

Pork was among the first of the meat animals to be preserved through processing. Today smoked ham and bacon are among the most popular of the

FIGURE 7.6 Inspection Mark Used on Processed and Fresh Meat Products

Did You Know? (7.2)

In the past meat buyers could not easily determine the origin of items they purchased. In fact, only since 2008 has the U.S. government required that country-of-origin labels be placed on meats sold to U.S. consumers. USDA regulations mandating that all buyers be fully informed about where the meats they were buying came from were originally proposed in 2002, but their implementation was delayed.

The law's leading opponents were grocery stores and large meatpacking companies, many of whom mix U.S. and Mexican beef for ground beef products, and other businesses involved in getting products to supermarkets. (Note: The law now allows the labels to list the United States as one of several countries of origin if the meat is mixed.)

In the past those opposing the implementation of the labeling requirements have said the tracking and paperwork needed to comply with the law were too burdensome and would lead to higher prices. In response to these concerns, regulators made the terms and paperwork required to comply with the law less troublesome.

As a buyer for a foodservice operation, it is important that you recognize that processed foods are exempt from these labeling requirements, as are all restaurants and other foodservice establishments.

It is also important to understand that, in addition to meats and poultry, all seafood sold to restaurants must indicate the country of origin. This can be especially important to informed buyers who may rightfully be concerned about the quality of seafood inspection and handling in some foreign countries.

processed pork items used in foodservice. Ham and bacon are made from fresh pork cuts. These are cured with salt then smoked.

Shoulders and rear legs (or "hams") are most often cured in this manner. In addition to ham and bacon, pork is widely used as an ingredient in sausage. Pork sausages, which are popular in many foodservice operations, may be purchased in a variety of market forms including bulk, links, or patties.

Lamb

For those consumers who appreciate its unique flavor, lamb is an extremely popular dish. A lamb is a young sheep, and you will find that buying it properly is important because those guests who enjoy it are very conscious of its quality factors. Sheep were among the very first animals domesticated. An archeological site in Iran produced a statuette of a wool-bearing sheep, which suggests that selection of sheep for clothing and food began more than six thousand years ago.

Interestingly, the terms *lamb* and **mutton** are used to describe the meat of domesticated sheep. Both terms refer to products generally known as sheep meat.

While not extremely common on many American-style restaurant menus, sheep meats are featured prominently in the cuisines of the Mediterranean, northern Africa, the Middle East, and certain parts of the China. In some countries, including India, the term *mutton* more frequently refers to goat (not sheep) meat, though in most Asian/Indian-style restaurants located in the United States, sheep meat (not goat) is generally served.

Lamb is technically defined as any sheep less than one year old. Lamb is known for its tender meat. Baby lamb is customarily slaughtered at between six and eight weeks old (at this age, the lamb is sometimes called hothouse lamb).

Buyer's Guide to Purchasing Term

Mutton   The meat of a full-grown sheep (usually more than two years old), eaten as food.

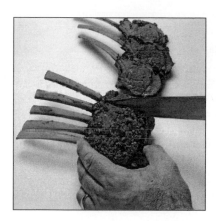

The Frenching process adds elegance to dishes such as lamb chops and rib roasts.
Richard Embery/Pearson Education/PH College

Spring lamb is usually three to five months old and has not been fed on grass or grains. Regular lamb is slaughtered at less than a year of age. Lamb between twelve and twenty-four months is called a yearling, and when it is more than two years old, it is referred to as mutton. At that stage in its life, it has a stronger flavor and less tender flesh than lamb.

Lamb carcasses generally are cut into four main parts. These are the shoulder, rack (the source of lamb rib chops), loin (the source of lamb loin chops), and the leg. Lamb, served in the form of rib or loin chops, which are cooked plain or after **Frenching,** are among the most popular of lamb cuts. Lamb leg served as roast is also popular.

Additional foodservice cuts of lamb that are commonly available include the neck, fore shank, breast (also called the brisket), and flank.

PURCHASING LAMB Approximately 50 percent of the lamb sold in the United States is imported from New Zealand or Australia. U.S. lamb, because it is fed on grain (not grass), tends to be smaller-boned and milder in flavor than imported lamb. As shown in Figure 7.7, there are five USDA grades for lamb based on proportion of fat to lean. Beginning with the best, they are Prime, Choice, Good, Utility, and Cull. When purchasing lamb, in general, the darker the color, the older the animal. Baby lamb will be pale pink, while regular lamb is pinkish red. Lamb can be purchased ground and in steaks, chops, and roasts in either fresh or frozen forms. Lamb variety meats can also be purchased.

Because the quality of lamb varies greatly according to the age of the animal, it is advisable to buy only lamb meat that has been identified as such by the USDA and that has been graded Prime or Choice.

Grade	Characteristics
Prime	Has abundant marbling and is generally very juicy and tender
Choice	Has less marbling than Prime grade but is still high quality
Good, Utility, and Cull	These grades are seldom sold to foodservice buyers

FIGURE 7.7 USDA Lamb Quality Grades

Buyer's Guide to Purchasing Term

Frenching (chops) A method of trimming individual or connected rib chops of meat (especially lamb), in which the excess fat is cut away from the bone, leaving the eye muscle intact.

Charcuterie

Before the days of refrigeration, those who raised, butchered, and sold meat at the retail and wholesale levels faced a significant problem. Because unprocessed meat could spoil quickly, keeping meats wholesome enough to eat safely could present challenges. While cooking and salting could alleviate this problem in many meats, other preservation techniques were also developed. The name given to cold cooked, cured, or processed meat and meat products was **charcuterie.** Today this French term refers to a delicatessen specializing in a variety of processed meats and meat dishes as well as the products sold in such shops.

Historically, however, charcuterie referred primarily to sausages, ham, pâtés, and other cooked or processed pork products. Today the art and science of the charcuterie includes the use of conventional pork products as well as **forcemeat** mixtures made from all types of meat, poultry, fish, and vegetables.

Charcuterie began as a necessary process to preserve meats before they could spoil. It was initially practiced as a way to use up various meat scraps and to preserve larger cuts such as hams and bacon. In many cases the products created proved equally as popular as the fresh meats from which they were made. Today the desirability (and purchase price) of gourmet items such as foie gras (a pâté made from goose liver, which can easily cost more than $100.00 per pound), other specialty pâtés, terrines, and galantines is heavily influenced by the quality of the original products used to make them as well as the finished item's primary ingredients. Properly prepared, the main ingredient of a charcuterie item will include the dominant meat (or seafood) from which the item is made and the fat that is added, for flavor, to the item. In addition, binders of starch or egg may be added as well as various seasonings that give the item its characteristic flavor and texture (e.g., chicken liver pâté). In some items garnishes of meats, fats, vegetables, or other foods are added in limited quantities to provide contrasting flavors and textures. Common garnishes include pistachio nuts, fatback, truffles, and diced ham or sausages.

Buyer's Guide to Internet Resources: Meats

Web Site	Topic
meat.tamu.edu/beefgrading.html	Federal grading standards for beef
www.ruthschris.com/menu/steaks	Steak descriptions from the Ruth's Chris Steakhouse chain
www.cryovac.com	Wet-aged beef packaging
www.americangrassfedbeef.com	Advantages of grass-fed beef
www.certifiedangusbeef.com	Definition of Angus beef
www.siouxpremepork.com	Premium pork products
www.theotherwhitemeat.com	General information about pork products
www.davidmosner.com	Natural veal and lamb products
www.boarshead.com	Processed meats of all types
www.Dibruno.com	Italian-style charcuterie

Buyer's Guide to Purchasing Terms

Charcuterie   The processing of meat, poultry, fish, shellfish, or vegetables prepared by salt curing, brining, and cold or hot smoking.

Forcemeat   A preparation made from uncooked ground meats, poultry, fish, or shellfish that is seasoned and emulsified with fat.

POULTRY

Poultry is the collective term used to describe domesticated birds bred for eating and for their eggs (and in some cases their feathers). The USDA recognizes six categories of poultry: chicken, turkey, ducks, goose, guinea, and pigeons. Each poultry type is divided into classes based on the bird's age, tenderness, and in some cases sex. Chickens and turkey make up the overwhelming majority of poultry sold in the United States.

The low cost, perceived healthfulness, and mild flavor of poultry products means they will likely make up a significant portion of your operation's entrée items and your meat purchases. In addition, because of the many processed forms of poultry available to foodservice buyers (and popularity with guests), poultry consumption continues to rise. In fact, while red meat still exceeds poultry in terms of the amount consumed per person, each year the gap has been narrowing and will most likely continue to shrink over the next decade, according to projections from the USDA.

Based on USDA data, in 2003 consumption of red meat, including beef, veal, pork, lamb, and mutton, was 118.5 pounds per person. Consumption of these items is projected to fall to just greater than 112 pounds in 2013. Meanwhile, poultry consumption, according to these same projections, will rise from 100.2 pounds per person in 2003 to 108.9 pounds per person by 2013.

Compared to other meats and seafood, poultry is fairly uncomplicated to buy. It is important to know that the meatiest parts of a bird are the muscles associated with flying. These are commonly known as white meat and consist of the breasts and, in nonflying birds, the wings. The walking muscles of a bird's legs consist of the two parts commonly known as the thigh and drumstick. White meat has less oxygen-carrying myoglobin than the walking muscles and, thus, is lighter in color. This is the common distinction between white meat and dark meat.

All poultry and poultry parts must be officially inspected to ensure that they are wholesome, properly labeled, and not adulterated. Every poultry processing plant's premises, facilities, equipment, and procedures must be inspected. When sold, an inspection stamp must appear on the label. This mandatory inspection is done by the USDA's Food Safety and Inspection Service. It must be done before poultry can be graded for quality. The USDA's Agricultural Marketing Service provides grading services, on a voluntary basis, to poultry processors and others who request it (and pay a fee for it). Most poultry sold to foodservice industry buyers is U.S. Grade A, the highest quality grade available.

Figure 7.8 illustrates the most common market forms of poultry sold to foodservice operators.

The USDA grade shield should be on the following ready-to-cook poultry products, whether purchased chilled or frozen:

Whole poultry carcasses

Poultry parts (with or without the skin and/or bones)

Poultry roasts

Poultry tenderloins (from the breast)

There are no grade standards for poultry necks, wing tips, tails, **giblets,** or poultry meat that is diced, shredded, or ground.

Buyer's Guide to Purchasing Term

Giblets   The edible internal organs of poultry, including the heart, liver, gizzard, and kidneys.

FIGURE 7.8 Basic Poultry
Market Forms
Source: USDA

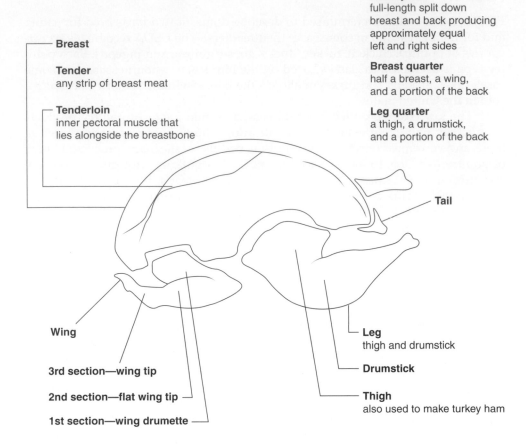

Breast

Tender
any strip of breast meat

Tenderloin
inner pectoral muscle that
lies alongside the breastbone

Poultry half
full-length split down
breast and back producing
approximately equal
left and right sides

Breast quarter
half a breast, a wing,
and a portion of the back

Leg quarter
a thigh, a drumstick,
and a portion of the back

Tail

Wing

3rd section—wing tip

2nd section—flat wing tip

1st section—wing drumette

Leg
thigh and drumstick

Drumstick

Thigh
also used to make turkey ham

While poultry grades are still important, increasingly, poultry is sold and purchased in a wide variety of preprocessed forms. Today you can select from processed poultry alternatives that range from items such as poultry-based hot dogs, hams, and bacon to breaded, battered, and preseasoned poultry parts and shaped meats.

Adding to the complexity of buying poultry, many poultry products of all forms may be injected with seasoning solutions that significantly increase product weight and, thus, affect taste and the cost per pound. As a result, when you buy poultry of any kind, you must be aware of this common practice that is discussed more fully as follows.

The popularity of poultry on
foodservice menus has continued to increase each year.

Felicia Martinez/PhotoEdit Inc.

Chicken

Chicken is the name given to the descendents of the red jungle fowl originally found in northern India and southern China. Chicken is the single most widely eaten form of poultry in the United States, as well as the rest of the world. Chickens contain white meat (breasts and wings) and dark meat (legs and thighs). Most chickens have a relatively low fat content and are quite tender. They are served roasted, fried, and stewed as well as, increasingly, in a large number of processed forms.

Chickens have very specific names based on the sex and age of the bird. A young chicken is called a chick. A male chicken is a cock or a cockerel. A female chicken is called a pullet or a hen. The age at which a pullet becomes a hen and a cockerel becomes a cock depends on the type of chicken raised. Typically, however, a chicken is a cockerel or pullet if it is less than one year of age. After one year of age, the chicken is referred to as a hen or cock. In the commercial industry, a female chicken is called a hen after it begins egg production (around five months of age). A sexually mature male chicken, also around five months old, is referred to as a rooster. A capon is a castrated male chicken.

Specific classes based on age also identify chickens. A broiler or fryer is a chicken eight weeks old or younger. A roaster is a chicken that is up to sixteen weeks old. Birds older than six months are simply termed mature. Chicken, sold either fresh or frozen, may be purchased in all of the product forms previously identified in Figure 7.8.

PURCHASING CHICKENS Because they are inspected and graded by the USDA, purchasing fresh chickens and fresh chicken parts is a relatively straightforward matter. The same cannot be said about processed chicken parts and products. Chicken meat is increasingly purchased by foodservice buyers in easier-to-cook or precooked and preprocessed forms. When you buy processed chicken products, you must carefully consider three major issues: (1) the method for removing chicken meat from the bone, (2) internal product modifications, and (3) external product treatments.

Meat Removal Not all boneless poultry meat is removed from the bone by knives. Mechanically separated poultry is a pastelike and batterlike poultry product produced by forcing bones with attached meat tissue through a sieve or similar device under high pressure to separate bone from the edible tissue. Mechanically separated poultry has been used in poultry products since 1969. The resulting meat has as different texture than regular poultry meat. As a professional buyer, you should always know if the processed chicken you are buying has been produced using mechanically separated poultry products.

Internal Product Modifications Food additives are not generally allowed in fresh-sold poultry. However, if chickens you buy are processed (injected with a basting solution, ground, canned, cured, smoked, dried, or made into luncheon meats), additives such as monosodium glutamate (MSG), salt, or sodium erythorbate may be added. When they are, these ingredients must be listed on the label in descending order from largest to smallest amount of ingredient. If injected with liquids, stocks, broths, and the like, the products should be labeled as such, and you should be able to easily determine the amount of solution (by weight) that has been added to the product you purchase.

External Product Modifications Many processed poultry products are battered (e.g., with wet batters) or breaded (e.g., with cracker meal, breadcrumbs, or cornmeal) for frying. The meat may be either cooked or raw prior to its coating. For battered and breaded poultry, the pieces are passed through a flour-based batter containing leavening then through the breading ingredients. Nuggets, fingers, strips, fritters, and patties are all examples of recognized forms of externally modified chicken products. The USDA requires that combined batter and breading for

Buyers at Work (7.2)

"This tastes different than what we used to buy from our other supplier," said Sofia to Lars, the sales representative from Braddock Foods, as she sampled the new product Lars was suggesting she buy.

"Look," said Lars, "you said you wanted a precooked, six-ounce, breaded chicken breast for your popular chicken fried chicken sandwich, right?" asked Lars. "And at a better price!"

"Yes," replied Sofia, "but you say your item costs 40 percent less than the item I'm currently buying. That seems like a big difference if your product is really the same. And it tastes . . . I don't know . . . softer and mushier somehow."

"Sofia, this is an all-white-meat product, same as the whole breasts you buy now. I'll bet your guests won't be able to tell any difference between this product and what you were buying before," said Lars confidently.

Assume you were Sofia:

1. What questions about this product's meat-removal system would you ask Lars?
2. What questions about product modifications may be appropriate?
3. How would you actually determine if "your guests won't be able to tell any difference" between the product Lars is selling and the one you previously purchased?

chicken nuggets, fingers, strips, and patties does not exceed 30 percent by weight. Chicken fritters may contain up to 65 percent batter and breading but must contain at least 35 percent meat. Because manufacturers can produce any chicken products they desire within these broad parameters, it is easy to see why processed chicken product buyers must be very careful when comparing alternative products across vendors.

Turkeys

Turkeys are members of the pheasant family and native to North America. When Europeans first encountered turkeys in the Americas, they incorrectly identified the birds as a type of guinea fowl, which was also known as a turkey-cock, imported to central Europe from Turkey. Despite the fact that they are not directly related to guinea fowl, the name of that country stuck as the name of the bird.

Turkey is the second most popular poultry meat sold in the United States, where it is served roasted whole and in an ever-increasing variety of processed products. A longtime food favorite in the southern United States, even deep-fried turkey (despite the dangers associated with cooking it), has also quickly grown in popularity, due in large part to its promotion by Food Network celebrities such as Alton Brown and Emeril Lagasse.

When purchased whole or in parts turkeys are classified as either a fryer/roaster (less than sixteen weeks old), young (eight months old or less), yearling (fifteen months old or less), or mature (fifteen months old and older). Like chicken, turkey contains both white (breast and wings) and dark meats (legs and thighs). In most areas of the country, all of these parts may be purchased fresh or frozen.

Because of its low cost and mild flavor, virtually hundreds of processed turkey products are available. Turkey ham, a meat product made from the thigh meat of turkeys, is cured and smoked like pork. The size and shape of the ham depends on how the meat is processed, and it is generally available in whole or half portions. Turkey ham is approximately 95 percent fat free and is a low-fat alternative to ham made from pork.

Turkey bacon is a meat product produced from smoked turkey that has a similar appearance and flavor to pork bacon. However, because it contains less fat than bacon made from pork, turkey bacon shrinks less when cooked (and produces a higher yield).

Turkey pastrami is an increasingly popular turkey product made from skinless thigh and drumstick meat that has been ground and seasoned. Like other types of pastrami, turkey pastrami is flavored with peppercorns and other seasonings then cured and smoked.

PURCHASING TURKEYS   In most cases the same purchase standards that apply to chicken and other processed meats apply to turkeys. A unique purchasing term associated with bone-in turkey products, however, is **self-basted.**

When bone-in products are sold as self-basted, the label must include a statement identifying the total quantity and common or usual name of all ingredients in the solution (e.g., *Injected with approximately 3 percent of a solution of* _____ [list of ingredients]). Basted and self-basted solutions in poultry products are limited to 8 percent of the raw poultry weight before processing.

Ducks

Despite their current limited popularity, as a professional foodservice buyer, you should know the principles of buying quality ducks and duck parts. The duck (*canard* in French) used most often in commercial foodservice is a roaster duckling. The USDA has established different classes for ducks. Broiler duckling or fryer ducklings are young ducks (usually less than eight weeks old) of either sex. Roaster ducklings are young ducks less than sixteen weeks old. Mature ducks are usually more than six months old. Government duck grades are USDA A, B, and C. However, in most cases you will not have the option to buy ducks that have anything other than a Grade A classification.

Ducks contain only dark meat and have an extremely high fat content. These two facts may contribute to the limited popularity of duck. Ducks also have a high bone and fat–to-meat ratio. This means there is less edible meat per pound of **dressed**-weight duck than for other types of poultry. As a result, buyers of this item must recognize that the edible portion yields of duck are approximately half that of commercial chickens. Thus, for example, while a four-pound roasting chicken could serve four people, an equal-sized duck would serve only two people.

PURCHASING DUCKS   Ducks are most often purchased whole or in halves. Duck breasts, which may be labeled as **magrets,** are also a common market form. Duck sausages and pâtés are also widely available. In most areas ducks and duck parts may be purchased either fresh or frozen.

Like other animals, the quality of duck meat is affected by the animal's age and what it has been fed. There are two groups of duck typically bred for meat: the Muscovy and the Pekin (not Peking). The Muscovy duck is the largest of the common duck breeds. The white Pekin duck, native to China, grows rapidly and is also a popular animal among breeders. You can choose either breed, but you should buy only those ducks that have been properly inspected.

Buyer's Guide to Purchasing Terms

Self-basted   A legally recognized food term referring to the fact that the product described has been injected or marinated with a solution containing butter or other edible fat, broth, stock, or water plus spices, flavor enhancers, and other approved substances.

Dressed   Meat, poultry, or fish that has been cleaned and prepared for cooking. This may involve removing the animal's skin, scales, or feathers; entrails; and other body parts such as head, tail, and feet.

Magret   A breast fillet of duck or goose intended for panfrying, roasting, or braising.

PROFESSIONAL PURCHASING PREVENTS PROBLEMS (7.2)

Properly Cooked Food Is Safe to Eat

A common problem: Food-borne illness outbreaks due to improperly prepared or stored poultry (and other meat) products.

Just as professional buyers must be familiar with meat cookery techniques to ensure tasty products, they must be knowledgeable about food-borne illness and how cooking helps to prevent illness. Food-borne illnesses are caused by eating food or drinking beverages contaminated with bacteria, parasites, or viruses. Harmful chemicals can also cause food-borne illnesses if they have contaminated food during harvesting, processing, or preparing.

Food-borne illnesses can cause symptoms that range from an upset stomach to more serious symptoms, including diarrhea, fever, vomiting, abdominal cramps, and dehydration. Most food-borne infections are undiagnosed and unreported, though the U.S. Centers for Disease Control and Prevention (CDC) estimates that every year about 76 million people in the United States become ill from food they have eaten. When a restaurant is identified as the source of a food-borne illness outbreak, the resulting bad publicity is devastating.

To help prevent outbreaks, it is important to recognize that harmful bacteria are the most common cause of food-borne illnesses. Some bacteria may be present on foods when you purchase them. Raw foods are the most common source of food-borne illnesses because they are not sterilized (examples include raw meat and poultry parts that may have become contaminated during slaughter and processing).

Professional buyers help prevent food-borne illness by ensuring production staff routinely cook foods to the appropriate minimum internal temperature before service: 145°F for roasts, steaks, and chops of beef, veal, pork, and lamb; 155–160°F for ground pork, ground veal, and ground beef; and 165°F for poultry. Where practical, require the use of a meat thermometer to be sure. Remember, foods may be considered properly cooked only when they are heated long enough and at a high enough temperature to kill any harmful bacteria that could cause illnesses.

GAME

Game refers to animals that, traditionally, have been hunted either for food or for sport.

Game animals are included in this chapter because, while less common, their meat is popular with a large number of consumers. Today the rising popularity of many game animals has increased these items' presence on foodservice menus, especially in the fine dining restaurant segment. It is important to understand that, in nearly all cases, the buying and selling of wild game (animals or birds) for commercial foodservice use is strictly forbidden. Such prohibitions help ensure a safe food supply. Farm-raised game, however, may be sold. Before they may be sold, some game animals are inspected by the USDA and others by the FDA.

Game for use in foodservice is typically divided into two basic categories: furred game and winged game.

Furred Game

Furred game animals can be large or small. Large, furred game animals commonly included on restaurant menus include antelope, buffalo, beefalo (a cross between bison and beef cattle), caribou, deer, and wild boar. Small game animals include

---

Buyer's Guide to Purchasing Term

Game   Animals hunted for food or sport.

rabbit, although squirrel, beaver, muskrat, opossum, raccoon, and other animal species infrequently appear.

The meat on game animals is typically dark and may have a strong flavor, but in the hands of talented chefs and cooks, it can be extremely tasty. Because of potential health and safety issues, if you buy these products, you must be extremely careful to ensure that the supplier of the furred game operates legally and supplies you with only government-inspected products.

Winged Game

Like furred game, the sale of wild winged game birds in the United States is illegal. Winged game birds are, however, very popular menu items. As a result, the game bird industry in the United States annually raises millions of birds for sale to commercial foodservice operators and direct to consumers. The most popular of these are pheasant, partridge, and quail, but they also include grouse, guinea fowl, squab (young pigeon), and ostrich. Winged game is generally available whole or precut and may be purchased fresh or frozen.

Buyer's Guide to Internet Resources: Poultry and Game

Web Site	Topic
www.tyson.com	Information about chickens
www.perdue.com	Foodservice-specific poultry information
www.jennio.com	Information about turkey products
www.mapleleaffarms.com	Foodservice-specific information about ducks
www.shafferfarms.com	Venison (deer) products
www.beefalo.org	Information about beefalo (animals bred by crossing bison and cattle) products

SEAFOOD

Seafood is very popular. The average American consumes 16.5 pounds of seafood per year, up from less than 15 pounds in 2000. Shrimp is the top choice, representing almost a quarter of the seafood that Americans eat, and interestingly, most of America's seafood arrives from foreign shores. According to the National Fisheries Institute, a seafood trade organization, 75 to 80 percent of all seafood is imported. The term *seafood*, unfortunately for hospitality food buyers, can mean many different things to different foodservice suppliers. For some, it refers to only specific species of fish with shells (shellfish) or other small marine creatures. For other sellers, seafood refer to virtually all types of freshwater and saltwater fish as well as to shellfish, whether caught in the wild or farmed in much the same way as cattle or chickens.

Today more seafood of outstanding quality is available, and more widely, than ever before. As a buyer, you may select from among seafood that comes from all over the world, thus allowing you the opportunity to offer new ingredients and creative menu items. At the same time, the variety and variability of seafood will make it challenging for you because these items are more fragile and availability is often less predictable than most meat products.

Both fish and shellfish have become increasingly popular on foodservice menus in recent years in part because of the reputation of seafood as a good source of protein, B vitamins, various minerals, and in the case of coldwater ocean fish, high levels of desirable omega-3 fatty acids. These nutrients cannot be made very efficiently by the human body and are essential to the development and function of the brain (thus fish are sometimes referred to as "brain food") and to

FIGURE 7.9   Black Sea Bass
(a type of round fish)
Source: USDA
© Culinary Institute of America

the health of the body's central nervous system. Other documented benefits of omega-3 fatty acids include lowering the incident of heart disease, strokes, and the artery-damaging form of blood cholesterol.

In addition to consumer perceptions of health benefits, fish are increasingly available on foodservice menus because of the ways they are packaged and stored. Fish are more perishable than other meats, and in the past that limited their use on commercial foodservice menus. Today, however, improved packaging and processing techniques have resulted in ample availability of most high-quality seafood (both fish and shellfish) at all times of the year.

Fish

Fish include those animals found living in both fresh and salt water. Fish, by definition, have fins and an internal skeleton of bones and cartilage. The number of different kinds of fish in the world is stunning. Of all the animals with backbones, fish account for more than half, or about twenty-nine thousand different species. Not all of those species are eaten regularly, nor are they all available for purchase by foodservice buyers. Of those that are commonly served, fish can readily be divided into two groups, based primarily on their shape and skeletal structure.

Round fish swim in a vertical position and have eyes on both sides of their head (see, for example, the black sea bass in Figure 7.9). Round fish are most often purchased as boneless fillets (horizontal cuts). In the case of larger round fish (e.g., tuna and salmon), the fish may be purchased either as fillets or as steaks (vertical cuts).

Unlike round fish, flatfish have asymmetrical, compressed bodies, swim in a horizontal position, and have both eyes on the top of their heads (see, for example, the brill in Figure 7.10). Flatfish tend to live on the bottom of ocean waters around the world. Typically, the skin on the top of their bodies is dark (to hide them from

FIGURE 7.10   Brill (a type of flatfish)
Source: USDA
Roger Phillips © Dorling Kindersley

predators). Because of their body shape, these species are not generally available in steak form and are sold either whole or, more commonly, as fillets.

Flatfish do not start out life flat. The larvae look like most other fish. They are the same color on both sides and have one eye on each side of the head. As the flatfish grow, their color and pigmentation patterns change, and one eye migrates across the top of their heads to end up on the same side as the other eye. Some flatfish are left-eyed and some are right-eyed. This means that some flatfish have both eyes on the left side (left-eyed), and some have both eyes on the right side (right-eyed). Many flatfish are found on muddy bottoms in shallow waters. Some flatfish migrate in the winter to deeper waters. Most feed on worms and small water creatures.

Even when segmented into round fish and flatfish, identifying fish by sight and name can be hard because of the large number of fish that look similar but are a separate species within a fish family. In addition, confusion can easily result when various names are given to fish based on the locality in which the fish is either caught or eaten.

Historically, in comparison with most food products, seafood has been poorly labeled. In the case of meats, for example, buyers know about the animal species (e.g., turkey, cow, chicken) and cut of the meat. In addition, in most cases, it is common to get information about where the meat was produced or how it was grown (e.g., organic, free-range, or grain fed). In contrast, buyers often do not know exactly which species of seafood they purchase (e.g., more than one hundred fish species are currently and legally marketed as "snapper" and more than twenty can be legally marketed as "red snapper").

In some cases neither a fish product's specific national origin nor how it was harvested may be included on the label. Add to this fact the reality that, in most cases, fish purchased today will not be delivered in its fresh, whole, and somewhat easily identifiable state, but rather in refrigerated or frozen prefabricated steak or fillet forms, and it is easy to see why buying fish can be so challenging. The FDA does publish a list of approved market names for fish in the "Seafood List: FDA Guide to Acceptable Market Names for Food Fish Sold in Interstate Commerce" (www.cfsan.fda.gov/~frf/seaintro.html). The list is updated regularly. Supplier deviations from these approved names are discouraged but historically have been difficult to enforce.

While it is not mandatory that fish be graded for quality, there are certain types of fish that are perceived as higher in quality than others are. **Sashimi** is a general term to describe fish that is of such high quality, it may be eaten raw.

The important thing to remember about sashimi is that, in nearly all cases, the fish should be saltwater fish, not freshwater fish, because freshwater fish may contain parasites that are killed by cooking. Saltwater fish do not contain these same parasites. Sashimi may be produced from a variety of seafood species (fish and shellfish). Among the most popular sashimi grade seafood are tuna, red snapper, halibut, bonito, eel, scallop, and shrimp. Despite the challenges and complexity of knowing what seafood to buy and the quality that will be delivered, fish buyers can learn to better understand how to purchase round fish and flatfish.

PURCHASING FISH   A detailed description of the types and market forms of round fish readily available to foodservice operators would fill its own book. If you will be purchasing large amounts of fish, you should seek out the detailed fish species-specific information you need to best accomplish this task (see this section's "Buyer's Guide to Internet Resources: Seafood"). Figure 7.11 lists thirty of the varieties of round fish commonly used in foodservice operations.

Buyer's Guide to Purchasing Term

Sashimi   High-quality, thinly sliced fish (usually sliced thinly into pieces approximately 1 inch wide by 1½ inches long, by ¼ to ¹⁄₁₆ inch thick), which is intended to be eaten raw.

Atlantic cod	Herring	Sardine
Atlantic salmon	John Dory	Scrod
Bass	Mackerel	Shark
Black sea bass	Mahi-mahi	Silver salmon (coho)
Catfish	Monkfish	Swordfish
Chinook (king salmon)	Orange roughy	Tilapia
Cod	Pacific cod	Trout
Eel	Pollock	Tuna
Grouper	Red snapper	Wahoo
Haddock	Rockfish	Whitefish

FIGURE 7.11   Popular Round Fish

Fewer in number, flatfish are also extremely popular on many foodservice menus. Buyers of flatfish also know that these items are among the most complex to buy. It is easy to realize why when you understand that, for example, the FDA permits use of the term *sole* (a popular flatfish) to be applied to more than fifteen different varieties of fish. These include English sole, rock sole, sand sole, and petrale sole as well as yellowtail flounder, starry flounder, and fluke. In addition to flounder and sole (often one and the same, but named differently on the menu) other popular flatfish commonly sold in the foodservice industry include halibut and turbot.

Shellfish

Like fish, shellfish can be more easily studied if they are first divided into two major classifications: **mollusks** and **crustaceans.**

Did You Know? (7.3)

The quality of fish and shellfish vary much more than does the quality of other meats and poultry. As a result, the eating characteristics of many fish and shellfish change significantly from one season to the next because these animals live out two life cycles. During the first phase, they grow and mature, storing up energy reserves and reaching the peak of their flavor and quality. At this time, their taste will be at its absolute best.

A subsequent life phase, however, finds them expending their stored energy to migrate and create masses of eggs or sperm to ensure future generations. It is important to understand that most fish do not store energy reserves in layers of fat like land animals. Instead, the proteins stored in their meat muscles provide their energy reserves. When migrating and spawning, they accumulate protein-digesting enzymes in their muscles and, thus, retrieve their stored energy. Then and immediately afterward, their flesh will be soft and spongy.

Because different fish species have different life cycles and, even within the same species, will have life-cycle variations based on where on the globe they are harvested, it is often very difficult for buyers to know whether a given fish variety will, in fact, be at its peak of quality and taste. In such cases, and when it is not possible for the buyer to personally inspect each fish product before it is purchased, the quality and reputation of an operation's fresh fish supplier is the key to ensuring consistent product quality.

Buyer's Guide to Purchasing Terms

Mollusk   Shellfish with soft, unsegmented bodies and no internal skeleton. Examples include conch, clams, and oysters.

Crustacean   Shellfish with hard outer skeletons or shells and joints that separate the "head" from the "tail" (as in shrimp and lobster) or "leg" from the "body" (as with crabs).

Atlantic oyster (bluepoint)	European oyster	Pacific oyster
Blue mussel	Greenshell mussel	Quahog (Atlantic clam)
Cherrystone clam	Littleneck clam	Scallop
Chowder	Manila clam	Soft-shell clam
Cockle	Olympia	Surf clam

FIGURE 7.12   Popular Bivalve Mollusks

MOLLUSKS   To best understand their unique characteristics, mollusks can be further divided into those that are univalve, bivalve, or **cephalopods.**

Univalve mollusks include abalone, the brownish gray shelled species harvested off the coast of California (California law does not permit it to be canned or shipped out of state), and conch (found off the waters of the Florida Keys and the Caribbean). Snails, too, although these are actually univalve land animals, are often considered univalve mollusks.

Bivalve mollusks are characterized by two shell halves attached by a central hinge made of muscle. Widely served to guests in a variety of market forms, you will most often buy these items when they are still alive, and they will be delivered to you in that same state. Clams and oysters are the bivalve mollusks you are most likely to purchase and serve. Figure 7.12 lists fifteen of the most popular bivalve mollusk types.

Cephalopods include octopus and squid (*calamari* is their Italian name), and they may be purchased fresh or frozen in blocks. Although it is the second most widely consumed shellfish in the world, squid is still a relative newcomer to American seafood cuisine. Still, squid is definitely catching on. Since 1990 U.S. squid imports have soared from thirteen thousand metric tons to more than forty thousand. Many species of squid are popular as food in cuisines as diverse and separated as Japanese and Spanish. In the United States, cephalopods are most often served fried or stewed. They can be stuffed whole, cut into flat pieces, or sliced into rings. The arms, tentacles, and even the ink of these animals are edible (see Figure 7.13). Tender fleshed, these mollusks, like all others, must be wisely handled and carefully cooked if they are to be served safely and at the peak of their quality.

CRUSTACEANS   Crustaceans are found in both fresh and salt water. They have a hard outer shell and jointed appendages and breathe through gills. They are among the most popular and expensive of all seafood. Some species (e.g., lobster) are purchased alive. Also, they are sold in a variety of market forms and in various sizes or **counts.**

FIGURE 7.13   Squid (Calamari): A Cephalopod Mollusk

Clive Streeter © Dorling Kindersley

Buyer's Guide to Purchasing Terms

Cephalopods   Marine mollusks with distinct heads and well-developed eyes. They lack an outer shell of any type. Examples include squid and octopus.

Count (crustaceans)   When used to label crustaceans, this term refers to the number in a pound. For example, 40–50 count shrimp means that, on average, forty to fifty individual shrimp of that size will weigh sixteen ounces. In general, shrimp of a lower count (larger size) are more expensive to buy than are shrimp of higher counts (lower size).

Live shellfish such as clams, oysters, and mussels must be carefully inspected on delivery.

Nicole Duplaix/National Geographic Image Collection

Blue crab	Maine lobster	Spiny (rock) lobster
Crayfish (crawfish)	Prawn	Stone crab
Dungeness crab	Shrimp	Tiger shrimp
King crab	Slipper lobster	
Langoustines	Snow (spider) crab	

FIGURE 7.14 Popular Crustaceans

When buying shrimp (one of the most popular crustaceans), counts can range from two hundred to four hundred shrimp per pound (Titi) to eight per pound (extra-colossal). Figure 7.14 lists some of the most popular crustaceans normally available to foodservice buyers.

It is important for foodservice buyers to understand that, unlike meats, most fish and shellfish inspections are voluntary. The National Oceanic and Atmospheric

Buyers at Work (7.3)

"I have only five cases of these, but I wanted to give you first crack at buying them," said Terry, the sales rep for Boone's Fish Products. "At this price, they are going to go really fast!"

Boone's is the seafood supplier for the Down Under Steakhouse. Holly is the manager/buyer at Down Under, and she is discussing shrimp that Terry is attempting to sell to her.

Normally, Holly orders twenty-four-count shrimp for her shrimp kebabs and shrimp salad. Both dishes are extremely popular with her guests. Terry is proposing that Holly buy five cases of thirty-six-count shrimp.

"I can give you a great price on these five cases," said Terry.

"But the shrimp are smaller—thirty-six count—right?" replied Holly.

"Sure, but you can just tell your cooks to add another piece to your kebab and shrimp salad when you make those dishes," said Terry.

Assume you were Holly:

1. If you actually bought the five discounted cases of shrimp, how do you think your guests would react to smaller but more numerous shrimp on their kebabs and shrimp salads?
2. What difficulties with cooking times or other areas of preparation could possibly arise if you instructed your cooks to begin using the smaller shrimp products?
3. How does this mini case illustrate the wisdom of establishing product specifications for the important foods you normally buy from your suppliers?

Administration (NOAA) conducts the voluntary seafood inspection program on a fee-for-service basis. The program provides vessel and plant sanitation; product inspection, grading, and certification; label review; laboratory analysis; training; and consultative and information services. Participants may use official marks on complying products, which indicate that they have been federally inspected, although few choose to do so.

It is also important for you to understand that well more than half of the fish consumed in the United States comes from other countries, will likely be fabricated within hours of being caught, and would then be ice packed or frozen right on the fishing vessel. It is easy to understand why thorough and consistent inspection and grading of products caught in the remote waters of far-flung fishing beds would be very difficult to achieve.

PROFESSIONAL PURCHASING PREVENTS PROBLEMS (7.3)

"Imitation" and "Flavored" Seafood Products Must Be Identified for Guests

A common problem: Ensuring accuracy in menus and full guest disclosure.

Must a "crab salad" be made from crab? While it would seem so, in some restaurants, unfortunately, it is not always so. *Surimi* is the term used to describe a food product typically made from white-fleshed fish (such as pollock or hake) that has been pulverized to a paste and attains a rubbery texture when cooked. Surimi can be made to taste a lot like crab (and other seafood). Surimi is a much-enjoyed food product in many Asian cultures and is available in many shapes, forms, flavors, and textures. The most common Surimi product in the Western market is imitation (artificial) crabmeat and legs, and it is widely sold to foodservice buyers.

In late 2006 the FDA ruled that producers of surimi (processed to appear and taste like crab, lobster, and other types of seafood) can label their packages *crab-flavored seafood* (or whatever it is made to resemble) rather than *imitation*. The *imitation* label previously was mandated by the FDA but only a few restaurants openly admitted to use of the product even though surimi has become even more popular as its quality has increased. (*Note:* To learn more about how this versatile and increasingly popular foodservice product is made and used on foodservice menus, go to www.pacseafood.com/products.html).

Some foodservice buyers choose between serving real or imitation crab depending on the menu application. For recipes such as sashimi and seviche, which are meant to emphasize a product's natural taste, king or snow crab makes the best fit. However, cost-saving surimi works well for California rolls, in which the flavor difference is barely detectable among additional ingredients such as avocado, rice, soy sauce, and wasabi.

Regardless of the purchase choice you make, guests always deserve to know what they are eating. It is never all right to misrepresent a menu item or ingredient. For example, "maple flavored" syrup is not maple syrup, nor is "crab flavored" seafood really crab. If an item is flavored or imitation, it should always be labeled as such on the menu. Knowledgeable purchasers understand well that accuracy in menu labeling is a matter of buyer integrity and professional responsibility.

RECEIVING AND STORAGE

Because of their high levels of fat and protein, all of the products examined in this chapter are exceedingly perishable. (Great care must be taken when receiving these products to help ensure that they are at their peak of quality at the time of arrival). Appropriate storage is also important to ensure that they maintain the highest possible quality levels.

In their fresh forms, meats, poultry, game, and seafood should be delivered to a foodservice operation at an acceptable temperature and in appropriate packaging. For most fresh items, a delivery temperature between 30°F and 34°F (−1°C

Buyer's Guide to Internet Resources: Seafood

Web Site	Topic
www.aboutseafood.com	Information from the National Fisheries Institute
www.cfsan.fda.gov/seafood1.html	Seafood-related general information from the FDA
www-seafood.ucdavis.edu/	Seafood safety information
www.pacseafood.com	Seafood cooking information
www.charlestonseafood.com/SeafoodNutrition.htm	Information about the nutritional aspects of seafood
www.shellfish.com	Resources and information about shellfish
www.alaskaseafood.org	Information about Alaskan seafood
www.floridaaquaculture.com/processing/handleintro.htm	Shellfish handling
www.landbigfish.com	500+ fish recipes
www.cookinglobster.com	Information on lobster and lobster cooking

to 1°C) is appropriate. Frozen foods should arrive at temperatures at or below 0°F. The use of thermometers to check the arriving temperatures of these foods is essential.

When products such as meats and poultry are delivered in vacuum-packed plastic, check the temperature by placing a thermometer between two packages (bags) making contact with the product inside. The thermometer should read 32°F (plus or minus one degree.) Fresh poultry and seafood that are delivered on ice should be received in clean, solid (not wet-soaked) containers. These products should be encased in crushed ice that shows no evidence of significant melting.

Fresh seafood products create special concerns for those receiving them. The FDA requires shellfish harvesters and processors of oysters, clams, and mussels put a tag on sacks or containers of live shellfish (in the shell) and a label on containers or packages of shucked shellfish. These tags and labels contain specific information about the product, including a certification number for the processor, which means that the shellfish were harvested and processed in accordance with national shellfish safety controls. When receiving items of this type, you should ensure that receiving personnel do the following:

- Discard cracked/broken shellfish—Throw away clams, oysters, and mussels if their shells are cracked or broken.
- Do a **tap test**—Live clams, oysters, and mussels will close up when the shell is tapped. If they do not close when tapped, they are dead and should not be accepted.
- Check for leg movement—Live crabs and lobsters should show some leg movement. These items spoil rapidly after death, so only live crabs and lobsters should be accepted.

Buyer's Guide to Purchasing Term

Tap test   A procedure used to check the delivery status of certain shellfish. When lightly tapped by hand or kitchen tool, live shellfish shells should close. If they do not, the animal inside is likely dead and should not be accepted or served.

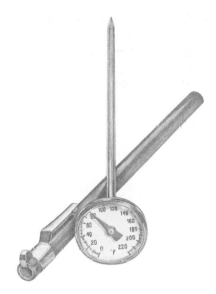

Quality tools for ensuring the proper temperatures of meats, poultry, game, and seafood on delivery are critical for receiving personnel.
Pearson Education/PH College

Delivery temperatures are especially important when buying seafood because, in some species, if the catch has been left out in the sun for too long or if the fish have not been transported under proper refrigeration, toxins known as scombrotoxins can develop. Serving fish with high levels of this toxin can result in food-borne illness in those who consume the items.

Storage

When possible, the storage area for meat, poultry, game, and seafood should be in close proximity to the area in which the product will be used. This reduces unnecessary time lost in transporting the items to remote storage areas to store or secure needed products. When a storage area is well located, properly labeled, kept clean, and monitored regularly, product quality can more easily be maintained.

Meat, poultry, game, and seafood received should be immediately placed in proper storage areas. For meats, poultry, and game, refrigerator temperatures of 41°F (5°C) and lower are best, as are freezer temperatures of 0°F (−17°C) or lower. Refrigerated and frozen seafood products may be held at these same refrigerator and freezer temperatures or, in the case of some crustaceans, in a regularly cleaned saltwater tank.

Properly wrapped meat cuts, frozen at 0°F (−17°C) or lower, will maintain their quality for several months. This varies, however, with the kind of meat. Figure 7.15 shows a range within which you can store meat with reasonable expectation that it will maintain its quality. Meats can be kept safely frozen for longer periods than indicated, but they will suffer quality decline.

Raw poultry may safely be kept in a refrigerator (40°F/4°C) for one to two days. Frozen poultry held in a freezer (0°F/−17°C) can be thawed then cooked

Product	Freezer (0°F/−17°C)	Refrigerator (40°F/4°C)
Beef, roasts and steaks	6–12 months	3–5 days
Lamb, roasts and chops	6–9 months	3–5 days
Pork, roasts and chops	4–6 months	3–5 days
Beef and lamb, ground	3–4 months	1–2 days
Pork, ground	1–2 months	1–2 days

FIGURE 7.15 Suggested Storage Times for Fresh Meats
Source: USDA

promptly after thawing. Thaw frozen poultry or parts in the refrigerator or in cold water, changing the water every thirty minutes. Cooked poultry may be kept in the refrigerator but should be used within two to three days or discarded.

Seafood products that have been received on ice (or refrigerated) can be safely stored using the following guidelines:

- If the seafood will be used within one to two days after purchase, store it in the refrigerator.
- If the seafood will not be used within two days after purchase, wrap it tightly in moisture-proof freezer paper or foil to protect it from air and store it in the freezer.
- Always thaw fish and seafood in the refrigerator. Thawing at temperatures higher than 40°F (4°C) causes excessive drip loss and adversely affects taste, texture, aroma, and appearance.

Purchasing Terms

Meat *168*	Steer *171*	Cured *177*	Magret *187*
Center of the plate *168*	Primal cuts *171*	Brined *178*	Game *188*
Quality grade *169*	Fabricated cuts *171*	Mutton *180*	Sashimi *191*
Yield grade *169*	Collagen *171*	Frenching (chops) *181*	Mollusk *192*
IMPS *169*	Corned beef *172*	Charcuterie *182*	Crustacean *192*
NAMP *169*	Box beef *173*	Forcemeat *182*	Cephalopods *193*
Wet aged (meats) *170*	IQF *173*	Giblets *183*	Count (crustaceans) *193*
Dry aged (meats) *170*	Maillard reaction *175*	Self-basted *187*	Tap test *196*
Boil-in-bag *170*	Myoglobin *177*	Dressed *187*	

Make Your Own Purchasing Decisions

1. Increasing labor costs and lack of skilled kitchen personnel have resulted in many foodservice buyers choosing to purchase prefabricated beef steaks and other meats (such as poultry breasts) to ensure quality and consistency. As a foodservice buyer, what unique quality assurance challenges will you face if you choose to purchase such products? How important will be your relationship with your meat supplier to effectively meet these challenges?

2. Like beef, pork is inspected by the USDA for wholesomeness and graded for yield. Under USDA regulations, however, pork (unlike beef) is not quality graded (it is graded only as Acceptable or Unacceptable). Identify two specific challenges facing foodservice buyers that directly result from the decision by the USDA to not establish varying acceptable quality levels for this item.

3. Some animal-rights advocates oppose, on moral or ethical grounds, the serving of certain types of dishes made with some types of goose livers. Others, for similar reasons, oppose the serving of veal.

How would you respond to guests such as those who may question your operation's use of these (or other) controversial menu item ingredients?

4. The quality of some imported seafood has increasingly become suspect with news reports of U.S. government inspectors rejecting large amounts of seafood products from some countries. Identify three specific steps you could take to help make certain that those for whom you buy fish and shellfish are protected, to the greatest degree possible, from inferior or potentially dangerous imported seafood products.

5. Many varieties of fish and shellfish have been overfished to the point that they are in real danger of being completely exhausted for commercial use (see, for example, the list found at www.fishonline.org/advice/avoid). Assume your guests' demand for such products remains strong and that these items are currently available for purchase from your supplier. What specific responsibility, if any, do you believe you have regarding the purchase and serving of such overfished species?

8

Produce, Dairy, and Eggs

Purchasing Pros Need to Know!

If you are like most food buyers, you will quickly realize that purchasing produce, dairy, and egg products is second in importance to only meats and seafood. In fact, in some foodservice operations, these items are featured even more than meats and seafood. The variety of produce, dairy, and egg products and the skill required to properly select them, however, often make their purchase even more challenging than center-of-the-plate items. In this chapter you will learn what you need to know to become an effective buyer of these versatile items.

Properly selecting produce, dairy, and egg products becomes even more important when you recognize the growing number of vegetarians who eat no meat or seafood of any kind. Even more people, for religious, ethical, sociocultural, or other reasons, reduce or eliminate animal products in their diets. In fact, for many, increased consumption of fruits and vegetables simply reflects how tasty they are. As a result, fruits and vegetables, in their vast number of colors, flavors, textures, nutritional contents, and market forms, comprise the majority of healthy protein and caloric intake for many individuals.

Most people enjoy eating foods in the fruits and vegetables (produce) categories examined in this chapter. This includes many items that, until recently, were not always available at all times but, because of advancements in growing, processing, and shipping, can now be purchased and served year-round.

In addition to produce, foodservice buyers purchase significant amounts of milk and the many products made from milk. These popular items include butter, yogurt, sour cream, ice cream, and cheese, each of which is sold in a wide variety of styles and market forms. This chapter will help you recognize the key factors you must know to buy these items effectively.

In addition to buying produce and dairy products, in most operations it is likely that you will also purchase large quantities of fresh or processed eggs. As a result, information about these critical foods is included in this chapter. This information is essential for you to know because eggs, while popular when served by themselves, are also a key ingredient in most baked goods as well as in numerous other menu items you will likely serve to your guests.

■ ■ ■

Outline

Produce
    Fruits
        Fresh Fruits
            Berries
            Citrus
            Exotics
            Grapes
            Melons
            Pomes
            Pit Fruits
            Tropicals

PRODUCE

Produce is the broad term generally used to describe fruits and vegetables. While most often reserved for foods that are fresh (those that have not been canned, frozen, or dried), the term can be used to describe fruits and vegetables in all of their many market forms. Tasty and nutritious when fresh, but of poor quality and nutritive value when they are past their peak, the purchasing of produce items can be a real challenge for you, but it is one you can master.

Biologists most often use the term **fruit** to refer to produce that develops from the ovary of a flowering plant and, therefore, contains one or more seeds. Thus, apples, oranges, pears, and grapes easily come to mind when fruits are considered. From a plant biology standpoint, however, tomatoes, eggplant, and some other items are classified as fruits. In the foodservice industry, however, most buyers would consider items such as these to be vegetables. In fact, regardless of their true botanical nature, in the hospitality industry, those produce items that taste sweet are generally referred to as fruits, while those that are not sweet are typically referred to as vegetables.

Buyer's Guide to Purchasing Terms

Produce   Agricultural products, especially fresh fruits and vegetables, grown for human consumption.

Fruit   The reproductive organ of a flowering plant. All species of flowering plants produce seeds (fruits) for reproduction.

Properly purchased and prepared fresh fruit and vegetables are healthful and fun to eat.

Slater King © Dorling Kindersley

Figure 8.1 lists the ten most popular fruits you are most likely to buy for foodservice use.

You should note that Figure 8.1 does not include lemons (a true fruit and one that is very frequently purchased for foodservice use), nor does it contain tomatoes or eggplants (also fruits). For many, but not all, foodservice buyers, lemons would be considered a vegetable, as would tomatoes and eggplants. Technically, however, the term **vegetable** refers to any herbaceous (nonwoody) plant that is commonly consumed for food.

Actually, the question of whether a specific produce item you will buy is a fruit or a vegetable will be less important to you as a foodservice professional than will the quality factors you must know to properly select the item. Examined strictly from a culinary perspective, the items listed in Figure 8.2 are generally considered vegetables and are the ones you are most likely to buy for use in foodservice.

Cooks as well as professional buyers know that vegetables typically contain less sugar and more starch than fruits. In most cases this means that vegetables taste best when carefully cooked and served at their peak of quality. Other vegetables (e.g., leafy greens, carrots, and celery) are very popular when eaten raw. Served cooked or raw, fruits and vegetables will likely make up a sizable portion of your food budget, so learning to choose these items properly can have a big effect on your operation's profitability as well as on its reputation with your customers.

FIGURE 8.1   Ten Most Popular Fruits for Foodservice Use

```
Banana
Strawberry
Orange
Watermelon (and other melons)
Cherry
Apple
Grape
Pineapple
Peach
Mango
```

Buyer's Guide to Purchasing Term

Vegetable   Any herbaceous (nonwoody) plant that can be wholly or partially eaten, including the leaves, stems, roots, tubers, seeds, or flowers.

Artichoke	Chicory	Lettuce	Rhubarb
Asparagus	Collards	Mushroom	Rutabaga
Bean	Corn	Okra	Shallot
Beet	Cress	Onion	Spinach
Broccoli	Cucumber	Parsnip	Squash
Brussels sprout	Eggplant	Pea	Sweet corn
Cabbage	Gourd	Pepper	Sweet potato
Carrot	Kale	Potato	Tomato
Cauliflower	Kohlrabi	Pumpkin	Turnip
Celery	Leek	Radicchio	Watercress
Chard	Lemon	Radish	Yam

FIGURE 8.2 A Foodservice Buyer's List of Most Popular "Vegetables"

Did You Know? (8.1)

For most produce buyers, the first step in becoming knowledgeable about produce standards and quality is obtaining *The Fresh Produce Manual*, published by the Produce Marketing Association (PMA).

Founded in 1949, PMA is a not-for-profit global trade association serving more than twenty-one hundred members who market fresh fruits, vegetables, and related products worldwide. Its members are involved in the production, distribution, retail, and foodservice sectors of the industry. PMA offers its members a wide variety of services, including the publication of many materials related to fresh produce quality and standards.

To learn about PMA and what it does for members, go to www.pma.com. To read about current fresh-produce data, you can go to www.producenews.com, publisher of *The Produce News*. As is true with many other food items, the USDA is also a good source of information www.usda.gov.

If you are responsible for buying a significant amount of produce, you may want to subscribe to a service that tracks product prices on a daily basis and provides historical data on produce prices. To view (and sample free for seven days) one such price-related site, go to www.todaymarket.com.

Fruits

Fruits are popular, in large part, because of their naturally occurring sugars. Sweet to the taste when at their peak of flavor, purchasing fruits can be especially challenging for you because fruits may have different names in different regions of the world or country (e.g., in the southern United States, the eggplant is commonly known as a guinea squash). Also, suppliers sometimes create names for fruits that they feel best describe the specific item they are selling. In fact, suppliers face their own challenges when selling fruits because no other food group offers a greater variety of colors, flavors, and textures than fruit. For convenience in learning about fruits, it is helpful to classify them as either fresh or processed items.

FRESH FRUITS Top-quality fresh fruits are tasty and nutritious. The quality of fresh fruit is initially judged by its outside appearance, and the USDA has established grade standards for most fresh fruits. Fruit grades are used as a basis for trading among growers, shippers, wholesalers, and retailers; however, they are used to only a limited extent in sales between wholesalers and restaurateurs because the use of USDA grade standards is generally voluntary. If, however, a container of fruit is actually marked with a grade, the packer must ensure that the contents conform to the official grade requirements of that marked grade.

As a foodservice buyer, you will most likely encounter USDA fresh fruit grades when you purchase apples or pears, but some other fruits occasionally

U.S. Fancy: Fancy means premium quality. Only the very best (a small percentage) of fruits achieve this grade.

U.S. No. 1: U.S. No. 1 means good quality and is the most commonly used grade for most fruits.

U.S. No. 2 and U.S. No. 3: U.S. No. 2 is noticeably superior to U.S. No. 3, which is the lowest grade practical to pack under normal commercial conditions.

FIGURE 8.3 USDA Fruit Grades
Source: USDA

carry grade designations. Figure 8.3 details the primary fresh fruit grades used by the USDA (grades for some specific fruits may vary slightly).

Fresh fruits are those that have not been subjected to any processing such as canning, freezing, or drying. Increasingly, consumers prefer **organic** fruits, and these are frequently available for use in foodservice operations, although buyers will pay a significant premium when choosing organic fruits.

In many cases fresh fruits can be purchased **ripe** or preripened (also known as unripened). Specific fresh fruit groups and their important characteristics can be examined in a variety of ways. One good way is to divide them into the following broad subcategories:

Berries   In a culinary sense, a berry is any small, edible fruit with multiple seeds. Berries do not ripen after they are picked, so they must be purchased fully ripened. These items will deteriorate rather quickly, even when stored properly, so it is essential that they be purchased ripe (but not overripe). Common berry varieties include blackberries, blueberries (also known as huckleberries), boysenberries, cranberries, currants, raspberries, and strawberries. Berries are a good source of vitamin C, but they generally must be used within one to three days of their purchase.

Citrus   Citrus fruits grow primarily in warm climates and are characterized by their thick rind coverings. Citrus fruits are acidic and a good source of vitamin C, and their flavors range from bitter to tart to sweet. Popular varieties include oranges, blood oranges (containing a red, not orange, pulp), grapefruits, lemons, limes, kumquats, tangelos, and tangerines.

Fresh citrus fruits are typically peeled before serving, and they can be easily split into segments. Orange and grapefruit pieces are frequently served alone or used in recipes, but their juices are also extremely popular as breakfast drinks. The juices of lemons and limes are used to flavor water and drinks as well, and these two fruits are often used as garnishes.

The rind of fresh citrus fruits (also known as the skin or zest), oils, juice, and pulp are all commonly used in the commercial kitchen. These fruits hold up well when properly stored but typically should be served within one week of their purchase.

Exotics   Exotic fruits come from a variety of locales. Many are available year-round and include gooseberries, guava, lychees, persimmons, pomegranates, prickly pears, rhubarb, and star fruits. These less common fruits most often find their way onto menus for use as garnishes and because of their unique flavors.

Buyer's Guide to Purchasing Terms

Organic   Food grown without artificial chemical pesticides.

Ripe   Mature and complete growth or development, beyond which decay will begin.

Trees bearing these citrus fruits and others like them require warm temperatures for growth and can be heavily damaged by freezing temperatures.

© Dorling Kindersley

Grapes   Technically a berry, grapes are the single largest fruit crop in the world, due in great part to their popularity in wine making. Table grapes (those grown for eating) include the Concord, a Native American variety used primarily for cooking, and the Thompson.

William Thompson was born in England and immigrated to the United States in 1863. He grafted three vine cuttings of a grape variety called Lady de Coverly to existing California grapevines. Over a four-year period, the grapes he produced were named Thompson seedless. Today the Thompson seedless grape is the most popular table grape sold for use in foodservice. The Thompson is also used for juice as well as wine making and accounts for 95 percent of the raisins produced in California. Thompson seedless–type grapes are white.

Flame grapes are a seedless blend of the Thompson, cardinal, and a few other varieties. They have grown rapidly in popularity to become the second most popular table grape after the Thompson seedless.

Grapes of all types keep well when properly stored and can easily last up to one week under refrigeration if overripe grapes are continually removed from the storage container.

Melons   Most people don't know that melons are in the same gourd family as squashes and cucumbers. Many melons originated in the Middle East and gradually spread their popularity across Europe. Melon seeds were transported to the United States by Columbus and eventually cultivated by Spanish explorers in California. Most are eaten without cooking, and their juices are also popular. Common types include cantaloupe, casaba, Crenshaw, honeydew, and watermelon.

Pomes   A pome, named for the French word for apple *(pomme)*, is a type of fruit that comes from a flowering tree. Pomes have thin skins and firm flesh. Within this family of fruits are apples of all types, pears, and quinces. The foodservice use of apples is extremely wide spread. The flesh of most pomes is eaten raw. Apples and pears are popular when cooked and can be served in a variety of baked items, desserts, and sauces.

In pomes such as pears, quinces, late apples, persimmons, and European pears, ripening takes place largely or entirely after they have been harvested, and these fruits soften after they have been picked. Some may change skin color. In properly controlled storage, pomes keep very well. In many varieties storage lives of several weeks are easily attainable.

Pit Fruits   These fruits are characterized by thin skins, soft flesh, and a woody pit (or stone) in the center of the fruit. Apricots, cherries, peaches, nectarines, and plums

Did You Know? (8.2)

In 2002 the USDA's National Organic Program (NOP) standards for food labeled *organic* went into effect. This standard applies to food grown in the United States or imported from other countries.

The NOP standards provide a national definition for the term *organic,* providing clear and consistent labeling requirements for use of the word. Before a product can be labeled *organic,* a USDA-approved certifier inspects the farm where the food is grown to make sure the farmer is following all the rules necessary to meet USDA organic standards.

For single-ingredient foods such as produce, a small sticker with the USDA Organic seal identifies foods that are 100 percent organic. For foods with more than one ingredient, there are four labeling categories:

1. *100% Organic*—Must be just that—100 percent organic ingredients
2. *Organic*—With the USDA seal must contain 95 percent organic ingredients by weight
3. *Made with Organic Ingredients*—Must contain 70 percent organic ingredients by weight
4. Products with less than 70 percent organic ingredients may not make any organic claims on the front of the package but may do so on the side of the package

It is important to note that the term *natural* does not mean organic. Neither do other truthful claims such as free-range and hormone-free. Only food that has been certified as meeting USDA organic standards may carry the USDA's Organic label (shown here).

How would you know about these new definitions and stay up to date with the latest information? It's easy. Visit the USDA Web page regularly. You can access it at www.usda.gov.

---

are popular varieties eaten raw or used for cooking. Storage lives of fresh pit fruits are relatively short, thus they should be purchased and used within days of delivery.

Tropicals   Tropical fruits are native to the world's hot tropical and subtropical regions. All can be eaten fresh, without cooking. Popular tropicals, most of which are now available year-round, include bananas, dates, kiwis (also known as the Chinese gooseberry), mangoes, papayas, passion fruits, and pineapples.

PROCESSED FRUITS   Because the storage lives of fresh fruits are often short, market forms often involve processing. Fruit suppliers process fruits for a variety of reasons, including reduced shipping costs, increased shelf life, improved utility, and product enhancement. Fresh fruits may be processed in many ways. In some cases the fruits are simply cleaned, trimmed, and packaged in bags, jars, or other containers. In other cases the foods are highly processed to enhance their form or useful life.

The most popular means of preserving fruits include the following:

Irradiation   Some fruits (as well as many vegetables and meats) can be subject to ionizing radiation to destroy parasites, insects, and bacteria. This treatment is classified as **irradiation** and is considered by the FDA as a food additive. Similar in many aspects to cooking foods with a microwave, irradiation also slows the ripening of the fruits treated.

Buyer's Guide to Purchasing Term

Irradiation   The use of X-rays for the purpose of preserving foods.

Irradiated fruits are generally purchased, stored, and used like any other fresh fruit.

Canning Many fruits are canned (or jarred). Pineapple and peaches are among the most popular. In **solid pack** canning, little or no water is added to the fruits before they are sealed in the cans and heated. **Water pack** canning is accomplished by first adding water or fruit juice to the products. **Syrup packing** involves the addition of various amounts of sugar and water to the foods prior to packing. In most cases the highest graded fruits are packed in higher sugar density (higher **Brix** level) syrups.

Freezing Freezing is a highly effective method for preserving fruits, even though the process negatively affects the texture of many fruits because freezing often damages the product's cell walls. The process does not, however, have a negative effect on the nutritive value of fruits. Many fruits are sold individually quick frozen (IQF), while others are sold as **purees.**

Drying Drying is one of the oldest known methods of preserving fruits. As fruits lose their moisture content, their flavor intensifies, there is a concentration of sugar content, and their storage lives are extended. Unlike dried beans and legumes, dried fruits are processed in a manner that results in products with 16–26 percent moisture. The result is fruits that are moist and soft. Raisins, prunes, apricots, and figs are among the most popular of the dried fruits.

Buyer's Guide to Internet Resources: Fruits

Web Site	Topic
www.thefruitpages.com	Information about fresh and processed fruit
www.ultimatecitrus.com	Information from the Florida Citrus Growers
www.fpfc.org	Fruits, vegetables, and floral products association
www.unitedfresh.org	Fresh produce
www.chiquitafi.com	Tropical fruits

Vegetables

The term *vegetable*, as commonly used, can include almost any nonwoody plant with edible parts used for food. A definition this broad, however, also includes fruits, nuts, and cereals, products that are not usually considered vegetables by foodservice buyers or by those guests for whom they buy.

Buyer's Guide to Purchasing Terms

Solid pack (canning) Canning foods with little or no water added.

Water pack (canning) Canning foods after the addition of water or juice.

Syrup pack (canning) Canning foods to which light, medium, or heavy sugar syrups have been added.

Brix A measurement of the ratio of dissolved sugar to water in a liquid. A 30 Brix (°Bx) solution contains 30 grams of sugar per 100 grams of solution. Put another way, there are 30 grams of sugar and 70 grams of water in the 100 grams of solution.

Puree Food prepared by cooking and straining or processed in a blender.

> **U.S. Fancy:** U.S. Fancy vegetables are of more uniform shape and have fewer defects than U.S. No. 1.
>
> **U.S. No. 1:** Vegetables of this grade should be tender, appear fresh, have good color, and be relatively free from bruises and decay.
>
> **U.S. No. 2 and No. 3:** While U.S. No. 2 and No. 3 have lower quality requirements than Fancy or No. 1, all grades are nutritious. The differences are mainly in appearance, amount of waste, and buyer preference.

FIGURE 8.4 USDA Fresh Vegetable Grades

A vegetable, as a culinary term, has come to mean those plants and plant parts eaten raw or cooked and served with a main meal. Using this definition, rice and sweet corn are examples of cereals that, while they are not vegetables in a botanical sense, are considered vegetables by most diners. Originating from almost any part of a plant, a vegetable can be a leaf (e.g., cabbage, lettuce, spinach), a seed (e.g., beans, lentils, peas), a root (e.g., beet, carrot, potato), a bulb (e.g., garlic, leek, onion), a flower (e.g., cauliflower, broccoli, artichoke), a fruit (e.g., cucumber, pepper, squash), or a stem (e.g., asparagus, celery, kohlrabi).

Vegetables are an important component of most menus. They add color, texture, flavor, and variety to appetizers, salads, and entrées and are often used as side dishes to accompany main courses.

The USDA has established grade standards for most fresh vegetables. Use of the grading standards is generally voluntary, but some state laws and federal marketing programs require grading of certain vegetables. If a package of vegetables does list a grade, the packer is legally obligated to verify that the contents meet the grade standards. Grade designations are most often seen on packages of potatoes and onions, but other vegetables occasionally carry a grade name. Figure 8.4 lists the USDA grades that have been established for fresh vegetables.

FRESH VEGETABLES There are few hard and fast rules for selecting fresh vegetables because each type has its own quality characteristics. The following are some broad guidelines for many of the most popular vegetables.

Artichokes The globe artichoke is the large, unopened flower of a plant belonging to the thistle family. The leaflike parts that make up the bud are actually the flower's petals. Size is not important with respect to quality. Poor-quality artichokes have large areas of brown on the petals and/or spreading petals (a sign of age that indicates drying and toughening of the edible portions).

Asparagus Asparagus, either green or white, is a member of the lily family, which also includes onions, leeks, and garlic. The edible portion of this plant is called a spear. Buy round spears with closed, compact tips and a fresh appearance. When green, a rich, dark green color should cover most of the spear. Reject spears with tips that are open and spread out, moldy, or decayed.

Beans The word *bean*, like the word *vegetable*, has an imprecise meaning. It is used to refer to the seeds of many different kinds of plants. Beans are widely used in quantity foodservice operations in one or more of their many forms. These include French beans, snap beans (string, stringless, and wax), bush beans, pole beans, and kidney beans just to name a few. Beans can be purchased in their fresh state or, in many cases, dried. Common dry types include pinto, navy, great northern, red kidney, and pink beans.

When buying fresh beans, look for a clean, bright appearance with good color for the variety of bean being selected. Reject wilted or flabby bean pods and those with serious blemishes or decay.

Beets Fresh beets are available year-round. Their color and flavor are unique, and they are popular in salads, as a base for soups, and as a side vegetable.

Buy beets that are firm, round, have a deep red color, and are smooth over most of the surface.

Broccoli   Broccoli is a popular member of the cabbage family and a close relative of cauliflower. Buy broccoli that is firm with a compact cluster of small flower buds (none of which should be open or showing a yellow color, which indicates excessive age). Also, reject broccoli with soft, slippery, and water-soaked spots on the bud cluster.

Cabbage   Cabbage is one of the most popular vegetables in the world. Essentially, there are three types: (1) smooth-leaved green cabbage, (2) crinkly leaved green (Savoy) cabbage, and (3) red cabbage. All types are suitable for many uses, although the Savoy and red varieties are more in demand for use in slaw and salads than in cooked dishes. Buy cabbage with firm, hard heads that are heavy for their size. Avoid cabbage with badly discolored, dried, or decayed outer leaves.

Carrots   Carrots are grown throughout the world in a variety of colors and in a wide variety of sizes. The type of carrot most often purchased in the United States is the Mediterranean. Freshly harvested carrots are available year-round. Buy fresh carrots that are well formed, smooth, and firm. If the tops are attached, they should be fresh and of a good, green color. Reject carrots with large, green, sunburned areas at the top (which must be trimmed) and roots that are flabby from wilting.

Cauliflower   A popular member of the cabbage family, cauliflower is believed to have originated in the Mediterranean regions. In addition to white cauliflower, green and purple types are also available. The white, edible portion is called the curd, and the heavy, outer leaf covering is called the jacket leaves. Buy cauliflower with a creamy-white color and compact, solid, clean curds. Reject cauliflower that has a spreading curd or that has dark spots on the curd, as these indicate excessive age.

Celery   Celery is popular for a variety of uses and is available throughout the year. Most celery is of the Pascal type, which includes thick-branched, green varieties. Fresh celery should have a solid, rigid feel, and the leaf tips (if any) should be fresh or only slightly wilted. Reject wilted celery and that with flabby upper branches or leaf stems.

Chicory, Endive, Escarole (and Other Greens)   These vegetables, used mainly in salads, are available practically year-round. The shape, texture, color, and flavor of each make them interesting for mixing with more traditional lettuce in salads. Actually, a large number of widely differing species of plants are grown for use as greens. The better-known kinds are spinach, kale, collard, turnip, beet, chard, mustard, broccoli leaves, chicory, endive, escarole, dandelion, cress, and sorrel. Buy fresh greens that are crisp and tender and have a good, green color. Reject wilted and yellowing plants or those with insect injury.

Corn   Worldwide, only wheat and rice are cultivated in greater quantities than corn. Much is used for cattle feed, but sweet corn is grown for human consumption. Fresh sweet corn is available in frozen form every month of the year, but in the United States, fresh sweet corn is most plentiful from early May until mid-September.

Cucumbers   Cucumbers can be purchased with or without seeds. Buy those with a good, green color that are firm over their entire length but not too large in diameter. Reject overgrown cucumbers that are too large in diameter, that are flabby, and/or that have evidence of spotty soft parts.

Lettuce   Lettuce is popular in salads. Four types of lettuce are generally available year-round: (1) iceberg (the most common), (2) butterhead, (3) romaine, and (4) leaf.

Iceberg lettuce is 90 percent water and has very little flavor. Therefore, the best-tasting salads are made with a combination of iceberg and other lettuce types and/or a mixture of one or more greens. Butterhead lettuce, including the big

Boston and Bibb varieties, has a smaller head than iceberg. This type will have soft, light green leaves in a rosette pattern in the center. Romaine lettuce plants are tall and cylindrical with crisp, dark green leaves. It is used to make the classic Caesar salad. Leaf lettuce includes many varieties—none with a compact head.

When buying fresh lettuces, look for good, bright color (in most varieties this means a medium to light green). Some varieties have red leaves. Slight discoloration of the outer, or wrapper, leaves will usually not hurt the quality of the lettuce, but serious discoloration or decay should be avoided because of the negative effect on the total yield of consumer-acceptable, visually appealing salad products.

Mushrooms   Mushrooms are naturally fat free and are popular by themselves and when prepared in a variety of ways. There are more than forty thousand known varieties. In the United States, the most common is the moonlight (button mushroom). Other popular mushrooms include portabello, porcini, and shitake.

Onions (Dry)   The many varieties of onions grown commercially fall into three general classes distinguished by color: yellow, white, and red. Yellow onions make up 88 percent of those grown (5 percent are white; 7 percent are red). Onions range in size from less than one inch in diameter (creamers/boilers) to more than four and a half inches in diameter (super colossal). The most common sizes of onions sold in the United States are the medium (2 to 3¼ inches in diameter) and the jumbo (3 to 3¾ inches in diameter). Onions should be hard, dry, and have small necks. Reject those that are wet, soft, or affected by decay.

Onions (Green), Shallots, and Leeks   Green onions, shallots, and leeks are similar in appearance but somewhat different in size and flavor. Scallions are a type of onion, and the term is often used when referring to green onions or shallots. Shallots are an onionlike plant that produces small bulbs and edible shoots. Leeks are larger than green onions but share the characteristic of large, green, edible shoots. Green onions are simply ordinary onions harvested very young. They have very little or no bulb formation, and their tops are tubular.

Peppers (Green)   Most of the green peppers used in the foodservice industry are considered sweet or bell peppers. While the taste of these vegetables is not actually sweet, the term is used to distinguish them from hot peppers. The best green peppers (as well as those with other colors) have a deep, characteristic color; glossy sheen; relatively heavy weight; and firm walls or sides.

Potatoes   Incan Indians in Peru were the first to cultivate potatoes, more than two thousand years ago. For practical purposes, most potatoes are of three types: russet, round white, and round red. Russets (sometimes called bakers) are the most popular type in the United States. Round white potatoes are used most often in the Eastern United States. Round red (redskin) potatoes are sometimes called new potatoes; however, technically, *new* refers to any variety of potato that is harvested before reaching maturity.

Squash   The squash varieties most used in restaurants are generally either a summer or a winter variety. The varieties of summer squash available include crookneck, straightneck, and zucchini. Winter squash includes the small-sized acorn (available year-round) and the butternut, buttercup, and Hubbard varieties. Reject squash with cuts, punctures, sunken spots, or moldy spots on the rind.

Sweet Potatoes   The sweet potato is not actually a potato (tuber) at all. It is a root, which is a member of the morning glory family. They are a Native American plant. Sweet potatoes are often confused with yams. However, yams are large, starchy roots grown primarily in Africa and Asia. Yams are rarely available in the United States; however, the term *yam* is commonly used. Two types of sweet potatoes are available in varying amounts year-round. Moist sweet potatoes are the most common. They have orange-colored flesh and are very sweet. Dry sweet potatoes have pale-colored flesh and are low in moisture.

Buyers at Work (8.1)

"This looks pretty bad," said Chef Alton as he carefully examined a head of iceberg lettuce taken from the twenty-four-head case that he was being shown by his receiving clerk.

"The whole case looks like that," said Shingi, the chef's receiving clerk.

Later, when Chef Alton called his produce sales representative, he found out why.

"I know it looks kind of 'rusty' in spots and the trim loss rate will be a lot higher," said Lani, the salesperson for the produce supplier, "but actually, Chef, it's called 'downy mildew,' and it happens when there is too much rain to harvest the heads at the right time. My own suppliers tell me it won't improve for several more days. I can't change that, but we do have other unaffected greens in stock. Right now I can send you butterhead, Bibb, loose-leaf, romaine, watercress, arugula, oak leaf, escarole, or radicchio. Would you like to place a reorder?"

Assume you were Chef Alton:

1. If the product specification for your salads called for iceberg lettuce, what are the advantages associated with keeping the iceberg lettuce and simply absorbing the higher trim loss?
2. What could be the disadvantages associated with keeping the iceberg lettuce and simply absorbing the higher trim loss?
3. Why would a knowledge of alternative greens and their characteristics be helpful to Chef Alton (and his customers) in this situation?

Tomatoes   Tomatoes, although technically a fruit, are one of the most popular and heavily used of all vegetables. The flavor of tomatoes varies greatly, and most buyers would agree that the best flavor usually comes from those that are locally grown. This type of tomato is allowed to ripen completely on its vine before being picked. Buy tomatoes that are smooth, well ripened, and reasonably free from blemishes. Reject too soft, overripe, or bruised tomatoes and those with severe growth cracks (deep, brown cracks around the stem) that can reduce yield.

PROCESSED VEGETABLES   Few, if any, menu ingredients have undergone more change in the past decade than have processed vegetables (and to a large, but lesser degree, fruits). Today an increased number of vegetables, processed in an ever-growing number of market forms, are readily available.

Three major factors have made this so. First, labor has passed food as the largest cost in many operations and has significantly increased demand for foods with "built in" labor. In many cases vegetables purchased raw must be cleaned, trimmed, chopped, diced, or otherwise handled. A supplier's central processing facility (or that operated by a multi-unit foodservice organization) can process fresh vegetable products much more cost effectively than can individual foodservice units. In addition, centralized processing can result in the increased consistency of sizes, shapes, and mixtures of products.

A second major factor in the increased sale of processed fresh vegetable items relates to consumers themselves. In the days when simply having adequate food stocks was an accomplishment, canned, jarred, dried, and in many cases poor-quality frozen products may have been tolerated because these methods, at least, provided a constant supply of products. Today, however, consumers demand fresher ingredients, of an increased variety, and of higher quality. The result is that food growers and suppliers are constantly challenged to manage their products in ways that result in fresher, better, faster-to-market produce. Central vegetable processing units, often located adjacent to the fields in which fresh produce is grown, helps them do just that.

Finally, and perhaps most significantly, the explosion in vegetable processing has been aided by recent, major advancements in packaging technology. The drying of vegetables entails methods that have existed for thousands of years. The canning process was invented in France in 1795 by Nicholas Appert, a chef who was determined to win a cash prize offered by Napoleon for a way to prevent military food supplies from spoiling.

In 1923 Clarence Birdseye, an American, invented and later perfected a system of packing fresh food in waxed cardboard boxes and flash freezing them under high pressure. As a result, the first quick-frozen vegetables, fruits, seafood, and meat were sold to the public beginning in 1930 in Springfield, Massachusetts, under the trade name Birds Eye Frosted Foods®.

In each of the above food preservation methods, processors sought to protect food from damaging contact with oxygen to prolong its life. Today food processors do the same thing using **modified atmosphere packaging (MAP)** technology.

Essentially, MAP lowers oxygen in a package from 20 percent to near 0 percent to slow the growth of microorganisms and the effects of **oxidation,** both of which damage fresh produce.

In the 1970s MAP reached the public when bacon and fish were sold in retail packs in the United Kingdom. Since then the interest in MAP has grown due to heightened consumer demand, and this has led to significant advances in the design and manufacturing of food packaging materials.

It has been estimated that 25 to 40 percent of all fresh produce harvested will not reach the market due to spoilage and mishandling that occur during distribution. Yet most consumers want fresh vegetables and fruits without the use of preservatives. The MAP technique is today's most commonly used packaging technology for fresh-cut produce. As a result, foodservice buyers selecting processed products can choose from a wider array of products than ever before.

Did You Know? (8.3)

Fruits and vegetables, as well as many other foods, are irradiated to provide the same benefits as when these products are processed by heat, refrigeration, or freezing, or treated with chemicals to destroy insects, fungi, or bacteria that cause food to spoil. This makes it possible to keep food longer and in better condition.

Because irradiation destroys disease-causing bacteria and reduces the incidence of food borne illness, hospitals sometimes use irradiation to sterilize food for immunocompromised patients. Also, irradiation is currently the only known method to eliminate the deadly strains of E. coli bacteria.

Irradiated foods are absolutely wholesome and nutritious. Nutrient loss with irradiation is less than or about the same as with cooking and freezing. Irradiation does produce chemical changes in foods. These changes have been carefully studied by food scientists, and they have determined irradiated foods are safe to eat.

Because irradiated food cannot be recognized by sight, smell, taste, or feel, they are normally labeled with a logo, along with the words *Treated with Radiation* or, more commonly, *Treated by Irradiation*.

Buyer's Guide to Purchasing Terms

Modified atmosphere packaging (MAP)   The practice of altering the internal oxygen ratios in a food package to improve the shelf life of the food.

Oxidation   The chemical reaction (and deterioration) that occurs when a substance is exposed to oxygen. Burning is an example of rapid oxidation; rusting is an example of slow oxidation.

PROFESSIONAL PURCHASING PREVENTS PROBLEMS (8.1)

Keep It Fresh

A common problem: Poorly prepared fruits and vegetables contribute to unhealthful consumer diets.

Americans simply do not eat enough fruits and vegetables, yet Americans truly love high-quality, fresh fruits and vegetables. As a foodservice professional, you know that the percentage of meals consumers eat away from home increases yearly. That is good news for the foodservice industry, but with the increase in business comes an increase in the responsibility to offer your customers healthful foods. For too long, some foodservice operators have neglected to offer quality fruit and vegetable alternatives on their menus because they say, "Customers don't want to buy those items."

The recent explosion in growth of salad and fresh fruit options offered by enlightened foodservice operators, however, proves that consumers *will* select quality fruits and vegetables that are well prepared. What they do *not* want are overcooked, highly processed, poor-quality products chosen only because they are easy to prepare or can be held for long periods of time at the proper serving temperature.

For buyers, that means choosing fresh fruit and vegetable products (whenever practical), and ensuring that the cooking, holding, and serving techniques used on all fruit and vegetable items help to guarantee these will be served at the highest quality levels. When they are, customer acceptance of these items will be just as high.

Buyer's Guide to Internet Resources: Vegetables

Web Site	Topic
www.doortodoororganics.com	Bulk organic produce
www.ams.usda.gov/fv/mncs/terminal.htm	Continually updated produce prices
www.efreshportal.com	General information about produce and nuts
www.freshcutproduce.com	Lists of available fresh-cut vegetables and fruits
hgic.clemson.edu/factsheets/hgic3063.htm	Freezing vegetables and fruits

DAIRY PRODUCTS

The term *dairy* generally refers to cow's milk and the basic foods that are produced from it. These products include cheeses, butter, yogurt, cultured dairy products, and ice cream. In some cases foodservice buyers purchase dairy products produced by mammals other than cows. Products made from goat, sheep, reindeer, buffalo, and camel milks are currently popular.

Dairy products are often consumed by themselves, as is the case with beverage milks, but are just as frequently used as ingredients in appetizers, baked goods, entrées, side dishes, and desserts. For some buyers, the amount of money spent on dairy products will exceed the amount they spend on meats or produce.

There is much for you to learn about buying dairy products, and there are various ways to approach the study of these popular items. One way to do so is to consider dairy products as belonging to one of the following three categories:

1. Milks and Creams
2. Cheeses
3. Other Milk-Based Foods

Because it may be served plain, flavored, hot, or cold, milk is one of the most versatile of all the popular beverages.

Magnus Rew © Dorling Kindersley

Milks and Creams

In addition to its widespread consumption as a beverage, milk contributes texture, flavor, and nutrients to a wide variety of other foods. While its protein, vitamin, and mineral (especially calcium) contents are significant, from a buyer's perspective, it is the milk's fat content that most influences what you will purchase and how much you will pay for it. In fact, the milk fat content of beverage milk actually defines the products purchased and how they are used in the kitchen.

In its natural form, cow's milk contains approximately 88 percent water, 3.5 percent fat (milk fat), and 8.5 percent other solids that include proteins, milk sugar (**lactose**), and minerals.

Unprocessed, or raw, milk is not generally available in the United States. As a result, you will choose from various forms of **pasteurized** and **homogenized** milks.

If you are buying milk for drinking or cooking, you will generally select from the following widely available forms:

Whole milk   Whole milk is usually homogenized and fortified with vitamin D. For shipment in interstate commerce, it must contain a minimum of 3.25 percent milk fat and 8.25 percent milk solids (not fat).

Low-fat milk   Low-fat milk has between 0.5 and 2 percent milk fat and is fortified with vitamin A. The addition of vitamin D is optional.

Skim milk   Also called nonfat milk, this product must have less than 0.5 percent milk fat and must be fortified with vitamin A. The addition of vitamin D is optional.

Buyer's Guide to Purchasing Terms

Lactose   The sugar found in milk. Natural cow's milk contains approximately 4.5 to 5.0 percent lactose.

Pasteurize   To expose a food, such as milk, cheese, yogurt, beer, or wine, to an elevated temperature for a period of time sufficient to destroy certain microorganisms that cause spoilage or undesirable fermentation.

Homogenize   To reduce fat particles to a uniform and smaller size and to distribute these evenly in a liquid (such as milk) to enhance its flavor and texture.

Flavored milks   Flavored milks are made by adding fruit, fruit juice, or other natural or artificial food flavorings such as strawberry, chocolate syrup, or cocoa to pasteurized milk.

Dry whole milk   Dry whole milk is pasteurized whole milk with the water removed. Dry milks with reduced fat levels or no fat are also readily available. "Instant" nonfat dry milk is made of larger milk particles that dissolve easily in water. The best instant nonfat dry milk will have a sweet, pleasing flavor and a natural color. It must also dissolve immediately when mixed with water. Dry milk products are used mainly in baking and other recipes in foodservice operations.

Evaporated milk   Evaporated milk is prepared by heating homogenized whole milk under a vacuum to remove half its water then sealing it in cans. Evaporated skim milk is also readily available.

Condensed milk   This concentrated canned milk is prepared by removing about half the water from whole milk then adding sugar. Sweetened condensed milk must have at least 40 percent sugar by weight and is used primarily in baking.

The U.S. Food and Drug Administration sets the standards for milk products as well as for **cream,** a milk form that, by definition, must contain at least 18 percent milk fat.

Foodservice buyers can usually select from the following widely available forms of cream:

Half-and-half   Half-and-half is made by homogenizing a mixture of milk and cream. It must contain at least 10.5 percent, but not more than 18 percent, milk fat.

Light cream   Also known as coffee cream or table cream, light cream must have at least 18 percent, but less than 30 percent, milk fat.

Light whipping cream   Also known simply as whipping cream, it must have at least 30 percent, but less than 36 percent, milk fat.

Heavy cream   Heavy cream must contain at least 36 percent milk fat.

Despite being pasteurized, all milk and cream products are highly perishable and must be carefully stored at or below 41°F (5°C) to maintain their best quality.

Buyer's Guide to Internet Resources: Milk and Other Products

Web Site	Topic
1. www.whymilk.com	Information about the nutritive value of milk
2. www.gotmilk.com	Milk recipes and health-related information
3. www.idfa.org	Dairy and foods from dairy products
4. www.creamsauces.com	Cooking with milk and cream
5. www.lactaid.com	Milk substitutes for lactose-intolerant diners

Buyer's Guide to Purchasing Term

Cream   A liquid dairy product with a high (at least 18 percent) milk fat content.

Cheeses

You know that milk and products made from milk are popular but also highly perishable. This has always been true, especially in warm climates where, in times before refrigeration, milk would spoil easily. Cheese products are the direct result of human efforts to prolong the life of dairy products. In fact, in European and European-influenced countries, cheese is one of the oldest and most widely produced foods.

Historically, cheese making produced products that served as a hedge against famine because they stored well and lasted a long time. In many ways cheeses can be simply considered as a more compact form of milk (and an item with a longer shelf life than the milk from which it is made). While the production of cheese was originally a humble process undertaken to prolong the life of local dairy products, today's foodservice buyers can choose from hundreds of cheeses made in a variety of styles and packaging forms to use in literally thousands of recipes or to serve alone.

Cheeses may be broadly classified as either natural or processed. Natural cheeses have been produced in the same manner for centuries. Essentially, all natural cheeses begin with a mammal's milk (cows, goats, or sheep are most popular). To make cheese, a protein found in milk (**casein**) is coagulated by adding an enzyme (usually **rennet**), which is a natural ingredient found in the stomachs of cattle, sheep, and goats. The stomachs of these animals would have been considered natural storage containers for early man, thus it is most likely that cheese making was originally discovered accidentally rather than on purpose.

As the milk **coagulates,** it naturally separates into curds, which are solid, and whey, which is the remaining liquid.

The whey is removed, and the solids are then either consumed immediately or specially treated in a variety of ways that may include cutting, kneading, seasoning, or cooking. After the whey is removed, the resulting solids product, known as green cheese, is treated and packed into molds to age (ripen). The rind (outside) of the cheese may, depending on how the cheese is made, range from very thin to very thick.

Many factors affect the quality of natural cheeses, including the type of milk used, the skill of the cheese maker, how long the cheese is aged, and even the atmosphere in the part of the world in which the cheese is produced.

Cheeses were originally produced to extend the storage life of milk, and the moisture level and fat contents of cheeses are good indictors of the final product's texture and shelf life. The higher the moisture content of a natural cheese, the softer and more perishable it will be.

Processed cheeses are made by combining aged and green cheeses and mixing them with emulsifiers and flavorings. The resulting mixture is then pasteurized and poured into molds. In most cases processed cheeses are less expensive to buy than natural cheeses. Processed "cheese food" is a variation of processed cheese. This product must contain at least 51 percent cheese but may also include

---

Buyer's Guide to Purchasing Terms

Casein   A protein found in milk. Natural cow's milk contains approximately 2 to 3 percent casein.

Rennet   An enzyme that causes the coagulation of milk. It is found in the gastric juice of the fourth stomach of certain animals such as cattle, sheep, and goats.

Coagulate   To thicken or make semisolid.

vegetable oils or milk solids designed to produce a cheese that spreads easily. These are often flavored with pimentos, fruits, vegetables, or meats.

For most foodservice buyers, the great majority of cheeses purchased are natural cheeses. There are thousands of natural cheese makers worldwide, and the number of distinct products they produce is vast. Natural cheeses can be classified based on where they are made, the ripening method used, or their fat content. For most buyers, the best way to classify cheeses is by their texture. Cheeses can be categorized as one of the following:

Fresh (or unripened)

Soft

Semisoft

Firm

Hard

FRESH (UNRIPENED)   Fresh, or unripened, cheeses are not cooked and have moisture contents between 40 and 80 percent. They are highly perishable and extremely popular. Among the most commonly purchased fresh cheeses are the following:

Cottage Cheese   Cottage cheese is a cheese product with a very mild flavor. It is drained, but not pressed, so some whey remains. It is not aged or colored. Different styles of cottage cheese are made from milks with different fat levels and in small or large curd forms. Cottage cheese is a soft, tasty, and easily produced cheese. It must have a milk fat content of at least 4 percent. Low-fat cottage cheese must have a milk fat content between 0.5 percent and 2 percent, and nonfat cottage cheese must contain less than 0.5 percent total fat.

Cream Cheese   Cream cheese is an unripened cheese containing at least 35 percent fat. Cream cheese is a uniquely American product, having originated in the United States in 1872 when a dairyman in Chester, New York, developed a 'richer cheese than ever before' made from cream as well as whole milk.

Feta   Feta cheese is increasingly served in foodservice operations. Feta is a Greek or Italian product originally made from sheep or goat's milk. Feta cheese is white, usually formed into square cakes, and can range from soft to semihard. Its tangy, salty flavor ranges from mild to sharp. The fat content of feta can range from 30 to 60 percent. It is now made in many countries, and increasingly it is produced from pasteurized cow's milk.

Mozzarella   Mozzarella is an Italian cheese that contains 40 to 50 percent milk fat. It becomes elastic and stretches when melted and is sometimes referred to as pizza cheese. Fresh mozzarella is a very mild cheese that many believe is best eaten within hours of its production.

Mascarpone   Mascarpone is also an Italian cheese and is best known for its use in sweet and savory sauces and desserts.

Queso Oaxaca   This fresh Mexican cheese is kneaded, soaked in brine, and shaped into a ball. It melts easily and is used in a variety of Mexican dishes, including quesadillas and dips.

Ricotta   Ricotta is a soft Italian cheese similar to cottage cheese. Ricotta has a milk fat content between 4 and 10 percent. Ricotta is often beaten smooth and mixed with condiments, such as sugar and cinnamon, and served as a dessert. This basic combination (often with addition of citrus flavorings and nuts) is also used as the filling of the crunchy Italian-style cannoli, but ricotta is also used in a variety of other Italian-style dishes, including pastas and desserts.

SOFT   Soft cheeses are best known for their thin skins and creamy middles. The moisture content of these cheeses range from 50 to 75 percent. Among the most commonly purchased soft cheeses are the following:

Brie   Containing approximately 60 percent fat, Brie is a French cheese made from cow's milk. Its soft, pliable rind may be eaten but is often cut away. Brie is often served as a dessert cheese and is commonly used as an ingredient in soups, sauces, or hors d'oeuvres.

Boursin   A French cheese with a high fat content (75 percent), Boursin is usually flavored with pepper, herbs, or garlic. It is delicious and rindless with a smooth, creamy texture that makes it popular as a sauce ingredient or when eaten alone.

Camembert   Camembert is a French cheese with a fat content of approximately 45 percent. Similar to Brie, this popular cheese is often served with fruit.

SEMISOFT   Semisoft cheeses are smooth and sliceable. The moisture content of semisoft cheeses ranges from 40 to 50 percent. These cheeses include what is commonly known as the "blue" or "veined" varieties, which refers to cheese types containing blue-colored molds that produce cheeses with a distinctive look and taste. The most commonly purchased of the semisoft cheeses include the following:

Gouda   Gouda is a Dutch cheese containing approximately 48 percent fat. Gouda is sold in various-sized wheels covered with red or yellow wax. The cheese itself is yellow with a mild, buttery flavor.

Havarti   Havarti, also known as Danish Tilsit, is a cow's milk cheese produced in Denmark. It has a mild and creamy texture and is often flavored with dill, caraway seeds, or peppers.

Fontina   This Italian cheese is from the Piedmont region of northern Italy, but imitation products are produced in Denmark, France, and the United States. Fontina is a popular after-dinner cheese.

Roquefort   Roquefort is a blue-veined sheep's milk cheese from France containing approximately 45 percent fat. Intensely flavorful with a rich, salty taste and strong aroma, authentic Roquefort is smooth and easy to spread (not crumbly).

Stilton   Stilton is a blue-veined cow's milk cheese produced in Great Britain. Produced in a manner similar to Roquefort, it has a pale yellow or white color and evenly spaced mold veins.

Gorgonzola   Gorgonzola is a blue-veined cow's milk cheese from Italy containing 48 percent fat. It is creamier than other blue-veined cheeses such as Roquefort or Stilton.

FIRM   Firm cheeses, such as cheddar, are solid and often flaky, while others, such as Emmentaler (better known in the United States as Swiss) are full of holes. Most firm cheeses have a moisture content in the range of 30 to 50 percent. Among the most commonly purchased firm cheeses are the following:

Cheddar   Cheddar cheeses are made from cow's milk and are extremely popular. The classic style of Cheddar cheese was originally developed in the village of Cheddar in Somerset, England. Today's styles include American, Colby, and longhorn. Cheddar cheeses are made in colors that range from white to very dark orange. Cheddar has a unique flavor that develops as the cheese ages. As a Cheddar cheese buyer, you will most often select from products labeled with adjectives such as *mild, medium, sharp,* and *extra sharp.* The milk fat content of Cheddar cheeses ranges from 45 to 50 percent.

Emmentaler   This Swiss-made cow's milk cheese is mellow and rich with a nutty flavor. It is ripened in three stages, and its characteristic holes are the result of gases that expand inside the cheese during the fermentation of bacteria added to the milk during production. Gruyere, made in Fribourg, Switzerland, is a firm cheese with a flavor and appearance similar to that of Emmentaler but with smaller holes.

Jarlsberg   Jarlsberg is a Swiss-type cow's milk cheese made in Norway.

Monterey Jack   Monterey Jack, or simply Jack, is a very mild, Cheddar-like cow's milk cheese originally produced in California. Its color ranges from pale ivory to white, and it is often flavored with peppers or herbs.

Provolone   This cow's milk cheese was originally produced in southern Italy and contains approximately 45 percent fat. Smoked provolone is perhaps the most popular of all the smoked cheeses.

HARD   Hard cheeses are carefully aged for extended periods of time and dried to the point that their moisture contents are approximately 30 percent. Hard cheeses are best when grated for use as needed. Among the most commonly purchased hard cheeses are the following:

Asiago   This sharp-flavored cow's milk cheese, when aged for one year, has a texture similar to Cheddar. When aged for longer periods, it becomes brittle, hard, and suitable for grating. Asiago melts easily and is used in a variety of recipes.

Parmigiano-Reggiano   Easily the most popular of the hard cheeses, this product is commonly, but most often improperly, known simply by its English-word variation, Parmesan.

Cheese of this style was originally produced near Parma, Italy. It is now one of the most widely copied cheeses in the world. The name Parmigiano-Reggiano is trademarked in Europe but not in the United States, so buyers of Parmesan cheese in the United States may be purchasing a very good or a very poor imitation of the original.

Romano   Romano is a sheep's milk cheese made in Italy. It contains approximately 35 percent fat. Romano is sharper and more brittle than other grated cheeses and is also lighter in color.

Buyers at Work (8.2)

"Well, what do we have in the box?" asked Raj, the general manager and buyer at Sofia's Italian Bistro.

"I have an American blue that I use for making salad dressing," replied Jeanette, the restaurant's kitchen manager.

"But we don't have any Gorgonzola at all for the Tuscan Gorgonzola Steak?" asked Raj.

"None," said Jeanette. "The distributor shorted us on your order this week."

Assume you were Raj and that you have included on the menu the words *melted Gorgonzola* as the topping for the popular Tuscan Gorgonzola Steak:

1. Would you use the American blue cheese as a substitute topping?
2. If so, would you inform your guests of the substitution?
3. As a professional buyer, what could you do to prevent such problems in the future?

The storage life of cheese varies based on the style and kind purchased, so it is important to know basic product information about each type of cheese you buy.

Philip Dowell © Dorling Kindersley

Buyer's Guide to Internet Resources: Cheese

Web Site	Topic
www.cheese.com	Alphabetical list of and information about 100+ cheeses
www.cheesesociety.org	Cheese buying and storage tips
www.ballardcheese.com	Cheese making information
www.fage.gr	Information on cheeses, butter, and yogurt
www.ilovecheese.com	American Dairy Association–supplied information about cheese

Other Milk-Based Foods

In addition to its use as a beverage and in cheese production, milk is used to make a variety of important foods widely used in the foodservice industry. Among the most popular of these are butter, yogurt (or yoghurt), sour cream, and ice cream. As a foodservice buyer, you may find these items to be challenging to purchase because of their high level of perishability and, with regard to ice creams, the vast array of quality levels generally available to you.

BUTTER   Butter is one of man's oldest processed dairy products. In fact, the first documented mention of butter making occurred more than thirty-five hundred years ago. The term *butter* is used in the names of a variety of products, including those made from pureed nuts (e.g., peanut butter), fruits (e.g., apple butter), and fats that are solid at room temperature (e.g., cocoa butter). In culinary usage, however, the word *butter,* unless qualified by another term, almost always refers to the dairy product.

Originally, butter was made from milk that had been collected over several days (to provide enough liquid to ultimately produce the solid butter). Because of the time that would pass, the milk would naturally **ferment.** The fats in the milk

Buyer's Guide to Purchasing Term

Ferment   The natural process by which microorganisms break down the carbohydrates in a food product; also called "fermentation".

were then separated from the liquid, and this resulting fermented cream was used to produce **cultured butter.**

The color of natural cultured butter is determined in most part by the feed of the animal from which it is made, although today the color of butters is most often manipulated in manufacturing to produce the uniform yellow butters common to foodservice customers.

With the advent of the pasteurization process, **sweet cream butter** began to be made. Sweet cream butter is produced from pasteurized cream. This type of butter first became popular in the nineteenth century, when refrigeration came into common use. Today in Europe cultured butters are still preferred, while sweet cream butters are more popular in the United States and the United Kingdom.

Butter of all types is typically sold in both salted and unsalted forms. Salted butters have either fine, granular salt or brine added to them during production. In addition to flavoring the butter, the addition of salt acts as a preservative.

Butter has a very high milk fat content (also called "butterfat"), which is one reason for its popularity. In the United States, all products sold as butter must contain a minimum of 80 percent milk fat by weight, not more than 16 percent water, and 2 to 4 percent other milk solids. The European-style cultured butters generally have a higher butterfat content (up to 85 percent).

Clarified butter is simply butter that has been heated to its melting point then most all of its water and milk solids are removed, leaving almost pure butterfat.

The advantages of this type of butter is its long keeping quality (several months when refrigerated) and its high **smoke point,** which allows it to be used in frying without burning as readily as nonclarified butter.

Ghee is clarified butter that is heated to remove all of its water and other solids. Because the resulting product is then composed entirely of butterfat, ghee can be kept, without refrigeration, for several months.

The USDA has established three butter grades. In general, butter buyers may select from the following:

U.S. Grade AA   This butter has a smooth, creamy texture and is easy to spread. It has a light, fresh flavor and may contain a small amount of salt. Grade AA butter is made from sweet cream and is available from most distributors.

U.S. Grade A   This butter is made from fresh cream, has a slightly stronger flavor, and possesses a fairly smooth texture. Grade A butter is also widely available.

U.S. Grade B   This butter is less commonly available to foodservice operators. It is usually made from sour cream, and its texture is coarser than that of regular butter. Its major application is in food manufacturing and processing.

The packages in which butter is sold display a shield surrounding their USDA-assigned letter grade (and occasionally the numerical score equivalent) indicating the quality of the contents. Grade scores are 93 or higher (for AA), 92

Buyer's Guide to Purchasing Terms

Cultured (butter)   Butter made from naturally or artificially fermented cream.

Sweet cream butter   Butter made from pasteurized cream.

Clarified (butter)   Unsalted butter from which the water and milk solids have been removed; also called "drawn" butter.

Smoke point   The temperature at which a heated fat begins to break down and create smoke.

Ghee   A form of clarified butter popular in Indian and other cuisines.

(for A), and 90 (for B). The highest attainable grade is AA, and the highest attainable **score** for butter is 100.

Unsalted butter is usually labeled as such and contains absolutely no salt. It is sometimes referred to as sweet butter, which is inaccurate because any butter made with sweet cream (instead of sour cream) is sweet butter. Therefore, you can expect packages labeled *sweet cream butter* to contain salt. Unsalted butter is often preferred for many cooking and baking purposes; however, it is more perishable than salted butter and, therefore, is often purchased and stored in a frozen state.

Butter may also be purchased in a variety of packaging types. These include blocks of varying weights, quarter-pound sticks, individually wrapped patties of various sizes, and preformed shapes (such as roses, balls, and chips).

Butter may be purchased in a variety of forms. Whipped butter is made by incorporating nitrogen gas (not air, as that would encourage oxidation and rancidity) into the butter. This process is typically done to increase the spreadability of the product. When purchased by weight, the whipping process does not affect the buyer's cost per ounce. If whipped butter is purchased by volume, however, the price is, of course, significantly affected.

YOGURT   Yogurt is a thick, tart, custard-consistency dairy product. There is evidence of yogurtlike products being produced as food for at least forty-five hundred years. Yogurt was known primarily in Asia and Eastern and Central Europe until the 1900s, when its health benefits were widely publicized. In 1919 Isaac Carasso, a Spanish entrepreneur in Barcelona, developed an efficient method for mass-producing yogurt. He named the business Danone after his son. In the United States, Carasso's company is better known to foodservice buyers as Dannon.

Commercially sold yogurt can be made from whole, low-fat, or nonfat milk, as well as soymilk. Therefore, yogurt contains the same amount of milk fat as the product from which it is made. Yogurt is produced by bacterial fermentation of milk sugar (lactose), which produces lactic acid. The resulting effect on the milk's proteins gives yogurt its characteristic consistency and tart, tangy flavor. In the United States, yogurt may be purchased plain or with a variety of fruit or spice flavorings.

The USDA recognizes three yogurt forms commonly available for foodservice buyers:

1. *Yogurt*   Contains not less than 3.25 percent fat, and not less than 8.25 percent milk solids (not fat).
2. *Low-fat yogurt*   Contains not less than 0.5 percent, nor more than 2.0 percent fat, and not less than 8.25 percent milk solids (not fat).
3. *Nonfat yogurt*   Contains not more than 0.5 percent fat and not less than 8.25 percent milk solids (not fat).

The caloric content of yogurt will vary based on its milk fat content and flavoring ingredients. While used infrequently for cooking in the United States, it is an extremely popular ingredient in many Middle Eastern cuisines. Also, yogurt has gained tremendous popularity as a breakfast and snack food. Typically, it may be purchased in bulk containers of one to five pounds, as well as in single-serving-sized containers of about six ounces (170 grams).

BUTTERMILK AND SOUR CREAM   *Buttermilk* was the term originally used to describe the liquid that was left over after producing butter from milk. Today the buttermilk

Buyer's Guide to Purchasing Term

Score (butter)   A numerical equivalent of a quality grade. For example, Grade AA butter may also be assigned a score of 93 or higher (out of 100).

Product	Minimum Milk Fat Content
Sour cream	Contains not less than 18 percent milk fat
Reduced fat sour cream	Contains 13.5 percent or less milk fat, but not less than 6 percent total
Low-fat sour cream	Contains 6 percent or less milk fat, but not less than 1 percent total fat
Nonfat sour cream	Contains less than 1 percent total milk fat

FIGURE 8.5 Minimum Fat Content of Sour Creams
Source: USDA

available to most foodservice buyers is actually an artificially **cultured dairy product** (in this case milk), to which lactic acid–producing bacteria have been added.

Sour cream (like yogurt) is also a cultured dairy product. Both buttermilk and sour cream are produced by adding a specific bacterial culture *(Streptococcus lactis)* to milk. The bacteria convert the milk sugar (lactose) to lactic acid. The acidity of buttermilk and sour cream explain their relatively long refrigerator shelf life because acid is a natural preservative that inhibits the growth of pathogenic bacteria.

Buttermilk is produced when the bacterial culture is added to fresh, pasteurized skim or low-fat milk to yield a thick milk product with a tart flavor. Sour cream is made by combining the same bacterial culture to dairy cream, and cream with a higher fat content that produces an even thicker product. The USDA has well-defined fat content minimums for regular sour cream (18 percent). Figure 8.5 lists the minimum fat contents of the most popular styles of sour cream.

Buttermilk is most commonly used in foodservices as an ingredient in baked products and quick breads (examples include pancakes and biscuits) because the acid in buttermilk reacts with baking soda in most quick bread recipes to form large quantities of gas bubbles that efficiently and quickly make these items rise (increase in volume).

Sour cream is a very commonly purchased foodservice item because it is used as an ingredient in many recipes. These include dips, salad dressings, soups, baked goods, toppings for baked potatoes, and many popular Mexican-style foods such as enchiladas, nachos, and quesadillas.

ICE CREAM Ice cream (or iced cream) will be challenging for you to purchase. In its basic form, ice cream is a frozen mixture of milk, sugar or other sweeteners, cream, and flavorings such as fruits, nuts, or vanilla. The last and perhaps most essential ingredient in ice cream is air, without which ice cream would not have the texture that makes it such a popular dish worldwide.

Prior to the development of modern refrigerators and freezers, ice cream was a luxury item reserved for special occasions simply because of the difficulty of making it. Originally, ice cream was made by hand in a large bowl placed inside a tub filled with ice and salt. The temperature of the ice cream ingredients is reduced by the mixture of crushed ice and salt. The salt water is cooled by the ice, and the action of the salt on the ice causes it to partially melt, absorbing heat from the ingredients, and bringing the mixture below the freezing point of pure water. The immersed container can also make better contact with salty water and ice than it could with ice alone. The development of industrial refrigeration by a German engineer during the 1870s eliminated the need to obtain natural ice for ice cream making and eventually led to the commercial mass production of ice cream.

Buyer's Guide to Purchasing Term

Cultured (dairy product)   The processed food created when specific bacteria are added to liquid dairy products.

In the United States, the ice cream you will buy must contain at least 10 percent milk fat and, at most, 50 percent air. Also, it must weigh at least 4.5 pounds per gallon. Ice creams termed premium and super premium have higher fat content (13 percent to 17 percent) and lower air content (called **overrun**).

Despite the fact that the USDA has established rigid standards for various ice cream quality levels, in common terminology, frozen custards, yogurts, and sherbets are also commonly referred to as ice cream. The USDA, as well as the governments of other countries, closely regulates product standards for these items as well. The following is a partial list of some of the most popular ice cream–like desserts as well as their identifying characteristics:

Low-fat ice cream (ice milk) This product contains less than 10 percent milk fat and lower sweetening content. It is made from milk, stabilizers, sweeteners, and flavorings, and contains not more than three grams of fat per four-ounce serving. Ice creams advertised as "reduced fat" or "light" must have a lower fat content than regular ice cream, but may not meet the standard for low fat.

Frozen custard Also known as French ice cream or New York ice cream, this product has must contain at least 1.4 percent egg yolks.

Frozen yogurt This product is a low-fat or fat-free ice cream alternative made with yogurt.

Gelato The Italian word for ice cream, gelato is an Italian-style frozen dessert that must have a 4 to 9 percent milk fat content.

Sherbet This product is made from milk, fruit or fruit juice, and stabilizers, and has a level of sweetening much higher than ice cream. It must contain 1 to 2 percent milk fat.

Sorbet Technically, sorbet is not a dairy product at all, as it is an ice cream–like product made with fruit puree and contains no milk.

Ice cream products are highly perishable and must be stored carefully and used quickly to maintain high quality. Increasingly, consumer demand in the hospitality industry is for higher-quality, more expensive ice cream products.

Did You Know? (8.4)

While the fat content of ice cream is often considered the important indicator of quality, purchasing pros know that overrun is equally or more important to your guests' perceptions of ice cream quality.

The percentage of overrun in ice cream products can ranges from 0 (no air) to 200 (a theoretical figure that would indicate 100 percent air). The legal overrun limit for ice cream is 100, or 50 percent air. Ice cream must have air in it or it would be hard as a rock. However, ice cream with an overrun of 100 would feel mushy in the mouth and would melt extremely quickly.

The most desirable overrun proportion is between 20 and 50 (10 to 25 percent air), which creates a product that is dense, creamy, and satisfying. Because the overrun amount is *not* listed on the package, the only way to be absolutely sure about it is to weigh the product.

Ice cream with an overrun of 50 (25 percent air) will weigh about 18 ounces per pint (subtract about one and a half ounces for the weight of the container). The net weight of other ice creams tested will be proportionally higher (or lower) with differing percentages of overrun.

Buyer's Guide to Purchasing Term

Overrun The term used to indicate the amount of air in a frozen dairy product such as ice cream.

Ice cream is highly perishable. To produce outstanding products like these, it should be stored properly and for no more than one week.

Dave King © Dorling Kindersley

Buyer's Guide to Internet Resources: Other Milk-Based Foods

Web Site	Topic
www.landolakes.com	Butter and butter recipes
www.dannonkitchen.com	Yogurt recipes
www.bluebell.com	Ice cream
www.haagen-dazs.com	Premium ice cream
www.icecreamusa.com	Ice cream and other frozen dessert items

EGGS AND EGG PRODUCTS

Many animals reproduce by laying eggs. Eggs are laid by a female bird, reptile, or fish, and the egg's contents, if fertilized, can develop into a new organism, with each egg holding one new animal. Foodservice buyers generally purchase unfertilized eggs laid by chickens (although duck, pheasant, and quail eggs, among others, are also widely available).

As a buyer, you will be able to choose from chicken eggs available in a variety of market forms. These include fresh eggs (also known as shell eggs), processed egg products of various forms, and egg substitutes, which are egg-alternative products that can be made in whole, or in part, from fresh eggs.

Fresh Eggs

From a culinary perspective, the three primary parts of a fresh egg are the shell, the yolk, and the white (**albumen**).

The shell, which is made of calcium carbonate, keeps the egg from drying out by retaining its moisture and protects the egg during handling.

The breed of chicken dictates the shell's color, which can range from white to brown. As a buyer, it is important for you to know that the shell's color has no effect on the egg's quality, flavor, or nutritive content. However, some food distributors consistently charge a premium for brown-colored shell eggs, and some guests prefer to see them when served as hard-cooked (boiled) eggs.

Buyer's Guide to Purchasing Term

Albumen   Another term for the white of a fresh egg.

Did You Know? (8.5)

Fresh shell eggs are sized by their minimum weight per dozen. As a result, buyers may compare prices based on the net cost per ounce or gram.

	Minimum Weight Per Dozen	
Egg Size	Ounces	Grams
Jumbo	30	850.5
Extra Large	27	765.5
Large	24	680.4
Medium	21	595.3
Small	18	510.3
Peewee	15	425.2

Source: USDA (ounce weights only)

The yolk of an egg contains approximately 75 percent of the egg's calories, most of the minerals, and all of the fat. The yolk also contains **lecithin,** the compound responsible for **emulsification** in mayonnaise and hollandaise sauce. The information in Figure 8.6 details the composition of a single large egg.

The feed eaten by chickens directly affects the color of egg yolks. As is true with shell color, however, the color of an egg's yolk is not an indicator of egg quality.

Eggs are typically sold to foodservice operators by the dozen and in various carton sizes. Egg cartons from USDA-inspected plants must display a **Julian date** (the date the eggs were packed).

Fresh shell eggs can be stored in their cartons in the refrigerator for four to five weeks beyond their Julian date with insignificant quality loss. Although not required, they may also carry an expiration date beyond which the eggs should not be sold.

FIGURE 8.6 Composition of a U.S.-Produced Large Fresh Egg

Note: g = gram, mg = milligram.

	1 USDA "Large" Egg
Weight	55 g (approx. 2 ounces)
Protein	6.6 g
Carbohydrate	0.6 g
Fat	
Monounsaturated	2.5 g
Polyunsaturated	0.7 g
Saturated	2.0 g
Cholesterol	213 mg
Sodium	71 mg
Calories	84

Buyer's Guide to Purchasing Terms

Lecithin A fatlike substance also called a phospholipid. A healthy human's liver produces this compound daily if that person's diet is adequate.

Emulsification The uniform dispersion of small droplets of one liquid into a second liquid with which the droplets cannot be readily mixed (e.g., oil and vinegar).

Julian date A dating system that starts with January 1 as number 1 and ends with December 31 as 365. These numbers represent the consecutive days of the year. For example, February 1 would be represented by the Julian date 32.

Did You Know? (8.6)

The term *free range* on labeled meat, chicken, or fresh eggs implies to consumers a method of raising animals in which the animal is permitted the freedom to roam around a large land area (the range). While the theory behind such an approach to raising animals may be comforting, in practice, there are few regulations imposed on what can be called free range, and the term may be used misleadingly by producers to imply that the animal product for sale has been produced more humanely than it actually has been.

The USDA requires that chickens raised for their meat have access to the outdoors in order to receive the free-range certification. Free-range chicken eggs, however, have no legal definition in the United States. As a result, the term may be used by a producer whose chicken cages are only two to three feet larger than those producers not using the term.

Likewise, free-range egg producers have no common standard on what the term actually means. Other terms such as *cage-free, free-running, free-roaming, naturally nested,* and the like also have no legal definitions that food buyers can count on. Until such time as a legal definition is imposed by the USDA, if it is important to you to offer your guests free-range items such as eggs, your guests will count on you to do the supplier research required to know exactly what you are buying.

The USDA has established three consumer grades for eggs: U.S. Grades AA, A, and B. The grade is determined by the interior quality of the egg and the appearance and condition of the egg shell. Eggs of any quality grade may differ in weight (size).

U.S. Grade AA   These eggs have whites that are thick and firm; yolks that are high, round, and practically free from defects; and clean, unbroken shells.

U.S. Grade A   These eggs have whites that are reasonably firm; yolks that are high, round, and practically free from defects; and clean, unbroken shells. This is the quality most often sold in stores.

U.S. Grade B   These eggs have whites that may be thinner and yolks that may be wider and flatter than eggs of the higher grades; the shells must be unbroken but may show slight stains.

U.S. Grade AA and A eggs are good for all purposes, but especially for poaching and frying, where appearance is important. U.S. Grade B eggs, if available, are suitable for general cooking and baking.

Processed Eggs

Most foodservice distributors sell a variety of processed egg products. These include whole eggs that have been shelled and whites-only and yolks-only products. Processed egg products are sold fresh (refrigerated), frozen, or dried. Processed eggs are shell eggs broken by special machines at the grading station then pasteurized before being packaged in cartons. Processed egg products may contain preservatives and flavor or color additives. Because of their built-in labor savings, these products generally cost more per ounce than do in-the-shell eggs.

Another special and popular form of egg processing exists when processors remove yolks from eggs and further process the whites only. Whites-only egg products such as ConAgra Foods' popular Egg Beaters is such a product. The processed egg products typically contain 99 percent egg whites. The other one percent comprises coloring, salt, and other ingredients. In addition, nutrients may be added to make up for those lost from the yolk, so egg products of this type will usually contain varying amounts of iron; zinc; folate; thiamin; riboflavin; vitamins A, E, B6, and B12; and have an equivalent amount of protein as whole eggs but with fewer total calories. Like shell eggs, it is important that proper storage and handling procedures are followed when using any processed egg product.

Buyers at Work (8.3)

"We could make the omelets a lot quicker if we used precracked eggs," said Lupita.

"That's true, but we would still need to have shell eggs on the line for guests who want fried eggs," replied Rolando. "We don't have enough space for both kinds.

Lupita and Rolando are the two chefs who work the Sunday morning omelet/egg station at the Hawthorn Plaza hotel. They are speaking to Luis Argote, the hotel's food and beverage manager (and its food buyer), about the property's Sunday brunch.

The brunch is extremely popular and it is common to serve more than five hundred guests each Sunday. Many of the guests elected to have their eggs or omelets prepared to order by Lupita or Rolando.

"It just takes too long to crack and whip eggs for omelets. The guests have to wait in line," continued Lupita. "If we bought precracked eggs, we could just dip the proper amount of egg mixture out of a container and right into the omelet pans!"

Assume you were Luis:

1. What effect would your decision to reject Lupita's suggestion have on your guests?
2. What, if any, effect on guests would result if you elected to use the processed egg product?
3. What are additional factors you might want to consider before deciding to implement Lupita's omelet production suggestion?

Egg Substitutes

Eggs contain **cholesterol** and, because significant numbers of people are allergic to eggs, the popularity of total egg substitutes has increased greatly in recent years.

Egg substitutes are generally of two types, and professional buyers must understand the difference between the two. The first type is a complete substitution made from soy or milk proteins. These cannot typically be used for baking or other uses where the egg is intended to provide thickening or leavening in the item to be produced.

The second type contains real albumen, but the yolk is removed and replaced with dairy or vegetable products. While these products taste different than whole eggs, the whites they contain do make them suitable for many cooking purposes.

The proper storage and rotation of fresh eggs is critical to their serving quality.

© Dorling Kindersley

Buyer's Guide to Purchasing Term

Cholesterol   A soft, waxy substance found in animal tissues and other foods of animal origin. Its level in the bloodstream can influence certain conditions such as plaque buildup in the arteries and heart disease.

Buyer's Guide to Internet Resources: Egg Products

Web Site	Topic
www.ams.usda.gov/AMSv1.0/getfile?dDocName=STELDEV3022056	Buying eggs
www.nestfresh.com	Organic eggs
www.eggbeaters.com	Processed eggs and egg substitutes
www.aeb.org	American Egg Board's information about eggs
www.iowaegg.org	Egg recipes

RECEIVING AND STORAGE

Like other fresh foods, produce, dairy products, and eggs should be carefully inspected on delivery, and there are also some special aspects regarding the receiving and storage of these items.

When receiving fresh produce, buyers and storeroom personnel must understand the common container sizes used to pack and ship these items. While many produce items are sold by the pound, many are also sold in container sizes and shapes that are not readily known by all buyers. Figure 8.7 lists some of the most frequently used of these as well as the approximate net weight of products these containers will hold.

Poly bags and other containers of precut or processed fruits and vegetables should be weighed to ensure the amount delivered matches the amount indicated on the vendor's delivery slip or invoice.

Proper storage of produce and dairy products is essential if they are to be served at their peak quality levels. It is important to remember that produce, dairy, and egg purchases will arrive at the operation in their best condition.

Items Purchased	Container	Approximate Net Weight in Pounds
Apples	Cartons, tray pack	40–45
Asparagus	Pyramid crates, loose pack	32
Beets, bunched	½ crates, 2 dz. bunches	36–40
Cabbage, green	Flat crates (1¾ bushel)	50–60
Cantaloupe	½ wire-bound crates	38–41
Corn, sweet	Cartons, packed with 5 dozen ears	50
Cucumbers, field grown	Bushel cartons	47–55
Grapefruit, Florida	4/5-bushel cartons & wire-bound crates	42½
Grapes, table	Lugs and cartons, plain pack	23–24
Lettuce, loose leaf	4/5-bushel crates	8–10
Limes	Cartons	10
Onions, green	4/5-bushel crates (36 green bunches)	11
Oranges, Florida	4/5-bushel cartons	45
Parsley	Cartons, wax treated, 5 dozen bunches	21
Peaches	2-layer cartons & lugs, tray pack	22
Shallots	Bags	5
Squash	1-layer flats, place pack	16
Strawberries, California	12 one-pint trays	11–14
Tangerines	4/5-bushel cartons	47½
Tomatoes, pink and ripe	3-layer lugs and cartons, place pack	20–33

FIGURE 8.7 Selected Produce Container Net Weights

From the time most of these items are delivered to the time they are served, quality levels will decline because fruits and vegetables lose moisture and continue to **respire** after they are harvested, which causes them to decline in quality as they age.

The ability of an operation to produce high-quality, fresh foods that maximize yield and flavor depends on the condition of the items on delivery and the ability to store, produce, and hold them, if necessary, before service. Vegetables with an especially high water content, such as lettuce and celery, quickly lose flavor and texture as they dehydrate. Therefore, water retention or replacement is important in maintaining quality vegetables. To best preserve most vegetables, store them in their original or airtight containers at normal refrigeration temperatures and buy only enough to last for a few days.

Some vegetables, such as tomatoes, do best if held at room temperature until fully ripe before being placed in the refrigerator. Others, such as sweet potatoes, should not be refrigerated at all. Avocados and bananas should not be refrigerated until they are completely ripe. Melons can also be held at room temperature until fully ripe before refrigerating them. Most fruits should be stored in their original containers, unwashed until ready to use, and can be held at standard refrigerator temperatures. When in doubt, discuss specific vegetable and fruit storage requirements with your produce vendor.

Fluid milks, butter, cream, yogurt, and most cheeses should be stored under refrigeration at 41°F (5°C). Dairy products easily absorb odors and should be stored in airtight containers. Butter should be stored in its original container to avoid absorbing flavors from other foods. To enhance their quality, keep frozen desserts in tightly closed cartons. Frozen desserts stored at temperatures below 0°F (−18°C) will keep for about a month but will have the best quality when stored for much shorter periods of time.

Canned milk, **aseptically** packaged milks, and dry milk powders do not need to be refrigerated.

After the can or box containing these items is opened, or after the dry milk product has been reconstituted, however, these become potentially hazardous foods that must be cared for just as if they were fresh milk products.

Unfortunately, the quality of fresh in-the-shell eggs on delivery is most often unknown. The age of eggs (how recently an egg was laid) is only one of many factors affecting its quality. For example, the National Egg Board states that a one-week-old egg, held under ideal conditions, can be fresher than a one-day-old egg left at room temperature for twenty-four hours.

The ideal conditions for eggs are temperatures that do not go above 40°F (4.5°C) and a relative humidity of 70 to 80 percent. The quality level of fresh eggs is very important. As eggs age, the white becomes thinner and the yolk becomes flatter. While these changes do not have an effect on an egg's nutritional quality, the fresher the egg is when poached or fried, the more it will hold its shape rather than spread out in the pan, which can certainly affect your guests' perceptions of product quality.

Buyer's Guide to Purchasing Terms

Respire   To take up oxygen and produce carbon dioxide through oxidation. Respiration rates can be controlled (slowed) when storing produce by reducing temperatures or by reducing the available oxygen levels.

Aseptic (packaging)   A system of packaging, in airtight containers, products that are free from organisms that cause disease, fermentation, or decay.

PROFESSIONAL PURCHASING PREVENTS PROBLEMS (8.2)

Care of Fresh Eggs

A common problem: Confusion over egg carton dating systems can result in improperly rotated fresh eggs.

Do all storeroom personnel know that a carton of USDA-graded fresh eggs with the date 210 is almost three weeks younger than one dated 190, but eggs dated 365 are two weeks older than those dated 014? In some cases they may not.

These three-digit numbers refer to the day of the year that the eggs are processed and placed into the carton. It must be displayed on each egg carton marked with a USDA grade shield. This three-digit Julian date represents the consecutive day of the year. For example, January 1 is shown as 001 and December 31 as 365.

Typically, eggs are packed within one to seven days of being laid. It is important to know that expiration dates are not required to be used (although, if they are used, they can be no more than thirty days from the day the eggs were packed into the carton). As a result, storeroom personnel must be trained in reading and understanding the unique date-marking system for fresh eggs if they are to be rotated properly.

Understanding Julian dates and their use in stock rotation is just one example of the specialized information knowledgeable buyers must possess and pass on to others in their operations if their food products are to be consistently served at the very highest quality levels.

Purchasing Terms

Produce *201*

Fruit *201*

Vegetable *202*

Organic *204*

Ripe *204*

Irradiation *206*

Solid pack
  (canning) *207*

Water pack
  (canning) *207*

Syrup pack
  (canning) *207*

Brix *207*

Puree *207*

Modified atmosphere
  packaging
  (MAP) *212*

Oxidation *212*

Lactose *214*

Pasteurize *214*

Homogenize *214*

Cream *215*

Casein *216*

Rennet *216*

Coagulate *216*

Ferment *220*

Cultured (butter) *221*

Sweet cream butter *221*

Clarified (butter) *221*

Smoke point *221*

Ghee *221*

Score (butter) *222*

Cultured (dairy
  product) *223*

Overrun *224*

Albumen *225*

Lecithin *226*

Emulsification *226*

Julian date *226*

Cholesterol *228*

Respire *230*

Aseptic (packaging) *230*

Make Your Own Purchasing Decisions

1. "Fresh" when discussing fruits and vegetables can mean anything from "never frozen" to "never processed." Choose one fruit and one vegetable (e.g., peaches and broccoli) and write a complete menu definition of "fresh" for those two items. Do you think the customers for whom you buy would completely agree with your definitions? What would you do to best ensure a complete understanding by those for whom you buy?

2. Consumers increasingly purchase organic fruits and vegetables for their use at home, as these products are perceived as more healthful (though more expensive) alternatives to highly processed fruits, vegetables, dairy products, and eggs. As a foodservice buyer, what specific implications do you believe this trend would have for your own purchasing activities?

3. Assume you are the buyer for a college foodservice program. Would you offer all possible versions of milk fat content milks (i.e., nonfat, 1 percent, 2 percent, and whole) to your residence hall students? What factors must buyers consider as they balance their guests' desires for variety with their operation's logistical limitations?

4. Buyers can often save money on fresh fruits and produce if they clean, trim, chop, or otherwise process these items on-site. The resulting items are often fresher products containing fewer

preservatives. The skilled labor required to process produce on-site, however, is often lacking in commercial kitchens. Assume you wished to institute a training program for your workers that would result in their acquiring the knowledge and skills needed to process most of your fresh produce products. What resources can you identify that would help you develop your training program?

5. Like many other food products, some fruits, vegetables, and dairy products are packaged under nationally labeled brands (e.g., Dole brand pineapples, Green Giant brand vegetables, and Ben and Jerry's brand ice cream). How important do you feel name brand products in these categories would be to your guests? How important would they be to you?

9

Groceries

Purchasing Pros Need to Know!

Groceries in this book refers to the many foods traditionally sold by grocers. Some hospitality buyers refer to these items as *dry goods*. In each case the terms indicate the variety of foods used to complement the service of the meats, seafood, produce, and dairy products you learned about in the previous two chapters.

Regardless of the term you prefer, in this chapter you will examine many of the food items that you will buy to serve your guests. The array of foods discussed in this chapter will not, perhaps, include all of the food items you may need to purchase (because specialized cuisines often incorporate unique grocery items), but they will include the vast majority of the grocery items you will spec and buy.

For example, bread is among the most important complements to a meal and to understand its many forms, one must understand the cereal grains from which it is made. This chapter examines wheat, corn, rice, and other cereals used to make breads as well as other starchy dishes. Despite its close association with Italian foods, pastas (and noodles) are a mainstay of many cuisines, and you should know how these popular starches are made and used in the foodservice industry. Potatoes are the starch most frequently consumed by American diners (due in large part to the popularity of French fries), and you will learn about the many available market forms of this widely served menu item. In addition to learning about starches, in this chapter you will be introduced to culinary fats and oils, some of the most important of food flavorings. These are used in all forms of cooking and baking, and a basic understanding of their sources will help you make good decisions when selecting these products.

Most diners like sweets. Natural and artificial sweeteners are important as food flavorings as well as for their role in baked products. Experienced cooks also know the importance of spices to enhance flavor and preserve foods. Thus, a basic understanding of these critical recipe ingredients is fundamental to purchasing them. Though sometimes neglected, in many dishes (e.g., pecans in pralines, walnuts or pistachios in baklava, and pine nuts in pesto) the meats from nuts (known as nutmeats) are an essential ingredient as well as an indispensable flavoring source.

Increasingly, foodservice professionals purchase a variety of foods that have labor built into them. These convenience foods affect many areas of today's foodservice menus, and knowledge of how they are made, packaged, and labeled is essential to good buying. Entrées, baked goods, soups, dressings, and condiments are good examples of foods that are often considered (and purchased as) convenience foods.

Some food products are not a specific type, but rather are common foods that are produced and handled in very special ways. Chief among these are kosher products (those permitted by Jewish dietary law) and halal foods (those permitted by Muslim dietary law). Your knowledge of these food types is increasingly important in a world where the diversity of foodservice customers is rapidly expanding.

■■■

Outline

Starches
   Cereal Grains
      Wheat

STARCHES

Grains (wheat, corn, rice, and others), **pastas,** and noodles are collectively known as starches. From a culinary perspective, a potato (the vegetable briefly examined in Chapter 8) is also considered a starch, as it will be in this chapter.

Some starches are vegetables, while others are grasses. Starches are the staple foods in nearly all cuisines. In general, they are high in carbohydrates, low in fat, and relatively inexpensive. As a result, in most cuisines, they have historically been considered an important part of a well-balanced meal. In addition, because of their health benefits, they are part of a well-balanced diet.

Cereal Grains

Of the approximately eight thousand species in the grass family, only a few are considered food. Aside from bamboo and sugar cane, **cereals** are the only grasses regularly eaten by humans. Cereal plants produce edible grains. The grain may be either a seed (e.g., rice) or a kernel (e.g., wheat).

The historical importance of grains is easier to appreciate when you consider that the major grains used in European cuisine (wheat, barley, rye, and oats) originally grew wild. During the times of harvest, groups of early humans working collectively could gather and store enough grain to feed the group until the next year. In many ways it was the ability to use them for different cooking purposes as well as their nutritional value and storability that permitted humans to move from nomadic (constantly moving), hunting societies to agrarian (farming) societies.

As the first farmers learned to tend wheat and barley fields planted for their grain size and ease of cultivation, these grains spread in popularity throughout western and central Asia, Europe, and northern Africa. Each of the popular grains had its own characteristics that directly affected its use in cooking.

Wheat, when mixed with water and flavorings (as well as other ingredients such as yeast, that created tiny bubbles in the dough), could easily be shaped, **leavened,** and cooked to produce a variety of light, tasty loaves of breads.

Barley had a short growing season and was hardy enough to grow in a variety of climates. Rye and oats were able to thrive in wet, colder climates (a major reason for their popularity in Irish and Scottish cuisines). Around the same time, other humans perfected the techniques required to grow rice in the wet, hot climates of tropical and semitropical Asia and Southeast Asia. The lasting effect of this grain on cuisines from those areas is unmistakable. In the western hemisphere, other groups (among them, the Incas of Peru and the Mayas and Aztecs of Mexico) were developing techniques to efficiently grow and harvest maize (corn), a grain so large and hardy that it dominates Central and South American cuisines and now ranks behind only wheat and rice as the world's third largest human food crop.

Grains of all types are similar in construction. Grain **kernels** are protected by a hull or husk, which is removed prior to eating the kernel.

Buyer's Guide to Purchasing Terms

Grain   The harvested seeds of grasses grown for food.

Pasta   Dough, usually made of wheat flour, water, and sometimes eggs, which is molded into any of a variety of shapes, then boiled or simmered.

Cereal   Any plant of the grass family that yields an edible grain (e.g., wheat, rye, oats, rice, and corn).

Leaven   To increase in size and lightness due to a chemical reaction in food.

Kernel   A single grain seed.

Did You Know? (9.1)

There are numerous steps involved from the time grain is planted until flour is available for baking. To see the "Grain Chain," go to: www.grainchain.com.

Understanding the three main parts of the edible kernel is essential to you when making informed cereal grain buying decisions:

Bran   The tough outer layer covering the endosperm.

Endosperm   The largest part of the kernel and the source of the grain's protein and starch content. This portion of the grain is used to produce **flour.**

Germ   Also known as the embryo, the germ is the smallest part of the kernel. It is the source of any fat found in the grain. Because of the tendency for fats to become rancid (spoil) quickly, this portion of the grain has historically been removed from the grain prior to grinding for flour.

Whole-grain flours (and foods) are those in which all three parts of the grain (bran, endosperm, and germ) are used in the product.

Humans began treating grains to remove the tough protective bran layers very early in time. Milling, the process of breaking grains apart, was used because removing the tough outer layers makes grains easier to chew, and removing the fat-containing germ prolongs the storage life of the grain.

Today the flours made by processing grains are produced by using steel rollers or stones to grind the grains. In both cases the miller (grinder) who processes the grain will expose it to one or more of the following processes:

- *Cracking*   The miller breaks open the grains.
- *Hulling*   The hull is separated from the grain.
- *Grinding*   The grains are reduced to powders of various sizes.
- *Pearling*   All or part of the hull, bran, and germ are removed from the grain.

Because most buyers believe stone grinding produces a product superior to that made with steel rollers, stone-ground products are always labeled as such and will generally be sold at a higher price.

While any grain can be used to produce flour, foodservice buyers are typically most concerned with the information needed to purchase wheat, rice, corn, and to a lesser degree, some other types of ground grains.

WHEAT   Wheat is the most widely cultivated food in the world. Its grain is highly prized for a variety of reasons, the most widespread of which is bread making. In

Buyer's Guide to Purchasing Terms

Flour   The finely crushed meal (powder) that results when an edible grain (or other food such as potato) has been ground; also called *farina* in Spanish and Italian and *farine* in French.

Whole grain   Foods that contain all three of the essential parts (bran, endosperm, and germ) and naturally occurring nutrients of the entire grain seed. If the grain has been processed (i.e., cracked, crushed, rolled, or ground), the resulting food product should deliver approximately the same balance of nutrients as that found in the original grain seed.

addition to the flours made from the endosperm of this grain, wheat germ and wheat bran are also popular, principally because of their nutritional value. Wheat germ and wheat bran can be purchased, cooked, and served alone, but they are most often added to other foods.

Some popular foods (e.g., the Lebanese dish tabbouleh and the northern African dish couscous) use coarsely processed wheat grains, but wheat is most often purchased in its finely ground flour form. In fact, even though flour can be made from many grains, in the U.S. foodservice industry, when buyers use the word *flour* they almost always are referring to wheat flour.

The type of wheat from which it is made determines the character of the wheat flour produced. The most defining characteristic of wheat is its **gluten** content.

Gluten helps make bread dough pliable (elastic) and gives the dough a chewy texture when it is eaten. Gluten provides many additional important qualities to bread. For example, gluten keeps the gases that are released during fermentation in the dough, so the bread is able to rise before it is baked. Also, gluten firms up when it is cooked, and this enables starches in the dough to help the bread maintain its proper shape when cooking.

Hard wheat produces a grain with a small kernel and high gluten content. Soft wheat produces flour that has lower gluten content. Flours with lower gluten-producing characteristics make tender baked goods such as cakes and pie crusts, while flours with higher protein contents produce heartier products such as yeast breads and bagels.

Figure 9.1 lists the various types and protein contents of the wheat flours you are likely to buy as well as the most common foodservice uses for these flours.

Flour develops better baking qualities if it is allowed to age for a few weeks after it is milled. Chlorine dioxide speeds this aging but also bleaches the flour. Bleaching destroys some of wheat flour's naturally occurring vitamin E, so some bakers (and their foodservice customers) prefer unbleached flours.

As a professional buyer, you should also be aware that wheat flour is often sold as **self-rising,** but the actual use of this type of flour in foodservice is limited because of the great variations in the ratio of salt and **leavening agents** used in their recipes.

Type	Protein Content	Used For
Cake	7–9.5%	Cakes
Pastry	7.5–12%	Pie crusts, biscuits
All-purpose	10–13%	General baked products, cookies
Bread	12–15%	Yeast breads
Whole-wheat	13–14%	Breads
High-gluten	14–15%	Bagels

FIGURE 9.1 Protein Content of Wheat Flours

Buyer's Guide to Purchasing Terms

Gluten   A special protein found in many (but not all) grains. Sticky when wet, it becomes firm when cooked.

Self-rising (flour)   All-purpose flour to which salt and a chemical leavening agent (usually baking powder) have been added.

Leavening agent   An ingredient that causes bread to increase in size and lightness (to leaven).

CORN   Corn (or maize from the Spanish *maíz*) is the only grain that is regularly eaten fresh like a vegetable (sweet corn), but was originally grown for its use as a ground product (corn flour). Corn is native to the Americas but was spread to the rest of the world in the late fifteenth and early sixteenth centuries by European explorers.

As a foodservice buyer, you will likely choose from three basic variations of ground corn flour:

1. *Cornmeal*   This product is made by grinding a special type of corn known as field corn, or dent. Ground field corn (cornmeal) may be yellow, white, or blue. It is used as a coating for fried foods or can be cooked and made into a variety of products.

2. *Hominy*   This product is made from dried corn that has been soaked in hydrated lime or lye. Doing so removes the germ and the hard outer hull from the kernels, making the kernels better tasting, easier to digest, and easier to process. When first cooked with an alkaline substance and very finely ground, this version of hominy is known as **masa harina** and is used a large number of Central and South American dishes.

   In most of the United States, hominy refers to whole corn kernels, which are hulled but not ground. In most of the southern United States, however, hominy refers to the coarsely ground kernels used to make the dish known as hominy grits, or more simply grits.

3. *Grits*   Grits are dried hominy that has been finely to coarsely ground. Grits are most often served as a breakfast cereal and are usually topped with butter or cheese. Quick-cooking and instant grits are also available to foodservice buyers.

RICE   Rice is the starchy seed of a semiaquatic grass. Rice is a staple dish in most East and Southeast Asian cuisines. It is a key ingredient, however, in many cuisines including French and Spanish.

Rice is the world's second largest grain crop (behind wheat). Rice is divided into three main types based on its seed size: long-grain, medium-grain, and short-grain. Long-grain is the most popular worldwide. Its grains remain firm, fluffy, and separate after cooking. Short-grain rice contains more starch, thus it tends to get sticky after cooking. Japanese sushi and Spanish paella are both made using short-grain rice.

Wild rice is a special variation of rice cultivated in the United States. The most highly prized variety is northern wild rice, an annual plant native to the Great Lakes regions. Wild rice is generally available in three grades: Giant (long grain and the highest grade), Fancy (medium grain), and Select (short grain).

To prepare it for use, the seeds of a rice plant are first milled to remove the outer husks of the grain (the bran). At this point in the process the product is called brown rice. This processing may continue with the removal of the germ, creating white rice. The white rice may then be buffed with glucose or talcum powder to produce polished rice. Next the rice may be partially cooked.

Buyer's Guide to Purchasing Term

Masa harina   Literally corn dough flour, it may be reconstituted with water or other liquids and used as a thickener and to make tortillas and tamales as well as other corn-based dishes.

"Converted rice" has been parboiled to remove the rice's surface starch. "Instant" or quick-cooking (minute) rice is created by fully cooking and flash freezing or drying the cooked product. Finally, rice may, in the same manner as many other grains, simply be ground to produce rice flour.

OTHER CEREALS Although wheat, corn, and rice are the most popular grains, others are also widely consumed and, thus, often purchased for use in foodservice. These include the following:

Oats Ninety-five percent of the oat crop grown in the world is used as animal food. The remaining 5 percent, however, constitutes important parts of American and European cuisines. Oats are consumed primarily as a breakfast cereal (oatmeal). **Rolled oats** are a popular oat form, as are **quick-cooking oats** and **instant oats.** Henry Crowell, the founder of Quaker Oats, who turned the commodity into a breakfast cereal by packaging it with cooking instructions and labeling it *Natural,* refined each of these forms. Today oats are also a very popular ingredient in breads, muffins, and cookies.

Barley Fast growing, hardy, and nutritious, in the Middle Ages, barley (as well as rye) was the mainstay grain of peasants' diets, while wheat flour was reserved for the wealthy. Today barley is used in Western cuisines primarily as an ingredient in soups. It is, however, an essential ingredient in Japanese miso (fermented soy paste). In Moroccan cuisine, as well other countries of northern Africa and western Asia, it is a popular ingredient for bread making.

Buckwheat While not actually a grain (it is the fruit of a plant most closely related to rhubarb), buckwheat nonetheless is often treated as a grain. It can be used to make noodles and bread; however, in the United States, it is most often encountered as an ingredient in pancakes and waffles, where it contributes tenderness and a nutty flavor.

Rye Popular for its use in bread making, rye flour is readily available to foodservice buyers. Interestingly, rye flour can absorb eight times its weight in liquid (in comparison, wheat flour can absorb only two times its weight). As a result, breads made with rye flour tend to be heavier than those of the same size that are made from wheat flour.

Rye flour may be purchased in four colors, or grades. These are white, medium, dark, and rye meal. Medium and dark ryes have the most intense flavors, and breads containing them will typically be labeled as such. Rye meal is simply whole rye grain that is ground in various coarseness levels. Some millers and food manufacturers refer to rye meal as pumpernickel. Others, however, use pumpernickel as a generic term to describe any dark rye flour.

Ready-to-Eat Cereals While not a separate type of grain, ready-to-eat cereals deserve the special attention of foodservice buyers. Despite their currently poor reputation for containing too much highly refined sugar and contributing only

Buyer's Guide to Purchasing Terms

Rolled oats Whole-grain oats that are steamed, rolled into flat flakes, and dried.

Quick-cooking oats Rolled oats cut into small pieces to reduce cooking time.

Instant oats Oats that are fully cooked before drying and must only be reconstituted with hot liquid prior to consumption.

"empty calories," ready-to-eat cereals began as a healthful alternative to the heavy American breakfasts of the mid-nineteenth century.

Dr. John Harvey Kellogg and his brother, Will Keith Kellogg; Charles William Post; and others were actually part of the first health movement in America. They warned about the dangers of fatty, protein-rich foods. Instead, they advocated a diet based primarily on vegetables, grains, and fiber. This group of innovators created the ready-to-eat cereal industry and invented such still popular cereal variations as shredded wheat, puffed rice, wheat and corn flakes, Grape-Nuts (invented by Post), **muesli,** and **granola.** Ready-to-eat cereals may be purchased in bulk or in single-serving containers.

Pasta

Pasta is one of the simplest ways to prepare cereal flours for food. Essentially, pasta consists of wheat flour mixed with water to make a paste, formed into small pieces, then boiled in water (not baked like most other doughs). *Noodle* is the German word for pasta. It is Italy, whose pasta makers had easy access to high-protein-content flours, that is most noted for pasta making. While pasta is primarily associated with Italian cooking, pastas are an important part of many cuisines. In China boiled grain pastes were used to make long noodles and thin sheets (wrappers), some of which were made of wheat flour and others made of rice or bean pastes.

Originally made from only wheat flour, today pasta is created from various combinations of flours, water, and egg yolks or whole eggs, and is produced in a wide variety of shapes and forms. Pastas, after cooking, are usually served with a sauce or are stuffed with meats, cheese, or vegetables, then sauced.

Italian-style pastas are made chiefly from **semolina,** the endosperm of durum, a high-protein wheat variety prized for its rich, cream color and smooth, durable doughs.

Couscous, a unique form of pasta associated with Moroccan cuisine but indigenous to Tunisia and Algeria as well, is also made from semolina.

Pasta is an ingredient in many common foodservice dishes and, thus, will be part of pasta products purchased canned or frozen. For most foodservice buyers, individual pasta products may be purchased dried or fresh.

DRIED PASTA   The dried pastas you will buy are available in a variety of flavors and shapes. In addition to white (traditional), green (spinach flavored), and red (tomato flavored) pastas, foodservice buyers can choose from whole-wheat products and other flavor combinations. While pastas can be made into literally hundreds of shapes, these can be considered more easily when divided into the three main groups of ribbons, tubes, and shapes, as shown in Figure 9.2.

FRESH PASTA   In addition to the dried pasta forms most commonly purchased, many operations choose to use fresh (not dry) and/or precooked pasta. Like their dried counterparts, these pastas are made from semolina. Fresh pasta cooks faster

---

Buyer's Guide to Purchasing Terms

Muesli   A mixture of thinly rolled grains, sugar, fruits, and nuts.

Granola   Rolled oats flavored with sweeteners (usually honey) and spices, enriched with vegetable oil, toasted, and mixed with nuts and/or dried fruits. The term was originally coined by the Kellogg brothers.

Semolina   The part of durum wheat used for Italian-style pasta making.

Pasta Group	Common Products
Ribbons	Lasagna
	Fettuccine
	Linguine
	Spaghetti
	Vermicelli (thin spaghetti)
	Capellini (angel-hair spaghetti)
Tubes	Manicotti
	Ziti
	Rigatoni
	Penne
	Spira
	Elbow
Shapes	Conchiglie (shells)
	Fusilli (spirals)
	Farfalle (bows)
	Rotolli (wheels)
	Orzo (rice grains)

FIGURE 9.2 Common Pasta Groups and Products

than dried pasta, and many kitchen managers believe its taste is superior. For operations serving stuffed pastas (for example manicotti, cannelloni, and tortellini), prefilled fresh pastas can save labor and help ensure product consistency.

For generations, culinarians have been instructed that pastas taste best when served **al dente.**

Today foodservice buyers can purchase expertly precooked pastas guaranteed to be prepared al dente. The results are product consistency and rapid preparation times. Precooked pastas need only be heated by plunging in boiling water or steaming (but not cooking) prior to their service. Many operators selecting precooked pastas also report reduced levels of product waste.

Packaged in a variety of forms, these precooked products, as well as fresh pastas, are increasing in quality, variety, and availability. Figure 9.3 lists some flavors of readily available fresh or precooked pastas.

Potatoes

Food historians generally agree that the potato originated in the Andes Mountains of South America. European explorers exported potatoes to Spain in the mid-1560s,

Egg	*Mushroom*	*Tomato-basil*
Tarragon	*Onion*	*Jalapeno*
Oregano	*Scallion*	*Chive*
Garlic	*Basil*	*Tricolor*
Green (bell) pepper	*Black pepper*	*Thyme*
Rosemary	*Sun-dried tomato*	*Cayenne*
Lemon-pepper	*Spinach*	*Red (bell) pepper*
Tomato	*Dill*	*Saffron*
Sage	*Lemon*	*Red (chili) pepper*
Whole wheat	*Buckwheat*	*Beet*

FIGURE 9.3 Fresh and Precooked Flavored Pastas

Buyer's Guide to Purchasing Term

Al dente Pasta that has been cooked just long enough to be firm to the tooth (not soft).

The best pasta dishes require careful cooking as well as the purchase of pastas made from high-quality semolina flours.

Ian O'Leary © Dorling Kindersley

where they quickly spread to the rest of Europe. Well suited to the climates of Europe, the potato was cultivated widely. Today the potato forms an important part of the traditional cuisine of the British Isles, Western and Eastern Europe, and of course, the United States. Versatility is one of the major factors driving the extreme popularity of potatoes. Potatoes can be served in a variety of ways. In some recipes the potatoes are peeled before cooking; in others (e.g., baked potatoes) the

---

PROFESSIONAL PURCHASING PREVENTS PROBLEMS (9.1)

Avoiding Pasty Pasta

A common problem: Improperly prepared cooked-to-order pastas reflect poorly on the operation and the buyer who originally purchased the pasta.

Because of the length of time required for cooking, it is often not practical to cook individual servings of dry pasta to order. The result is that precooked or partially cooked pasta is used in cook-to-order foodservice operations. This practice is certainly reasonable; however, if not implemented properly, it can result in over- (or under-) cooked pastas that can reflect poorly on the operation and its pasta buyer (you).

To avoid this situation, it is important to fully understand that, when pasta cooks in water, the proteins and starch granules absorb water and expand. This causes the pasta's outer protein layer to rupture and the dissolving starch to be released into the cooking water. Deeper in the noodle, there is less water readily available, so the center of noodle stays drier and more intact than does the surface.

Cooking pasta al dente means stopping the cooking process when the center of the noodle remains slightly underdone and offers resistance to chewing. At this point, the water content of the noodle surface is 80 to 90 percent. At the same time, the water content at the center of the noodle is between 40 and 60 percent. It is critical to understand that, unless the cooking process is stopped completely at this al dente stage, the pasta center will continue to absorb water or, if no water is available, seek to equalize the water content of the outer and inner noodle, creating a product that is too dry on the outside and too mushy on the inside (neither of which is a good thing).

While buyers may not be the individuals in their operations responsible for food production, pasta cooking is one area in which buyers must work closely with cooks to ensure cooking procedures are in place to make certain quality standards are consistently met.*

*For a good discussion of pasta production techniques appropriate for foodservice operations serving cook-to-order pastas, see Labensky and Hause, *On Cooking,* 4th ed. (Upper Saddle River, NJ: Pearson Prentice-Hall, 2006).

potato is served with its outer covering (skin) left on during cooking and service. Many potato dishes are served hot, but some very popular styles are served at room temperature (e.g., potato chips) and others are served cold (e.g., potato salad). One of the most common methods of serving potatoes is the simple mashed potato. In this form, the potato is first boiled then, when cooked through, is blended with butter, seasonings, and milk. In addition to mashed potatoes, plain or seasoned boiled or steamed potatoes are also very popular. Potatoes may be served whole, sliced, or diced, and baked, roasted, or fried.

In the United States, French fries (called "pommes frites" in France and "chips" in Great Britain) are the single most popular method of serving potatoes. This potato preparation style could actually be best translated as potatoes "fried in the French style" because many foods, including seafood, vegetables, and meats are cooked in the same manner (i.e., deep-fat fried). Today, however, foodservice buyers can choose to purchase fresh potatoes for French frying or they can select from a variety of processed potato products intended to shorten frying times. Those buyers seeking to serve French fries with a reduced fat content can select items that are to be baked in an oven or even microwaved. This is possible because, unlike many other foods, potatoes can be easily cooked in a microwave and still retain nearly all of their nutritional value and texture. Properly done, microwaving produces a potato very similar to a steamed potato while retaining the appearance of a conventionally baked potato. Creative foodservice operators continue to explore the use of battered, breaded, and preseasoned French fries, a testament to the consumers' desire to sample all things French fried.

While the number of ways potatoes can be prepared is a challenge to foodservice buyers, so is the fact that there are more than five thousand varieties of potato. For most buyers, however, it is easiest to choose potatoes when it is recognized that potatoes can be classified as being of either a **mealy** or **waxy** type.

In some food reference sources, new potatoes are considered to be a separate variety of waxy potato. Technically, however, the term *new* refers to immature potatoes of all varieties, harvested in the spring and early summer. New potatoes have flimsy, parchmentlike skins that can be easily peeled off with the fingers. New potatoes of most varieties are prized for their high moisture content and creamy texture. Experienced buyers know that the term *new* does not refer to a specific potato variety and, thus, are careful when choosing potatoes that are labeled as such.

In most cases foodservice buyers choose mealy potatoes for use as bakers and for French fries. Waxy potatoes (sometimes called boiling potatoes), such as red skins, are used for dishes in which the end product is best if the potato keeps its shape after cooking. Yukon gold and white potatoes (as well as Peruvian purple and blue) are considered all-purpose potatoes because their moisture and starch contents fall midway between those of the waxy and mealy potato varieties. Figure 9.4 is a summary of the most common potato preparation methods and the common potato varieties best suited for them.

As a professional foodservice buyer, you will purchase fresh potatoes on many occasions, but you will also likely choose from a large number of alternative potato market forms. For example, in commercial kitchens, dried potatoes are very popular for making items such as scalloped and au gratin potatoes. Freeze-dried, powdered,

Buyer's Guide to Purchasing Terms

Mealy (potato)   A potato variety with a low moisture and high starch content (e.g., Idaho and russet). These are good for baking and frying.

Waxy (potato)   A potato variety with a high moisture and low starch content (e.g., red skins and whites). These are good for salads, soups, and stews.

Use	Recommended Potato Type
Baking	Russet (Idaho)
Salads, gratins, and scalloped potatoes	Yellow Finn, red skin, white round, and purple
Mashing	Russet, Yukon gold, and purple
Soups, stews, and chowders	Yukon gold, Yellow Finn, red skin, white round, and purple
Panfrying	Red skin, white round, new, and white fingerling
French fries	Russet and purple
Roasting	New potatoes of all varieties
Steaming/boiling	Red skin and Yukon gold
Potato pancakes	Russet and Yukon gold

FIGURE 9.4   Recommended Potatoes to Purchase for Various Uses

or granulated potato products are frequently chosen to make mashed potatoes. Also, reconstituted, dehydrated potatoes are commonly used to make hash browns.

In most cases, however, if you buy processed potatoes, they are likely to be purchased frozen. The number and types of frozen potato products are vast, and many are highly specialized. All professional buyers, however, should understand the basics of buying frozen French fries, easily the most popular market form of the most popular potato item sold to foodservice operations.

The USDA has established specific standards for frozen French fries, and these standards can be reviewed at www.agribusinessonline.com. In addition to the many other quality characteristics that are important, length is the characteristic most affecting product price because customers overwhelmingly prefer longer French fries over shorter ones, and buyers readily pay a product premium to satisfy this preference. As a result, length standards for frozen French fries are strictly defined.

The USDA standards for French fry length are determined by establishing the percentages (by actual count) of the individual potato strips making up the container of French fries. Standardized USDA definitions for frozen French fry packages are as follows:

Extra long   Eighty percent or more are two inches in length or longer; and 30 percent or more are three inches in length or longer.

Long   Seventy percent or more are two inches in length or longer; and 15 percent or more are three inches in length or longer.

Medium   Fifty percent or more are two inches in length or longer.

Short   Less than 50 percent are two inches in length or longer.

Buyer's Guide to Internet Resources: Starches

Web Site	Topic
www.flour.com	Regular and organic flours for baking
www.usarice.com	Rice recipes and cookery information
www.zerega.com	Custom made Italian-style pastas
www.vegkitchen.com/recipes/asian-noodles.htm	Asian-style noodle definitions and recipes
www.larsenfarms.com/retail_choosing.asp	Information about buying fresh potatoes
www.simplot.com	Information about processed potatoes of all types and market forms

Experienced buyers know that potato strip length is a critical factor when buying frozen French fries. As a result, they are careful to always include length standards in any frozen French fry specification they develop. Doing so helps ensure the buyer receives and serves products with high levels of length uniformity and that guest satisfaction with this extremely popular potato form remains uniformly high as well.

FATS AND OILS

One good way for professional food buyers to understand **fats** is simply to recognize that they are not water. In fact, they are so unlike water that the two cannot actually be mixed. Culinarians use this knowledge to their advantage when they fry foods to brown them, when they create **emulsions** in items such as dressings, and when they thicken sauces with microscopic but intact fat droplets.

Fat is the term most often used to identify those lipids (the Greek term for fat) that are solid at room temperature. *Oil* is the term used to identify those fats that are liquid at room temperature. Both fats and oils are members of the triglyceride family of chemical compounds. Therefore, oils can quite correctly be considered simply liquid fats.

Despite the fact that most fats do not actually have a sharply defined temperature at which they completely change from solid to liquid (they soften gradually over a broad temperature range), many foodservice buyers use these traditional solid and liquid categories when discussing them.

Because of their importance in the human diet and their proven relationship to obesity, heart disease, cholesterol levels, and other health-related issues, it is more important than ever that you understand fats and oils.

Solid fats contain more saturated fats and/or trans fats than oils. Trans fats occur naturally, in small quantities, in meat and dairy products. Most trans fats

Did You Know? (9.2)

There are actually four types of fats: (1) monounsaturated, (2) polyunsaturated, (3) saturated, and (4) trans.

Monounsaturated fat and polyunsaturated fat are the "good" fats and can be eaten in moderation with no known negative effects on health.

It is generally accepted that consumption of saturated fat should be kept low, especially for adults.

Trans fats are recognized as particularly unhealthful, and their use in commercial foodservice operations is increasingly restricted or prohibited.

Because of the different types of fats, it is wise for foodservice buyers to better understand the composition of the fats used in their own operations.

To learn more about the composition of fats and oils commonly purchased for foodservice use, you can go to www.hsph.harvard.edu/nutritionsource/fats.html.

When you arrive, read about the relationship between cholesterol and fats and scroll down to read about the percentage breakdowns of "Specific Types of Fat in Common Oils and Fats."

Buyer's Guide to Purchasing Terms

Fat   A natural oily substance found in animals and plants. Fats are a major class of energy-rich food and do not dissolve in water.

Emulsion   A mixture (suspension) of tiny droplets of one liquid in another liquid (e.g., an oil-and-vinegar emulsion).

consumed by foodservice customers, however, are industrially created as a side effect of partial hydrogenation of plant oils.

Hydrogenation is a process of changing the chemical properties of liquid oils to make them solids.

The hydrogenation technique was perfected in Germany in the early 1900s and was first commercialized in the United States in 1911 as the product Crisco.

Partial hydrogenation changes a fat's molecular structure, raising its melting point, and reducing its rancidity. Unfortunately, this same process also results in a proportion of the changed fat becoming trans fat. This is a critical fact to know because, unlike other fat forms, trans fats are not beneficial for health.

Despite their reduced usage in foodservice, trans fats can be found in many commercial cakes, cookies, crackers, icings, margarines, and microwave popcorns. Eating trans fats has been found, among other things, to increase the risk of coronary heart disease, and as a result, health authorities worldwide recommend that consumption of trans fat be eliminated or severely restricted.

In December, 2006, the New York City Board of Health voted to make New York the nation's first city to ban artificial trans fats in foods served at restaurants. The board, which passed the ban unanimously, barred restaurants from using most frying oils containing artificial trans fats by mid-2007 and mandated the elimination of artificial trans fats from all of foods served by July, 2008. Other communities have followed New York's lead.

Solid Fats

Solid fats are fats that are firm at room temperature and include butter and shortening. Solid fats come from many animal foods and, as previously noted, can be made from vegetable oils through hydrogenation. In commercial foodservice, the most commonly used solid fats include the following:

- butter
- beef fat (tallow, suet)
- chicken fat
- pork fat (**lard**)
- margarine

In most cases solid, nonhydrogenized fats have low smoke points (see Chapter 8). As a result, these fats are purchased primarily for the characteristic flavors they give soups (chicken fat), sauces, and baking (butter) and for flavoring other foods (beef and pork fats).

Margarine is a solid fat and has a long and interesting history. In 1869 Napoleon offered a prize to anyone who could make a butter substitute suitable for the armed forces of France, as well as for the country's poor. A French chemist invented a substance that was first extracted from beef fat then flavored. The resulting product was called "oleomargarine," and was, over time, shortened to "margarine." The term *margarine* now refers generically to any of a range of broadly similar fats and oils made into solids (although liquid margarines are also available). Some foodservice buyers commonly shorten the name *oleomargarine* to *oleo*.

Today margarine can be made from any of a wide variety of animal or vegetable fats and is often mixed with skim milk, salt, and man-made emulsifiers. Margarine made from vegetable oils is especially important in today's foodservice

Buyer's Guide to Purchasing Terms

Hydrogenation   A process that converts liquid oils to solid oils.

Lard   A highly purified form of pork fat.

industry and is a substitute for butter: a situation that is appreciated by vegetarians as well as those individuals who must avoid dairy-based products.

While the USDA has not developed grades for margarines, it has established specifications to ensure quality (www.ams.usda.gov/dairy/vegoil.pdf). The three main categories of margarine most purchased by foodservice buyers are as follows:

1. Solid, uncolored, or colored margarine used for cooking or baking. This product is also known as *shortening*, a term that refers to a hydrogenated vegetable oil that is solid at room temperature.
2. Traditional margarines for such uses as spreading on bread, English muffins, and the like. These items contain a relatively high percentage of saturated fats and can be made from either animal or vegetable oils.
3. Margarines high in mono- or polyunsaturated fats, which are made from safflower, sunflower, soybean, cottonseed, or olive oil and are often considered to be more healthful than butter or other types of margarine.

Liquid Fats (Oils)

As you've learned, oils are fats that are liquid at room temperature. Oils can come from many different plants as well as from fish. For purposes of buying foodservice oils, they can best be considered as either cooking oils or flavoring oils.

COOKING OILS   Many oils used for cooking, baking, or as an ingredient in other recipes are obtained from plants and have characteristics that make them appropriate for specific recipes or cooking styles. These include quality oils made from the following:

- canola
- corn
- peanut
- safflower
- soybean
- sunflower
- coconut

Olive oil is a popular product that is so widely used for cooking (and other purposes) in commercial kitchens that it deserves the special attention of professional food buyers. The olive (*Olea europaea*) is a species of small tree native to coastal areas of the eastern Mediterranean. Olives and oil are so closely associated that *oil* is actually a variation of the tree's name (*Olea*).

Olive oil is the only oil that is extracted from a fruit rather than a seed, nut, or grain. Extra virgin, virgin, and pure, the label designations of olive oil, refer to the acidity levels of the oil. Low acidity oils labeled extra virgin (maximum 1 percent acidity), or virgin (maximum 3 percent acidity) are best and the most expensive. These oils are typically used for salads and to make dipping sauces for breads, with less expensive olive oils most often used for frying.

FLAVORING OILS   By themselves, most oils add flavor to foods. Also, other ingredients such as garlic, spices, and herbs may be steeped in oils to add a more complex flavor. Other oils, such as those from nuts (almonds) and seeds (sesame), provide a strong flavor and the aroma of the item from which they are taken. Some specially produced flavored oils are also known as **infused oils.**

Buyer's Guide to Purchasing Term

Infused oils   Products prepared by extracting aromatic oils from other sources and emulsifying them with high-grade olive or canola oils. Commonly produced infused oils include those made with garlic, basil, citrus, and other spices.

PROFESSIONAL PURCHASING PREVENTS PROBLEMS (9.2)

What's in the Bottle?

A common problem: Confusion over olive oil labeling can result in poor purchasing decisions.

The International Olive Oil Council (IOOC) is an intergovernmental organization based in Spain. The IOOC promotes olive oil use around the world by tracking production, defining quality standards, and monitoring authenticity. More than 85 percent of the world's olives are grown in IOOC member nations. Twenty-three countries are members. However, the United States is not, and the United States does not recognize the international olive oil labeling standards mandated by IOOC.

As a result, olive oil suppliers selling to the U.S. market choose label wording differently than they do when selling to better-regulated IOOC countries. A few examples will help make this clear:

Imported from Italy creates an impression that the olives were grown in Italy. In the United States, however, it means only that the oil was bottled in Italy. The oil could originate from any country.

100% Pure Olive Oil is often touted as good quality, while it is actually the lowest quality commercially available. (Better grades would have *virgin* or *extra virgin* on the label.)

Light Olive Oil despite the implication to the contrary, refers only to a lighter color, not a lower fat content. All olive oil, which is all fat, has 120 calories per tablespoon.

While the USDA is considering adopting labeling rules that parallel the IOOC standards, until this occurs, terms such as *extra virgin* may be applied to *any* grade of oil, making the term of dubious usefulness. Thus, when it comes to quality olive oils, it is easy to see why U.S. foodservice buyers should definitely have as much (or more) product knowledge as their suppliers.

Buyers at Work (9.1)

"You are just the buyer," said Chef Wieland angrily. "I'm the chef."

Wieland Ludwig was indeed the chef at the Michigan Avenue Plaza, a mega-hotel of more than three thousand rooms and a property that served more than ten thousand banquet meals per week.

Wieland was talking to Karla Varela, the departmental food buyer, who, like Wieland, reported directly to the hotel's food and beverage director.

"Chef," Karla explained carefully, "I'm just as concerned about food quality as you are. But like I just said, currently, all we use is extra virgin olive oil. And we use a lot! With the new banquet menus we have just implemented, I was simply asking if there are any recipes or frying applications that might work just as well with virgin oil. If there are, we might save a lot of money!"

Striking the proper balance between buying the best and most expensive and the appropriate quality level can often be a buyer's greatest challenge.

Assume you were advising Karla:

1. What approach might you suggest to use to discuss the olive oil issue with the chef?
2. Do you think it makes sense for Karla to review menus regularly for potential areas of product cost savings? Who should be involved in that process?
3. Would you suggest that Karla discuss this issue with her boss? Would you foresee any negative impact of such a course of action?

Because of the manner in which bottles are labeled in the United States, buyers must be very knowledgeable when selecting quality olive oils.

Clive Streeter © Dorling Kindersley

Did You Know? (9.3)

The use of olive oils has become increasingly prevalent in the foodservice industry, but other exotic oils also are finding their place in creative American cuisine. Look for these oils to continue their rapid increases in popularity:

Almond oil—Nutty-rich flavor enhances salads and other dishes and also has a very high smoke point

Avocado—High smoke point, very nice for sautéing and for use in salad dressings

Grape seed (grapeseed)—Light, nutty flavor that is high in vitamin E and has a high smoke point; an outstanding, healthful sautéing oil

Hazelnut—Unique flavor that is excellent in baked goods, cookies, and candies

Walnut—Very rich and nutty flavor, good for salads, pastas, and drizzled on steaks

Truffle—Very expensive, rich, and savory, it is best when used (by the drop only) on potatoes, pastas, and vegetables

Safflower—All-purpose cooking oil with neutral flavor and high smoke point

Sunflower—Very light flavor, very high smoke point

Buyer's Guide to Internet Resources: Fats and Oils

Web Site	Topic
www.foodsubs.com/Oils.html	Substitutes for oils and fats in cooking
www.margarine.org	Margarines
www.peanut-institute.org	Peanut oils
www.internationaloliveoil.org	International olive oil standards
www.aboutoliveoil.org	The North American Olive Oil Association
www.oliveoilsource.com	Olive oil information and recipes
www.boyajianinc.com	Infused olive and Asian oils
www.theoilsite.net	Cooking oil information
www.omega9oils.com	Healthful cooking oils

FLAVORINGS

Regardless of the cuisine, food flavorings are an important part of what makes food taste good and, in many cases, authentic. For example, most diners expect to taste cumin (a spice), and cilantro (an herb) when eating Southwestern-style and Mexican foods. In a similar manner, sesame-ginger is a common seed-spice combination used in Asian cookery. Also, curry (a savory spice mixture) gives a distinctive flavor to Indian dishes. In the United States, toasted pecans will top praline-style desserts, and cinnamon is a must when creating tempting yeast-raised breakfast rolls!

In all of the above examples, selected foods are used to flavor, enhance, or in some manner complement the taste of other foods. In this section you will learn about three broad categories of important food flavorings: (1) sweeteners, (2) herbs and spices, and (3) **nutmeats.**

Sweeteners

Sweet (sugary) foods are favorites among foodservice guests. Some foods are naturally sweet and, after some processing, are eaten essentially as they occur in nature (e.g., honey, molasses, and maple syrup). In other cases (e.g., chocolate) a food with a unique flavor is sweetened with sugars to enhance the flavor of the original food. In still other cases, sweeteners such as sugar are used in combination with other foods because they provide texture, flavor, and color. In baked goods, sugars and other sweeteners enhance product tenderness because they weaken gluten strands in the flour used, provide food for yeast, assist in the leavening process, and even serve as a preservative.

Sweet foods are so popular that many nutritional experts in the United States are concerned about their overconsumption. This is especially true when it comes to sweetened drinks and some other snack foods. In fact, many school districts now significantly restrict the sale of both these items during school hours, citing an increasing incident of obesity and poor diets among their reasons for doing so. For professional foodservice buyers, the need to purchase sweet products will undoubtedly continue. It is important, however, to recognize your own responsibility for purchasing food items that taste good while also contributing to the good health of your customers.

Sugars make food taste sweet. Chemically, sugars, like the starches you learned about earlier in this chapter, are carbohydrates. They may be classified as either single (simple) sugars such as glucose and fructose, which occur naturally in honey and fruits, or more complex sugars such as sucrose and lactose (milk sugar).

Sugar is made by some plants to store energy that is not immediately needed. In this regard, the energy is stored in much the same manner as animals store fat. When people consume sugar, they receive the same energy boost the plant originally intended for itself. Sucrose is the most commonly purchased plant sugar in the foodservice industry. Worldwide, sugar cane accounts for approximately 70 percent of the sugar grown commercially and is produced in warm-climate areas where cane grows readily. Sucrose extracted from special varieties of beets (most sugar beets contain approximately 17 percent sugar by weight) account for the remaining 30 percent of the total available. Sugar beets can grow in colder climates where sugar cane would not grow. Sugar taken from either plant is equally suitable for foodservice. The **refined** sugars are chemically identical and may be efficiently extracted from either plant source.

Pure, refined sucrose is most often purchased in granulated (table sugar) or powdered forms. Powdered sugars (also known as confectioner's sugar because of its use in candy and dessert making) are available in varying degrees of fineness. For example, 10X is the most commonly sold form of powdered sugar (numbers

---

Buyer's Guide to Purchasing Terms

Nutmeat   The edible portion of nuts.

Refined (sugar)   The process of converting plant sugars into concentrated sugar forms readily usable for food and beverage flavoring.

Did You Know? (9.4)

The definition of *honey* stipulates an absolutely pure product that does not allow for the addition of any other substance. This includes water or other sweeteners, according to the National Honey Board.

   Honey, a USDA-graded product, is truly an amazing item. One of its defining characteristics is the fact that it simply cannot spoil. To learn why, as well as to investigate other aspects of honey, go to the National Honey Board's Web site at www.honey.com.

lower than 10 indicate greater sugar coarseness, while numbers higher than ten indicate a product that is even more finely powdered).

   Bar sugars are very fine (superfine) granulated sugars (not powdered sugar) that are popular with bartenders because they instantly dissolve in liquids. Brown sugar is simply refined cane sugar with some **molasses** added to it. Light brown sugar contains approximately 3.5 percent molasses, while dark brown sugar contains about 6.5 percent molasses. The variation in molasses used to produce the sugar accounts for the differences in color.

   Sugars for foodservice use may be purchased in dry or liquid form. The table sugars derived from cane or beets are popular, but so are liquid sweeteners. Except for leavening baked products, liquid sweeteners can be used in the same manner as crystallized dry sugar. Some liquid sweeteners can, just like crystallized sugar, be made from sugar cane. Other liquid sweeteners are made from a variety of plants and grains or by honey bees. The most common of these **syrups** are the following:

CORN SYRUP   This product is made by extracting starch from corn kernels and treating it with acid or an enzyme to develop a sweet syrup. Corn syrup is very thick but is less sweet than refined sugar or honey.

HONEY   Honey is made by bees and is a strong sweetener consisting of fructose and glucose. Its flavor and color vary depending on the season, type of flower or plant from which the nectar used to make it is extracted, and its age. Depending on the source and its quality, variations in the price of different honeys can be large.

MAPLE SYRUP   This distinctive syrup is made from the sap of sugar maple trees. One sugar maple tree produces about twelve gallons of maple sap each year, and it takes thirty to forty gallons of sap to produce one gallon of maple syrup. As a result, pure maple syrup (USDA Grades AA and A are best) is quite expensive. Maple syrup is often blended with other, less costly syrups, such as corn syrup, to produce maple-flavored syrup. It is important for foodservice buyers to note, however, that some maple-flavored syrups may contain only artificial maple flavoring and coloring and, thus, no maple syrup at all.

MOLASSES   True molasses is a by-product of cane sugar refinery. Some molasses, however, is made from corn syrup and is popular because of its lighter color and milder flavor. Blackstrap molasses is a very dark, distinctively flavored molasses preferred in the American South. Sorghum molasses is actually the product that results when the sweet sap of a brown corn plant (sorghum), normally grown as cattle feed, is boiled down to a syrup consistency.

Buyer's Guide to Purchasing Terms

Molasses   The thick, dark- to light-brown syrup that is separated from raw sugar in the manufacture of refined cane sugar.

Syrup   A thick, sticky solution of sugar and water that is often flavored.

CHOCOLATE Chocolate is the most popular sweet flavoring sold in the United States. Chocolate is made by combining cocoa powder produced from cacao beans, sugar, and in many cases milk or milk solids. Chocolate is used to flavor drinks (see Chapter 10) as well as a variety of candies, baked goods, and desserts. As a buyer, you will likely purchase chocolate in a variety of forms, including powdered cocoa, chips, chunks, pellets, blocks, and bars. The styles of chocolate typically purchased for foodservice vary based on the amount of chocolate liquor (ground cacao bean) they contain. These styles include the following:

Cocoa Cocoa is made from pulverized cacao from which all of the cocoa butter has been removed. No sugar has been added to it.

Unsweetened Chocolate This product contains 99 percent chocolate liquor. It also contains no sugar, is bitter (not sweet), and is used primarily for baking and cooking.

Bittersweet Chocolate This product contains 35 to 70 percent chocolate liquor. It contains sugar, cocoa butter, and vanilla. It is also known as semisweet.

Sweet (Dark) Chocolate This product is similar in makeup to bittersweet chocolate but contains 15 to 35 percent chocolate liquor. It is dark in color but lighter in flavor than bittersweet.

Milk Chocolate This product contains approximately 20 percent chocolate liquor and includes milk or milk solids as well as sugar. Its sweet taste and smooth flavor make it a favorite for use in candy as well as beverages.

White Chocolate This product is made from cocoa butter mixed with sugar, milk solids, and vanilla. It contains no chocolate liquor.

Couverture Couverture is bittersweet, milk, or white chocolate with a very high percentage of cocoa butter. It is used primarily in doughs and batters to add moisture and creaminess. It is also popular with confectioners for use in making candies and icings.

Despite the popularity of sugar and sweeteners of all types, due to a variety of health-related concerns expressed by guests, the foodservice industry's use of artificial sweeteners has increased dramatically in recent years. Artificial sweeteners are chemicals that offer the sweetness of sugar without the calories. Because the substitutes are much sweeter than sugar, it takes a much smaller quantity to create the same sweetness sensation. As a result, menu items made with artificial sweeteners contain fewer calories than do similar items made with sugar.

Artificial sweeteners are often used as part of a weight-loss plan or as a means to control weight gain. People with diabetes may also prefer artificial sweeteners because they make food taste sweet without raising blood sugar levels. If you are like most foodservice buyers, you will find the following artificial sweeteners to be the most commonly requested by your guests as well as the most popular for use in lower-calorie recipes:

Aspartame (sold as NutraSweet or Equal)

Saccharin (sold as Sweet'N Low or SugarTwin)

Acesulfame potassium (sold as Sunett or Sweet One)

Sucralose (sold as Splenda)

Of course, simply removing sugar from items such as cookies, cakes, and chocolate candy will not make them low-calorie, low-fat foods. If too many are eaten, customers and patients will still get more calories than needed and may be discouraged from consuming other, more nutritious foods such as fruits, vegetables, and whole grains. As a result, the extensive use of these products in noncommercial and institutional foodservice settings such as schools, colleges, health-care facilities, and correctional facilities must be carefully assessed.

In addition to cream and sugar, providing sugar substitutes is essential to high-quality coffee and tea service.

Michael Littlejohn/Pearson Education/PH College

Buyers at Work (9.2)

"What do you call it?" said Sara, the director of purchasing for the Blossom Garden chain of two thousand restaurants.

Sara was in her office meeting with Harriet Haley, corporate account sales representative for Confection Creations, a company that specialized in high-quality premade desserts. Harriet was attempting to convince Sara that a newly developed product made by Confection Creations would be an excellent addition to the Blossom Garden's dessert menu.

"We call it the Mocha Chocolate Bomb," replied Harriet.

"Well, it is tasty . . . and attractive," said Sara, "but it's really big."

"Exactly! It's sixteen ounces of cake, chocolate, and icing that your guests will love," said Harriet. "There's enough in one serving for four people! One-quarter pound of cake each—half a pound if only two share it! Think about the marketing possibilities. And the profits!"

Assume you were Sara:

1. What further questions would you ask of Harriet?
2. How could she measure her guests' interest in large, showy desserts such as the Mocha Chocolate Bomb?
3. What, if any, guest health concerns should you consider as you make a decision about the addition of this specific menu item? Do you have any obligation to serve reasonable portion sizes to help ensure your guests eat healthful diets?

Herbs and Spices

Herbs and spices have, for centuries, been used to improve the taste of foods. In the foodservice industry, the use of quality herbs and spices enhances both the flavor of food and the reputation of the operation using them. As a result, professional buyers should have a thorough knowledge of the use and quality levels of each herb and spice most used by their own operations.

In foodservice an **herb** refers to a large group of **aromatic** plants whose flowers, leaves, or stems are used to enhance food flavors.

Buyer's Guide to Purchasing Terms

Herb An aromatic flower, leaf, or stem.

Aromatic *As a noun:* A food used to enhance the natural taste or aromas of another food. Aromatics include herbs, spices, and some vegetables. *As an adjective:* Fragrant or spicy.

Allspice	Chipotle	Mace	Pepper, white
Anise	Chives	Marjoram	Poppy seed
Basil	Cilantro	Mint leaves	Rosemary
Bay leaf	Cinnamon	Mustard	Saffron
Caraway seed	Cloves	Nutmeg	Sage
Cardamom	Coriander	Oregano	Savory
Celery seed	Cumin	Paprika	Sesame seed
Chervil	Dill	Parsley	Tarragon
Chili pepper, ancho	Fennel	Pepper, black	Thyme
Chili pepper	Ginger	Pepper, red	Turmeric

FIGURE 9.5   Commonly Purchased Herbs and Spices

Most herbs may be purchased either fresh or dried. Fresh products are generally more attractive and tend to have a flavor that is milder than the same herb when dried. Dried herbs have greater shelf lives and are typically less expensive than fresh. Fresh herbs are most often preferred by those operations where food quality standards are extremely high.

Spices used in foodservice are strongly flavored or aromatic portions of plants. Spices can include bark, roots, seeds, bulbs, or berries.

Most but not all spices grow in tropical or warmer climates. Spices are almost always used in their dried (not fresh) forms and can typically be purchased either whole or ground.

The skillful use of herbs and spices gives many foods and, in some cases, entire food operations and cuisines their distinctive reputations. Consider, for example, the effect of curry (a spice blend) on Asian and Indian foods, Cajun seasonings (peppers) on foods of that style, and tarragon (an herb) on such classics dishes as béarnaise sauce.

The knowledge you need to effectively purchase herbs and spices is significant. This is made even more apparent when you learn that some plants (e.g., dill) are classified as both an herb (its leaves) and a spice (its seeds) and that the quality of available herbs and spices can vary tremendously. While it is by no means intended to be exhaustive, Figure 9.5 lists forty of the herbs and spices most commonly used in commercial foodservice and, thus, those most likely encountered by professional foodservice buyers.

Nutmeats

Nutmeats play an important role in many foodservice operations. Interestingly, not everyone agrees about the definition of a **"nut"** (technically, a nut is a fruit or seed, but not all fruits and seeds are nuts).

Fortunately, however, foodservice buyers need not concern themselves with a definition that would be acceptable to a plant scientist. In the kitchen, the term *nut* is commonly applied to many seeds and pods that are not true nuts. Because nuts (like many spices and herbs) generally have a high oil content, they are popular as a food flavoring as well as when **shelled** for eating by themselves.

Buyer's Guide to Purchasing Terms

Spice   An aromatic bark, root, bulb, or berry.

Nut   A hard-shelled, dry fruit or seed with a separable rind (shell) around an edible kernel.

Shelled (nut)   The food term used to describe a nut in its ready-to-eat form; also commonly known as "nutmeat."

A large number of shelled nut varieties are used in cooking, eaten raw, roasted as a snack food, or pressed for oil that is used in cooking (e.g., walnut, peanut, and almond oils). Popular fruits and seeds that most culinarians consider "nuts" include the following:

Pine nuts (Korean pine nuts)   Purchased shelled and unshelled, these are used to make pesto (a combination of basil leaves, garlic, olive oil, pine nuts, and spices) and as a salad topping

Almonds   An edible seed used in making nougat and almond spreads, as well as in baking

Cashews   A high-fat-content and flavorful nut used in Asian cooking as well as spreads, candies, and snacks

Coconut   Used in making desserts, some entrées, and drinks

Corn nut   A roasted maize (corn) seed

Peanuts   Used whole or in pieces for baking and as a spread in a variety of recipes

Pistachio   Used for making ice creams and candies

Additional popular nuts include beechnuts, Brazil nuts, chestnuts, filberts, hazelnuts, hickory, and macadamia nuts. Grade standards have been established by the USDA for a number of kinds of nuts; however, use of the standards by suppliers is not mandatory. Nut prices alone are not reliable bases for judging the quality of either shelled, unshelled, or roasted nuts. The best aid to professional buyers is a statement on the label, which shows the nuts are of a certain U.S. grade, that they have been subjected to USDA inspection, or both.

Buyer's Guide to Internet Resources: Flavorings

Web Site	Topic
www.sucrose.com	Cane and beet sugar information
www.hfcsfacts.com	High fructose corn syrup
www.ghirardelli.com/foodservice	Gourmet foodservice chocolates
www.admfoodservice.com/products/cocoa.aspproducts/cocoa.asp	Wholesale chocolate and cocoa products
www.dietitian.com/sugar.html	Nutrition and artificial sweeteners
www.freshherbs.com	Fresh herbs and their uses
www.spiceadvice.com	Herbs, spices, and condiments facts
www.mccormick.com	Information about herbs, spices, and condiments
www.thenutfactory.com	Nutmeats and their culinary uses
www.netrition.com/nuts.html	Nutrient content of various nutmeats

CONVENIENCE FOODS

Earlier in this text you learned about the make or buy decisions routinely faced by professional foodservice buyers. Convenience food manufacturers create products with the hope that you will decide to buy rather than make.

This is because convenience foods, by definition, are those in which labor has been added to one or more ingredients to reduce the amount of labor that must be used in the buyer's own kitchen. Despite the common preference of many kitchen managers to make their own products fresh and on-site, there are a large number of practical reasons foodservice operations choose to use quality convenience foods.

Consider, for example, the skilled labor required to make an item such as mayonnaise. For some very special foodservice operations, making classic mayonnaise on-site and from scratch is important. Those same operations will, of course, employ the skilled cooks and chefs that know how to make this complex emulsion properly.

For most operations, however, mayonnaise is an item that requires skill to produce and must be of consistent quality, therefore, the purchase of a ready-to-use, high-quality convenience product simply makes most sense.

Interestingly, in many segments of foodservice, the word *convenience*, when attached to foods, is negative and made-from-scratch foods are considered superior. As a professional food buyer, you should recognize that this perception actually reflects a lack of understanding of both culinary history and today's professional food industry.

In fact, nearly all foods eaten are made from scratch; some are simply made from scratch in one location then transported to another. For example, a gourmet-style blueberry muffin is always made from scratch in a bakeshop located somewhere. The bakeshop may be large or small, and the product may be transported across town or across the country. If, for example, the muffin were made by talented bakers at 5:00 a.m. and transported that same morning to a local hotel for use in its continental breakfast program, would it be true that the item is of poor quality because it was not produced on-site in the property's kitchen? The answer clearly is, "No."

Understanding that all foods are created from scratch somewhere within the foodservice industry supply chain means that the essential issue for a foodservice buyer to consider is simply this:

Is it in the best long-term interest of my business to buy a convenience item or to produce that same item on-site and from scratch?

Considered from that perspective, the issue of purchasing any high-quality convenience item is not any different than a restaurant owner/operator who purchases maple-smoked hams (a convenience item) from a talented charcuterie, freshly made cheeses (another group of convenience items) from a local dairy farm, and daily baked breads (also convenience items) from the neighborhood bakery to make, from scratch and on-site, a delicious panini grilled ham and cheese sandwich. Consider if the same owner/operator rejected the notion of any convenience foods and attempted to smoke hams, make cheese, and bake bread in the restaurant's own kitchen. Would a quality product result at a price the restaurant's guests could readily afford? It is not likely.

Of course, not all convenience items (nor all scratch-made items) are of good quality. Just as food production managers should avoid purchasing raw ingredients that result in poor-quality items made on-site, professional buyers should avoid choosing poor-quality convenience items. Dedicated buyers can do just that if they learn about the characteristics of the convenience items that are important to them.

While the number of quality convenience items available for purchase continues to increase each year, for many foodservice buyers, the majority of convenience items purchased will fall into one of the following categories:

- Soups and bases
- Baked goods
- Entrées
- Vegetables and fruits
- Dressings and condiments
- Desserts

Soups and Bases

A soup is simply any liquid food made by combining ingredients such as meats, vegetables, and **stock** and cooking these ingredients until their flavors are fully extracted.

Stews are simply a variation of soup that are thicker and often contain larger pieces of ingredients. Traditionally, soups are classified as either clear soups or thick soups. Clear soups include bouillons and consommés. Thick soups include cream soups, purees, bisques, and chowders. All of these soup types are available in convenience food forms.

The advantages of purchasing convenience soups are product consistency as well as the labor savings involved in not having to cook these menu items for the long periods of time they often require. Disadvantages include perceived (or real) concerns regarding the quality of such products as well as consumer acceptance of them.

It is important for you to recognize that foodservice industry manufacturers have come a long way from the days when convenience soup products essentially meant canned chicken noodle or beef vegetable soups with ingredients of questionable origin and quality. Today those foodservice operations that serve significant amounts of soups, sauces, or sauce-based products are among the biggest beneficiaries of the improvement in today's convenience items of this type.

Now available fresh, canned, frozen, boil-in-bag, dried, or as a concentrate, soups are popular with guests, and many of the convenience soup items offered are of extremely high quality. The range of quality and cost of these products is wide; however, as a well-informed buyer, you can achieve excellent product consistency and competitive per-serving soup costs when you carefully choose these convenience items.

For those operations that prefer to make their own soups and sauces on-site, the variety and quality of food **bases** on the market has never been greater. Quality soup or sauce bases contain no artificial ingredients, preservatives, or colorings. The fat and sodium (salt) contents of convenience soups and bases are also areas where professional food buyers must pay careful attention before selecting products.

Baked Goods

By sheer sales volume, one of the largest categories of convenience foods purchased is that of breakfast-style pastries, doughs, and breads. For many buyers, these are among the most valuable of their convenience items.

Few items create the consistently positive response from guests as does the smell of fresh baked goods. When a consistent, high-quality baked product is desired, however, it makes little sense for many foodservice operations to make the investments required to produce their own doughnuts; bake their own sandwich breads and buns; or make items such as bagels, Danish pastries, and muffins on site.

Several factors contribute to the difficulties encountered when seeking to produce high-quality baked goods on-site. Chief among them is the lack of skilled labor capable of producing high-quality baked goods. Unfortunately, there are few professional schools in the United States training individuals for careers as **pâtissiers.**

Buyer's Guide to Purchasing Terms

Stock   Water in which bones, meat, fish, or vegetables have been slowly simmered.

Base (food)   Stock concentrates of freshly cooked meat, poultry, seafood, or vegetables.

Pâtissier   Pastry chef; an individual capable of producing a wide range of high-quality baked products.

In addition, for many operations, the small number of items needed daily and the need for significant investment in the specialized baking and **proofing** equipment required results in a situation in which convenience items such as partially baked breads and **"scoop and bake"** products can be purchased and served at a lower cost with higher quality than many similar made-from-scratch items.

In many foodservice settings, the quality of bread served as a meal accompaniment is exceptionally important. Even those simple operations that use only traditional-style sliced white breads (for toast) and buns (for hot dogs and hamburgers) know that freshness and taste are critical to ensuring high levels of guest satisfaction with these products.

Fortunately, the variation of available bread products is tremendous (as is their cost variation). Professional buyers can typically choose from ready-to-bake, partially baked, and fully prebaked, and refrigerated, frozen, or fresh delivered baked goods. The choice of these items should be carefully coordinated with kitchen production managers to ensure the proper product in the proper prebaked or baked state is selected.

Entrées

The greatest advancements in convenience food manufacturing are currently occurring in this important menu category.

Convenience entrées are popular with some foodservice operators because they save labor, reduce spoilage costs, and ensure product consistency. These frozen and, increasingly, modified-atmosphere-packaged (see Chapter 8) center-of-the-plate items require minimum preparation and in many cases are simply heated before they are served.

Convenience entrée items have lagged in quality behind other categories for important reasons that have caused difficulty in their manufacturing. While cooking

Advances in entrée production and packaging have greatly increased the number of highly acceptable items found in this convenience category.

Dave King © Dorling Kindersley

Buyer's Guide to Purchasing Terms

Proof (baked goods)   To allow an unbaked product to rise by enhancing the production of yeast in the product.

Scoop and bake   A generic term used to describe a variety of baked goods batters and mixes that are purchased in final form but are portioned (scooped) and baked on-site. Examples of scoop-and-bake products include muffins, brownies, and cookies.

develops the characteristic flavors of meats, it also promotes the development of stale, leftover product flavors when the meat is cooked, cooled, and reheated. The primary source of these off-flavors is naturally occurring unsaturated fatty acids, which are damaged by exposure to oxygen as well as chemical reactions related to the iron occurring naturally in the meats. The negative effect on meats of these acids and iron reactions occurs slowly under refrigeration but more rapidly when reheated. This is why poultry and pork (with higher levels of unsaturated fats in their tissue) are affected more than beef and lamb products (although these items also are affected).

Convenience food manufacturers have made great advancements in controlling (but not completely eliminating) this leftover effect. They do so with the addition of herbs and spices when cooking, use of oxygen-resistant wrappings, and the virtual elimination of all air (oxygen) from the packaging used for the item. Thus, despite the advantages and tremendous increases in product quality related to convenience entrées, professional foodservice buyers must address several concerns when they purchase them:

- Assurance that the item is made from high-quality products, not substandard ingredients
- The item's fat and trans fat content as well as sodium (salt) levels
- Detailed labeling, including information about ingredients that could result in the operation's legal liability if not disclosed to guests prior to service (e.g., monosodium glutamate [MSG] or peanut products)
- Disclosure of the use of any **genetically engineered food** ingredients in the item's preparation
- The type and amount of preservatives, if any, used in the product's manufacture

Vegetables and Fruits

Vegetables, both canned and frozen, are among the foodservice convenience items with the longest history of use. As you learned in Chapter 8, many vegetables (as well as fruits) maintain their quality characteristics well during canning and freezing. Today, however, the convenience forms of vegetables and fruits most often used in foodservice are related to precut or otherwise processed and bagged fresh products.

The use of these items controls for the waste that can occur during trimming and cleaning, as well as provides for uniform product size. The use of these very cost-effective products is practical in a large number of foodservice settings and illustrates some of the best uses of convenience foods.

Dressings and Condiments

Some food production managers and buyers use the term *dressing* when referring to any sauce added to a dish before it is served. Of course, the term is also used when describing a popular accompaniment to poultry. Most guests, however, associate the term *dressing* with salads. While some operations take great pride in producing their own salad dressings on-site, the majority of operations purchase premade salad dressings or dressing mixes. In fact, some dressings are so widely known and so popular (e.g., the Hidden Valley company's Ranch brand dressing) that a foodservice operation is nearly compelled to offer it or to provide a very similar substitute.

Buyer's Guide to Purchasing Term

Genetically engineered food   An item produced from crops or animals whose genetic makeup has been altered through a process called recombinant DNA (gene splicing) to give the food a desirable trait.

Ketchup (catsup) Chutney	Louisiana-style hot sauce Tabasco sauce*	Bacon bits A-1 Steak Sauce* Heinz 57* Barbecue sauce	Soy Sauce Hoisin sauce Plum sauce Teriyaki sauce Tahini
Mustard (yellow) Mustard (brown) Mustard (Dijon)	Relish (pickle) Relish (corn) Relish (mango)	Worcestershire sauce Lea & Perrins*	Picante sauce Taco sauce Salsa
Cocktail sauce Tartar sauce Oyster sauce	Chili sauce Wasabi Horseradish sauce	Sauerkraut Pickles Onions	Jams Jellies Honeys Honey mustards
Mayonnaise-based salad dressings	Malt vinegar Vinegar-based salad dressings	Mayonnaise Hellmann's/Best Foods* Salad dressing Miracle Whip*	Salt Pepper Sugar

*Denotes name brand item.

FIGURE 9.6   Selected Popular Foodservice Condiments

Similarly, the term *condiment* can be widely interpreted. Strictly speaking, a condiment can be defined as any food that enhances another food.

From the perspectives of most foodservice guests, however, condiments are those items routinely expected to be made available as accompaniments to the foods they are served. Some of these (e.g., salt and pepper) are so popular they are, in most operations, left on diners' tables at all times. Others, such as ketchup (catsup) and mustard and pickle **relish** may or may not remain on the table based on the style of foodservice operation, but they are served almost immediately with certain foods (e.g., the service of ketchup with French fries). Other popular condiments such as steak sauce, salsa, and vinegar are frequently available but are typically served only on request.

Figure 9.6 lists some of the condiments most popular in commercial foodservice operations. The list is not intended to be exhaustive, but instructive, as it lists many (but not all) of the items you might purchase in individual **PCs (portion-control packets),** bottles and jars of various sizes, or even one-gallon or five-gallon containers.

Note that, in some cases, the condiment named in Figure 9.6 is generic (e.g., ketchup), while in other cases, a very popular condiment refers specifically to a particular branded item (e.g., A-1 Steak Sauce). When purchasing condiments, one of a buyer's greatest challenges is to determine whether guests will change their perception of an operation based on its use of generically branded versus name-branded condiment offerings.

Buyer's Guide to Purchasing Terms

Condiment   Any food added to a dish to enhance flavor (e.g., herbs, spices, vinegars, and dressings).

Relish   A condiment containing vinegar, salt, and sugar as well as chopped fruits or vegetables (e.g., products made from pickles, corn, and onions).

PC (portion control packet)   Individual serving–sized packages of seasonings, dressings, and condiments such as jams, jellies, syrups, and sauces. PCs (or PC packets) typically range in size from 0.25 to 2.0 ounces.

Quick-service restaurants must offer a wide variety of PC condiments to satisfy the tastes of all their take-out and dine-in customers.

Dennis MacDonald/PhotoEdit Inc.

Did You Know? (9.5)

Why are so many grocery items such as condiments, canned fruits and vegetables, and even flours and pastas privately labeled? Because product-marketing dollars greatly impact the private label process. This is because, in most cases, large food manufacturers pay food distributors a predetermined dollar amount for each case of their brand name product sold. Thus, when companies such as Birdseye, Hunts, Campbell's, Heinz, and others benefit from their products being sold to a food distributor's customers, the manufacturer will pay (or rebate) to *the distributor* an amount per case sold that is agreeable to both. These payments, or invoice reductions, are known in the food-distribution industry by the term *marketing-dollars*.

Of course, marketing-dollars are a real cost, which food manufacturers must ultimately pass on to customers in the price of the products they sell. When a product is privately labeled, however, the food manufacturer pays no brand name–related marketing-dollars to the distributor. Instead, they can charge less, which results in passing all or most of the marketing-dollars savings directly to the product's end user *(the foodservice operation).* Those who buy for large foodservice organizations know this and, as a result, pursue private-label options anytime they believe the marketing-dollar costs they will ultimately save exceed any additional costs or charges incurred by private labeling.

Desserts

Some of the most dramatic advances in high-quality foodservice convenience items are in the frozen gourmet dessert industry. Products in this category include cakes, torts, cheesecakes, **petits fours,** bundts, tarts, and the like. The proper preparation of these types of items often requires employees with highly advanced baking skills.

While sometimes costly on a portion cost basis, the regular offering of these specialty products can easily raise guests' perceptions of a foodservice operation's quality, while their strategic use can elevate selected days and distinctive gatherings to true "special event" status.

Buyer's Guide to Purchasing Term

Petit four   Very small, usually iced, cakes that are generally served after a meal or as part of a larger dinner or dessert buffet (plural: petits fours).

High-quality convenience items such as this permit some buyers the ability to offer their guests menu selections that far exceed their own operations' ability to make the item from scratch.

Dave King © Dorling Kindersley

Buyers at Work (9.3)

"What's wrong with the biscuits we make now?" asked Jeanette. Jeanette was the early-morning baker at the one-thousand-employee Delhi auto parts plant, where for fifteen years she had prepared muffins, cakes, cookies, and the buttermilk biscuits that were a favorite with those morning shift employees who elected to eat in the employee cafeteria.

"There's nothing wrong with them, Jeanette," replied Azhur Zafar, the plant's director of foodservices. "You know the staff employees here love your biscuits. It's just that Birdsong Foods has just come out with a new Thaw and Bake biscuit that could really save us a lot of time. And the quality is pretty good. I've tried them!"

Assume you were observing the conversation between Jeanette and Azhur.

1. What job-related concerns might Jeanette have about switching to this convenience item? What product-related concerns might she have?
2. Assume as well that the new biscuit product was good but no better than the made-from-scratch biscuits currently being produced and served. What might be motivating Azhur to consider buying this new product from Birdsong Foods?
3. If you were asked, what specific issues would you advise Azhur and Jeanette to jointly consider and discuss prior to switching to this particular convenience product?

SPECIALIZED FOOD PRODUCTS

Some products purchased for use in foodservice are not special foods, but rather are foods processed in special ways. For foodservice buyers, two of the most important of these food types are **kosher** and **halal.**

Buyer's Guide to Purchasing Terms

Kosher   The name of the Jewish dietary laws; food prepared in accordance with these laws is considered kosher.

Halal   An Arabic term meaning *permissible,* in English it is used most frequently to refer to foods that are permissible according to Islamic dietary laws.

Kosher

The market for kosher foods in the United States is large, with more than twenty-three thousand certified kosher foods available. When a food is labeled as Kosher, this means it has been prepared according to strict rules of food preparation noted in the Bible and formalized in Jewish law. These foods are often labeled with a symbol of a U surrounded by a circle. The practice of kosher does not allow the mixing of meat and milk in the same meal. Food labeled "Pareve" does not contain either meat or milk and, therefore, can be combined with most other foods during a meal.

Halal

Halal, for Muslims, means "allowed" or "lawful" foods. Halal foods are increasingly in demand and are regularly purchased by some foodservice operators. A simple and effective means of guaranteeing halal status of all foods purchased is to insist on halal certification. The Islamic Food and Nutritional Council of America (IFANCA) has a halal certification program, and their approved items contain a *Halal M* stamp on the package. Other genuine halal foods may be designated as such by a seal with a capital *H* inside a triangle.

It is important for foodservice buyers to note that, even if purchased as genuine kosher or halal, foods of these types must be properly handled after they are delivered to the foodservice operation to maintain their status because, for example, mixing a kosher or halal food with one that is not would result in the loss of the original item's kosher or halal status. Also, the very fact that the foods are kosher or halal may affect their proper storage after delivery (e.g., fresh poultry processed under kosher and halal laws are lightly salted, a process that increases the oxidation of fat in the bird and results in these items not keeping as long as conventionally processed birds).

PRODUCT RECEIVING AND STORAGE

Because groceries cover such a wide range of products, some will be delivered fresh, while others will arrive frozen, refrigerated, or packaged for holding in dry-storage areas. Personnel assigned the task of receiving all grocery products must be vigilant. Frozen foods must immediately be placed in frozen food holding units, and refrigerated foods must be promptly put away. Also, for nearly all grocery items, a **FIFO** storage system should be used.

In a FIFO system, receiving clerks rotate stock in such a way that products already on hand are used prior to more recently delivered products. To do so, receiving clerks must take care to place new stock behind or underneath old stock. Sometimes, however, employees do not do this. Consider, for example, the storeroom clerk who receives six eighty-pound bags of all-purpose flour. The FIFO method dictates that these six bags be placed under or behind the five bags already in the storeroom. Will receiving clerks place the six newly delivered bags underneath or behind the five older bags when it means moving the five older bags as well as the six that have newly arrived? They will, but only if proper receiving procedures are enforced. If they are not, employees may be tempted to

---

Buyer's Guide to Purchasing Term

FIFO (first in, first out) Short for "first in, first out"; a storage system that seeks to issue products already in storage prior to the issuing of more recently delivered products.

take the easy way out and simply place newer products on top of or in front of previously received products.

When stored, frozen and refrigerated grocery products should be held at temperatures consistent with other frozen and refrigerated food products. In many cases, however, buyers will find that many groceries are stored in dry-storage areas.

Dry-storage areas should generally be maintained at a temperature ranging between 65°F and 75°F (18°–24°C). Temperatures lower than those recommended can be harmful to food products. Excessively high temperatures must be avoided as well. In many cases dry-storage areas can be very warm, especially when they are poorly ventilated and/or located near cooking and baking equipment that generates significant heat. In addition, because many dry-storage areas are either not air-conditioned or are poorly air-conditioned, it is a good idea to continually monitor temperatures with a wall thermometer.

Shelving in dry-storage areas must be easily cleanable and spaced properly. Local health codes vary, but shelving should generally be placed at least six inches above the ground to allow for proper cleaning beneath the shelving and to ensure proper ventilation. Dry-goods products should never be stored directly on the ground. Product labels should face out for easy identification.

For items such as flours and grains stored in bins or large containers, mobile storage and transport equipment should be used when possible to minimize heavy lifting and resulting employee injuries. If possible, grains should be dry-stored in a cool, dark place. For flour products, airtight containers are recommended to prevent insect infestation. Whole grains containing the grain oil (germ) must be refrigerated to prevent rancidity.

PROFESSIONAL PURCHASING PREVENTS PROBLEMS (9.3)

Disappearing Spice Oils

A common problem: Spices that are too old lose their potency, resulting in lower product quality and higher-than-necessary costs.

The goal in spice and herb storage is to handle them in such a manner as to retain their characteristic aromas and taste. The oil-based flavor compounds that create aroma and taste are highly susceptible to evaporation and product deterioration if exposed to air, heat, or light.

Spices and herbs stored in open or loosely closed containers in hot, brightly lit kitchens can quickly lose their essential oils and, as a result, will not flavor products as they should.

When buyers purchase herbs and spices in large containers and expose those containers to the harsh storage conditions of many commercial kitchens, the result is significant loss of flavoring ability and (because cooks must use more to achieve the same flavoring results) increased portion costs.

As a professional purchaser, it is important for you to understand that to preserve most herbs and spices sellers of these items must dry them out so they do not rot. They must do so, however, as gently as possible so moisture is removed without removing the item's characteristic flavor. When you purchase these items, you must continue their special care.

On delivery, spices are best stored in glass containers that do not allow light to penetrate and under refrigeration. Under these conditions, whole spices (whose cells are intact) can keep for up to one year, while ground spices (whose finely ground particles have a large surface area and lose their flavor molecules to the air more rapidly) can last for a few months.

What should you do? Buy quality flavoring products in container sizes that are appropriate for usage levels and, on delivery, promptly date the containers. Store excess herb and spice inventories under refrigeration and regularly review container product dates to ensure older products are used before newer ones. The result is herbs and spices that perform at their peak and produce lower costs, better-tasting products, and increased guest satisfaction.

Buyer's Guide to Internet Resources: Other Foods

Web Site	Topic
www.stockpot.com	Frozen soups
www.campbellsoupcompany.com	Convenience soups and broths
www.soupbase.com	High-quality soup and sauce bases
www.bridgford.com	Frozen bread doughs
www.stouffers.com	Frozen entrées
www.barberfoods.com/fs_home.asp	Convenience entrées and vegetables
www.dressings-sauces.org	Popular dressings and sauces
www.richs.com/foodservice	Convenience desserts and toppings
www.koshertoday.com	Kosher foods
www.ifanca.org	Halal foods

Purchasing Terms

Make Your Own Purchasing Decisions

1. Despite their tremendous popularity, the health-related concerns of eating French fries and other fried foods (especially those produced using trans fat–containing oils) are increasing. Federally defined levels of obesity in some states are now estimated at more than 30 percent of the entire state population and are expected to rise. As a buyer, what, if any, are your responsibilities to address the issue of increasing guest weights and decreasing health levels, within your own buying practices?

2. While it may be relatively easy to write purchase specifications for needed canned, frozen, or otherwise processed items, the reality for many buyers is that they will choose these items from only the list of products already offered for sale by their primary and secondary food vendors. As a purchaser, what alternative courses of action are available to you if you truly require a processed food item that is not readily available to you?

3. Assume that you are the new buyer for a 125-unit group of Fresh to Go soup and salad restaurants noted for their made on-site soups and fresh salads. Assume also that you are considering the purchase of high-quality, dried and ready-to-simmer soup mixtures sold in five-pound bags. The instructions on the bags direct production staff to simply boil the bag's contents for ten minutes to rehydrate the ingredients and complete the soup. Can this soup still be considered to be made on-site? How would you decide? Should customers be informed of this change if you make it? Are there any ethical issues in this decision?

4. Many large foodservice chains such as McDonald's, Arby's, and Chick-fil-A choose to put their own restaurant's name on items such as PC mayonnaise, ketchup, and sauces despite the fact that the product itself may have a formulation identical to that of a well-known name brand product and, in fact, may actually be made and packaged by the name brand food manufacturer. Assume you were a professional food buyer for a large chain. What would be the advantages of using such a private-label approach? What are potential disadvantages to such an approach?

5. The purchase of quality center-of-the-plate items, produce, and dairy products is very important in most foodservice operations. For many buyers, however, more than 50 percent of their total food budget will be spent on grocery items. Why do you think this category of foods has not received the attention of more high-profile items? What are the implications of this for cost control? For guest satisfaction? Give a specific example of a grocery purchase decision that would have a significant effect on each of these two important considerations.

10

Beverages

Purchasing Pros Need to Know!

It would be difficult to overestimate the importance of knowing how to skillfully purchase the beverages used in foodservice operations because the service of quality beverages always enhances the service of quality foods. Also, in operations such as the increasingly popular gourmet coffeehouses, wine bars, cocktail lounges, pubs, and taverns, guests may actually choose which establishment to visit based on the quality of beverages it serves. Buyers for traditional restaurants also recognize that the first menu item served to nearly all guests will be a beverage. Because most foodservice guests drink beverages, ensuring that the quality of these products is outstanding will reflect positively on the image of the operations that sold them.

The number and type of beverages offered by even the smallest foodservice unit can be extensive, thus there is much to know about them. One way to study beverages more easily is by first categorizing them as either nonalcoholic or alcoholic, and both types will be examined in this chapter.

In all foodservice operations, coffee is one of the beverages most served, and you should know about the various roasts, grinds, and packaging alternatives from which you will choose. While less popular in the United States, tea drinkers are steadfast in their preference for this beverage, so information on teas and iced teas is included in this chapter, as is information about chocolate-flavored beverages. Carbonated beverages (soft drinks) are the most frequently ordered beverage in many foodservice operations, however, bottled waters are a fast-growing category also, so key information will be presented on these two categories as well.

Alcoholic beverages are crucial to many hospitality operations, and restaurants that offer alcoholic beverages are maintaining a hospitality tradition that stretches back to the beginning of the enjoyment of food. Beer is likely the oldest alcoholic beverage produced, and it is sold in a variety of styles and packaging types. Beer is the first alcoholic beverage you will learn about in this chapter.

For many foodservice buyers, wine knowledge is indispensable. This chapter presents key information about wine types, the packaging forms available, and the special storage techniques important for maintaining quality in these beverages. The final alcoholic beverages examined in this chapter are grouped under the broad classification of "spirits." Spirits are differentiated by their flavors, the food product used to make the beverage, the amount of alcohol they contain, and the specific ways they are produced.

It is easy to see that the range of beverages available for purchase is large. As a result, learning the specialized knowledge required to properly select, store, and serve these products will take time, but it is critical for all those who will purchase beverages for use in the foodservice industry.

■ ■ ■

Outline

NONALCOHOLIC BEVERAGES

Few activities are more enjoyable and relaxing than enjoying beverages in a social setting. As a result, many of your guests may be just as likely to come to your operation for the quality of beverages you serve as for the quality of your food. This is true whether the beverages you serve do or do not contain **alcohol.**

As a professional purchaser, it is important to remember that the vast majority of beverages served in the hospitality industry *do not* contain alcohol.

According to the American Beverage Association (the nonprofit industry group of nonalcoholic beverage manufacturers and suppliers), carbonated soft drinks, bottled water, coffee, and milk account for approximately 60 percent of the beverages consumed by the average American. Fruit beverages (such as juice), **sports drinks,** tea, and other nonalcoholic drinks account for another 25 percent.

Beers, wine, and spirits, as important as they are to the hospitality industry, account for only about 15 percent of all beverages consumed. It is also important for you to recognize that nearly 100 percent of your guests who purchase food will purchase a beverage as an accompaniment to the food. Not all customers who purchase beverages, however, will purchase food. A few examples of this include customers at bars, lounges, and pubs, as well as those

---

Buyer's Guide to Purchasing Terms

Alcohol   A colorless liquid produced by the fermentation of sugar or starch, which is the intoxicating ingredient in beer, wine, and spirits.

Sports drink   A beverage designed to rehydrate, as well as replenish, the drinker's electrolyte, sugar, and other nutrient levels.

frequenting coffeehouses or those simply stopping at a local foodservice operation to purchase a **to-go** beverage.

Because the presence and importance of quality nonalcoholic beverages in hospitality is so prominent, you should have a good understanding of the quality factors related to purchasing coffee, tea, soft drinks, and bottled water products.

Coffee

Coffee lore and tradition states that the first coffee trees were discovered in east Africa, in an area south of the Sahara Desert and near modern-day Ethiopia. Today coffee is grown in many parts of the world, with Brazil, Vietnam, and Colombia the largest exporters. Coffee is enjoyed by foodservice guests in virtually all settings. As a result, every foodservice buyer should have a thorough understanding of the procedures required to make a good cup of coffee.

This starts with the selection of quality coffee beans ground at the restaurant or the purchase of vacuum-packed, preground coffee from a reputable coffee supplier. The number of choices (roasts, grinds, brands, and price levels) is large, and the serious buyer should become familiar, at least to some degree, with the history, type of beans available, production process, and service of both regular and **decaffeinated** coffee.

It is likely that the first parts of the coffee tree used for food were actually the cherrylike fruits it produces. Initially these fruits were eaten, and the leaves from the trees were used to make a flavored tea (by boiling the leaves in water). Coffee trees produce a cluster of red berries, each of which contains two seeds (coffee beans). It is these beans that are roasted to produce ground coffee.

Knowledgeable coffee buyers know that there are actually two very different species of plants grown for their coffee beans. The *Coffea arabica* plant produces what is known in the industry as arabica beans. These trees are native to the cool highlands of east Africa. *Coffea canephora* is a larger tree, native to the hotter areas of west Africa. This plant produces the robusta bean.

Approximately 70 percent of the coffee beans grown worldwide are arabica. Today most of the coffee grown in Central and South America are arabica, while the coffees produced in most of Africa and Indonesia are robusta. Arabica coffees are highly prized for their complex taste and balanced flavors. Arabica beans also contain less **caffeine,** more oil, and less sugar than robusta beans.

There is no question that the keys to making good coffee include those related to both art and good science. The original version of roasted, brewed coffee was developed by the Arabs. In fact, in the Middle East, Turkey, and Greece, the originally developed brewing style still thrives.

To make their coffee, the Arabs first roasted coffee beans then ground them to a fine powder, added sugar and water, then boiled the mixture one or more time until it foamed. The resulting beverage was decanted into very small cups and drunk immediately (before the sediment it contained could increase its already considerable bitterness).

Buyer's Guide to Purchasing Terms

To-go (menu item)   The hospitality industry term for menu items intended to be consumed off premises; also called as "take-out."

Decaffeinated   A beverage product in which its naturally occurring caffeine has been significantly reduced. A regular cup of brewed coffee contains sixty to 180 milligrams of caffeine; decaffeinated coffee will contain two to five milligrams.

Caffeine   A natural stimulant found in coffee, tea, and cola nuts.

High-quality coffee drinks are both popular and highly profitable.

Around the 1700s, significant European modifications to coffee drinking included the invention of the drip pot, a device used to isolate, or filter, the ground beans from the water used for coffee making. Essentially, with a drip pot, hot water is passed over ground coffee beans, and the resulting liquid is then filtered through cloth or paper and allowed to collect in a separate container.

The development of the drip procedure did three important things:

1. It allowed the use of water heated below its boiling point.
2. It limited the contact time between water and ground beans.
3. It produced a brew without sediments that could be held for a period of time without becoming bitter.

The importance of this advancement by the French is even more apparent when you recognize that the method described above is essentially the same one foodservice operators use to brew their coffees today.

The Paris Exhibition of 1855 marked the next major advancement in coffee production. It was at that event that **espresso** was introduced.

When using specially designed espresso machines, water is forced through ground coffee at a very high pressure, causing maximum extraction of the ground coffee's oils, which are then emulsified into tiny droplets and mixed with the brewing water. The result is a velvety texture and a pleasant, rich taste that lingers on the tongue. Today made-on-premises fresh-brewed coffee is still produced using either a variation of the drip-pot production system or the espresso method, although most of the growth in brewed coffee sales will be found in espresso-style coffee offerings.

ROASTING COFFEE BEANS Raw, green coffee beans are very hard and have little flavor. Roasting transforms the hard beans into fragile, easily opened flavor packs. Proper roasting releases and enhances the flavors in coffee. Continued roasting darkens the beans and causes a distinct visible gloss as increased oils come to the beans' surface. Coffee beans can be roasted until they are only a very light brown color, or they can be further roasted until they are almost solid black. As the degree of roasting increases, changes in the molecular structure of the bean will

Buyer's Guide to Purchasing Term

Espresso   Roughly, Latin for "to press out at the moment," the term now refers to machine-produced coffee.

result in some subtle (and some not-so-subtle) changes in the taste of the coffee brewed from the roasted bean.

The skill of the coffee bean roaster, the degree to which a coffee bean is roasted, and how the bean is cooled and handled after roasting can have as great an effect on the quality of coffee as does the original bean. Poor roasting techniques can damage the best coffee beans, and thoughtful roasting can minimize the deficiencies of lower-quality beans.

As a professional buyer, you will typically be able to choose from a variety of different roasting styles. Unfortunately, there are no international standards for roasting levels, thus individual roasters are free, when it comes to roasting styles, to label the beans they sell however they choose to do so. The most commonly used terminology for coffee bean roasting, however, includes the following:

City Roast   Also known as "American" roast, this roasting style is the one used for most of the coffee sold in the United States. (Most canned coffee sold in grocery stores is city roasted.) While it is the most common, it is not particularly the most distinctive, nor would most serious coffee drinkers feel it produces the best cup of coffee. In fact, perhaps the greatest advantage of this roast level is that most American coffee drinkers do not find it objectionable. Thus, it consistently produces a safe, if not outstanding, cup of coffee. The wide distribution of this coffee style may help explain why Americans lag far behind many other countries in per-person consumption of coffee.

Brazilian   This roast is darker than city roast. When this roast is used, the beans will just begin to show surface oils. (As roasting time increases, oils from within the bean move to its surface.) It is also important to remember that, in this context, the term *Brazilian* refers only to a roasting style, not to coffee beans grown in Brazil.

Viennese   Also known as medium-brown roast, this style typically falls between a city roast and a French roast.

French   This roast, also known as a "New Orleans" roast or "dark" roast, approaches espresso in flavor without sacrificing smoothness. Beans roasted French style will be the color of semisweet chocolate with visible oil on the surface.

Espresso   Espresso, or Italian roast, is the darkest roast. Beans roasted in this style will look almost burned. The beans will be black or nearly black with very visible shiny oils on their surfaces.

Did You Know? (10.1)

Despite the proven positive effect on health of regular coffee consumption, many foodservice guests request decaffeinated coffee. Decaffeinated coffee was invented in Germany around 1908. Decaffeination can be achieved through a variety of processes, all of which are relatively harmless to the drinker's health but quite harmful to coffee quality. The basic process for decaffeination consists of soaking coffee beans in water to dissolve the naturally occurring caffeine, extracting it from the water, then resoaking the coffee beans in the decaffeination water to reabsorb the flavor compounds that were lost in the initial caffeine extraction. In the process, not all of the caffeine is removed from the coffee nor, unfortunately, can all of the flavor compounds be returned to the beans. No coffee is caffeine free. Removing all of the caffeine from coffee would be extremely costly, so it is important for you to recognize that, by weight, the amount of caffeine found naturally in coffee is about 1 percent for the arabica and 2 percent for the robusta coffee beans. When, for example, you buy coffees labeled *97% Caffeine Free*, it is 97 percent of that 1 percent or 2 percent caffeine by weight that has been removed. Because the chemical composition of decaffeinated (decaf) coffee is significantly altered, the flavor and aroma of beverages brewed from decaf coffee are changed (in a negative manner) as well.

PROFESSIONAL PURCHASING PREVENTS PROBLEMS (10.1)

Choosing the Right Grind

A common problem: Coffee quality is negatively affected if the grind purchased is inappropriate for the brewing method used.

It is important to understand that you could make coffee from whole roasted beans, but it would take hours and not taste very good. You could also make coffee from pulverized beans (some specially built coffee vending machines do it), but it would likely taste bitter using the coffee equipment in your foodservice operation. You want ground coffee of consistent particle size with no powder. The best grind is the one with particle sizes that work best in your operation.

Most suppliers will carry three sizes, so you can choose the best one for you. These are regular, drip, and fine. Each of these grinds contains particles of many sizes. The difference is in the proportion of each size particle they contain. Regular grind is the coarsest, followed by drip, then fine. For most foodservice operations, drip is likely best because it is ground to match the way most operations' coffeemakers work (using a drip-extraction method). A fine grind is usually used for making espresso. For those operations grinding their own beans, the general rule is that if your coffee tastes weak, you may need to produce a finer grind, and if the coffee tastes bitter, experiment with a slightly coarser grind.

GRINDING COFFEE BEANS   While few foodservice operators roast their own coffee beans, many do grind their own beans. The aroma the process produces is unmistakable, and the improved quality is definitely appreciated by serious coffee drinkers.

Coffee beans are ground to increase the surface of the roasted beans. Increased surface area results in an increase in extraction of coffee flavor. There is no best grind for a coffee bean. The key to a quality ground coffee is to create consistent particle sizes appropriate to the brewing method used. Too much variation in ground particle size makes it hard to control flavor extraction during the brewing process. When not consistent in size, smaller particles may be overextracted (which leads to bitterness), and larger ones will be underextracted (which leads to weakness). As a result, the product produced from inconsistently ground coffee beans is most often bitter and weak.

Many foodservice operators feel the product they brew will be superior if the beans from which it is made are ground just before they are used for brewing. Sometimes that is true, but it is most dependent on the type of grinder used. Typical propeller grinders (such as those found in most homes) smash all coffee particles until the machine blades are stopped, regardless of how small the pieces become. As a result, coarse and medium ground coffees end up containing some finely ground powder. More expensive burr grinders (used by commercial coffee suppliers) allow smaller pieces to escape through grooves built into the grinding surface, resulting in a more even and desirable final particle size.

COFFEE MARKETING FORMS AND PACKAGING   Coffee beans for grinding are typically sold by the pound. Preground coffee beans can be purchased in individual packages designed to produce from two cups to several gallons at a time. While there are some industry guidelines, the strength at which your consumers will prefer their coffee will vary based on your operation's geographic area, the brewing style used, the equipment used, and even the time of day the coffee is to be consumed. (Many foodservice operators offer more intense coffees for after-dinner consumption than those they serve before meals.)

Despite variations of these types, many operators find that when using a drip method, a ratio of two level tablespoons of coffee to six fluid ounces of water

Did You Know? (10.2)

Serving a great-tasting cup of coffee is important to foodservice operations of all types. In most cases brewed coffee of poor quality is the result of mistakes made in brewing, holding, and service, not in the purchasing process. Essentially, all methods of brewing coffee are the same: ground coffee is soaked in hot water until the water tastes good. The only equipment needed to make great coffee is water, a pot, heat, and a straining system (to remove the grounds). Simple as that seems, bad brewed coffee is common. To ensure only quality coffee is served to guests, foodservice buyers should work with those responsible for making the coffee to ensure they follow the ten steps to serving great coffee:

1. Ensure purchased coffee is stored in a cool and dry storage area.
2. Keep coffee brewing equipment meticulously clean.
3. Use fresh water for brewing, as free of impurities and alkalis as possible and avoid using softened water.
4. Use a clean/new filter each time coffee is brewed.
5. When using drip-type brewers (the most common type used in foodservice) ensure water brewing temperatures are as close to 200°F (93°C) as possible.
6. Remove and dispose of used grounds as quickly as possible to avoid increasing bitterness during holding times.
7. Hold coffee at 175°F to 185°F (80°C to 85°C).
8. Discard brewed coffee after holding twenty to thirty minutes in open-top containers or two hours in closed-top containers (vacuum pots).
9. Never mix old brewed coffee with new.
10. Serve coffee at 155°F to 175°F (70°C to 80°C); deliver prepoured coffee immediately to guests to ensure proper serving temperatures are maintained.

Most of the coffee consumed in the United States is brewed with paper filters, a method that produces coffee in the classic American style: clear, light bodied, with little sediment or oil. Other brewing methods produce coffee richer in flavor, oils, and sediments. Foodservice operators who use nonpaper filter brewing methods do need to keep this difference in mind.

(one "coffee cup") makes a good cup of coffee. Because a pound of coffee contains approximately eighty level tablespoons, one pound of ground coffee used in a drip coffeemaker will produce forty cups of coffee; however, many buyers find that their consumers prefer a milder brew.

Espresso machines use a ratio of one-quarter ounce of coffee to approximately one and a half to three ounces of water, depending on the strength desired. Foodservice operators who attempt to stretch their coffee budgets by reducing the amount of coffee used to produce each cup brewed risk creating coffees that, while less costly, are significantly less flavorful.

Premade (prebrewed) coffees are sold in powdered form (instant coffee), frozen concentrates (for vending machine dispensing), and in bottles as well as cans. Many times these products are convenient and may, for a variety of reasons, have a role to play in a foodservice operation. They simply will not, however, produce a drinkable beverage of the same level of excellence as that obtained by freshly brewing high-quality, well-roasted, properly ground beans. How important is high-quality, fresh-made coffee to the success of a foodservice operation, and equally important, will coffee drinkers pay a premium for superior coffee products? Just ask Starbucks.

Tea

The use of tea to flavor beverages is a technique nearly five thousand years old and was discovered, according to Chinese legend, in 2737 B.C. by a Chinese emperor when some tea leaves accidentally blew into a pot of water he was boiling.

Buyers at Work (10.1)

"It will be terrible," said Andrew Hayman, the front office manager of the 105-room limited service Sleep Well Inn.

"I'm just telling you what the corporate office's e-mail said. It came while you were on vacation," replied Marisha, Andrew's assistant manager.

"So now we are required to have coffee available in the lobby 24/7? Do you know what that's going to taste like at three a.m. after it's been sitting for two hours? And who's supposed to make it?" asked Andrew.

I don't drink coffee, so I don't know," said Marisha, "but I do know the e-mail said we had to have a 24/7 hot coffee service in place by the first of next month or we'll lose twenty-five points on our next corporate property inspection."

Assume you were Andrew and were responsible for implementing this new requirement:

1. What coffee service options would be available to you?
2. How would you ensure the coffee you elected to serve is of good quality?
3. What guest service challenges would you face as you implement this new requirement? How can effective procurement procedures and your knowledge of coffee brewing help you address these new challenges?

The credibility of such a story is enhanced when you realize that, in many areas of the world, boiling water before drinking it was (and still is) an essential act for ensuring good health. The tea tree *(Camellia sinensis)* is native to Southeast Asia and southern China.

In the 1600s tea became popular throughout Europe and the American colonies. Until the late nineteenth century, however, all tea in world trade came from China. About that time, the British, very large consumers of tea, intensified tea production in their own colonies (especially India). Interestingly, the United States has made two significant contributions to the tea industry: in 1904 iced tea was created and served at the World's Fair in St. Louis, and in 1908 Thomas Sullivan of New York developed the concept of tea in a bag (teabags). Today more coffee than tea is consumed in the United States; however, tea drinkers constitute a committed and sizable consumer group.

VARIETIES   Beverage teas are of three basic types: black, green, and oolong. In the United States, more than 90 percent of the tea consumed is black tea. This type of tea has been fully oxidized (fermented), results in a hearty flavor, and has an amber color.

Some popular black teas include English breakfast (a good breakfast choice since its hearty flavor mixes well with milk), Darjeeling (a blend of Himalayan teas suited for drinking with most meals), and orange pekoe (a blend of Ceylon teas that is the most widely used of the tea blends).

Green teas are gaining popularity in the United States due, in part, to recent scientific studies linking its consumption with reduced cancer risk. Green tea is made by cooking fresh tea leaves, pressing them to remove excess moisture, then drying them by hot air or frying in a hot pan. Green tea has a delicate taste and is light green or gold in color. It is often served as a complimentary beverage in Chinese or other Asian-style restaurants.

Oolong tea, popular in China, is partly oxidized and is a cross between black and green tea in color and taste. Most recently, tea manufacturers have begun to offer flavored varieties of black, green, and oolong teas. These are increasingly popular. Also, a significant number of foodservice guests now request **herbal teas.**

While flavored teas evolve from these three basic teas, herbal tea contains no true tea leaves but is popular because, like regular tea, it is considered healthful and contains no calories.

Hot-tea drinkers make up a small but significant number of foodservice guests. The popularity of iced tea, however, is much greater. Approximately 85 percent of the tea consumed in the United States is iced tea. In fact, iced teas are so popular that they are typically one of the limited beverage choices available at quick-service restaurants, as well as nearly all other types of foodservice operations (although **chai** teas are gaining in popularity).

Quality iced tea begins with quality teas. It should taste fresh, clean, and be sparkling clear (unclouded). Any variety of dry tea may be used to make iced tea. The best iced teas, once made, are allowed to slowly cool to room temperature before refrigerating to prevent the tea from acquiring a cloudy appearance (although prolonged storage in a refrigerator may still render the tea cloudy).

The methods buyers use to purchase dry tea leaves and iced tea products are significantly different. Dry teas may be purchased in bulk, loose leaf form but are more commonly purchased in a variety of package sizes, each containing individual and single-serving tea bags. Because tea leaves that are steeped in boiling water expand as they absorb moisture, many tea purists prefer not to make tea from tea bags (insisting that such bags restrict the tea's ability to expand and, thus, do not allow for maximum flavor extraction). Despite the potential effects on product quality, however, the overwhelming majority of foodservice operations serving tea in individual portions offer guests tea bags. Professional foodservice buyers purchase these either as single-serving tea bags wrapped in paper or as single-serving tea bags sealed in foil pouches to minimize excessive drying of the tea bag's contents.

Unlike hot teas, iced teas are typically brewed by the foodservice operation and served ready to drink. Iced tea can be served either presweetened (popular in the American South and Southwest) or unsweetened (popular in the remaining regions). As a result, foodservice operators may offer one or both of these products on their menus. Of course, those who offer unsweetened teas will also offer one or more types of sugars or sweeteners (see Chapter 9) for those guests who prefer sweetened ice tea.

If your operation will serve iced tea, you may purchase loose-leaf teas and make your own product, specially sized iced tea bags that contain enough tea leaves to make iced tea in large quantities, powders that must simply be mixed with water, or you may elect to offer a variety of premade, or ready-to-drink, tea forms. The most popular ready-to-drink teas currently available are sold in cans and/or bottles. These typically are purchased in cases of varying unit counts with individual product serving sizes ranging from eight to twenty-four ounces each.

Buyer's Guide to Purchasing Terms

Herbal tea   A beverage that is prepared in the same manner as tea but which contains no actual tea leaves. Instead, these teas are made by steeping the flowers, berries, peels, seeds, leaves, or roots of plants in boiling water (e.g., lemon, blackberry, peach, peppermint, and apple-cinnamon).

Chai (tea)   The Chinese word for *tea*, it is made from brewed tea and milk.

Ready-to-drink iced tea is sold in several flavored varieties, the most popular of which are lemon, raspberry, and peach.

Because of its wide popularity and low cost, foodservice operators who provide guests with machine-dispensed beverages often include iced tea as one of the product offerings. When they do, iced tea concentrates will be purchased and dispensed in the same manner as are the operation's soft drinks.

Chocolate

Chocolate is one of the most remarkable foods purchased by professional foodservice buyers. Like many other foods, the variation in quality and price among chocolate products is significant. Unlike other foods, however, chocolate's flavor is exceptionally rich, complex, and versatile. It is arguably the single most popular flavor in the world. As you learned in Chapter 9, chocolate is highly prized as a flavoring when making candies, cookies, cakes, and pastries, but it is also extremely popular as a flavoring for cold milk and as a hot beverage.

Chocolate is made by drying, fermenting, and roasting the **cocoa beans** from which it is produced.

Cocoa beans are harvested from the cocoa tree (called *Theobromo cacao,* or "food of the gods"), which originated in South America. Today Africa grows the majority of the world's cocoa.

Cocoa seeds, and the chocolate used to make drinks, can best be understood by considering the seed's fat and nonfat contents. When the fat (called cocoa butter) is removed from cocoa seeds, a bitter powder remains. This **cocoa powder** is the product most often used to make **hot chocolate,** a drink popular in cold and warm climates. Standard cocoa powder has a cocoa butter content of 10 to 12 percent (USDA standard).

While it can be made from a variety of chocolate products melted into milk, the typical manner in which hot cocoa or hot chocolate is purchased is in its dry powdered form. It is available in regular and sugar-free formulas. Some manufacturers offer a product that includes dried marshmallows. Most often it is packaged in various carton sizes containing single-serving units, each weighing approximately 0.75 to 1.5 ounces each and producing one eight- to ten-ounce cup of hot chocolate beverage.

The mixture of cocoa powder, sugar, and dried milk solids used for hot chocolate production has a relatively long shelf life. It can easily be prepared by guests (who simply stir the powdered mix into very hot water). It is relatively inexpensive because it does not contain significant amounts of the highly valued cocoa butter needed by chocolatiers for making other superior-quality chocolate products such as fine candies and gourmet pastries.

Buyer's Guide to Purchasing Terms

Cocoa bean   The seed of the cacao tree. When dried and ground, it is further refined to produce a variety of chocolate forms.

Cocoa powder   The dry powder made by grinding cocoa seeds and removing most of the cocoa butter from the dark, bitter cocoa solids. Cocoa powder has a bitter flavor and is often called simply "cocoa."

Hot chocolate   The sweet drink made from mixing cocoa powder, sugar, and milk. In some areas of the country, it is also known as "hot cocoa" or even more simply "cocoa."

Buyer's Guide to Internet Resources: Coffee, Tea, and Chocolate

Web Site	Topic
www.coffeeresearch.org	Coffee production and brewing information
www.ncausa.org	National Coffee Association (U.S.A.) information
www.supreme-mfg.com/liquidcoffee.htm	Liquid coffee concentrates
www.integratedcoffee.com/aboutICTI.htm	Decaf and caffeine-free coffees
www.1st-line.com/machines/comm_mod/ grinder/index.htm	Commercial coffee grinders
www.bunnomatic.com	Coffee brewing equipment for foodservice use
www.teausa.org	Tea products and brewing
www.stashtea.com	Tea history and product definitions
www.lipton.com	Tea and human health
www.conagra.com	Swiss Miss powdered beverage chocolate

Soft Drinks

Soft drinks are widely served in nearly all foodservice operations. Also known collectively as carbonated beverages, soft drinks are produced by injecting (under very high pressure) CO_2 (carbon dioxide) gas into sweetened and/or flavored water.

Carbon dioxide dissolves fairly quickly when the carbonated beverage is *not* kept under pressure (as is the case when it is served to guests). As the CO_2 gas dissolves, it is released as bubbles that float to the top of the beverage. This action gives soft drinks their characteristic "fizz." After a few hours at room temperature, nearly all of the CO_2 in the beverage is released, and the soft drink will become **flat,** less flavorful, and in many cases will taste overly sweet.

Soft drinks taste good for several reasons. Sweeteners and carbonation are important for flavorful soft drinks, but so is **carbonic acid.** This acid occurs naturally as the carbon dioxide in the beverage dissolves, and it is the cause of the slightly sharp, burning sensation for which carbonated soft drinks are known.

As a buyer of soft drinks, the choices of container sizes available to you will be many. Soft drinks are sold in two-liter and one-liter plastic bottles, twenty-four-ounce and twenty-ounce bottles, and twelve-ounce cans. They are packaged in a variety of quantities including six-packs, twelve-packs, and cases of twenty-four

Buyer's Guide to Purchasing Terms

Soft drink   A carbonated beverage produced by combining CO_2 gas, purified water, and flavored sugar syrups; also called "soda" or "pop" in some parts of the United States.

CO_2   Carbon dioxide; the colorless, odorless gas used to carbonate water in soft drinks and beer. In its solid form, CO_2 is called "dry ice."

Flat (soft drink)   The term used to describe a soft drink or other carbonated beverage that contains too little carbon dioxide.

Carbonic acid   A very weak acid that gives carbonated beverages their characteristically sharp taste. It is created by the dissolving of carbon dioxide (CO_2) in water (H_2O) to create carbonic acid (H_2CO_3).

or thirty-six containers. Increasingly, smaller-sized (eight ounces) soft drink containers are also available.

It is also important for you to know that soft drinks are more than merely a group of pleasant beverages. Consider, for example, that more foodservice guests elect these products as their beverage of choice than both coffee and tea combined. In fact, soft drinks are the single most popular U.S. beverage category. (For purposes of this discussion, the term *soft drink* is restricted to flavored, CO_2-carbonated beverages. It should be noted, however, that some foodservice buyers also consider sparkling waters, lemonade, and fruit punch to be soft drinks.)

Consider also that carbonated soft drinks are the single biggest source of calories (about 7 percent) in the American diet. Currently, teenagers get 13 percent of their calories from carbonated and noncarbonated soft drinks. Consumption of carbonated soft drinks peaked in 1998, when consumption was 56.1 gallons per person. Soft drinks provide large amounts of sugars (mostly high-fructose corn syrup) to many individuals' diets. For example, soft drinks provide the average twelve- to nineteen-year-old boy with about fifteen teaspoons of refined sugar a day, and the average girl with about ten teaspoons a day. Those amounts roughly equal the government's recommended daily limits for teens' sugar consumption from all foods.

Rising soft drink consumption has become such a concern that some nutritionists have recently questioned the wisdom of their unrestricted service. Soft drinks obtain nearly all of their calories from the addition of refined cane sugar or corn syrup. (*Note:* Diet soft drinks do not contain these levels of sugars.) Also, soft drinks contain few, if any, vitamins, few minerals, no fiber, no protein, and in most cases no other essential nutrients. So popular are these beverages that some nutritionists believe the drinks are a significant factor in the increase in obesity and diabetes in the United States because their excessive consumption may displace more healthful beverage choices such as water, milk, and fruit juices. As a result, soft drink availability in school foodservice and health-care settings is increasingly restricted.

Did You Know? (10.3)

Despite their current high level of popularity, the consumption of soft drinks, especially among the young, continues to rise dramatically. Consumption of soft drinks was 48 percent higher in 1996–98 than in 1977–78. During this same time, restaurants and fast-food establishments, as sources of soft drinks, increased more than 50 percent, from 14.4 percent in 1977–78 to 22.1 percent in 1994–98. At the same time, the obesity rate of young children in the United States has soared, with many nutritionists blaming much of this trend on excessive consumption of soft drinks. In fact, carbonated soft drinks are the single largest source of calories in the American diet, according to a 2005 report called "Liquid Candy," produced by the nonprofit Center for Science in the Public Interest (CSPI). Currently soft drink companies annually manufacture enough product to provide more than fifty-two gallons to every man, woman, and child in the United States.

In response to health concerns about children's diets, Burger King Holdings Inc., the world's second largest hamburger chain, set nutritional guidelines to follow when targeting children younger than twelve in advertising. Also, the company's Kids Meals include low-fat milk (not soft drinks). The meal consists of flame-broiled chicken tenders; organic, unsweetened applesauce or apple slices; and low-fat milk, for a total of 305 calories. McDonald's Corp. offers four Chicken McNuggets, apple slices with a low-fat caramel dip, and low-fat milk in its Happy Meals (for a total of 370 calories per meal). By comparison, a large soft drink (thirty-two ounces) by itself contains 310 calories and, while it may be tasty, contributes virtually no nutritional value to the drinker.

The lesson for those foodservice buyers responsible for the health of their customers should be that soft drinks have a place in a balanced diet, but true concern must be shown for limiting the consumption of these beverages to healthful amounts.

Did You Know? (10.4)

Most buyers know that 7-UP and Sprite both refer to citrus-flavored soft drinks and the Coke and Pepsi "cola wars" are legendary, but as a beverage category, the question often arises: What's in a name?

When it comes to soft drinks, the answer is often "geography."
Soft drinks are called *pop* in most of the upper Midwest of the United States.
In the lower Midwest, the term *soft drink* is most common.
Soda is the name of choice in the Northeast, the Southwest, and most of Florida.
Soda pop is used by some consumers, especially in the mountain west.

Other common names include *drink* or *cold drink,* which are commonly used in some parts of the South (especially Louisiana) while *Coke,* the name of a specific Coca-Cola Company product, is the generic term for soft drinks used in much of the South. Thus, it is common to hear Southern restaurant guests ask their servers the very sensible question: "What kind of Coke do you serve?"

Interestingly, foodservice buyers selecting soft drinks do not have the luxury of choosing from a large number of suppliers. In fact, just two companies account for more than 75 percent of the U.S. soft drink market: Coca-Cola and PepsiCo. When the London-based Cadbury Schweppes company is included, the three companies account for more than 90 percent of all soft drink sales. Soft drinks may be purchased in a variety of flavors, with cola by far being the best selling. Other popular flavors include citrus, root beer, strawberry, cherry, and variations of Mountain Dew (a PepsiCo product) and Dr Pepper (a Cadbury Schweppes product).

In the United States, prepackaged soft drinks may be purchased for sale in foodservice operations; however, because of the lower costs per serving that can be achieved, many operators choose to produce the carbonated beverages they sell with their own on-site production systems.

When produced on-site, individual servings of soft drinks are made using special equipment that injects CO_2 gas into purified water and flavored sugar syrups. This equipment, typically provided and maintained by soft drink manufacturers, requires the purchase of **bag-in-box** soft drink syrups and mixes.

When using an on-site soft drink–production system, selecting the actual drink types that will be sold is usually dependent on the vendor that provides and/or services the dispensing equipment used by the property. For example, a Coca-Cola distributor who supplies a free machine to a foodservice operation will likely do so only if that operator agrees to exclusively serve Coca-Cola products.

Like all machines, soft drink–production equipment must be maintained and, because of its function, adjusted on a regular basis to ensure that the proper amount of syrup is mixed with the proper amount of water. Improper calibration (adjustment) can result in excessive product usage and cost (from using too much syrup) or a poor-tasting product (from using too little syrup).

Bottled Waters

Worldwide, water is humanity's most important and most widely consumed beverage. It is a uniquely American custom that, in most restaurants, complimentary

Buyer's Guide to Purchasing Term

Bag-in-box The term used to describe the five-gallon syrup containers used in most modern soft drink–dispensing systems. It is so named because the soft drink syrup is sealed in a plastic bag that is then placed in a cardboard box for easy transporting.

PROFESSIONAL PURCHASING PREVENTS PROBLEMS (10.2)

"Flat!" "Fizzy!" or "This Just Doesn't Taste Right!"

A common problem: Guest complaints related to the carbonation level of on-site-produced soft drinks.

Many factors affect the taste of on-site-produced soft drinks. Water quality, syrup proportions, degree of carbonation, and serving temperatures are just a few of the many components affecting the taste of the final product.

Invariably, some customers' view of the right taste of a soft drink will vary from those of an operation's managers as well as those of other customers. In cases such as these, the guest will typically return the beverage with the statement, "This just doesn't taste right!" which typically indicates that the drinker feels the product does not meet the expected quality standard.

In many cases these guests may be quite right. Soft drink–production equipment can malfunction; gas cylinders providing carbon dioxide for mixing can run out, as can syrup supplies. As a result, it is a good idea for purchasers to ensure that adequate supplies of gas and syrup products are on hand and that dispensing equipment is cleaned, calibrated (adjusted), and serviced on a very regular basis.

---

water is immediately offered to guests when they are seated. Increasingly, however, some American restaurants offer for sale both **still** (noncarbonated) and **sparkling** (carbonated) bottled water to guests to meet the increased demand for these products. Today a foodservice operation that offers its guests a choice of coffee, tea, and soft drinks should also plan to sell one or more brands of domestic and/or imported bottled water.

In the United States, the FDA regulates bottled water as a food product. Bottled water companies must follow the FDA's standards of labeling, which mandate that beverage companies label their waters to define where the water came from and if it has been treated or carbonated.

Bottled waters are classified with tightly defined terms such as *purified*, *spring*, and *artesian* (described below). All bottled water sold in the United States, whether imported or domestic, must meet the same regulations. The most popular of the bottled waters used by foodservice operations are classified by the FDA as one of the following:

Artesian   Bottled water may be labeled as *artesian* if it comes from a well that taps a confined aquifer (a water-bearing underground layer of rock or sand) in which the water level stands at a height above the top of the aquifer.

Purified water   Water that has been produced by distillation, deionization, reverse osmosis, or other processes and that meets the U.S. definition of purified water may be labeled as *purified* bottled water. These waters are taken primarily from metropolitan water sources, run through commercial filters, and are purified of chlorines and other items inappropriate for drinking water. These are typically sold in large (five-gallon) containers.

Mineral water   Waters containing not less than 250 parts per million total dissolved mineral solids may be labeled as *mineral* water. Mineral water is

---

Buyer's Guide to Purchasing Terms

Still (bottled water)   Water that is not carbonated.

Sparkling (bottled water)   Water that is carbonated.

distinguished from other types of bottled water by its relative proportions of mineral and trace elements, but no additional minerals can be added to them.

Spring water   These waters originate from an underground formation from which water flows naturally to the surface of the earth. Spring water must be collected only at the spring or through a well drilled directly into the spring.

Sparkling water   Sparkling waters are those that, when bottled, contain the same amount of naturally occurring carbon dioxide that they had when they were taken from their source.

Soda waters, seltzer waters, and tonic waters customarily used in the preparation of alcoholic drinks are not considered bottled waters. These are regulated separately; most often contain added sugars; and by law, are considered soft drinks.

Most of the bottled water sold in the United States is noncarbonated (still), but sparkling waters are also popular. In theory, any type of bottled water that is sold may first be carbonated. Some of these products are also flavored with ingredients such as citrus or other fruits. Flavored carbonated waters are similar to soft drinks but are lighter in flavor and contain less sugar. They are not likely to be completely calorie free but are lower in carbohydrates and calories than traditional soda-type soft drinks.

As with soft drinks, bottled water products from PepsiCo (Aquafina) and Coca-Cola (Dasani) sell best. When combined, however, the Nestlé Waters company's brands of Poland Spring, Arrowhead, Ozarka, Deer Park, Zephyrhills, Ice Mountain, and others outsell both the PepsiCo and Coca-Cola products. Professional foodservice buyers know that local consumer preferences are very important when choosing bottled waters that will be highly accepted by guests.

Buyer's Guide to Internet Resources: Soft Drinks and Bottled Waters

Web Site	Topic
www.cocacola.com	Coke products (soft drinks)
www.pepsico.com	Pepsi products (soft drinks)
www.cadburyschweppes.com	Dr Pepper products (soft drinks)
www.sellbottledwater.com	Tips for selling bottled waters, including water and food pairings
www.sanpellegrino.com	Naturally carbonated spring water
www.evian.com	Fine-dining bottled waters (palace-style bottles)
www.beverageinstitute.org	Nutrition information, ingredients, and facts about a variety of nonalcoholic beverages

ALCOHOLIC BEVERAGES

For many professional buyers in the hospitality industry, some of the most complex, challenging, yet interesting purchase decisions to be made relate to the buying and serving of **alcoholic beverages.**

Alcoholic beverages contain ethyl alcohol (also known as ethanol), a colorless product created by fermenting a liquid containing sugar. When making alcoholic

Buyer's Guide to Purchasing Term

Alcoholic beverage   A drinkable liquid containing ethyl alcohol.

beverages, fermentation is the chemical reaction that splits a molecule of sugar into equal parts of ethyl alcohol and carbon dioxide. The carbon dioxide escapes into the air, and the ethyl alcohol remains in the liquid. This chemical reaction is caused by yeast. The yeast may occur naturally in the liquid to be fermented or may be introduced into the process by the beverage maker. Ethyl alcohol is, in itself, neither poisonous nor harmful to one's health. (In fact, the positive effects of moderate alcohol consumption are well established.) From a buyer's perspective, any drinkable liquid that contains significant amounts of ethyl alcohol is legally considered an alcoholic beverage.

The history of alcohol and the alcoholic beverage service industry has been a long one. Babylonian clay tablets and Egyptian papyri make mention of taverns. Evidence of more than one hundred bars was found in the ruins of Pompeii (destroyed by a volcano in the first century A.D.), which was a community of only twenty thousand people.

Throughout history, alcoholic beverages have had many uses. In some societies alcoholic beverages were thought to possess magical or holy powers. They were an important part of medical treatment well into the 1800s. Alcoholic beverages were considered a basic and essential food in many cultures. Because these beverages were not associated with diseases caused by drinking contaminated water, they became an accepted part of everyday meals. Alcoholic beverages were particularly important for travelers, who had to be especially cautious about contracting an illness from water containing bacteria for which the traveler had not built up an immunity.

As the ruins and records from the ancient past have shown, taverns have been an integral part of society from at least the beginning of recorded history. Ancient taverns were the forerunners of their modern restaurant counterparts in many ways beyond their beverage service. They were important meeting centers and places to celebrate special occasions. Some featured entertainment; others offered gambling. Most taverns provided food and beverage service and, in many cases, lodging. Taverns also played an important role in the early political development of the United States because they served as public gathering places for those individuals who desired political separation from England.

Slowly, hospitality facilities that served only alcohol or sold alcohol and food became separated from other facilities that offered lodging. By the end of the 1800s, corner saloons, private clubs, cafés, cabarets, and music halls all became popular in the United States. Also developing about this time were restaurants that served beer, wine, and other beverages along with a variety of foods.

By 1900, there was a neighborhood saloon on just about every corner in many cities, and small towns usually had at least one. Some of these saloons became known for their shady customers and for the prostitution and gambling that sometimes accompanied them. Consequently they developed bad reputations, and when that fact was combined with a vocal minority of citizens morally opposed to alcohol consumption, the stage was set for **prohibition.**

The Eighteenth Amendment to the Constitution, which prohibited the manufacture, sale, transportation, and importation of alcoholic beverages was passed in 1919. It went into effect in 1920 and lasted until 1933. The amendment was effective only in stopping the legal manufacture, sale, and transportation of alcohol. Many people still drank poor-tasting, illegally produced alcoholic beverages for

---

Buyer's Guide to Purchasing Term

Prohibition   A law in the United States, made possible by the Eighteenth Amendment to the Constitution, which eliminated all businesses that manufactured, distributed, or sold alcoholic beverages.

the thirteen years the amendment was in effect. Ultimately, the American public's desire to drink alcoholic beverages was again made legal, and the Eighteenth Amendment was deemed a failure. In 1933 Congress passed the Twenty-first Amendment to repeal the Eighteenth Amendment. Despite the repeal, the use of alcoholic beverages was not quickly reaccepted in many parts of American society, and the sale of alcoholic beverages is still highly restricted (or even prohibited) in some areas.

The Twenty-first Amendment allowed individual states, counties, towns, and precincts to control the sale and usage of alcoholic beverages through the issuing of liquor licenses. As a result, a variety of alcohol-related laws exist throughout the United States. In the mid-1930s, only twenty-eight states allowed the sale of alcoholic beverages. Today despite restrictions of many kinds, the sale of alcoholic beverages is legal throughout most of the country. However, there is still a societal concern about the consumption of alcohol, and its use and sale are still highly regulated as are those establishments that serve it.

To understand the societal concern regarding the sale of alcoholic beverages, it is important to understand the effects of alcohol. When it is consumed, the alcohol in an alcoholic beverage is absorbed and can create significant changes in the person who is drinking it. When consumed, alcohol passes from the stomach to the small intestine, where it is rapidly absorbed into the blood and distributed throughout the body. Because it is absorbed quickly and thoroughly, alcohol can affect a drinker's nervous system even if it is consumed in small amounts. In small to moderate amounts, alcohol reduces inhibitions, which makes many people feel more outgoing. As the amount of alcohol consumed increases, a person's speech becomes slurred, motor skills are impaired, and the drinker may even have trouble walking steadily. Memory loss, blurred vision, and impaired judgment increase with increased alcohol consumption. With excessively high concentrations of alcohol in the body, a person can pass out and die.

Professional food and beverage managers would all agree that they should not allow alcoholic beverages to be served to guests who have consumed too much alcohol (and, thus, are intoxicated). The question of what constitutes too much alcohol, however, can vary by locale. The American Medical Association has defined the **blood alcohol concentration (BAC)** level of impairment for all people to be 0.04 grams/100 milliliters of blood (0.04). In a few states, it is illegal for a drinker to drive a motor vehicle if the concentration of alcohol in his or her blood exceeds 0.10 percent. In most states, legislatures have reduced that level to 0.08 percent. Federal grants for highway construction are tied to reduced BAC limits for legal intoxication. As a buyer, the effects of alcohol consumption, recovery from its effects, and legal standards for service should be well understood.

The liver is responsible for the elimination (through metabolism) of 95 percent of ingested alcohol from the body. Healthy people metabolize alcohol at a fairly consistent rate. As a rule of thumb, a person will eliminate one average drink (between 0.5 ounce and 1.0 ounce of pure ethyl alcohol) per hour. Food consumed with alcohol results in delayed alcohol absorption. This is true for two reasons. First, because alcohol is absorbed most efficiently in the small intestine, the digestion of food prevents the stomach's contents (including the alcohol) from being rapidly released into the small intestine. The result is a lower rate of alcohol absorption. Second, alcohol elimination rates are inversely proportional to alcohol concentration in the blood. When food is present in the stomach, less alcohol is absorbed, and that which is absorbed is eliminated at a faster rate than if the drinker

Buyer's Guide to Purchasing Term

Blood alcohol concentration (BAC)   The amount of alcohol in the blood.

had not eaten. For this reason, food, in nearly all cases, should be offered to those consuming alcohol even if the food offered consists of only bar-type snacks or light appetizers.

Until the early seventeenth century, the only alcoholic beverages were those made by fermentation. Beer and wine are the result of this fermentation. Scottish and Irish people first distilled (removed water from) beer and created the first whiskey. The new product was called "usquebaugh," which means "water of life." From the 1600s to the 1800s, the use of the stronger distilled alcoholic beverages spread throughout the world. Corn and malt, flavored with juniper berries, were distilled to produce gin, which became popular in England and Holland. Vodka, distilled from various grains including potatoes, became a national drink in Russia and Poland, and rum, made from molasses or sugar cane juices, was produced throughout the Caribbean.

Government regulations set minimum and maximum amounts of alcohol for various types of alcoholic beverages. Generally speaking, alcoholic beverages can contain from 2 percent alcohol to more than 75.5 percent.

The number and kinds of alcoholic beverages available for sale today is vast. It has been said that an alcoholic beverage has, at some time, been produced from virtually every fruit or grain in and every flavor known to man. Of course, some of these have become more popular than others. All alcoholic beverage products produced fall into one of three basic categories:

1. *Fermented* **Fermented alcoholic beverages** are made from grains or fruits that have an alcoholic content of 3 to 15 percent.
2. *Distilled* A **distilled alcoholic beverage** results when the alcohol content of a fermented beverage is increased through distillation.
3. *Compounded* A **compounded alcoholic beverage** results from combining a fermented or distilled beverage with a flavoring agent(s).

Within the three basic beverage categories, buyers have the ability to choose from a wide variety of products. As a group of products, alcoholic beverages are commonly further classified as a **beer, wine,** or **spirit.**

Licensing

Some foodservice operations are permitted to serve all three types of alcoholic beverages, while others may serve only beer, wine, or both. The social responsibilities

---

Buyer's Guide to Purchasing Terms

Fermented alcoholic beverage An alcoholic beverage made by the fermentation of carbohydrates found in grains or fruits (e.g., beer and wine).

Distilled alcoholic beverage An alcoholic beverage that results when the alcohol content of a fermented beverage is increased through distillation (e.g., vodka and bourbon).

Compounded alcoholic beverage An alcoholic beverage that results from combining a fermented or distilled beverage with a flavoring agent(s) (e.g., gin [flavored with juniper] and other beverages flavored with flowers, fruits, plants, or spices).

Beer An alcoholic beverage fermented from cereals, malts, and hops (a flower added to flavor the beverage).

Wine An alcoholic beverage produced from fermented grapes.

Spirit An alcoholic beverage produced by distilling (removing water from) a liquid that contains alcohol. Sometimes referred to as "hard liquor" or "liquor" because of the large proportion of alcohol they contain.

of buyers, restaurant managers, and owners of properties that serve alcoholic beverages are high, and societal pressure for responsible service will remain and even intensify in the future. For that reason, it is important that buyers understand the basics of licensing requirements for those operations selling alcoholic beverages. The requirements for obtaining a **liquor license** vary from state to state.

In general, licensing related to alcoholic beverage services will determine the following:

- *What is sold*   Holders of liquor licenses are not free to sell any alcoholic beverages they choose. In fact, the type of license granted indicates whether the licensee is permitted to sell beer only; beer and wine only; or beer, wine, and spirits. In addition, the selling of these products, regardless of their type, will be allowed only if the products have been purchased from a state-approved alcoholic beverage supplier. This ensures product wholesomeness, allows the state to carefully monitor alcoholic beverage sales, and assists in the collection of applicable taxes.
- *Where it is sold*   In most cases a liquor license designates a very specific geographic location in which alcohol may be served. This may be identified as an individual building address or even a particular section(s) of a building. In all cases buyers and managers should know exactly where their license allows them to serve alcohol and where the boundaries of that permitted area are located. In most cases the license will require that guests not be allowed to remove alcohol from these designated premises.

   Some licenses may allow the restaurant manager to serve in alternative locations. For example, a restaurant manager may hold a license authorizing beverage service at catered events in off-site locations. The terms of the license will clearly spell out the circumstances in which off-site alcoholic beverage service is allowed.
- *When it is sold*   Operating hours for businesses that serve alcohol are strictly controlled. While few localities place restrictions on when food may be sold, all states regulate the time of day alcohol may be sold; at what time service must stop; and on what days of the week, holidays, or special occasions (such as election days), if any, that service must be restricted/curtailed.
- *How it is sold*   Holders of liquor licenses may be instructed by their state about how alcohol can or cannot be sold. For example, in many locales, guests may not be served more than one alcoholic drink at a time or, perhaps, only guests seated at a table or bar may be served. In other locales these practices may be permitted. Businesses holding liquor licenses of any type must be aware of all restrictions on how these products can be sold.
- *To whom it is sold*   In all fifty states and the District of Columbia, those who would purchase alcoholic beverages must be twenty-one years old or older to do so. Restaurants and bars are responsible for taking reasonable steps to ensure they serve alcohol to only those who are legally entitled to make these purchases. However, restaurant managers are likely to encounter other guests who are older than twenty-one but who are still prohibited from purchasing alcohol, specifically those who appear to be obviously and visibly intoxicated.
- *In what quantity it is sold*   In most jurisdictions, beer may be sold by the glass or the pitcher, wines can be sold by the glass or bottle, and spirits are

---

Buyer's Guide to Purchasing Term

Liquor license   A state-authorized permit that allows the holder of the license (licensee) to sell alcoholic beverages in accordance with state, local, and federal laws; sometimes called a "liquor permit."

typically sold by the drink. This is not, however, always the case. Depending on local regulations, restrictions on the quantity of alcohol that can be sold at one time to a specific individual may be quite extensive. To purchase properly, you must understand all applicable restrictions that are placed on the quantity of alcohol you can serve to any purchaser of alcohol.

Beer

Beer is generally recognized to be the world's oldest and most popular alcoholic beverage. In ancient times, the Egyptians made it from barley, Babylonians made it from wheat, and the Incas made it from corn. In fact, barley used for beer for brewing was so important to the early Romans that they pictured the grain on their gold and silver coins. So popular is beer in the United States that total 2007 beer purchases exceeded 2.9 billion cases with domestically made beer accounting for more than 85 percent of those sales.

Today's beer is most often produced by fermenting grain starch (commonly barley). The type of grain or other starch used for fermentation, any flavorings (commonly hops) added, and the specific production techniques used by the beer's brewer cause these products to have varying characteristics, colors, and flavors.

Beverage buyers today can choose from many hundreds (or more) of brands of beer. According to data compiled by the Beer Institute (an industry trade association), more than twelve hundred breweries and **microbreweries** are currently producing beers in the United States.

There are two general styles or classifications of beer that you can purchase for foodservice operations: **lagers** and **ales.**

The lager beers commonly sold include bock, dark lager, light lager, light beer, dry beer, ice beer, malt liquor, and the very popular **pilsner.** Ales include light ale, brown ale, porter, and stout.

Lagers and ales are brewed in basically the same way, but different types of yeasts and different methods of fermentation yield different bodies and tastes. When guests order a "beer" in the United States, they are usually ordering a lager product. In this country, ale is typically ordered by brand name. Most ale has a higher alcohol content, more body, and a stronger taste than lager beer.

Most of the popular lager-style beers sold in the United States are pilsners. All pilsners are characteristically amber colored, light flavored, and contain less alcohol than malt and bock beers. While not true worldwide, the preference of American drinkers and diners is overwhelmingly for extremely mild pilsner-style beers. These "American-style" lagers are often the subject of disdain among "true" beer drinkers because lighter beers are considered to have less character than most European styles of beer. While it is true that these beers are different from their heavier-bodied counterparts, American-style beers are increasing in popularity worldwide.

A very light color and body and the frequent use of rice or corn in their brewing are the factors that characterize American-style beers. So popular are they that

---

Buyer's Guide to Purchasing Terms

Microbrewery   A very small commercial beer brewery.

Lager   A bright, clear, light-bodied beer brewed from malt, hops, and water. The mixture is then fermented, lagered (stored) to develop flavor, then carbonated.

Ale   A heavier brew than lager made from malt or malt and cereals. It is fermented at a high temperature. The resulting beer is full bodied and more bitter than a lager.

Pilsner   Beers of the style made popular by the Pilsner Urquell brewery in Plzeň, Bohemia (now the Czech Republic).

the five top-selling beer brands in the United States (Bud Light, Budweiser, Miller Light, Coors Light, and Corona Extra) are all of this type.

Light beers are the best-selling beers in most areas of the United States. These light beers are essentially pilsners brewed with extra enzymes to give them a lower calorie and carbohydrate content. In addition, many light beers have lowered alcohol content. Light beers really came of age in about 1973, when Miller released Lite, the first of the light beers to use an enzyme called amyloglucosidase. This enzyme effectively allowed the fermentation of all the beer's fermentable sugar, resulting in a beer that was both lower in calories and slightly higher in alcohol content. While some brewers reduced the alcohol content to a level at or below their regular beers, many consumers enjoy the fact that they can get the same beer taste they seek at a much-reduced calorie content because regular beers contain 150 to 180 calories per serving, while light beers have 68 to 134 calories per serving.

The popularity of specific pilsner-style beer brands can vary greatly based on the location of a foodservice operation, so experienced buyers look to their beverage suppliers for advice and survey their own customers to determine the most popular beer brands to purchase and offer for sale.

Less popular in the United States but more popular worldwide are the dark varieties of ales such as porter and stout. Porter originated in England in the eighteenth century. Dark brown, heavy bodied, and malty flavored, these beers have a slightly less sweet taste and reduced hop flavor than do light ales.

Stout is a heavy beer made with roasted malted barley. The traditional English stouts are sweet because they use lactose (milk sugar) in their production and are sometimes called cream stouts. Porters, stouts, and ales are gaining in popularity in the United States as microbreweries broaden the taste preferences of American beer drinkers.

The two primary issues beverage buyers must consider before purchasing beer, as well as many other alcoholic beverage products, are the following:

1. What should be purchased?
2. How should it be purchased?

Many beverage buyers are challenged when selecting the proper mix of traditional and lower-calorie (light) beers, as well as low-carbohydrate beers, pilsners, ales, and other beer products. After the decision about which products to purchase has been resolved, however, the issue of how they should be

---

Did You Know? (10.5)

There are four ingredients used to make all types of beer: (1) malt (typically barley malt), (2) water, (3) hops, and (4) yeast. Often a fifth ingredient, an additional grain called malt adjunct, is added to the mixture. The following steps are then taken by the beer's brewer:

1. The barley is soaked in water and heated to make a malt. This gives beer its taste and color and contributes to the body and the head (foam).
2. The malt's starch is broken down to sugar. Grain residue is then removed from the brew.
3. The liquid is boiled for several hours and hops are added. This gives beer its sharp flavor. The hops are then removed, and the brew is cooled.
4. Yeast is added to cause fermentation. At this point, lager or ale is produced depending on which yeast and fermentation process is used.
5. The brew is cooled and stored for two to four weeks. Then the beer is pasteurized, bottled, and capped. Draft beer (also called "keg" or "tap" beer) is an unpasteurized product. It requires special handling and should be kept refrigerated at all times. Even if a keg is kept under proper refrigeration, its shelf life is only thirty to forty-five days, so it should be used as quickly as possible.

	CAPACITY
Contents in ounces	1984.0
Contents in gallons	15.5
Contents in liters	58.7
Full keg weight	160.5 pounds
Empty keg weight	29.7 pounds
Beer weight	130.8 pounds
	SERVINGS*
Number of 10-oz. servings	198
Number of 12-oz. cases equivalent	6.8 cases
Number of 12-oz servings	165
Number of 16-oz. servings	124

*The number of servings contained in a keg will be affected by the quality of the operation's beer dispensing lines, product temperature, CO_2 levels, and bartender's skill. If keg beer is purchased, it should only be in response to a customer demand that ensures sufficient turnover to warrant the required investment in proper dispensing equipment and its maintenance.

FIGURE 10.1 Keg Specifications for U.S. Half-Barrel

purchased still remains. In many cases beer can be purchased by the **keg,** in bottles, or in cans.

Because bottles and cans of beer are pasteurized, they have a longer shelf life than does keg beer (which has not undergone pasteurization). Keg beer is typically significantly less costly per ounce to buy, and profit levels for its sale are higher than for canned or bottled beer. Spoilage, however, can be a problem, and there must be adequate refrigeration space for holding and serving from kegs. In addition, beer lines and taps must be cleaned frequently. While keg sizes can vary, the most popular keg size sold in the United States is the half-barrel. Figure 10.1 lists detailed information about this popular keg size.

It is critically important to understand that how a beer is served has a great deal to do with the way it will taste. To be served properly, all beer should be stored

Draft beer is extremely popular. Many customers prefer it to canned or bottled beer, and it can be highly profitable.

Lockyer, Romilly/Getty Images Inc. -Image Bank

Buyer's Guide to Purchasing Term

Keg A container for beer. Kegs vary in size but nearly always contain unpasteurized beer. Beer served from kegs is called "draft" or "draught" beer.

and presented to the guest at the right temperature. Beer glasses must be clean, or the head of foam will lose its firmness and break up. Keg beer should be poured only when it can be served immediately. The glass should be held at a forty-five-degree angle for half the pour then straightened for the last half of the pour. When the head has risen slightly higher than the rim of the glass, the pour should be stopped, resulting in a head that normally measures from one-half to one inch.

Buyer's Guide to Internet Resources: Beers

Web Site	Topic
www.realbeer.com	Beer brewing information
www.beerhistory.com	Historical facts about the U.S. beer industry
www.beerinstitute.org	Beer industry advocacy/lobbying activities
www.budweiser.com	Budweiser beer products
www.millerbrewing.com	Miller beer products
www.coors.com	Adolf Coors beer products
www.brewpubzone.com	Lists of U.S. microbreweries
www.inbev.com	World's largest brewer
www.pilsner-urquell.com	First Pilsner-style brewery
www.probrewer.com	Keg (draft) beer troubleshooting tips

Wine

The history of man is intertwined with the history of wine. While no one knows when wine was first made, even the earliest literature makes reference to its production. Wine has been made since the beginning of time, but it was not until the mid-1800s that the science of wine production became known. Louis Pasteur, the famous scientist, was the first to discover and prove that fermentation was caused by yeasts in the air. The knowledge of why fermentation started helped wine producers improve their products greatly.

Some areas of the world produce spectacular wines, while other areas produce either no wine or wines that are not popular enough to be sold world-wide. Many countries, however, produce good, solid, highly drinkable wines. Wine is particularly fascinating to people because no two wines are ever identical. There are subtle differences in wines, even those made from the same grapes. Location, climate, soil, winemaker, and the wine's age are but a few of the characteristics that influence the taste of wine.

Good wine appeals to the eye, the nose, and the mouth. To the eye, the wine should appear clear and brilliant. Red wine should appear rich, and white wines should sparkle. To the nose, the wine should be pleasant, with a hint of flowers, spice, or other characteristic common to the wine type. The aroma, or **bouquet,** should linger and, above all, be an indicator of the taste to come.

Finally, the flavor of the wine should be appealing to the drinker. From inexpensive to the very highest price, wines are available for every taste and preference. Some food and beverage buyers are confused by the great variety and seemingly complex information associated with wine. You should not be. In most cases you

---

Buyer's Guide to Purchasing Term

Bouquet   The aroma of wine.

can do a good job buying wine if a few wine basics are understood and the preferences of your own customers are taken into account.

Wines can be classified in a variety of ways. Country of origin, type of grape used to make the wine, and alcohol content of the finished product are just a few of the ways wine buyers classify wines. Wines can also be grouped based on their sugar content. As a result, wines may be classified as dry (not sweet), semidry, or sweet. These terms are used to describe the sweetness of a wine and refer to the residual sugar content (the amount of grape sugar remaining in the wine after fermentation has occurred) in the wine. Dry wines are the least sweet and have a sugar content below 0.8 percent, while semidry wines have 0.8 to 2.2 percent grape sugar, and sweet wines have more than 2.2 percent sugar. Of the many ways wines may be classified, for the professional buyer, color is probably the most common way.

A wine's color depends on how long the grape skins remained in the beverage during fermentation. Because all grape juice is clear in color, any juice can be used to make white wine. If grape skins are allowed to stay in contact with the juice during production, the juice will take on the color of the grape skins. If the red grape skins stay in contact for a long time, red wine will result. If they are allowed to stay in contact for only a short time, a light red, or **rosé,** wine will result.

While the study of wine can be a lifelong endeavor (and passion), professional buyers who understand the basics of red and white wines are in a good position to make good buying decisions for their own foodservice operations.

RED WINES   Red wines have traditionally been associated with hearty, full-bodied flavor. The classic red wines are made from the Cabernet Sauvignon (pronounced cab-er-nay so-veen-yohn) grape. This is the red wine made famous by the Bordeaux region of France. These wines are complex, outstanding products that make excellent food accompaniments and are fine for drinking by themselves. They are typical of the red wines sold to accompany beef, wild game, and dark meat entrées that require a bold, hearty flavor.

Another outstanding grape used for making red wines is the Pinot Noir (pronounced pee-no nwar). It is from this grape that the famous French burgundies are made. Interestingly, this is the same grape used to make champagne (a sparkling wine discussed later in this chapter).

Other important grapes used for making red wine include the Merlot (pronounced mer-low); the Gamay and Napa Gamay, grown in France and California, respectively; the Australian Shiraz (called Syrah in France); and the Zinfandel (pronounced zin-fan-del), a grape grown in California and popular for making a very light red, or blush, wine.

Light red wines can range from just barely pink to nearly red. They are called white Zinfandels (if they are made from that type of grape), blush, or rosé wines. They are especially popular for drinking in warm-weather climates. In addition, these light red wines are frequently drunk when eating light foods such as fish and poultry. Most rosés taste light and fresh, with sweet, fruity flavors. The most popular of these are Zinfandels, named for the grape used to produce them.

Zinfandel grapes, the most widely planted grape in California, can be used to produce rich, red wine but are most often used to create the blush wines associated with its name. Red wines that are made from a blend of different grapes may be labeled as simply *red* or *table red*. These wines are less expensive than those made exclusively with one grape type and are often very popular because of their

---

Buyer's Guide to Purchasing Term

Rosé   A very light red–colored wine; sometimes called a "blush" wine.

lower price. The most important thing for the professional buyer to remember is that wines selected for sale should match the tastes and price range of their intended consumers.

WHITE WINES   While red wines have traditionally been associated with robust food, white wines, with their more delicate taste, are most popular for drinking by the glass in bars and lounges, at receptions, and with light foods. White wines (served chilled) compliment delicate foods, such as fish, poultry, and pork and are often served as a meal accompaniment to these dishes.

White wines range in flavor from those that are dry and tart to others that are sweet and mellow. Their colors range from pale yellow to very deep gold. White wines have a more delicate flavor than red wines. They vary in alcohol content from a low of 10 percent to as much as 14 percent. Most of the white wines served in the United States come from Italy, Germany, France, Chile, Australia, and California and other domestic sources.

Grapes used to produce fine white wines vary according to the country that makes the wine. In the Rhine and Moselle valleys of Europe, the Riesling grape is most often used to produce the sweet, flavorful wines associated with German whites. The trebbiano grape of Italy produces Soave and is used to make Chianti, a fruity, Italian, flavored wine. Pinot Bianco, Pinot Grigio, and Traminer are other popular Italian grapes used for making white wine.

Chardonnay is by far the most popular white wine sold in the United States today. This complex wine is aged in oak. While many white wines are fermented in stainless-steel tanks, fermenting and aging in oak and other woods give wines unique and quite complex flavor, color, and aroma characteristics. Like many red wines, Chardonnay wine will improve with age prior to its bottling. Chardonnay is made from the same grape used in the Burgundy and Champagne regions of France. It is, however, truly an international sensation, and excellent Chardonnay wine is produced in France, the United States, Argentina, Australia, Bulgaria, Romania, Mexico, and even Japan.

OTHER WINES   While classifying wines as red or white is very helpful to buyers, variations of these wine types do exist and must be understood. For example, **sparkling wines** are characterized by the presence of carbonation in the wine.

Did You Know? (10.6)

A wine's age affects its quality. Wine aging starts in the fermentation tank in which the wine is made. After it has fermented to the degree desired by the winemaker, the grape skins that affect wine's color are removed and the young wine is held in a neutral storage container such as a stainless-steel vat, or in wood (most often oak).

Inexpensive wine is typically filtered and goes straight from a steel storage tank to the bottle, but higher-quality products are aged in wood casks. When stored in wood, a gradual oxidation also occurs, resulting in less bitterness in the wine, increased color, and greater stability. The wood also imparts its own flavors as the wine reacts chemically with it.

Even after it is removed from the wood and bottled, chemical compounds in the wine continue to change in complex ways. In most cases, these changes add softness, richness, and complexity to the wine.*

*For a detailed examination of the affects of age on wine flavor, including the best time to drink various wine types, go to www.wineaging.com.

Buyer's Guide to Purchasing Term

Sparkling wine   A naturally or artificially carbonated wine.

Sparkling wine is generally white but can vary in color from light to dark red. Champagne, a type of sparkling white wine, is actually made from grapes that are bluish-black on the outside and red on the inside. Their juice, however, is white and produces white sparkling wine if it is not allowed to be colored by the dark skins of the grapes. Sparkling wines are simply those that are carbonated (bubbly). Their alcohol content is the same as that of regular wine. Champagne is the most popular sparkling wine, and the name *Champagne* legally applies to only a specific sparkling wine made in France.

Some wines are considered neither red nor white nor sparkling but are still important wine products. These include the following:

Vermouth   Vermouth can be either sweet (Italian) or dry (French). These are **fortified wines,** those whose alcohol levels have been increased after fermentation is complete. In the case of vermouth, the alcohol level is increased to around 18 percent (36 **proof**).

Vermouths are flavored with a product other than the grapes used for their production. French vermouth is steeped in a combination of nutmeg, coriander, orange peel, tea, and other spices and flavorings. Italian vermouth, which is often colored red, is flavored with quinine as well as a variety of herbs and spices. The most common uses of vermouth in the United States are as an ingredient in the martini, a mixture of gin or vodka and dry vermouth, and the Manhattan, a combination of whiskey, bitters, and sweet vermouth.

Sake   Sake is often called rice wine because the term *sake* means "essence of rice spirit." In fact, sake is a product made from rice, but it is made more like a beer than a wine. Sake is served warm to release its entire aroma. At 14 to 16 percent alcohol content, it has the strength of a wine and can be enjoyed straight or mixed with vodka or gin in place of vermouth in a martini.

Sherry   Sherry is a blended wine, made famous by the sherries originally produced in Spain. There are a great number of varieties, from the very dry varieties to the sweet, deep golden cream varieties. Sherries contain from 13 percent to 20 percent alcohol and are drunk both before and after dinner.

Port   Port is a variety of wine produced in Portugal. It became widely distributed and popular in English-speaking countries during the early 1700s. All port bottled in Portugal is certified as Porto by the Portuguese government. The rest of the port made outside Portugal is called port or port wine. Port is a rich, popular after-dinner drink.

Other popular fortified wines include marsala, Madeira, and muscat.

In the United States, wine coolers are popular. The term *wine cooler* has come to mean a variety of flavored wines. Typically a mixture of wine and fruit juices, these easy-to-drink wines are sweet and appeal to many guests who would not ordinarily order wine. Wine coolers have about half the alcohol content of table wines (about six percent), and are available in many flavors, including citrus, orange, strawberry, peach, and raspberry. They are typically served well chilled or over ice.

Buyer's Guide to Purchasing Terms

Fortified wine   A wine whose alcohol content has been increased. Fortified wines are also called "dessert wines" in the United States but are called "liqueur wines" in Europe.

Proof (alcohol)   A measure of the alcoholic strength of a beverage. Proof is equal to two times the percent of alcohol present in the beverage (e.g., a beverage containing 25 percent alcohol would have a proof of 50 (25 percent alcohol content $\times$ 2 = 50 proof).

Purchasing Wines

Like many foods, wine labels carry a great deal of information about a wine that can be helpful to buyers. Some labels, like those found on German wines, can be very detailed. Other wine labels carry less information. Among the information that can generally be found on wine labels are the following:

- **Vintage,** the year the grapes used to make the wine were grown
- Where the majority of grapes used to produce the wine were grown
- The type of grape used
- Vineyard owner's name and address
- Bottler's name and address
- Shipper's name and address
- Governmental inspection/authorization information

Most foodservice operators will offer guests wine menus (lists) consisting of wines sold to guests by the bottle or **by the glass.**

Because wines are frequently purchased and sold to diners by the bottle, you should be well acquainted with the most common bottle sizes used by wine suppliers. These are listed in Figure 10.2.

Increasingly wines may be sold to foodservice operators in boxes rather than bottles. The box containers sold typically contain two to five liters of wine. Boxed

Wine labels can provide valuable information to knowledgeable buyers.

© Dorling Kindersley

Buyer's Guide to Purchasing Terms

Vintage   The year in which the majority of grapes used to make a wine were grown. In the United States, 85 percent of the contents of a wine bottle must have been grown in the year stated on the wine's label.

By the glass (wine)   Wine priced for and sold to guests by the single serving (rather than by the bottle).

FIGURE 10.2 Common Wine Bottle Sizes

Note: 1 U.S. quart = 0.946 liters
1 U.S. gallon = 3.785 liters

Bottle Size (Capacity)	Name	Description
0.100 liters	Miniature (mini)	A single-serving bottle
0.187 liters	Split	¼ standard bottle
0.375 liters	Half-bottle	½ standard bottle.
0.750 liters	Bottle	Standard wine bottle
1.5 liters	Magnum	Two bottles in one
3.0 liters	Double magnum	Four bottles in one

wines are actually bagged wines, as wineries selling boxed wines package their products in vacuum-sealed bags. These are designed to minimize the presence of oxygen and prevent oxidation that can cause wines (as well as other foods) to deteriorate. Well-designed bag-in-box wine containers can keep wines at top quality for up to four weeks after they are opened.

PROFESSIONAL PURCHASING PREVENTS PROBLEMS (10.3)

I'll Take the House Wine, Please

A common problem: Guests are hesitant to purchase some wines offered simply because they are unfamiliar with them.

Wine buyers can be challenged by the vast number of products available to them. For customers, the problem is even greater. The "unique" wine discovered and offered for sale by a knowledgeable wine buyer may be truly remarkable or offer great value, but it is unlikely many guests will know that. In fact, they may be unfamiliar with most of the wines you will buy and offer for sale to them. While not all buyers are responsible for wine list development or sales, guests can be encouraged to order wines with which they are not very familiar if the following are true:

1. Wines are selected that complement the menu items served in the foodservice operation (e.g., Italian wines with Italian food).
2. The wines are modestly priced in relation to the menu prices (but consider some higher-priced wines for guests who know about and prefer a higher-quality wine).
3. You select some popular-priced wines that can be sold by the glass.
4. The wine's characteristics and flavor are clearly described on the wine menu.
5. Recommendations printed on the food menu (or made by servers), suggest complementary pairings between the specific wines you offer and your individual menu items. Always remember, however, that your guests' preferences for any wine with any food at any time during the meal is the best rule for selling more wine.

Wine sales will increase when detailed information about the wines offered is provided on the wine list.

Steve Mason/Getty Images, Inc. -Photodisc.

Buyers at Work (10.2)

"Why not buy some more types?" asked Dave Abbott, the salesperson for Umberto Wines. "They won't spoil. You just will be offering your guests more choices. Do that, and you'll see your wine sales increase. I promise you that!"

Dave was attempting to convince Sasha Abhyankar, manager of the Fifty Yard Line Steakhouse, that he should significantly increase the number of wines offered to the guests of the restaurant.

"I don't know, Dave," replied Sasha. "We have six good reds, five whites, and two blush wines on the menu now. Additional choices may just confuse my guests or just result in their switching from their current wine selection to a different wine. That doesn't mean increased sales . . . just increased inventory."

Assume that you were Sasha:

1. What signs would indicate to you that the number of wines offered on your menu is insufficient and, thus, should be expanded?
2. What signs would indicate to you that the number of wines offered on your menu is too large and, thus, should be reduced?
3. What role would you want your salesperson and Umberto Wines to play in this assessment?

Buyer's Guide to Internet Resources: Spirits

Web Site	Topic
www.winespectator.com	Comprehensive information about wine
www.wineintro.com/basics	Wine basics
www.winespectator.com	Extensive information about wine
www.wine-searcher.com	Comprehensive information about wines available for purchase
www.winemag.com	American wines

Spirits

Spirits are the most potent of alcoholic beverages because water and alcohol boil at different temperatures, so when carefully managed, **distillation** allows the concentration of alcohol in a beverage to increase.

The boiling point of water is 212°F (100°C), while alcohol boils at 173°F (78°C). When distillers boil a liquid mixture containing alcohol at a temperature above the boiling point of alcohol but below the boiling point of water, the alcohol will vaporize, but the water in the mixture will not. If they can then capture the alcohol and convert it back to a liquid before the vapor escapes into the air, they will have created the basis for a distilled beverage.

The Arabs are generally credited for the term *alcohol*, a discovery they made when using the alembic still, the heating device first used to distill alcohol. While

Buyer's Guide to Purchasing Term

Distillation   A method of separating chemical substances based on differences in their boiling points.

Did You Know? (10.7)

In 2007 the U.S. Treasury Department was considering a new rule that would require companies to put alcoholic content, serving sizes, and nutritional information on all alcoholic drink packaging. According to the proposed rules, labels on alcoholic beverages, from beer cans, to wine bottles, to spirit containers, would include a statement of the drink's percentage of alcohol by volume.

The labels would also include a serving facts panel, which would list the number of calories, carbohydrates, fat, and protein for a standard serving size. Companies could also choose to disclose the amount of pure alcohol, or ethyl alcohol, per serving.

Currently, liquor and wine labels must include at least the percentage of alcohol by volume, but that information is not allowed on beer labels except in states that require it. (However, if a brewer wants its beer to be labeled as a light beer, the label must show its caloric content and the percent of alcohol per volume.)

Most industry observers support this proposed rule because they agree that consumers have a right to learn more about the products they are buying. Buyers of beverages for sale in the hospitality industry should monitor this (as well as other) proposed regulation as it represents the type of continued governmental action that can directly affect foodservice purchasing.

beer is the result of the fermentation of grain and wine is the result of the fermentation of grape juice, spirits are the distillation of these and other fermented sugar products. For example, vodka is a spirit made from grain, rum is made from sugar cane, and brandy is the result of distilling grape juice. Other popular spirits you will likely buy in quantity include whiskey, gin, tequila, and **liqueurs.**

Most spirits are approximately one-half water and one-half alcohol (80 to 100 proof). Taste differences occur among types of spirits (e.g., gin versus vodka), within product categories (e.g., Irish whiskey versus Scotch whisky), and among different brands of the same product (e.g., one brand of vodka versus another). In most cases the manager's first purchasing decision relates to which liquors will be the restaurant's **well brands** and which will be its call brands. The former typically cost less and are sold for less than their call-brand counterparts.

The very best of the call brands are sometimes referred to as "premium" or "super premium," depending on the product's cost and selling price potential. In most operations that serve spirits, buyers offer guests their choice of well, call, and selected premium products.

Specific well brands may be selected because they cost the operation less than better-known and more popular call brands. If, however, the well brands selected are viewed by guests as too "cheap," the operation's reputation may suffer. Guests who do not specify a brand generally do not care which is used as long as the quality of the beverage is acceptable. In practice, a buyer's liquor distributor can advise about well brands in keeping with the quality image desired by an operation as well as appropriate call and premium products that could be offered.

Buyer's Guide to Purchasing Terms

Liqueur   A spirit (usually sweetened) and flavored with fruit, spices, nuts, herbs, or seeds.

Well brand   The brand of liquor that is served when the guest does not indicate a preference for a specific brand. Sometimes called the "house" or "pour" brand. For example, a guest ordering a "vodka tonic" would be served the operation's well vodka in the drink.

As is true with beer and wines, the amount of product knowledge you can obtain about spirits is vast. There is, however, some basic information that all potential buyers should know about the most popular spirits:

Vodka   Vodka is the best-selling spirit in the U.S. market today, accounting for approximately 25 percent of all the spirit beverages sold. It is distinguished by its aroma; texture; weight; and smooth, silky character. It is also noted for its bite, which makes it a good accompaniment to oily and smoked foods such as caviar and salmon. It is famous for the warming sensation it provides the body as it is drunk, perhaps a reason for its popularity in cold climates. Vodka was invented in Poland but was adopted by the Russians as their official drink. In fact, the word *vodka* is a variation of *voda*, the Russian word for water. Contrary to popular opinion, the best vodka is made not from potatoes, but rather is distilled from fermented grain. Unlike whiskey or gin, which are lightly flavored by the distiller, vodka is produced with the objective of creating a tasteless, colorless, odorless product. To achieve this result, the vodka is filtered through charcoal. It requires no aging and mixes easily with other beverages because of its neutral qualities. Most recently, flavored vodkas have appeared on the market. These products are flavored with a variety of ingredients, including berries, oak, honey, pepper, currants, pineapple, and citrus.

Gin   In the 1950s gin outsold vodka in the United States by nearly a three-to-one margin. Today it is still favored by many older drinkers as well as those who enjoy the simplicity of the gin martini, a popular **mixed drink.**

The flavor of gin comes from juniper berries. The beverage was invented in Holland in the 1600s. Today gin is available in two basic types: Dutch and English. Dutch gin is meant to be drunk straight and cold and is not typically mixed. English (dry) gin is made in both England and the United States and is used most often in mixed drinks.

Rum   Rum is a spirit with a significant history in the development of the New World. It is said that Columbus brought sugar cane cuttings to the West Indies from the Caribbean Islands in the early 1500s. Molasses, which is produced when sugar is refined, became to Caribbean countries what malted barley was to the Scots and grape juice was for the French and Italians: the essence of a unique and flavorful distilled spirit. Rums of many flavors and colors are produced throughout the Caribbean as well as Central and South America. They can be either light or full bodied. The great majority of rum sold in the United States is of the light variety. Darker rums tend to be fuller flavored than the lighter varieties. Spiced and fruit-flavored rums are also popular. The two most often requested are Captain Morgan's (flavored with apricot, fig, vanilla, and other ingredients) and Malibu Rum, flavored with coconut.

Tequila   Tequila is a spirit product produced in Mexico. Tequila is aged in oak and can only be produced in a very tightly controlled area of the country—Tequilas—the official district surrounding the town of Tequila, Mexico. Tequila is made from the blue agave plant and, to earn its name, must contain at least 51 percent fermented agave juice. Tequila is the principal ingredient in the very popular margarita, a fruit juice and tequila mixed drink that can be served frozen or over ice.

Buyer's Guide to Purchasing Term

Mixed drink   A beverage created by combining one or more spirits with various other beverages and/or flavorings; sometimes called (incorrectly) "cocktails."

Whiskey Whiskey is a brown (colored) spirit, rather than a white (clear) spirit, such as those discussed previously. Currently the sale of brown spirits is declining as the sale of white spirits (vodka, gin, rum, and tequila) is increasing. For professional spirit buyers, however, a basic understanding of whiskey is still essential. Scottish and Canadian distillers spell whisky without an "e," while Irish and American distillers include the "e."

There are two general types of whiskey: straight and blended. Straight whiskies are unmixed or are mixed with whiskey from the same distiller. Blended whiskies are a mixture of similar straight whiskies from different distillers. By government standards, an American whiskey can be labeled as *straight* if it contains at least 51 percent of a single grain (e.g., corn, rye, or other grain). Whiskies are typically categorized according to country of origin:

- *Scotch whisky* This is the whisky of Scotland, and it is light bodied and smoky flavored. Barley, and sometimes corn, is the grain used to produce it. Most Scotch whisky is blended rather than straight and is bottled at 80 to 86 proof. The base grain is dried over open, peat fires that give the product its smoky taste. The grain is then combined with water (mash), fermented, distilled, and aged at least four years.
- *Canadian whisky* This is a blended whisky and is light in body. It may contain corn, rye, wheat, and barley as base grains. It is aged six years or more and bottled at 80 to 90 proof.
- *Irish whiskey* This uses the same ingredients and is made the same way as Scotch whisky. The main difference is that the malted barley is not exposed to peat smoke when it is dried, so there is no smoky taste. The product also goes through a triple distillation process and uses several grains in addition to malted barley. The result is a very smooth, high-quality whiskey that is offered for sale after aging a minimum of seven years.
- *U.S. whiskey* These include bourbon, rye, corn, bottled-in-bond, blended, and light whiskies. Bourbon is the most popular and is a straight whiskey distilled from a fermented mash containing a minimum of 51 percent corn. It is aged in charred oak barrels from two to twelve years. Bourbon has a strong flavor and a full body. It is generally bottled at 80 to 90 proof. Blended whiskey is a combination of straight whiskies. Nearly one-half of the U.S. whiskies consumed are blends. These are designated by the words *American Whiskey* on their labels.

Brandy Brandy is a distilled spirit made from a fermented mash of fruit: generally grapes, but also apples, cherries, apricots, and plums. The word itself has its origins in Holland, where it is derived from *brandewijn*, or "burned wine," a reference to the fact that the wine product from which the brandy was made was heated when distilled. If brandy is made from grape juice, the term *brandy* stands alone on the label. If it is made from other fruits, the name of the fruit appears with the term *brandy* (e.g., apricot brandy). Brandies must be bottled at 80 proof or more. Different types of brandies include the following:

- *Cognac* Considered the finest of brandies, it is produced in the Cognac region of France. Cognac is the distillation of grape juice only
- *Apple Brandy* The American name for Calvados, the French equivalent of apple brandy
- *Kirsch or Kirschwasser* German brandy made from a wild black cherry
- *Ouzo* Greek brandy that is colorless and has a licoricelike taste
- *Per William* Made from Swiss or French pears
- *Elderberry* Made from the elderberries

- *Fraise*   Made from strawberries
- *Framboise*   Made from raspberries
- *Slivovitz*   Made from plums

Liqueurs   Liqueurs (sometimes called "cordials") are spirits that have been redistilled or steeped with fruits, plants, flowers, or other natural flavorings then sweetened with sugar. When the sugar content is high, the liqueur has a creamy quality and is designated *creme de* (as in creme de cacao). Some popular liqueurs include the following:

- *Anisette*   Red or clear color with an anise or licorice flavor
- *Amaretto*   Almond flavor but made from apricot stones
- *Coffee liqueur*   Made from coffee beans
- *Creme de bananes*   Yellow color, banana flavored
- *Creme de cacao*   Brown or clear color with a chocolate-vanilla flavor
- *Creme de menthe*   Green or clear color with a mint flavor
- *Creme de cassis*   Deep red color with a red currant flavor
- *Curaçao*   Orange, blue, or clear color with an orange peel flavor
- *Triple sec*   A white curaçao (orange flavor)
- *Kummel*   Clear color with a caraway seed flavor
- *Maraschino*   Clear color with a nutty, cherry flavor
- *Sambuca*   Licorice flavored, usually clear in color.
- *Sloe gin*   Red color with a plum flavor, made from the sloe berry
- *Schnapps*   In the United States, the term *schnapps* was traditionally used only to describe a peppermint-flavored liqueur. Schnapps in Germany, however, is a generic term for distilled spirits. Today popular schnapps flavors still include peppermint and spearmint, however, cinnamon, banana, peach, strawberry, apple, raspberry, root beer, licorice, cola, and even a peppermint-flavored product that contains real twenty-three-carat-gold flakes are also popular.

Professional spirits buyers may choose from a variety of container sizes when purchasing products. In the United States, spirits may be purchased in any of the bottle sizes listed in Figure 10.3. The common, but now very inaccurate, names for these bottles predate the U.S. beverage industry's 1980s conversion to a complete metric measurement system.

Despite their vast popularity, it is a fact that not every individual wants to or can drink alcoholic beverages. Health concerns, the presence of medication, and even religious beliefs may cause a person to abstain from consuming alcohol. The use of nonalcoholic beverages in bars and restaurants can be traced back to the classic Shirley Temple, which consists of ginger ale and cherry juice over ice cubes, to which a garnish, usually a cherry, has been added.

Beginning in the 1970s, bartenders noticed an increase in the sale of garnished soda waters. At the same time, specialty food shops began successfully

Common Bottle Name	Metric Capacity	Fluid Ounce Capacity
Miniature	50 ml	1.7
Half-pint	200 ml	6.8
Pint	500 ml	16.9
Fifth	750 ml	25.4
Quart	1.0 liter	33.8
Half-gallon	1.75 liters	59.2

Note: 1 liter equals 1,000 milliliters; 1 fluid ounce equals 29.4 ml

FIGURE 10.3   Spirit Bottle Sizes and Capacities

The number of spirit products available for purchase is vast, and buyers must carefully select the ideal variety of different products and brands.

Lon C. Diehl/PhotoEdit Inc.

Buyers at Work (10.3)

"Do you have Tanqueray Rangpur?" Allisha asked the bartender at the Dueling Piano Bar, the city's most popular hangout for young professionals.

"I'm not familiar with that one . . . but we do have Bombay Gin. Will that do?" replied Josh the bartender.

"It's not even close," answered Allisha. "What's wrong with this place? Everybody is drinking Rangpur. It's better than flavored vodka . . . they are so last year!"

"I'm really sorry," replied Josh. "I'll tell the manager to look into it."

Assume you were the beverage manager at the Dueling Piano Bar and were responsible for beverage product selection and purchasing.

1. What factors would you consider before determining if this new beverage item is one that you wished to carry?
2. Do you think that trendy operations would use different selection criteria than would more traditional beverage outlets when choosing which beverages to offer? What might those different criteria be?
3. Assume you decided not to carry Tanqueray Rangpur gin. What, specifically, would you want Josh to say to Allisha if she returned to the bar at a later date and again asked for that product?

merchandising winelike bottles of carbonated grape juices and beerlike cans containing partially brewed mixtures of water, malt, corn, yeast, and hops.

The increased demand for these products and consumer acceptance of light beers and other low-calorie products showed that there was a potential market for dealcoholized beverages. To meet this demand, a new class of nonalcoholic (NA) beers and, to a lesser degree, wines, has been introduced. NA beverages are fermented in the traditional way but then have a major portion of their alcoholic content removed. The result is tasty products that are not classified as alcoholic beverages because they contain less than 0.5 percent alcohol.

The most important reason for the increase in popularity of these NA products is that they allow consumers to enjoy a beverage environment in those situations where it would not be wise to consume alcohol. Thus, the designated driver out with friends can enjoy the beer taste he or she likes without the worry of drinking and driving. Similarly, the office worker can enjoy a lunch-hour NA beer or two and return to work with perfect concentration.

From the point of view of the professional beverage manager, NA products provide an excellent alternative for the guests who have consumed all the alcohol they would like on a given occasion. This means the customer can continue to dance, play darts, watch the game, or engage in other activities provided by the beverage operation. In many markets and locations, these NA products may be significant sellers and should be seriously considered for purchase by all those responsible for beverage procurement.

Buyer's Guide to Internet Resources: Spirits

Web Site	Topic
www.tastings.com	The Beverage Testing Institute
www.discus.org	Distilled Spirits Council of the United States
www.diageo.com	Large spirits manufacturer; products include Smirnoff vodka, Johnnie Walker scotch, Cuervo tequila, and Tanqueray gin (among others)
www.webtender.com	Mixed drink and cocktail recipes
liquor.legalview.com	Liquor service and liability information
www.libby.com	Bar glassware

RECEIVING AND STORAGE

Unlike many other foodservice products, the quality variation of beverage products is small. In most cases the specific beverage product purchased determines product quality, which will not vary from one supplier to another. For example, a case of branded tea bags purchased from one supplier will (if the product has been properly stored) be identical in quality to the same tea brand purchased from any other source.

After beverages have been properly received, they should be appropriately stored in a timely manner. When receiving alcoholic beverages, special procedures are needed after the products received are checked against the products ordered. These include ensuring that beverage employees, not delivery personnel, move products to inventory areas. There is an increased chance of theft when non–beverage operation staff members are allowed into storage areas containing large quantities of expensive and theft-prone products. In addition, prompt placement into storage areas reduces the chance for employee theft when products are left in unprotected areas.

In most cases, the storage of nonalcoholic beverage products is relatively uncomplicated. Coffees and teas are most likely to deteriorate during storage. Those items, as well as canned and bottled beverage products, should be stored in a well-ventilated, clean, and dry or refrigerated storage area. Received products should be properly rotated when stored, and special attention must be paid to the expiration or **pull dates** (if any) on the beverages' containers.

Buyer's Guide to Purchasing Term
Pull date   The date after which a packaged alcoholic beverage should not be served to guests; also known as the package's expiration date.

Whenever possible, wine bottles should be stored on their sides to help prevent their corks from drying and, as a result, causing the wine to deteriorate.

SGM/Stock Connection

Most wines and spirits are relatively nonperishable, and the shelf life of canned and bottled beer products is relatively long. However, it is always important to manage the storage of these products to ensure maximum product quality. The following are recommended storage procedures for alcoholic beverages:

For Beer: Store keg beer between 36°F and 38°F (2.2°C–3.3°C).

- Store canned and bottled beer at 70°F (21.1°C) or lower, and rotate stock as it is delivered.
- In all cases expiration (pull) dates on beer products should be carefully monitored.

For Wine: Store bottled wine on its side.

- Store red wines at temperatures between 50°F and 70°F (10°C–21.1°C) and, if at all possible, at **cellar temperature.**
- Store white and sparkling wines in refrigerators if they are to be used within a few months of purchase or at 50°F and 70°F (10°C–21.1°C) if they are to be held longer.
- Avoid excessive light, humidity, and heat in wine storage areas as these can damage wines and their containers.

For Spirits: Store spirits in clean, dry, well-ventilated storage areas.

- Store sealed cases with date of receipt marked on the case to allow for easy rotation.
- Store individual bottles with date of receipt upright on shelving that allows for easy rotation.
- Despite the relative nonperishability of spirits, avoid excessive heat in the dry-storage area as this can harm the beverages.

Buyer's Guide to Purchasing Term

Cellar temperature   A constant storage temperature between 55°F and 60°F (12.8°C–15.6°C).

Purchasing Terms

Make Your Own Purchasing Decisions

1. Some foodservice operators feel bottled water sales will continue to increase, while others believe environmental concerns will limit consumer interest in this menu item. Which view do you believe is most valid? Cite evidence to support your position.

2. With the significant rise in cases of childhood obesity and diabetes in the United States, many health professionals question the wisdom of offering youngsters soft drinks in the huge sizes popular today. What, if any, responsibility do those in the hospitality industry have to restrict the soft drink consumption of those they serve? Would your answer vary if you purchased food and beverages for a school foodservice program?

3. The current methods used to produce cocoa in some countries (especially those in Africa) has caused many professional foodservice buyers to question the wisdom of purchasing chocolate products produced from cocoa grown in these countries. To better understand the issue, enter "cocoa production exploitation" in your favorite Internet search engine. Read a minimum of two articles on the issue. Would you buy, for your own operations, chocolate products produced from African cocoa? Why or why not?

4. Traditionally, those restaurants that offer Coca-Cola beverage products do not offer beverage products produced by the PepsiCo (Pepsi) bottling group (and vice versa). Why do you believe this is so? Is this a good situation for guests? Explain your answers.

5. The question of the appropriate number of well, call, and premium alcohols to purchase when stocking a bar is one that challenges all beverage buyers. Assume you were in charge of menu development and beverage purchasing for a popular two-hundred-seat white-tablecloth steak and seafood restaurant. Choose one liquor (gin, vodka, whiskey, or other very popular spirit) and explain the factors you would consider as you determine the appropriate number of different brands and quality levels of this beverage you would offer your guests.

11

Buying Nonfood Items

Purchasing Pros Need to Know!

In previous chapters you learned about many of the food and beverage products you will buy. In addition to those items, however, you must know a great deal about the products, supplies, and tools needed to serve your menu items. In this chapter you will learn about four major categories of nonfood products that are critical for the successful operation of a food facility: (1) dining room supplies, (2) take-out supplies, (3) various items used in the back of the house, and (4) cleaning supplies.

The dining room supplies you choose will do much more than merely provide the utensils guests need to consume their food. The number and quality of service items provided with meals communicates a great deal to customers about an operation's quality. The thoughtful selection of china (dishes), glassware, flatware (silverware), and where applicable, table linens that meet guest expectations is very important. If the quality level of these or other products is inappropriate, your guests' image of your operation may suffer (if the quality is too low) or excessive costs will be incurred (if the quality of items purchased is higher than necessary).

While dining room supplies are important, the fact is that many of today's foodservice clients purchase menu items to be eaten away from the place of purchase. "Take out" foods and beverages are those purchased by customers for consumption at their homes, in their cars, on commuter trains, in offices, or in many other places. As this segment of the foodservice industry continues its rapid growth, buyers must make good decisions about the items that must be supplied to go along with the take-out foods. In this chapter you will learn about the most important of these items.

Every kitchen requires nonfood items if quality products are to be produced and served cost effectively. These include smallwares such as portion-controlling scoops and ladles, storage containers, and cooking pots and pans. Also, hand tools, including various spoons, measuring tools, and of course knives must be provided in sufficient quality and quantities to ensure workers have the tools they need to do their jobs.

Foodservice professionals know the importance of cleaning supplies, the final category of nonfood items presented in this chapter. The proper selection of cleaning supplies helps ensure the service of high-quality, safe-to-consume foods and beverages. Just as important, appropriate selection and use of cleaning supplies helps ensure healthful working conditions for all employees.

■■■

Outline

DINING ROOM SUPPLIES

The buying of quality food and beverage products is an important start to operating a quality foodservice establishment. Just as a kitchen or bar needs the products and supplies necessary to produce quality menu items, so, too, does the dining room area need the resources required to serve those items. While there are many ways to categorize the nonfood items needed, one convenient way to do so is by segmenting these products into those used by guests and those used by the staff who will actually serve the guests.

In many foodservice operations, the items supplied to guests will include **tabletop** items as well as, in many operations, **single-service** (disposable) items.

Quality tabletop items set the mood for fine dining and will complement the menu items served in this establishment.
Roger Mulkey/Creative Eye/MIRA.com

Buyer's Guide to Purchasing Terms

Tabletop (items)   Reusable products used to serve menu items to customers including china, glassware, flatware, and linens.

Single-service (items)   Also commonly called "disposable" items, these are non-reusable products used to serve menu items to customers. These items typically include dishes, cups, flatware, and napkins made of plastic, foam, aluminum, and/or paper.

In addition to the tabletop and single-service items provided, some foodservice operations supply guests with a limited number of on-the-table items. For example, in many foodservice operations, salt and pepper shakers may be continually left on the dining tables for the use of all guests.

In addition to the items guests use when dining, there are nonfood items used by those who serve guests. For example, in many facilities, those who serve guests will be required to wear a uniform that may be provided, in all or in part, by the employer. As a professional hospitality buyer, you must understand the basics of uniform selection and procurement. Other nonfood items routinely used by dining room staff vary based on the service levels provided. However, they frequently include minor service items such as corkscrews, knives, and writing utensils or other devices required for guest order taking.

For Guests

It is as difficult to describe the typical nonfood item supplied to guests as it is to describe the typical foodservice guest. The nonfood items needed to provide a customer with a take-out bagel and cup of coffee are vastly different from those required to serve the same guest an elegant, four-course dinner with a selection of various wines. Despite the variations, however, buyers can better understand these important items when they are separated into the following categories:

- Tabletop items
- Single-service items
- Condiments and their containers

TABLETOP ITEMS   The number and types of tabletop items used in the foodservice industry are large and can range from the inexpensive plastic baskets and forks used by some casual barbecue operations for the service of chicken, ribs, and beef brisket to the most elegant (and costly) fine porcelain china and silverware used in **five-star** restaurants.

While there are specialized items (e.g., the metal pails used by some casual seafood restaurants to serve bottled beer on ice), most tabletop items can be classified in one of the following groups:

- Dishware
- Glassware
- Flatware
- Linen

The most distinguishing characteristic of these nonfood items is the ability of the operation to reuse them. For some of the items, it will be true that lower-quality items may be less expensive but may not last as long (may not be reused as often) as higher-quality, more expensive items. As a result, an item's **cost per use** is an important consideration.

Buyer's Guide to Purchasing Terms

Five-star (restaurant)   An extremely high-quality restaurant. Stars are a familiar and popular restaurant rating symbol, with ratings of one to five stars commonly used. Some rating entities use diamonds in place of stars, but their intent is the same. Ratings of these types appear in consumer guidebooks and are issued by a variety of entities, including AAA and Mobile. The greater the number of stars or diamonds awarded, the higher the operation has been ranked by the reviewers.

Cost per use   The average purchase cost incurred when using a tabletop item one time.

To illustrate, consider the foodservice buyer who is faced with the decision of choosing between two different brands of drinking glasses. Assume that the less expensive of the two glass alternatives costs $3.00 per unit (glass) and has an expected life of four hundred uses. The cost per use in this situation would be computed as follows:

$$\frac{\$3.00 \text{ per unit}}{400 \text{ uses}} = \$0.00750 \text{ cost per use}$$

The more expensive **glassware** item is more durable and has an expected life of eight hundred uses.

This item, however, costs $5.00 per unit. The cost per use associated with the more expensive glass would be computed as follows:

$$\frac{\$5.00 \text{ per unit}}{800 \text{ uses}} = \$0.00625 \text{ cost per use}$$

The cost difference in this analysis would be computed as follows:

Alternative #1 cost per use	$0.00750
Less	
Alternative #2 cost per use	($0.00625)
Difference	**$0.00125 per use**

While cost per use is only one of several factors that likely would be important to the buyer making this purchase decision, it is clear that the more expensive (initial cost) glass would, in this specific case, be least costly to the operation over the long run. In fact, the savings per unit with the second alternative equals 20 percent (.00125/.00625 = 20 percent), an amount that would be quite significant in a large-volume operation.

Dishware Dishware (dinnerware) refers to reusable foodservice dishes most often made of plastic, metal, **ceramics,** glass, or in some cases ceramics and glass.

Dishware refers to the items guests use while dining and include plates, bowls, cups, saucers, and the like.

Dishware can be made from a variety of materials. **Porcelain** in its many forms is an extremely popular material used for making dishware; however, many other types of ceramics can also be used. In the hospitality industry, china (a type of porcelain) is so popular that it is a term often used to mean the same as dish.

Although porcelain is frequently referred to as china, the two are not identical. They are similar in that both can be **glazed** or unglazed.

Buyer's Guide to Purchasing Terms

Glassware The collective term used to indicate the front-of-the-house objects made of glass (as well as other materials) and used by guests for drinking.

Dishware The collective term used to indicate the front-of-the-house objects made of paper, plastic, metal, ceramic, or glass and used for presenting food to guests; also called "dinnerware."

Ceramic Inorganic, nonmetallic materials whose formation is caused by heat. Foodservice examples include bone china, porcelain, clay, and stoneware.

Porcelain A clay-based ceramic made by heating selected and refined materials to a very high temperature. Porcelain is very popular for its use as a material in dish making. Because of its origins, it is often called "china."

Glaze When used to describe ceramic dishes, the shiny material coating the outside of the dish.

China is softer than porcelain. This difference in hardness is due to the higher temperatures at which true porcelain is heated (2650°F/1454°C for porcelain versus 2250°F/1232°C for china). Due to its resulting greater hardness, porcelain has some medical, dental, and industrial applications that china, limited to domestic and artistic use, does not have. Moreover, while porcelain is always translucent, china is opaque.

While the terminology used to describe various ceramic dishes can vary somewhat, the categories of ceramics you are most likely to encounter include the following:

China A high-quality clay that may contain bone (calcium phosphate) and is heated to 2250°F (1232°C) or above. Porcelain (china) was first made in China, and it is a measure of the esteem in which the exported Chinese porcelains of the seventeenth and eighteenth centuries were held in Europe that in English *china* became a commonly used word for the Franco-Italian term *porcelain*.

Stoneware Made from clay of a less fine quality than china. It is heated to about 2200°F (1205°C) or above.

Pottery Clay baked at approximately 1500°F (816°C) or above.

Terra-cotta Clay baked at approximately 1000°F (538°C) or above.

Bone china (first developed in Great Britain) is an extremely popular foodservice form of china and is characterized by its whiteness, translucency, and strength. Production of bone and other types of china usually involves a two-stage firing where the material is first heated to a temperature of 2336°F (1280°C), glazed, then fired (heated) to a lower temperature (below 1976°F, or 1080°C).

While china is very popular as a material used in dishware making, there are others. Glass dishes are made from glass material containing boric oxide, soda, and silica (sand). Glass dish variations developed by manufacturers such as Corning and others have proved durable and are commonly purchased under a variety of trademarked names. In addition, many foodservice operators find that serviceware made of paper, plastic, or metal serve their dishware needs as well. When selecting dishware, you should always look for items that complement the type of service offered by the operation and are of appropriate quality, price, and durability.

Glassware *Glassware,* as the term is used in the hospitality industry, refers to drinking vessels. Of course, these items are commonly made of materials other than glass, including Styrofoam, plastic, and metal. Glass is such an extremely popular material for making drinking vessels, however, that the term *glass* is most often used to refer to these items regardless of the material from which they are made. Most glassware is classified as either a tumbler (a flat bottomed glass with no handle), stemware (a glass bowl placed above a glass stem) as shown in Figure 11.1, or mug (a glass with a handle). Within these three broad categories, manufacturers offer literally hundreds of different sizes, shapes, and styles of glassware.

Actual glass is a popular glassware material that can be formed into a variety of smooth shapes. Some glass is brittle and can break into sharp pieces, while other glass types do not. When it is compressed, pure glass can withstand a great amount of force without breaking. The properties of specific glass types can be modified or changed with heat treatments and the addition of various chemicals and materials.

The glassware most commonly used in foodservice is made by fusing (heating) sand (silica) in combination with soda and lime. Additions of metals (such as lead) change the properties of the glass. Lead crystal (also called **crystal)** is glass that has been hand or machine cut with facets.

Buyer's Guide to Purchasing Term

Crystal Glass of fine quality and a high degree of brilliance.

FIGURE 11.1 Stem-Style Glassware

Lead oxide added to the molten glass gives lead crystal a much higher level of light reflection than normal glass and, consequently, a much greater sparkle. The presence of lead also makes the glass softer and easier to cut. Crystal can consist of up to 33 percent lead, at which point it has the most sparkle. True crystal, however, is very fragile and quite expensive. Many foodservice buyers find that a lower cost, more durable type of glassware is sufficient to meet their operational needs.

Glassware need not be made of glass. For example, products made of plastic are extremely durable. Glassware made of paper is inexpensive and, because it will not be reused, also saves washing and sanitizing costs. These glassware choices, however, tend also to be associated by customers with lesser-quality or faster-service foodservice operations. As a result, they should be chosen by buyers only when their use clearly fits the style of operation in which they will be used.

Flatware Knives, spoons, forks, and their variations are known, collectively, as flatware. Internationally, flatware is most commonly referred to as **cutlery,** the term used to identify any hand utensil used for serving or eating food.

PROFESSIONAL PURCHASING PREVENTS PROBLEMS (11.1)

Chips, Cracks, and Breaks . . . Oh My!

A common problem: Cracked or chipped dishware and glassware not only reflect negatively on the management of a food and beverage operation, it also presents a real danger to guests.

Regardless of the quality level purchased, dishware and glassware can become cracked or chipped and even broken. In some cases the damage is caused by guests, but more often the cause is rough treatment in the dishwashing area or even simple employee carelessness.

Regardless of cause, professional buyers know the importance of ensuring that glassware and dishware is regularly and carefully inspected for damage. The failure to do so risks the negative reaction of guests, and potentially the personal-injury lawsuits that could result if a guest is cut by (or even consumes) pieces of defective dishware and glassware items.

Buyer's Guide to Purchasing Term

Cutlery Various utensils, such as knives, forks, and spoons, used at the table for serving and eating food; also called "flatware" or, in the United States; "silverware."

Did You Know? (11.1)

The foodservice industry is diverse and, as a result, uses a variety of specialized glass shapes. These special glass shapes often have their own names. The following are some of the specialty glassware names you will likely encounter throughout your own hospitality career.

Common Glass Name	Description/Use
Water goblet	A large, stem-style glass (also may be used for iced tea)
Juice glass	A small (four- to six-ounce) tumbler-style glass used for serving juices.
Sherbet	A stem-style glass used for serving ice cream or sherbet.
Shot glass	A small glass for measuring/serving up to three ounces of liquor.
White wine glass	A stem-style glass shaped especially for the service of white wine.
Red wine glass	A stem-style glass shaped especially for the service of red wine.
Snifter	A short stem-style glass with a wide bowl that narrows at the top used for serving brandy and other liquors.
Champagne (flute)	A stem-style glass with a tall, narrow bowl used for champagne.
Champagne (cocktail)	A stem-style glass with a wide, shallow bowl used for champagne, martinis, and various cocktails.
Margarita	A large (fifteen-ounce capacity), specially shaped glass for serving margaritas.
Pilsner	A short-stemmed, specially cone-shaped glass for serving beers, stouts, and ales.

Interestingly, in the United States, *cutlery* is used most often to identify knives, while the term *silverware* or *silver* is often used to mean flatware. This is because, traditionally, good-quality flatware was made from silver. Because of silver's expense, however, from the mid-1800s until today, a process using electro-plated nickel silver (EPNS; commonly called "silver plating") places a thin silver coating on nonsilver utensils. Today most foodservice cutlery, including very high-quality designs, is made from stainless steel. While the useful life of stainless-steel cutlery does not necessarily exceed that of silver, experienced buyers know that, when extremely high-quality (and durable) dining room supply items are purchased, guest theft of such items often increases.

When producing cutlery, manufacturers punch the individual items out of sheets of stainless steel. Flatware that is not punched out of such sheets is made from stainless steel that has been rolled to various thicknesses. The thickness (and, thus, weight) of the flatware is measured by its **gauge.** Good-quality flatware will be at least twelve gauge (0.1094 inches thick) and can range up to two gauge (0.656 inches thick).

It is important to know that, regardless of thickness; stainless steel is a composite of different metals and can vary greatly in terms of its composition. The main ingredient in stainless steel is chromium, to which nickel has been added to provide resistance to rust and corrosion. The numbers 18/0, 18/8, or 18/10 on

Buyer's Guide to Purchasing Term

Gauge (stainless steel)   In stainless-steel flatware, a measure of thickness. Flatware thickness typically varies from twelve gauge (thinner) to two gauge (thicker).

flatware describe the composition of stainless steel used to make it. A common misperception is that these numbers refer to the weight of stainless flatware. The numbers have nothing to do with weight. Instead they refer to the percentage of chromium and nickel that is used in the manufacture of the stainless steel. A label of *18/10* on stainless steel flatware means 18 percent chromium and 10 percent nickel. Flatware labeled *18/0* or (simply *18*) has a nickel content of 0 percent. The higher the nickel content, the more protection from rust and corrosion.

18/10 and 18/8 are the optimal amounts of chromium and nickel for stainless-steel flatware and are regarded as the highest level of quality. Most of the least-expensive stainless steel flatware is made from 18/0 stainless steel. If these numbers are not mentioned, it is most likely that the flatware is 18/0 (the lower level of quality). If the flatware is 18/8 or 18/10 your supplier will certainly emphasize that point, but it should be noted that even the best stainless-steel flatware is subject to occasional pitting and corrosion.

The number of types of flatware pieces used by an operation can be significant. For example, a buyer selecting spoons may choose from a manufacturer's selection of soup, table, tea, dessert, demitasse, bouillon, grapefruit, egg, and caviar spoons. In addition to knives, spoons, and forks, some foodservice operators purchase sporks (a combination spoon and fork), splades (a spork with a cutting blade on one side), or knorks (a fork with a cutting blade on one side).

Linen   Linen refers to the cloth tablecloths and napkins used in foodservice. Linen is so important to some foodservice operations that, in the minds of many customers, the finest dining experiences are to be had at "white tablecloth" restaurants. With their crisp, white linens and clean, elegant look, these establishments project an upscale image that complements great food and justifies higher menu prices. Actually, table linens (tablecloths and napkins) establish a mood and enhance the decor at any restaurant, from casual cafés to formal fine-dining rooms.

In most cases restaurants rent the linen products they select, while some large hotels and other facilities may have on-site laundry operations that allow them to purchase their linens. From a buyer's perspective, the two most important characteristics of linen are the fiber(s) from which it is made and its size.

Traditionally, the best foodservice linens were those made from cotton or from cotton blended with other fibers. High-quality cotton products will have about two hundred threads per square inch of fabric and, when washed, will shrink less than 10 percent from their original size. Today, because of their resistance to wrinkles and ease of care, nylon, rayon, acrylic (for flame resistance), and polyester are popular linen fibers. While not typically as absorbent as cotton, these man-made fibers are more durable and often more stain resistant.

Size is the second major consideration when selecting linens. Figure 11.2 indicates the size of tablecloth that should be purchased or rented based on an operation's dining table size.

Dining Table Size	Select Tablecloth Size
24" square	42" square
30" square	52" square
36" square	62" square
42" square or round	62" square
48" square or round	71" square
60" round	85" square or 90" round
	120" round (to the floor)
72" round	85" square or 90" round
	132" round (to the floor)
30" × 48"	52" × 72"
30" × 72"	52" × 96"
30" × 96"	52" × 114"

FIGURE 11.2   Table Size/Tablecloth Size Guide

FIGURE 11.3   Banquet Table with Thirty-Inch Drop

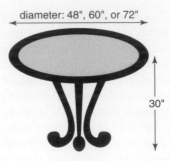

diameter: 48", 60", or 72"

30"

Note that the size of tablecloths needed exceeds the size of the table because of the **drop** typically desired by buyers.

To determine the size tablecloth you should buy or rent, you must first determine the amount of drop you seek. The standard foodservice banquet table (as illustrated in Figure 11.3) is thirty inches high.

Drop must be measured on each side of a table. To illustrate, if, when using a standard-sized banquet table, your desired drop is half the distance to the floor, you will need fifteen inches of drop. Thus, if you seek to cover a fifty-five-inch square table and want to provide (the industry standard) fifteen-inch drop, you will need fifty-five inches to cover the tabletop, as well as an additional fifteen inches on each side of the table, computed as follows:

Top coverage   = 55"
plus
Drop from edge of table = 15 (×2)

Or

Top coverage   = 55"
plus
Edge drop   = 30"
equals
Size needed   = 85"

Thus, you would need an eighty-five-inch-square tablecloth to cover a fifty-five-inch table and provide fifteen inches of drop on each side of the table.

Like tablecloths, napkins can be procured in a variety of sizes; however, standard rental sizes are twelve, fourteen, and sixteen-inch squares. They should be made from fabric material that weighs at least four ounces per square yard. White napkins are by far the most popular color chosen, due in part to the color variations that frequently result from the repeated washing of colored napkins.

SINGLE-SERVICE ITEMS   As more foodservice customers consume their foods away from where they are purchased (in some cases due to the casualness of the operation itself), professional foodservice buyers are purchasing increasing numbers of single-service (disposable) dishware, flatware, and glassware items, as well as napkins.

Dishware may be made from paper, plastic, aluminum, or foam. Flatware is typically made from plastics and may be purchased in bulk cartons, wrapped in a

Buyer's Guide to Purchasing Term

Drop (tablecloth)   The amount by which a tablecloth overhangs the table on which it is placed.

grouping (e.g., a knife, spoon, fork, and often a napkin), or individually wrapped. Glassware may be made from Styrofoam or from waxed or unwaxed paper, and paper napkins are a standard item in many facilities, including some that are considered fine dining.

In all cases you should know that quality single-service products, like reusable products, can be purchased at a variety of quality levels. The level chosen will, in many respects, dictate the value perceived by the operation's customers. For example, paper napkins of increasing thickness (ply) can be perceived by guests as an indication of increased quality.

CONDIMENTS AND THEIR CONTAINERS   As you learned in Chapter 9, a condiment is any food added to a dish to enhance flavor (e.g., spices, herbs, vinegars, and dressings). Thus, technically, condiments are edible food items. They are included here as a category, however, because they also are tabletop items. Thus, for example, salt and pepper (the two most popular condiments) consist both of the individual products and their serving containers. These can range from the simple (and disposable) types used by quick-service restaurants, to the very ornate grinders used in fine-dining restaurants.

Buyers of these items recognize that their purchase can be critical to guest satisfaction. For example, consider the quick-service restaurant that elects to offer portion-controlled (PC) ketchup on request for take-out orders. The size of the packet or container, the brand (or private label), and even the ease of package opening will all send a message to customers that can reinforce, or significantly detract from, a desired customer perception of value.

Ketchup, mustard, salt, pepper, soy sauce, salsa, salad dressings, and a variety of other condiments, as well as the **caddies** that hold them (see Figure 11.4) are important to many operations.

The thoughtful purchase of these items, in keeping with carefully established specifications, is no less critical than that of the ingredients used to make the operation's main menu items.

FIGURE 11.4   Condiment Caddy

Buyer's Guide to Purchasing Term

Caddy (condiment)   A container designed to hold tabletop condiments.

Even in very casual dining settings, the selection of popular and attractively packaged condiments on dining tables will directly affect your customers' perceptions of food quality.

Bob Daemmrich/Stock Boston

Buyer's Guide to Internet Resources: Dining Room Supplies

Web Site	Topic
www.oneida.com	Dishware and glassware
www.aplasticplate.com	Melamine (plastic) reusable dishware
www.loveglassware.com	Glassware manufacturing information
www.libbey.com	Glassware types and styles
www.westernsilver.com	Silver-plate and silver flatware items
www.hiramwild.com	Custom flatware
www.restauranttablecloths.com	Tablecloths
www.fergusonirishlinen.com	Superior-quality table linens
www.dartcontainer.com	Single-use foodservice products
www.creativecaddies.com	Custom-made condiment holders and dispensers

For Staff

As important as tabletop, single-service, and condiment items are to the image portrayed by your foodservice operation, the nonfood items you will provide to those who serve your guests are equally important. This is so because the staff-related supplies you choose will reinforce the quality and value message you seek to communicate to your guests. In addition, the uniforms supplied to staff (as well as other front-of-the-house tools you give them) will significantly affect your employees' attitudes about their jobs and, as a result, will directly affect how they feel about delivering quality service.

UNIFORMS   Those foodservice buyers who understand consumer behavior would agree that a critical component for success in today's highly competitive hospitality environment is the implementation of a well-conceived uniform program. Such programs help ensure that each employee projects an identically inviting public image. When employees wear professional-looking uniforms, they reflect an image, or brand, that can project instant quality and credibility to guests.

The psychological importance of uniforms can be easily illustrated by examining professional sports teams. Consider the loyal fans of your favorite team. Individual players on the team are traded, change teams, and eventually retire; meanwhile, fan loyalty toward the team remains a constant over many years.

Consider the message this employee's uniform conveys about the operation's food quality, cleanliness, and management. Contrast that message with the one that would be sent by employees wearing mismatched, dirty, and worn-out uniforms.

Michael Newman/PhotoEdit Inc.

Why? Because the loyalty is linked to the team's image, and a big part of the image is the team uniform, regardless of who is wearing it. In a similar manner, guests frequenting a foodservice operation come to associate the uniform with the operation, an important factor to recall in an industry where employee turnover rates can be quite high. A business's employees can change, but its uniforms can keep its customers coming back time and time again.

Few topics generate more front-of-house employee interest and concern than the uniforms they are required to wear. Uniform and apron standards vary greatly by company. In some cases employees may be required to personally provide and maintain one or more uniform items (e.g., dark shoes or khaki slacks). In other cases employees may be issued uniforms, but they are responsible for the uniform's cleaning and maintenance. In still other cases, uniforms may be supplied and maintained by the employer.

Certainly, how employees look in the uniforms they wear is important, regardless of the desired appearance of employees; however, it is important for professional buyers in hospitality to understand the employment laws that relate to uniforms and uniform standards. For example, under California labor law, an employer that requires its employees to wear uniforms is responsible for providing those uniforms and maintaining them in good repair. This means, of course, that the uniforms belong to the employer, and the company could charge the employee a reasonable deposit while the uniform is in the employee's hands. An employee who does not return the uniform when asked will find that his or her employer can legally keep the deposit or deduct the cost of the uniform from the employee's last paycheck. Other states also have laws that may affect uniform choices. You must know the laws that are in place in the state in which you work. For multiunit operations, you must understand applicable uniform-related laws in each state in which your organization operates units.

OTHER STAFF SUPPLIES In addition to uniforms, other significant items provided to front-of-house employees are those related to one or more of the following activities:

- *Recording guest orders* These include guest checks, paper, pens and pencils, and/or handheld recording order devices.
- *Serving guests* These server-used supplies include such items as serving trays, jack stands (for the holding of serving dishes until placed in front of

Did You Know? (11.2)

In the hospitality industry, the selection and purchase of employee uniforms can be a complex issue. In addition to evaluations of the price and quality, some additional purchase-related factors experienced buyers consider include the following:

1. *Compliance with company policies*   Company-mandated dress requirements including employee uniforms must not illegally discriminate. Issues related to male and female dress requirements and even company-permitted uniform variations intended to accommodate diverse religious beliefs are among the compliance issues to be considered as buyers select uniforms.
2. *Guest impressions and expectations*   Employee uniforms send an important and distinct message about the operation's image. Consider, for example, the different dining expectations of customers when they are greeted by a hostess in a tuxedo shirt and formal jacket and by the same employee dressed in a short-sleeved sport shirt and khaki pants.
3. *Modesty*   A professional image extends to issues of conservatism in dress. Because of differences in employees' height, weight, and even body shape, buyers must carefully consider potential employee concerns regarding the appropriateness of selected uniform components.
4. *Safety*   Uniforms that look good on employees are certainly desirable, but the uniforms must be functional as well. Uniforms must consider worker safety. Components that restrict movement, consist of excess materials that could get caught in operating equipment, or constitute a tripping hazard should be avoided.
5. *Ease of care*   If employees will be responsible for the cleaning and maintenance of their uniforms, careful consideration must be given to the issue of fabric care. Not all employees possess the knowledge or laundering equipment necessary to properly care for some uniform fabrics, and this limitation is always considered by experienced buyers. Easy-care fabrics such as those which are easily washable and resist wrinkling are highly desirable materials for uniform construction.

Buyers at Work (11.1)

"I think our girls will look stupid in that, and they'll hate it. I'm just telling you, if you want an all-out server mutiny on your hands, go ahead and pick TL5301," said Sofia Lopez.

Sofia was talking to Ben Schnelling, the new manager of the Stillwater Grill Steak House restaurant. Ben was recently hired by the restaurant's owners to update the successful operation's menu and dining room feel. The owner's wanted a more upscale look in the dining room, as well as a more innovative and complex menu.

As part of the upgrade process, Ben asked Sofia, the restaurant's dining room manager, her thoughts about his choice of new staff uniforms. Ben liked item TL5301, which was displayed prominently on the cover of his chosen uniform vendor's new spring catalogue. Featuring a traditional, tuxedolike look, Ben felt the long skirts and long-sleeved blouses of TL5301 would make the female servers look very elegant.

Sofia, however, truly hated the look Ben was proposing, questioned its legality (because the female server uniform consisted of a skirt, while the male servers would be wearing pants), and was convinced the female members of her current dining room staff would hate it as well.

Assume you were Ben:

1. What input do you feel staff should have in decisions such as the uniforms they will wear?
2. How important do you feel Sofia's support would be in the successful implementation of a change in employee uniforms?
3. How would you answer a female server who questioned the gender inequity of the uniform? If you allowed a female server to wear pants, does it follow that you would allow a male server to wear a skirt? Explain your position.

Ashtrays (where permitted)	Ramekins	Salsa bowls	
Sauce cups	Bread baskets	Bud vases and candles	
Tabletop butter warmers	Individual coffee and tea pots	Condiment dispensers/ holders	
Cream pitchers	Tabletop napkin dispensers	Syrup dispensers	
Tortilla servers	Cup dispensers	Menu holders	
Jack stands/tray holders	Wine service items (buckets and stands)	Youth seating and booster chairs	

FIGURE 11.5   Miscellaneous Service-Related Items

guests), and miscellaneous dishware and meal service items (see Figure 11.5) required to serve food and beverages to guests.

- *Collection of payment*   These typically include small trays or payment folders for the presentation of customer bills and the return of payment cards or change (if guests paid their bills in cash).

PROFESSIONAL PURCHASING PREVENTS PROBLEMS (11.2)

"I'll Be Right Back with That . . ."

A common problem: Guest's credit and debit card information can easily be compromised by dishonest foodservice employees who take possession of payment cards during the payment collection process.

While representing only a tiny fraction of all payment card transactions, many guests are rightly concerned about the identify theft that can occur when their cards are handled by hospitality industry servers, bartenders, and cashiers. As a result, big changes are taking place in the recording of guest orders and the collection of guest payments. One of the most rapidly advancing areas is that of pay-at-the-table systems, which allow guests to pay for their meals in a manner similar to that of self-check grocery store lines. In these systems, payment cards are swiped, data entered, and receipts printed all at the table.

Pay-at-the-table systems have many advantages. When guests are provided POS-interfaced devices that allow them to pay for their meals at their dining table, those tables can be turned faster. Transaction times are reduced (because servers need not make multiple trips to the table), and guests' feelings of security are greatly enhanced (because only they are handling their payment card and/or entering their personal identification number (PIN). In addition, with these systems, end-of-shift closings and tip reconciliations can be performed more quickly and payment card transaction (discount) fees may be reduced.

When combined with handheld order-taking devices, pay-at-the-table systems may quickly make servers' paper guest checks and pens and pencils as obsolete as mechanical cash registers. As a professional buyer, it is the existence of issues such as this one that reinforce the importance of continually monitoring guests' changing needs as well as advancements in hospitality-related technology.

Buyer's Guide to Internet Resources: Staff Supplies

Web Site	Topic
www.restaurantuniformsonline.com	Foodservice industry uniforms
www.cintas.com	Hospitality industry uniforms
www.waitstuff.com	Front-of-house waiter supplies
www.foodservicedirect.com	Guest check presentation folders/tip trays
www.practicallynetworked.com/ support/wireless_secure.htm	Developing a secure wireless network for use with at-the-table payment systems

TAKE-OUT PACKAGING

For most professional foodservice buyers, an understanding of the purchasing requirements for food and beverages served to diners who will eat away from the operation are crucial. This is because of the increasing size of the **take-out** market.

The National Restaurant Association (NRA) estimates that more than half of the food sold by its members is either takeout or delivery. Annual growth in the take-out market yearly exceeds that of the foodservice industry overall. The importance of this market is easy to recognize when you consider that the total take-out sales for the top five quick-service restaurants (McDonald's, Burger King, Wendy's, Subway, and Taco Bell) exceed their dine-in sales.

It is also important that buyers recognize take-out foods (those in which customers preorder their food but on arrival take their orders out of the restaurant to eat them) are often sold in restaurants that offer table-service options as well. Increasingly time-pressed consumers have expanded the number of foodservice operations in which they have an interest in buying take-out products. As a result, even high-end steak and seafood houses report increased interest in take-out options related to their products. Thus, buyers may be assigned the task of selecting appropriate packaging and condiment items for takeout sold in facilities offering extensive dine-in options, as well as for the specialized and popular take-out option known in the hospitality industry as **drive-thru.**

Traditional Take-Out Packaging

Take-out food is often considered fast food, but that is not always the case. While quick-service restaurants do, of course, offer take-out foods, take-out outlets can also be small businesses serving traditional food, which can be of extremely high quality. Examples include the sandwiches sold by high-end delicatessens, home replacement meals sold by full-service restaurants, Asian foods, and pizza. Increasingly, full-service restaurants have also sought to increase their sales by offering many of their menu items on a to-go basis.

Take-out foods may be picked up by guests or may be delivered by a restaurant to its customers. In some cases operations are so geared to take-out and delivery customers that they provide no facilities for dining on-site. Then foodservice buyers must concern themselves with both the packaging materials in which food will be held (e.g., pizza boxes and sandwich wrapping materials), and the heating/holding devices to keep foods at the proper temperature until they are delivered. Also, certain types of food that are normally served in sit-down settings can still be packaged to go based on orders taken by telephone, fax, or Internet. Then the nonfood packaging materials needed to ensure high-quality product delivery are of great importance. Bags, wraps, glasses, cups, flatware, plates, bowls, and other containers all must provide guests with sanitary and food- and Earth-friendly product characteristics.

Buyer's Guide to Purchasing Terms

Take-out (foods)   Food and beverages sold with the intent that guests will not consume them at the point of purchase; also called "carry-out" and "grab-and-go."

Drive-thru   Food and beverages sold to customers who do not leave their vehicle to enter the restaurant, but rather place their orders, receive, and pay for their items at specially designated drive-thru windows.

PROFESSIONAL PURCHASING PREVENTS PROBLEMS (11.3)

Recycling and Other Green Alternatives

A common problem: In the past packaging waste generated when selling take-out foods has been considered "Earth unfriendly" by many environmentally conscious groups and individuals, sometimes resulting in a poor image for those companies in the foodservice industry.

For decades, expanded polystyrene foam (Styrofoam) was the packaging material of choice for many foodservice operators. Styrofoam, however, is made from crude oil and can leach toxic chemicals into the food it contains. Also, it takes hundreds of years for one container made of Styrofoam to break down in a landfill. The reaction of some consumers is typified by the following statement posted on the Internet site of California Citizens against Waste:

> "America's fast food culture is hurting more than our waste lines. With it's grab-and-go, overly packaged food stuffed with unnecessary condiments, fast food outlets are our country's primary source of urban litter and a significant hurdle to local communities' waste diversion goals.
>
> "Litter characterization studies across the country have recognized fast food restaurants as the primary identifiable source of urban litter. *(Source: www.cawrecycles.org, retrieved October 1, 2007.)*

Despite some views to the contrary, the hospitality industry has many creative and responsible members who have responded to this problem. In 2006 Starbucks introduced a new disposable cup containing 10 percent post-consumer recycled content. After much research, tests, and a series of focus groups, two different environmental and economic improvements were implemented. These were the use of reusable cups (low-tech) and the development of a new, environmentally preferable single-use cup (high-tech).

In addition to using recycled packing products, the use of 100 percent biodegradable take-out packaging materials is increasing. ASTM International is one of the largest voluntary standards development organizations in the world. It is a trusted source for technical standards for materials, products, systems, and services. ASTM has developed standards for 100 percent biodegradable packaging materials that are increasingly purchased by environmentally aware foodservice operations. ASTM requires that packaging materials that meet its standard biodegrade in a commercial compost facility completely within sixty to 180 days, without releasing any toxic residues. This can be achieved by making take-out containers (and flatware items) from various materials such as paper, bagasse (sugar cane), and potato starch. As increasing numbers of buyers use such products, the reputation and image of the foodservice industry regarding excessive packaging waste will surely improve.

Drive-Thru and Take-Out Packaging

Take-out operators are making prepared food fresher, cheaper, faster, tastier, and more convenient than ever. As a result, more consumers are asking themselves: Why do it myself? The time required for shopping, cooking, and washing dishes at home is rapidly disappearing, and more customers elect to simply drive through and pick up their meals. As those in this industry segment know well, the drive-thru segment flourishes or suffers based on the operation's ability to fill orders accurately and, most important, rapidly.

By outfitting their employees with headphones, developing advanced point-of-sale systems, and installing speakers in their kitchens to improve communications, operations can dramatically improved their speed of service. Packaging materials that hold foods in top condition until customers consume them are a critical part of this segment's success or failure. In most cases this results in the need to design menu items and select packaging materials that allow guests to eat their meals in their vehicles and often with only one hand.

Buyer's Guide to Internet Resources: Take-Out Packaging

Web Site	Topic
www.dartcontainer.com	Paper, foam, and plastic take-out products
www.genpak.com	Single-use take-out products
www.fpi.org	Information about the Foodservice Packaging Institute
www.creativefoodpackaging.com	Green and biodegradable take-out packaging
www.ecowise.com	Biodegradable take-out packaging

BACK-OF-HOUSE SUPPLIES

Just as professional buyers must supply front-of-house employees with the tools they need to serve menu items to guests, back-of-house employees must also be supplied with the items needed to prepare these products for service. The purchase of large pieces of stationary equipment is addressed in Chapter 13. In this chapter you will learn about the kitchen supplies (**smallwares** and kitchen hand tools) purchased by foodservice buyers as well as examine the many office supplies necessary to support an operation's basic administrative needs.

Kitchen Supplies

The kitchen and bar-related tools and supplies professional foodservice buyers must purchase to support the production of their food and beverage products will depend entirely on the needs of the operation. Clearly, the kitchen supplies needed by a take-out pizza parlor will be different from those needed by a large hospital's foodservice department. However, all buyers must be concerned with selecting quality products that enhance (not detract from) their intended use (e.g., sharp knives work better and are safer to use than dull knives). Also, quantity concerns are important (e.g., a shortage of proper storage containers will increase food costs because of product deterioration resulting from improper storage).

Smallwares purchasing can be challenging simply because of the wide price range related to many items. For example, from some manufacturers, a ten-inch sauté pan could be purchased for as little $15.00. Alternatively, the French-made Mauviel Cuprinox 2.5-mm 10-inch Copper Fry Pan sells, in quantity, for $189.00 each. Which is best? The answer, of course, is that it depends. The point for professional buyers to remember is that the price and quality variations they will encounter when buying smallwares are extremely significant. As a result, great care must be taken to carefully specify the precise quality desired before selecting product suppliers for these items.

The number of smallware items available to foodservice professionals is as varied as the foods they prepare; however, Figure 11.6 lists some broad categories of the most commonly purchased cookware and bakeware items.

KITCHEN HAND TOOLS Like smallwares, the price and quality variations when purchasing kitchen hand tools can be great, especially relative to knives, the

Buyer's Guide to Purchasing Term

Smallwares The collective term used to identify the pots, pans, storage, and related products used to prepare, store, and serve food and beverages.

Bain Marie pots
Frying pans
Sauté pans
Sauce pans
Stock pots
Double boilers
Baking pans
Roasting pans
Pie pans
Cake pans
Spring pans
Muffin tins
Loaf pans
Sheet trays
Line (hotel) pans
Display trays and pans

FIGURE 11.6 Common Cookware/Bakeware Categories

kitchen hand tool of most importance to **chefs** and many other food production workers. The total number of different and specialized foodservice hand tools is extensive and ranges from the common (vegetable peelers) to the unique **(mandoline).** Figure 11.8 lists twenty of the most popular categories of kitchen hand tools.

FIGURE 11.7 Line (Hotel) Pans of Various Sizes

Buyer's Guide to Purchasing Terms

Line pan   A stainless-steel or foil pan, with reinforced corners, used to hold and display food on a steam table or in a chafing dish. May also be called a "steam table" pan or even more commonly a "hotel" pan (see Figure 11.7). A full-size line pan measures 20.75 inches by 12.75 inches and may vary in depth from one-half inch to six inches. Line pans are also sold in half, third, and smaller sizes.

Chef   In general usage, the term used for a professional cook. Often the title is used by those individuals certified as a chef by a member organization of the World Association of Chef Societies (WACS), of which the American Culinary Federation (ACF) is a member.

Mandoline   A device used for safely and rapidly cutting vegetables such as roots, onions, potatoes, cucumbers, and the like into uniform slices of various thickness.

Bag squeezers	Garnishing tools	Meat tenderizers	Scoops	Strainers
Can openers	Ice cream dippers	Measuring tools and devices	Serving spoons	Tongs
Coring tools (vegetable)	Ladles	Mixing spoons	Skimmers	Turners/spatulas
Dishers	Mashers	Rubber spatulas	Spreaders	Whips

FIGURE 11.8   Selected Kitchen Hand Tools

Experienced foodservice buyers know that, in addition to the categories listed in Figure 11.8 kitchen knives are, by far, one of the most important of kitchen hand tools. Despite very similar appearances, knives can vary tremendously in construction and quality. It is essential that foodservice buyers understand the materials and techniques used to produce quality hand knives.

Knives   Technically, any sharpened blade with a handle could be considered a knife. Not all knives, however, are equal in quality. Also, those knives used in commercial kitchens come in a variety of shapes and sizes. It is important for you to know that the best metal-blade knives are forged, not stamped. A fully forged knife is a single piece of metal beaten and ground into shape in several stages involving high heat and many tons of pressure, while stamped knives are simply cut out of sheet metal. Forged knives are more expensive than stamped items but are considered by professionals to be well worth their higher prices. Forged knives are stronger tools because forged metal is finer-grained and sturdier.

Quality knives also have sharp blades; however, other parts of the knife are equally important. Figure 11.9 shows the main parts of a knife that is typically known as a chef's knife.

A. *Tip*   The tip, or point, of the knife is helpful for scoring shallow cuts and is used for piercing. Care must be taken, however, because abuse or improper storage can sometimes result in breakage of this somewhat delicate part.

B. *Spine*   The spine is opposite the sharpened part of the blade; it is the unsharpened top. The spine, tapered thicker than the blade, adds heft and stability. It may be used to apply pressure when cutting but is most often used to push cut or chopped items around a cutting surface.

C. *Bolster*   The bolster gives the blade weight, balance, and (most important) keeps fingers from slipping onto the blade. Bolsters are found on only forged knives, not stamped knives. It is one of the important elements designating a quality knife. Bolsters that extend the full length of the blade are best.

D. *Heel*   The heel is used for chopping small bones and for cutting through tough items that involve using weight or force.

E. *Rivets*   The rivets, or binding posts, affix and secure the handle to the blade. If visible, they should be completely flush with the handle's surface so food cannot be trapped and create a food-borne illness hazard.

F. *Handle*   The handle should be sturdy and easy to grip. Handles can be made of wood, metal, or synthetic material. Wood handles provide an

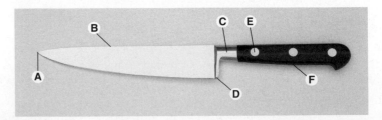

FIGURE 11.9   Basic Chef's Knife Parts

excellent grip but also require more maintenance than a plastic or stainless-steel handle. Some critics also argue that wood-handled knives absorb microorganisms. If used, wood handles must be well sealed from moisture and may require periodic oiling to keep from drying out. Some plastic materials are considered a better choice than wood or metal because they can withstand high temperatures, are dishwasher safe, and can provide better friction for grip. Wood handles injected with plastic materials have been developed because they possess the best attributes of wood handles and molded plastic handles. They have an excellent grip but do not require the maintenance that an all-wood handle requires. They are also not as porous as wood-handled knives, preventing the absorption of microorganisms. Some popular knives have stainless-steel handles. These last longer than other types and add weight to the knife, but critics contend that these handles become very slippery (and, thus, more dangerous to use) when wet.

In addition to the knife parts listed in Figure 11.9, the **tang** is also noteworthy. In cheaper, lower-quality knives, this part of the knife is often a cost short cut because it is not always visible. In quality knives, the tang usually extends all, or nearly all, the way to the butt (end) of the handle. The tang is important for knife balance and to ensure that the blade will not break off the handle during heavy or prolonged use.

As important as how knives are made is the material from which they are made. High-carbon steel (also called "cutlery steel") is considered to be the best steel from which to make knife blades, but it is not widely available. Professionals generally agree that this is the best metal used for cutlery because it holds an excellent edge and is quite easy to sharpen. It is somewhat brittle, however, and can break when dropped. Also, it has a tendency to rust if it is not dried thoroughly after use. Lastly, because of steel's reaction to acids and alkalis in foods such as tomatoes and citrus fruits, these knives discolor easily. (*Note:* This does not affect the other good qualities of this type of knife.)

Quality knives allow staff to do their work safely and more productively.

Corbis Digital Stock

Buyer's Guide to Purchasing Term

Tang (knife)   The portion of a knife's blade that extends into the handle.

Unlike carbon steel, stainless-steel blades do not discolor or rust. This metal alloy is so hard that it strongly resists sharpening. Although it remains sharp longer, once it loses its edge, it is no longer useful. Recent advances in technology have produced some never-need-sharpening knives that do hold up for many years. Note that knives in this class almost always lack the quality, balance, and feel of good-quality knives. They remain a viable alternative, however, for those operators who do not wish to care for, or sharpen, their cutlery.

High-carbon stainless-steel knives combine the best attributes of carbon-steel and stainless-steel blades. They have the toughness and ability to hold an edge and do not discolor. This alloy has become the most popular of metals used in knife construction because of its rust- and stain-resistant qualities. It does not hold its edge quite as well as high-carbon steel and is not quite as easy to sharpen. Nevertheless, its convenience and ready availability make it the most frequently chosen knife material.

Titanium knife blades are made from a combination of titanium and carbide metals. When compared to steel, titanium is lighter, more wear resistant, and holds its edge longer. The titanium blade is more flexible than steel and works best for knives used for tasks such as boning and filleting. Titanium-coated or titanium-edged knives do not have the same quality as those made entirely of titanium or titanium and alloys, and they have a relatively short useful lifespan because the edge hardness is usually lost after only a few sharpenings.

Ceramic knife blades are both strong and brittle. They are stronger than steel and have an edge that can be significantly thinner than steel. This makes cutting easier, and the edge can last significantly longer with proper care. Because of their brittleness relative to steel, ceramic knives are best used for slicing (not chopping) because they can be made very thin and with a very sharp edge. Because of the lightness of ceramics, they do not have the familiar heaviness expected of a metal knife. Sharpening of this knife blade is done using diamond sharpeners because diamonds are one of the few materials harder than ceramic. Although they are much more delicate than steel knives, they tend to hold their edge up to ten times longer. Once the blades have dulled, however, they must be sharpened by a professional.

Because steel-bladed knives are the type most commonly encountered by foodservice buyers, it is important to know the difference between **hollow-ground** and **taper-ground** steel knives. Hollow-ground blades are manufactured using a process that melts two separate pieces of metal and presses (fuses) the pieces together. After the pieces are connected, a beveled (sloped) edge is produced. Although these blades often have very sharp edges, the blade frequently lacks the balance and useful life of a taper-ground blade. Hollow-ground blades are most often found on knives that are used less frequently.

Taper-ground knife blades are manufactured with a single piece of metal and have been ground so they taper smoothly from the spine to the cutting edge. The taper-ground knife is a more stable tool due to the rigid structure of a finely tapered, single sheet of metal. Thus, the taper-ground blade is made to withstand more cutting action as it cuts cleanly through a variety of foods and food textures

---

Buyer's Guide to Purchasing Terms

Hollow ground (knife)   A knife blade that is made using a process that fuses two separate pieces of stamped metal together, which is then ground to create a beveled edge.

Taper ground (knife)   A knife blade that is manufactured with a single sheet of metal that is ground (tapered) from the spine to the cutting edge of the blade.

Did You Know? (11.3)

Knife edges should be regularly realigned using a **butcher's steel**, or a device similar to it to keep the knife sharp and safe. A sharp knife is safer because of the effortless way in which one can use it; accidents can occur with dull knives because of the extra effort that it takes to push the blade through the food and the slipping that can then result.

A butcher's steel does not technically "sharpen" a knife. It simply removes burrs from the knife's edge, reducing resistance and drag when cutting and, as a result, producing a knife that does feel sharper. It really takes an expert with the appropriate specialized tools, however, to properly sharpen knives. A butcher's steel removes only a minimal amount of metal from the edge. Over a period of time, enough metal is removed that the edge requires sharpening by grinding.

Production workers who try to use electric grinding wheels to sharpen their knives don't do their operation any favors! Electronic sharpeners at preset angles and rolling sharpeners should not be used because they usually are made of ceramic or other hard substances that will remove too much metal. They shorten the life of the knives and may create hot spots, indicated by bluing marks, that remove the temper from the blade, making it difficult to keep sharp. True kitchen professionals identify a reputable sharpening service that can sharpen (and repair) their knives as needed and gladly pay for their professional services.

---

when slicing or chopping. This type of blade is most often desired on knives that are intended for heavy usage.

Cutting Boards   The purchase of cutting boards is closely related to that of knives. Wooden or plastic cutting boards minimize resistance against the edge of a knife and help maintain its sharpness, but plastic is the preferred cutting board material of most health department officials because it is more easily cleaned than wood.

Ceramic, stone, metal, or other too-hard plastic surfaces, while more cleanable than wood, can quickly dull a knife's sharp edge. Regardless of the cutting board material chosen, it must be approved by local health inspection authorities and be easy to sanitize. Plastic cutting boards can go in the dishwasher, but like any other cleaned dish, they should be allowed to air dry thoroughly and should be stored in a well-ventilated area between uses.

Office Supplies

Most hospitality buyers tend to minimize the importance of office supplies. In the past that certainly made sense. If a facility could secure pads of paper, pens or pencils, and perhaps adding machine tape, the needs of the "office" were essentially met. Contrast that to today's situation, however, and you can readily see the importance of securing a steady and cost-effective supply of printers, printer ink cartridges, paper, miscellaneous writing supplies (for dining room and kitchen staff), wireless network connectors, and computer display terminals (to name only a few items). While small in the dollar amount needed to create them, foodservice activities generate a tremendous amount of paper and reports, and an appropriate source of the supplies and tools needed to support these activities must be assured. In most cases this can be accomplished by establishing an account with one or more local office supply vendors.

Buyer's Guide to Purchasing Term

Butcher's steel   A long, thin, pointed rod made of extremely hard, high-carbon steel (some are made of diamond steel or ceramic) used to keep a fine edge on sharp knives; also, often called a "sharpening steel" or simply a "steel."

CLEANING SUPPLIES

In many respects the purchasing of appropriate cleaning supplies, including the tools employees use for cleaning and the chemicals that help them do their jobs more effectively, is very straightforward. When making purchasing decisions about cleaning supplies, however, professional buyers must be aware of the **Occupational Safety and Health Administration (OSHA)** requirements that can affect their decisions.

OSHA standards directly affect the products you should buy and the information you must supply to the workers who will use the products. While sometimes criticized as overly aggressive, OSHA has had a significant effect on hospitality workplaces in a relatively short period of time. Among the changes in safety regulation brought about by OSHA are the following:

Guards on all moving parts　In the past many (but not all) manufacturers produced foodservice equipment such as slicers and meat saws with guards to prevent accidental contact with their blades. With OSHA, the use of guards was expanded to cover essentially all parts where contact is possible.

Personal protective equipment (PPE)　In the hospitality industry, broader use of gloves, coveralls, and other protective equipment when handling hazardous chemicals and blood was an important OSHA initiative.

Lockout/Tagout　In the 1980s OSHA developed requirements for locking out energy sources in an "off" condition when performing repairs or maintenance.

Hazard communication　Also known as the "Right to Know" standard, this rule was issued in 1983 and requires the development and communication of information on the hazards of chemical products used in the workplace.

Blood-borne pathogens　In 1990 OSHA issued a standard designed to prevent hotel, health-care, and other workers from being exposed to blood-borne pathogens such as hepatitis B and HIV (the AIDS-causing virus).

It is important to understand that the main purpose of the Occupational Safety and Health Act is to help ensure safe and healthful working conditions. As a result, OSHA is very aggressive in enforcing the rights of workers. Every hospitality operation is legally required to comply with the extensive safety practices, equipment specifications, and employee communication procedures mandated by OSHA. As a buyer, your interaction with OSHA can best be viewed as that of two partners working toward the same goal. Thus, OSHA's activities will help ensure that you and your organization

- provide a safe workplace for employees by complying with OSHA safety and health standards.
- provide workers with tools and equipment to do their jobs that meet OSHA specifications for health and safety.
- establish training programs for employees who use hazardous chemicals.

While there are other OSHA requirements (e.g., businesses must report to OSHA within forty-eight hours any worksite accident that results in a fatality or requires the hospitalization of five or more employees, and they must maintain

Buyer's Guide to Purchasing Term

Occupational Safety and Health Administration (OSHA)　OSHA is an agency in the U.S. Department of Labor. Established in 1970, its mission is to prevent work-related injuries, illnesses, and deaths by issuing and enforcing rules (called "standards") for workplace safety and health.

on-site records of work-related injuries or illnesses), a buyer's most significant concerns relate to OSHA-approved tools and chemicals.

Before examining cleaning tools and chemicals, however, it is important for you to know that OSHA may use federal or state inspectors to monitor the safety-related efforts of businesses. These inspectors are allowed to visit your business to ensure your compliance with their regulations. When initially developed, few businesses viewed OSHA as a partner in their worker safety efforts. Today astute managers recognize that compliance with OSHA standards results in fewer accidents, lower insurance costs, and a healthier workforce.

Cleaning Tools

In many cases the cleaning tools needed by employees are readily available from a variety of suppliers and may be purchased with various food products offered by them. Thus, for example, scrub brushes, mops, mop buckets, griddle bricks, scrapers, and cleaning cloths of all types are simply specified in the same manner as any other item and purchased as needed. In other cases, however, consideration of OSHA requirements regarding cleaning tools and equipment is very important. Suppliers may (or may not) provide adequate information when advertising their items. When in doubt, however, it is your job as a professional purchaser to ensure that, if an OSHA standard exists for it, any cleaning tool purchased meets or exceeds the standard or recommendation.

Cleaning Chemicals

Buyers are responsible for providing workers with the products they need to **clean** and **sanitize** surfaces that normally come into direct contact with food (such as dishware, knifes, and cutting boards) as well as those that do not (such as walls, floors, and tables). All surfaces in an operation must be kept clean; however, any surface that comes into direct contact with food must be cleaned and sanitized.

Cleaning chemicals are those that help remove food, soil, rust, minerals, and other deposits. These must be safe for employees to use. Surfaces may be sanitized by using heat, chemicals, or both. The chemical products you will purchase for sanitizing must also be safe to use.

The best manufacturers of cleaning and sanitizing chemicals provide free container labels that will help you comply with the OSHA Hazard Communication ("Right to Know") requirement. On the labels they supply, chemical manufacturers would assess the health risk, flammability, and physical hazards associated with their products and assign a number (from zero to four) to each of these areas; often on a color-coded label. A score of zero in one of the measured categories means there is very little risk associated with the use of the product, while a score of four indicates a very severe risk. In most cases hospitality industry buyers choosing cleaning and sanitizing chemicals should avoid any product with a score higher than two in any of the assessed areas. In most cases manufacturers' product labels also indicate the need for any protective clothing (e.g., gloves or masks) that should be worn when using the labeled product.

The number of chemical compounds needed to ensure clean and healthful kitchen facilities is significant, and these may be purchased from full-service food

---

Buyer's Guide to Purchasing Terms

Clean   To make a surface free of all food and other types of soil.

Sanitize   To reduce the number of microorganisms on a surface to a safe level.

suppliers or from companies that specialize in chemical supply. In either case buyers should recognize that this is another area of purchasing that OSHA heavily influences. This is primarily because of the requirement that **Material Safety Data Sheets (MSDS)** for each chemical product used in the workplace be made readily available to all workers prior to their exposure to or use of the chemical.

Currently OSHA's requirements regarding MSDSs are that, for each chemical sold, its MSDS must address

- the material's identity, including its chemical and common names.
- hazardous ingredients contained in the product (even in parts as small as 1 percent).
- cancer-causing ingredients (even in parts as small as 0.1 percent).
- a list of physical and chemical hazards and product characteristics (e.g., if the product is flammable, explosive, or corrosive).
- the known health hazards, including the following:
  - Acute effects, such as burns or unconsciousness, which occur immediately
  - Chronic effects, such as allergic sensitization, skin problems, or respiratory disease, which build up over a period of time
- if the material is a known carcinogen.
- limits to which a worker can be exposed, specific target organs likely to sustain damage, and medical problems that can be aggravated by exposure.
- usage and storage precautions, safety equipment, and emergency and first-aid procedures.
- specific fire-fighting information.
- precautions for safe handling and use, including personal hygiene.
- identity of the organization responsible for creating the MSDS, date of its issue, and emergency contact phone number.

Acquiring and making available an OSHA-approved MSDS for each cleaning product purchased for use by employees is an important job responsibility for all hospitality buyers.

Vincent P. Walter/Pearson Education/PH College

Buyer's Guide to Purchasing Term

Material Safety Data Sheet (MSDS)   A written statement describing the potential hazards of and best ways to handle a chemical or toxic substance. An MSDS is provided by the manufacturer of the chemical or toxic substance to the buyer of the product and must be made available in a place where it is easily accessible to those who will actually use or come into contact with the product.

Did You Know? (11.4)

Dishwashing in foodservice operations is critically important to ensure the safety and health of guests. While proper dishwashing may be accomplished using a variety of methods, experienced buyers recognize the following:

When dishwashing by hand:

- Use a three-compartment sink to (1) wash, (2) rinse, and (3) sanitize.
- The interior and exterior of all sinks must be clean and free of grease buildup.
- All faucets must be clean and functioning properly.
- Drains must be fully operational and not leaking.
- Scrape all utensils and dishes first to remove debris.
- Wash in water 100°F–120°F (38°C–49°C).
- Use recommended amounts of detergent in the wash sink.
- Change rinse water as needed.
- To sanitize dishware, immerse in 170°F (77°C) water for thirty seconds or in an approved chemical sanitizer for one minute or more (follow manufacturer's instructions).
- Air-dry all items.

When dishwashing by machine:

- For best results, follow all directions on the machine carefully.
- Place dishes and utensils in racks, trays, or baskets so all surfaces can be touched by a direct spray of wash and rinse water.
- Add liquid or powder detergent when necessary.
- Unless otherwise specified, wash water should be 140°F–160°F (60°C–71°C).
- Add liquid sanitizer when necessary.
- Automatic detergent dispensers, wetting agent dispensers, and liquid sanitizer injectors (if any) must be properly installed and maintained.
- Unless otherwise specified, rinse water should be 180°F (82°C).
- All dishwashing machines should be thoroughly cleaned at least once a day or more if the machine is used heavily.
- Air-dry all items.
- Consult frequently with your mechanical dishwasher cleaning and sanitizing products supplier to ensure optimal operation of dishwashing equipment.

Buyer's Guide to Internet Resources: Back-of-House Supplies and Cleaning Supplies

Web Site	Topic
www.lincolnsmallwares.com	Maker of quality smallwares products
www.don.com	Seller of smallwares and cookware products
www.coppercookware.us	Commercial-quality copper-clad cookware (pots and pans)
www.onlinestainless.com	Stainless-steel flatware
www.dexter-russel.com	U.S.-made knives
www.zwilling.com	J. A. Henckels Swiss-made knives
www.kikuichi.net	Carbon steel knives made in Japan
www.staples.com	Office supplies
www.americanhotel.com	Cleaning tools and supplies
www.ecolab.com	Cleaning and sanitizing chemicals

Buyers at Work (11.2)

"I thought you would be happy," said Rhonda Magana as she talked to Shanna Alexander, director of purchasing for the 850-room Barcelona San Cabo resort.

Shanna had just returned from a vacation to the Puerto Plata area of the Dominican Republic. Rhonda was filling Shanna in on what had happened during the seven days Shanna had been gone.

Shanna was not sure if she was pleased. While she had been gone, Rhonda had assumed the buyer duties related to the cleaning supplies purchased by the resort. Now Rhonda was telling Shanna about the "good deal" she had gotten on the floor cleaner used on the hotel's lobby floor, tiled hallways, and kitchen floor areas.

"There are twelve plastic bottles in each case, just like the old cleaner, but it's a brand-new product and it costs 10 percent less per case than what we used to use," Rhonda said proudly, "so I bought a lot of it."

Assume that Shanna finds the old cleaning product was sold in liter bottles, and the new product is sold in quarts. Assume also that, due to differences in concentration levels, the surface area that could be cleaned by the old product was 125 square feet per container and the area that can be cleaned by the new product is one hundred square feet per container.

1. What is one cost-related concern Shanna might have about the new product?
2. What could be one OSHA-related concern Shanna might have about the new product?
3. What weaknesses in the hotel's purchasing system do you think Shanna may discover based on this incident?

It is important for buyers to recognize that it is part of their professional responsibility to ensure that employees who may be exposed to hazardous chemicals have access to the protective information they need prior to using the chemical. This can be a challenge when purchasing for facilities that employ large numbers of diverse employees, many of whom do not speak or read English. Despite the challenges, however, providing such information is both the right thing to do and the legal thing to do. In this regard, experienced professional buyers recognize that their chemical suppliers can be a great asset in complying with the letter and spirit of the law because they (the suppliers) are required to provide these documents for the products they sell.

RECEIVING AND STORAGE

In most cases the proper receiving of nonfood items requires the same attention to detail and skill required for food purchases. Verification of quantity, quality, and price at time of delivery is very important. Typically, nonfood items will be stored in secure dry-storage areas. As you learned in Chapter 9, dry-storage areas should generally be maintained at a temperature ranging between 65°F and 75°F (18°C–24°C). Temperatures lower than these could be harmful to some nonfood products (as can excessively high temperatures or excess humidity); however, spoilage or product deterioration is not often the issue with nonfood items.

Of greater concern to hospitality buyers and managers is the security of nonfood items. Because many of the nonfood items you will buy (such as dishes, glassware, flatware, kitchen knives, and the like) are valued by employees, these items can be prime targets for pilferage and theft. As a result, highly valuable nonfood items should be kept in locked and secured areas and should be issued only with the approval of management. Even less costly nonfood items, such as paper and plastic products, should be inventoried regularly and stored in areas that serve to discourage their unauthorized removal from the operation.

The proper storage of cleaning and sanitizing supplies requires that they be kept physically separated from food products to avoid contamination. In most cases local health codes require segregated storage areas for those chemicals deemed to be hazardous to foods. To avoid potentially disastrous mistakes, cleaning and sanitizing chemicals should never be stored in containers whose labels indicate they previously held foods. Also, to comply with OSHA requirements, all chemical storage containers should be clearly and properly labeled in a manner that communicates the specific dangers of using the product.

Purchasing Terms

Tabletop (items) *305*	Porcelain *307*	Drive-thru *318*	Butcher's steel *325*
Single-service (items) *305*	Glaze *307*	Smallwares *320*	Occupational Safety and Health Administration (OSHA) *326*
Five-star (restaurant) *306*	Crystal *308*	Line pan *321*	
	Cutlery *309*	Chef *321*	
Cost per use *306*	Gauge (stainless steel) *310*	Mandoline *321*	Clean *327*
Glassware *307*	Drop (tablecloth) *312*	Tang (knife) *323*	Sanitize *327*
Dishware *307*	Caddy (condiment) *313*	Hollow ground (knife) *324*	Material Safety Data Sheet (MSDS) *328*
Ceramic *307*	Take-out (foods) *318*	Taper ground (knife) *324*	

Make Your Own Purchasing Decisions

1. In many instances buyers of dining room supplies must make a trade-off between durability and price. In most cases a more durable tabletop item will cost more than a less durable item. Professional buyers should, of course, calculate and assess cost per use when making their purchase decisions. However, what other factors (in addition to cost) should buyers consider when assessing the wisdom of purchasing longer-life versus shorter-life dining room supply items such as flatware, glassware, and dishware?

2. While buying one standard glass size in large quantity might be less costly to the operation, bartenders and bar managers often want many different glass shapes and sizes to best market the products they sell. Assume you were the individual responsible for making glass purchasing decisions for a very large and busy foodservice operation that sold a significant amount of alcoholic beverages. What factors would you consider as you sought to determine the optimum number of different glass sizes and types to use when serving beverages to your customers?

3. Environmentally friendly packaging products are increasingly important to foodservice consumers. In many cases, however, these products are still more expensive on a per-unit basis than are less-Earth-friendly products. What are the specific factors that you, as a professional purchaser, should consider when assessing the advantages and disadvantages of using these more costly packaging products?

4. Foodservice operations that rely on carry-out sales for a large portion of their business often can face difficult decisions when developing product specifications for service related to their dine-in customers. As a professional buyer, what specific challenges exist in seeking service items (dishware, glassware, and flatware) that can cost effectively meet the expectations of both take-out and dine-in guests?

5. Hospitality buyers can play an important part in ensuring that workers using chemicals and other cleaning supplies understand the hazards associated with using those products. Assume you were a buyer in a large, multi-unit hotel company. Assume also that you knew there were many employees of different nationalities working for your company who used these supplies and could not read English. In such a case, what do you believe would be your responsibility to help communicate to them the information typically contained in an MSDS? How could that be done?

12

Buying Technology and Services

Purchasing Pros Need to Know!

Advancements in technology have caused rapid change in our society as well as the hospitality business. It is critical that professional buyers stay current with technology-related product and service advancements. Selection can be more complex than purchasing other hospitality goods and services, but fortunately, buyers need not be technology experts to effectively purchase them. In this chapter you will learn about the significant factors you must know and consider when selecting such products.

It is also important to remember that, despite their complexity, technology products are essentially machines that are subject to malfunction, breakdown, or simply wearing out. As a result, vendors providing service and repair to technology products must be carefully chosen. This is especially true with those technology-related items that are marketed exclusively to the hospitality industry. In this chapter you will learn how professional buyers evaluate some of the most important technology products used in foodservice.

In addition to technology-related products, all hospitality buyers must purchase essential services. For example, foodservice units must have fresh water to serve guests, cook foods, and clean the facility. In a situation such as this, it is unlikely you will be allowed to choose from alternative water supply sources. Similar circumstances are likely to exist in the case of electrical supply, energy sources, and waste removal. In such cases buyers must be even more vigilant than normal because, historically, in situations where a supplier has a monopoly on a service or product, the normal market conditions (competition) that help control price increases and ensure the quality of services may be absent. As a result, buyers faced with buying from a single-source (monopoly) supplier must be especially aware of potential service, billing, and payment issues.

In addition to the essential services that must be purchased by their businesses, hospitality buyers face many instances in which they will decide if the operation's own staff will perform a specific service in-house or if the service will be purchased from an outside vendor. Identifying those services that should be outsourced, the manner in which bids for the needed services will be secured, and how final service provider selection will be made are important considerations. You will learn about these responsibilities in this chapter.

Buying professional services can be very different from buying products. When purchasing services, ensuring that the actual service provided was exactly the service you intended can become difficult. In such cases buyers must confirm that the vendor follows the contract's terms, and more subjective quality assessments may also be made. You will learn about these concerns in the concluding portion of this chapter.

■ ■ ■

Outline

Considerations in Technology Procurement
    Cost
    Complexity
    Warranty/Maintenance

CONSIDERATIONS IN TECHNOLOGY PROCUREMENT

In Chapter 4 you learned that a *supplier* is any business (large or small) that sells products to a hospitality business. You also learned that a *service provider* (see above comment) is any business that sells services to a hospitality organization. Those companies that specialize in technology often uniquely combine both of these characteristics. Thus, for example, in a restaurant, a telephone service provider may install and maintain telephone lines (a physical product) and offer a variety of calling/billing plans (a service).

Important issues to consider when buying technology and other services are similar but not identical to those you consider when buying foodservice products. For this reason, it is essential you know how to choose, monitor, and evaluate companies providing technology and other essential services and those you voluntarily elect to outsource. There is little doubt that the future of hospitality management and operations will continue to be heavily influenced by technological advancements. While you need not become a technology expert to be an effective buyer, you must become an expert in evaluating the appropriateness of purchasing and using advanced technological systems. In most cases hospitality operators desiring advanced technology to improve their operations are interested in achieving one or more of the following goals:

- Higher revenues
- Lower operating costs
- Improved guest satisfaction
- Increased employee (or management) productivity
- Better communications
- Creation of a competitive advantage

All of the above are worthy objectives; however, while rapid advances have made many technology-based products and services you can buy more valuable, versatile, and flexible, there can be disadvantages as well in applying them in your business.

Sometimes advanced technology systems are so complicated, they can be used by only a few, highly trained individuals. This may be acceptable (as, for example, when only one manager is trained to change menu prices in an operation's new POS system). Alternatively, highly technical advancements may lead to great frustration (as, for example, when on a busy night, a wireless POS system ceases operation for unknown reasons).

In the foodservice industry, technological improvements can involve everything from advancements in a programmable cooking unit used in the kitchen to property-specific employee training, delivered via the Internet, in a multi-language format.

While an operation's effectiveness can often be greatly improved by well-designed and well-integrated technology, there are limitations to the role technology can reasonably be expected to play. An overreliance on technology or a misapplication of its features often results in frustration and wasted time and money. To avoid such a situation, you must carefully consider the following essential elements before selecting and purchasing any technology designed to enhance your operation:

- Cost
- Complexity
- Warranty/maintenance
- Upgradeability
- Vendor reliability

Cost

It can be difficult to justify the cost of any investment in technology. Consider an item as simple as the telephone. When telephones first appeared, it may have been difficult to actually prove cost effectiveness even though they were judged an important technological advancement for a hospitality operation. Today, of course, few businesses could be operated without a voice-transmitting communication device and few managers could survive without their cell phones. Web sites constitute a more recent example. When they first emerged, these were considered in exactly the same manner as telephones. Today, of course, few managers would recommend that a hospitality operation disregard the importance of a professional Web site.

Cost, of course, plays an important role in the decision of how much technology a facility can afford. When it is possible to demonstrate that a proposed technological advancement will pay for itself relatively quickly (e.g., in reduced labor costs or increased revenues), the decision can be an easy one. Often, however, it is difficult to identify actual savings. Technology vendors can be helpful, but experienced buyers recognize that the goal of these vendors is to sell their products, so their advice and any estimated cost reduction/savings calculations must be carefully evaluated.

Complexity

While the manufacturers of many technology products maintain that their offerings are simple to use, experienced technology users know that many times the capabilities of a product can far exceed the skill level of the person using it. In fact, some technology systems are so advanced that their implementation and routine operation requires very high levels of skills. Maximizing the capability of a software program designed to perform recipe conversions, for example, may require knowledge of computer entry techniques, mathematics, and basic cooking skills. If a member of your production staff does not have the advanced computer skills and the math or language mastery needed to use the technology purchased, difficulties using the program will likely arise. These problems can often be reduced or eliminated through the implementation of thorough employee training programs, and your chosen technology vendor should provide you with or help you to secure this training at little or no cost.

Warranty/Maintenance

Because technology items are, essentially, nothing more than highly advanced machines, they need routine maintenance and they can break down. When they do, it will be critical that you receive quality repair service in a timely manner and at a fair price. Typically, a technology purchase will include a warranty or guarantee. Buyers should study their warranties carefully. Items of particular importance will be the following:

- A listing of precisely which items are covered under the terms of the warranty
- The length of the warranty
- The hourly rate charged for repair service for items not covered by the warranty
- Expected response time of the service/repair technicians when service is required

Many standard warranties specify twenty-four-hour response time for service problems. In many cases that timing may be acceptable. Consider, however, the very crowded restaurant whose POS system goes down on a busy Friday evening. In such a case, the restaurant's manager would certainly want it repaired sooner than twenty-four hours.

Upgradeability

While it is difficult to predict what new technological developments may occur in the future, advancements that are compatible with current systems will likely prove to be less expensive than those that require completely new software or hardware. Therefore, many buyers prefer to work with larger and more established technology vendors as these organizations generally ensure that advancements in their products are compatible with those they already have marketed. Smaller and newer technology companies may offer you some features that are desirable. However, their systems may be subject to complete obsolescence if newer technology makes the old systems incompatible with more recent versions offered by alternative vendors.

Vendor Reliability

Where reliability of advanced technology products is concerned, two areas are of importance: reliability of the product (or service) and reliability of the vendor. To help ensure that a vendor's products or services are reliable, buyers should insist that their potential vendors provide a list of current customers who can be contacted for information about the reliability of the products they have purchased.

Vendor reliability is also very important. There is no more important consideration when selecting a new technology than the quality of the vendor supplying it. While a variety of factors can influence vendor reliability, the following three essential reliability factors are worthy of close examination:

1. Location and response time
2. Quality of service staff
3. Vendor reputation

LOCATION AND RESPONSE TIME   Generally, the closer the location of the vendor to your operation, the more successful that vendor will be in providing reliable service. Long-distance vendor relationships certainly can work, but only if the vendor is highly motivated and has **field representatives** who can quickly come to a buyer's site if needed.

Location is important because of its direct effect on response time, which is critical when an advanced technology system is down. Regardless of the warranty in place, service response time, rather than who is to pay for that service, can be of critical importance in a downtime emergency.

Buyers should be cautious if the service person or field representative provided by a vendor works as an independent contractor or for a company not directly related to the one from which they are buying. Subcontracted service can be acceptable, but is often a sign that buyers may have difficulty acquiring a prompt response to potential problems. The best advanced technology companies provide their own service representatives in a timely fashion.

QUALITY OF SERVICE STAFF   Experienced hospitality purchasers know that service interruptions in advanced technology products will occur. When a problem develops, it is the quality of the service/repair department, not the vendor's sales department, that will be of most importance. Before selecting a technology vendor, buyers should insist that they meet with the service person(s) who will be responsible for their account. They should ask the questions needed to ensure that the service provider understands the buyer's operation well enough to be of true assistance when needed.

Many buyers maximize vendor reliability by doing business with only very well-established companies. They believe that well-established companies are likely to be better at what they do and are more likely to be in business in the future. Of course, they understand that even Microsoft was once a start-up company. However, in general, it is a good idea to do business with technology suppliers who have an established record of accomplishment. Technology start-up companies, like all new businesses, often experience high failure rates, a situation that can leave their customers struggling to find alternative repair and maintenance services.

VENDOR REPUTATION   Perhaps the most important factors in selecting technology vendors are the same ones buyers should use when evaluating any supplier. The

---

Buyer's Guide to Purchasing Term

Field representative   A vendor's employee assigned to the on-site management and service of the vendor's accounts.

If technology systems fail during peak volume periods, vendor response time is of critical importance to managers and guests.

Lon C. Diehl/PhotoEdit Inc.

integrity of an advanced technology vendor is as critical as your own. Honesty, fairness, consistent quality, and a willingness to stand behind their promises are characteristics that buyers should seek in all vendors, but especially those involved in advanced technology products and services. Vendors with solidly positive reputations for integrity maximize a buyer's chances of purchasing a reliable technology system from a reliable vendor who provides reliable service.

Buyers at Work (12.1)

"I can't believe this," Carl Graves, the general manager of the Tidewater Restaurant, said for the tenth time. Carl was talking with Mike Freeport, the restaurant's assistant manager. It was just after 2:00 a.m. on Saturday morning, and neither Carl nor Mike had ended their Friday night work shift.

Mike got off the telephone with BecoLabs, the company that had recently installed the new low-temperature dish-washing machine and chemical-dispensing system used at the Tidewater to wash dishes for the five hundred to seven hundred diners the restaurant served on a typical Friday or Saturday night.

The system had been suggested to be more energy efficient and less expensive than the older system it replaced. Mike felt the decision to go with the new machine was a good one when he made it two months ago. The problem now, however, was that the machine had stopped working completely at around 9:30 p.m. The lights on the digital control panel had flickered twice then gone out, and the machine went dead. Only by using every available dish in the restaurant and by heavily utilizing the bar area's glass washer was the restaurant able to provide enough dishware, flatware, and glassware to get through the evening.

"We were lucky," said Carl. "If the system had gone down two hours earlier, we would never have been able to keep up. When are they coming to fix it?"

"I don't know," said Mike. "I got a recording."

"Well, if we don't hear back from them that they can fix the problem by early tomorrow, I'm not sure how we will get these dishes done and get through Saturday's dinner rush," said Carl.

"Paper plates?" suggested Mike.

"Not funny, wise guy," replied Carl. "This could get really bad."

Assume you were this restaurant's general manager:

1. At this point in time, how important is this product's warranty to your problem? Why?
2. At this point in time, how important is product upgradeability to your problem? Why?
3. At this point in time, how important is vendor reliability (especially response time) to your problem? Why?

ADVANCED TECHNOLOGY PRODUCTS
FOR FOODSERVICE OPERATIONS

Like buyers in virtually every other business, those in hospitality encounter a seemingly endless variety of new product and service innovations brought about by technological advancements, and their usefulness, if any, to the buyer's organization must be assessed. Implementation of advanced technology systems generally has a cost, which must be recovered if the purchase is to make sense financially. Also, some implementation costs may be nonmonetary. Consider, for example, the hospitality manager considering the elimination of employee-punched time cards in favor of newly developed laser time clocks that scan employees' fingerprints (or irises of their eyes) to establish the employees' identities and times they report to work. Because it prevents **"buddy-punching,"** the system's cost may easily be justified in labor savings. However, the effect on employee perceptions must also be considered (e.g., will employees feel that managers do not really trust them, and if so, how could that affect employee morale?).

Other costs of hospitality-related technology advancements may come in the form of guest relations. For example, some restaurants are experimenting with allowing guests to place their orders directly on computer screens located at their tables. This order method is faster for the guests than waiting for a server to take orders. However, some industry observers question the wisdom of using this self-order technology because of the lack of personal contact that accompanies such high-tech systems.

Despite their potential disadvantages and some concerns associated with them, technological advances in hospitality are likely to continue at a fast pace. As a professional purchaser, you must make a strong effort to remain current about changes that will affect your own industry segment. (Specific methods for doing so are described later in this chapter.)

For most hospitality buyers, the advancements in technology that will be most important to understand are those related to the systems they currently use. The major technology systems used in food and beverage operations vary greatly by industry segment. Buyers for quick-service restaurants may be very interested in software and hardware innovations designed to speed the processing of drive-through orders. Buyers for full-service restaurants, however, may be more interested in advancements in handwriting recognition systems that allow servers to write an order at the guest's table then send it, via wireless technology, to the kitchen simply by pressing "enter" on a handheld order pad. Buyers in health-care foodservice settings may seek and evaluate advancements in nutritional assessment software that go far beyond calculating nutrients of menu items. Advanced software programs could include automation of ingredient, recipe, and menu functions and resident-specific tracking (e.g., for food preferences/allergies, nourishments, room and meal service locations, medical and weight histories, and the like).

Despite the diversity of need for, and the variation in speed of, innovation across industry segments, the majority of foodservice buyers will likely encounter selected technology-related systems regardless of their industry segment. Four of the most common products of which you should be aware are the following:

1. Point-of-sale (POS) systems
2. Beverage dispensing systems

Buyer's Guide to Purchasing Term

Buddy-punching   The usually prohibited practice of one employee punching a time card in (or out) for another employee.

3. Merchant services (payment card processing)
4. Security/surveillance systems

Point-of-Sale (POS) Systems

You have learned that a restaurant's point-of-sale (POS) system is used to record financial information. In the most basic POS systems, the financial information maintained includes the number of customers served, the amount of money spent by the guests, a record of the items these guests purchased, and specific information about how the guests paid for their purchases.

Advanced POS systems may be **interfaced** with product ordering and/or payroll systems and allow the capabilities of the POS to expand greatly. Buyers investigating POS alternatives should consider the technological advancements that relate to the hardware and software components of these systems. Advances in the hardware used in POS systems develop rapidly. The hardware advancements likely to be the most important to your operation relate to the following components:

Monitors   All computer monitors display information held in the POS system. Monitors may also be designed to serve as data input devices. In kitchens, monitors display guest orders in the sequence in which they were received, and they can be programmed to highlight special order status (e.g., those guest orders for delivery, for carry-out, or for those guests dining in). This allows production personnel to know which guest orders should be prepared first. It also allows them to combine orders, where practical, to increase the efficiency of their production efforts.

Display monitors used in kitchens are designed to withstand the extreme heat, smoke, and humidity conditions that often exist. In dining areas monitors are increasingly designed to feature touch-screen entry and are designed to maximize server effectiveness through the thoughtful placement of data entry functions, easy-to-view content displays, and efficient print functions.

Input devices   Input devices are used by servers to place guests' orders. In those operations without a POS system, communicating guest orders to the kitchen simply involves writing the orders down and giving them to kitchen production personnel. When using a POS, guest orders have traditionally been communicated by entering the orders onto a keypad or touch screen (see Figure 12.1). More recently, however, new handheld input devices have been developed that are interfaced with a wireless connection to the main POS terminal. This allows servers to enter guest orders without having to return to a central POS station or to wait in line while other servers manually enter orders into a POS data entry terminal. Typically, these handheld devices use a touch pad for information entry, but some have recently been developed that can be programmed to recognize an individual server's handwriting.

Receipt printers   Receipt printers serve two functions. In kitchens where no display monitor is used, dependable printers can provide production personnel with hard copy orders even in the extreme conditions of the cooks' preparation areas. In the dining room, printers quickly and quietly print guest orders and receipts with speed, accuracy, and reliability.

Buyer's Guide to Purchasing Term

Interfaced   Electronically connected for the purpose of sharing files, information, or data.

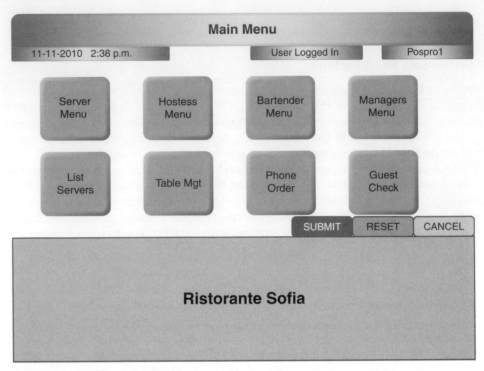

FIGURE 12.1 POS Data Entry Screen
Source: POS screen courtesy of Panda Pros

Payment card readers Card readers that allow servers to authorize credit, debit, and other types of payment cards have advanced greatly in speed and ease of use. They are typically designed as an integral part of the POS system and completely eliminate the sometimes difficult process of interfacing separate payment card readers with the POS system.

In the early days of POS system development, the software was limited primarily to programs that added revenue totals, maintained guest check totals, identified the number of guests served, and indicated how customers paid for their purchases. Today additional software programs designed as stand-alone personal computer programs or included as part of a larger POS system are readily available. A buyer's choice of POS and the software it contains will depend greatly on the type of foodservice operation using it. For many buyers, however, helpful POS software programs that are readily available include those that do the following:

- Maintain revenue totals from different POS locations within one restaurant
- Maintain revenue totals from different POS locations within a restaurant chain or group
- Compare products produced (from guest checks) in the kitchen or at the bar to actual inventory reductions
- Prepare purchase orders based on recorded item sales
- Reconcile (match) guest check totals with total revenues collected
- Identify revenue collection and menu item sales differences by outlet, day, shift, hour, and/or server
- Reconcile credit card deposits with credit card sales
- Maintain payroll-related records
- Maintain accounts receivable records
- Create the revenue portion of the income (profit and loss) statement after reconciling bank deposits, charge card sales deposits, returned checks, and bank deposits

---

PROFESSIONAL PURCHASING PREVENTS PROBLEMS (12.1)

"Complex Doesn't Always Mean Good!"

A common problem: POS systems purchased for operations frequently are not fully used due to these systems' high level of complexity.

Selecting a new POS system will be one of a professional buyer's most important decisions. With virtually hundreds of brands on the market, the features and capabilities available to you can be overwhelming. A common mistake is a buyer selecting a system that offers countless features, despite the fact that only a few features are ultimately used. As with many advanced technology programs, the features offered by the system may simply exceed the ability of users to fully understand, appreciate, and use them. As a result, when selecting a new POS, experienced buyers always do the following:

- Investigate fully both the initial and the ongoing training systems that will be included with the system's purchase
- Assess the ability of the operation's current (and future) staff to use the system's most advanced features
- Pay for only those system features deemed essential by the business's owners
- Recognize that manufacturers of POS systems (to a degree much more than many other technology tools you will purchase) seek to distinguish themselves by the *number* of functions their products can perform; ease of use and dependability, however, are the POS features most highly prized by experienced hospitality buyers
- Seek input about the proposed POS purchase from actual users (i.e., unit managers, supervisors, servers, and bartenders) before a final decision is made

---

Buyers selecting POS-related software programs should remember that interfacing (connecting) the various software programs will be very important. For example, a POS containing a software program that computes total server tips collected from guests as part of their charge card payments in a specific payroll period is good. If that program interfaces with an operation's payroll-generating software, that is even better.

PROFESSIONAL PURCHASING PREVENTS PROBLEMS (12.2)

"Interfacing POS Data with a Supplier's Order System"

A common problem: The hospitality industry lags behind many others in automating its purchasing functions.

Historically, foodservice operations have not been at the forefront of automation. Nowhere is this more evident than in the automation of the purchasing function. In fairness to hospitality operators, however, three essential components are required to interface the product needs of a foodservice operation with its suppliers' available inventory.

The first of these three required components is an Internet connection. While that might seem obvious, it was not so long ago that the average foodservice facility did not have access to the Internet. Payment card transactions were processed using telephone lines, and some industry professionals considered the idea of each restaurant having its own Web site unnecessary. Increasingly, however, foodservice managers at the unit level now have easy access to the Internet.

The second required component is a functioning interface between the restaurant's POS (which requires that it have one) and the vendor's ordering system. When such interfaces exist, data from the POS (e.g., the number of twelve-ounce steaks sold in a specific time period) can easily be used to prepare the restaurant's steak order for the upcoming order period.

Finally, and perhaps most important, hospitality managers/buyers must be comfortable using the vast capabilities of the Internet and their own POS systems in an electronically interfaced environment. Previous generations of managers and buyers did not necessarily have that comfort level. Today's more computer-literate hospitality professionals, however, are likely to make great strides in this area by readily accepting (and even demanding) rapid advancements in online purchasing capabilities.

Beverage Dispensing Systems

Many restaurants and bars, and especially those that are very-high-volume operations, automate all or part of their drink production processes. In these systems the production of drinks such as scotch and water, gin and tonic, rum and cola, beer, and even wine are dispensed in a predetermined amount by an electronic dispensing device activated by the bartender. Buyers can chose from an array of technology and automation levels, as well as price.

In the best systems, the automated dispensing equipment is interfaced to the bar area's POS system. This helps ensure that each drink produced by the system is correctly priced and automatically charged to the proper guest. This also reduces opportunities for bartenders to give away free drinks. Automated dispensing systems that record the number of drinks produced, the amount of alcohol of each type dispensed, and the revenue value of the drinks prepared increase an operation's ability to effectively control products and revenue. They also can supply accurate product usage information that may be helpful in the purchasing process. Additional benefits from using an automated beverage-dispensing system can include the following:

- Elimination of pouring too little or too much alcohol in a guest's drink
- Reduced product spillage
- The elimination of drink pricing errors
- Accurate record keeping of all products sold
- Reduced incidence of bartender production errors
- Less required supervision of bartenders
- Lower and more consistent product costs
- Reduced cost per product ounce when buying (because liquor may be purchased in larger containers for dispensing)
- Reduced liability potential resulting from failure to strictly control the amount of alcohol in each drink

Advances in automatic dispensing equipment have eliminated many of the difficulties associated with these systems when they were first introduced. Equipment breakdowns and malfunctions have been greatly reduced, as have the costs required for system maintenance and upkeep. Buyers for properties with high-volume sales should investigate potential advantages and disadvantages of alternative dispensing equipment technology available. Managers and purchasers must also consider guest relations aspects of these systems. For example, some guests seated at bars where this equipment is used may question the serving size and brand (quality) of alcoholic beverages dispensed through the system. Other guests may feel drinks produced in such a system are weak and, thus, do not represent a good value for the money the guest spends.

In busy operations such as this one, automated beverage systems can speed service times and improve accuracy in guest billings.

Michael L. Abramson/Woodfin Camp & Associates, Inc.

Merchant Services (Payment Card Processing)

Today fewer customers than ever carry large amounts of cash, and many foodservice operations do not accept personal checks. Most foodservice operations, including quick-service restaurants (QSRs) now accept a variety of "plastic" forms of bill payment. Since the 1960s **credit cards** were the most common form of payment card accepted at most restaurants. Today **debit cards** are increasingly used by guests to pay their bills. Merchants that accept payment cards for purchases are charged a fee by the banks for the right to allow their customers to pay by credit or debit card.

Examples of credit cards are Visa and MasterCard. Travel and Entertainment (T&E) cards use a prepayment system in which the card issuer collects full payment from the card users on a monthly basis. These card companies do not typically assess their users interest charges. Instead, they make their profit by collecting fees from the merchants accepting the cards. Examples of T&E cards are American Express (Amex) and Diners Club. (Note: In some cases, the fees charged by T&E card issuers have been raised so high that some properties no longer accept them.)

Increasingly, debit cards are used for guest payment. Funds needed to cover the user's purchase are automatically transferred from the user's bank account to the entity issuing the debit card. As with bank cards and T&E cards, merchants accepting debit cards are assessed a fee for the right to do so.

The collection and payment of the fees assessed to those foodservice operations accepting payment cards and the transfer of funds to the operator's account are handled by a foodservice buyer's **merchant services provider (MSP).** An MSP plays an important role as the foodservice operation's coordinator/manager of payment card acceptance and funds collection.

Payment card issuers and the MSP charge the foodservice operation. All businesses that accept cards—credit or debit—are charged fees for every transaction by the card's issuer. The percentage charged is different for various types of businesses. For example, restaurants are charged different fees than are department stores. In most cases the average charge ranges from 1.0 percent to about 3.0 percent of each transaction's value (including charged tips). The rate charged varies depending on whether a credit or debit card is used, whether it is swiped or hand-entered into a system, and whether a customer's billing information is provided at the time of purchase.

The MSP also assesses a variety of fees including those for setup, for each transaction, for programming, for printing and mailing monthly statements, and for managing the card company's usage assessments and fund transfers (payments). In most cases foodservice operations have little option but to accept the most popular of payment cards. The quality of MSP selected and the fees it charges, however, can vary greatly. Essentially, the MSP serves as an intermediary for payment card transactions, taking care of the money transfers between the customer's and merchant's banks. Generally, the MSP will keep 10 to 20 percent of all the fees foodservice operators pay for card services, and the card company (Visa, MasterCard, and others) receives the balance. At the end of the month, the foodservice operator receives a statement displaying the total transactions and the various fees paid (because the fees are withdrawn by the MSP before any revenue is deposited in the foodservice operation's bank account).

As with any technology vendor, hospitality buyers should select MSPs they can trust and that charge a fair rate for their services. The MSP rate varies based on the average size bill paid by the operation's guests, the total number of payment card transactions processed annually by the operation, the business's own credit worthiness, and how the foodservice facility will connect its POS system to the

---

PROFESSIONAL PURCHASING PREVENTS PROBLEMS (12.3)

"Turn Tables Turn"

A common problem: Guests waiting for servers to return from the processing of their payment cards slow restaurant table turns and decrease operational revenues, especially on busy nights when table space is at its most valuable.

Everyone who has dined out frequently has experienced it. You are finished with your meal, and the check has been presented to your table. The totals on your bill are correct, so on the reappearance of your server, you present your payment card. The server takes your bill and payment card away, and you wait (patiently or impatiently) for his or her return. In the meantime, your table cannot be cleaned and readied for the next group of guests. It is truly a lose-lose-lose situation (for the diner, for waiting guests, and for the operation).

Rather than lose valuable minutes as servers go to tables, pick up credit or debit cards, access a POS system terminal, process the transaction, and return the card, some hospitality purchasers are choosing pay-at-the-table wireless processing devices for interface with their POS systems (e.g., see www.verifone.com). These handheld units, issued to each server, allow for immediate debit or credit card payment processing right at the guest's table.

In an era where identity theft is of increasing concern (it has been estimated that 70 percent of credit card fraud originates in restaurants), an added benefit to guests and to the operation is the fact that the guest's payment card never leaves the guest's sight. The result is a higher degree of guest comfort with the security of the transaction and a reduced opportunity for dishonest servers to record guest payment card information for their own illegal purposes.

The net effect of wireless pay-at-the-table systems is a faster table turn. The result is a win-win-win situation (for seated guests, for waiting guests, and for your operation).

MSP. The technology chosen for the interface (manual, dial-up, or high-speed dedicated leased line) also has a significant effect on the total fees charged to the restaurant.

Surveillance Systems

Electronic surveillance can play a big role in some restaurant operations. These systems serve two essential purposes. The first is to aid in the protection of guests. Guests who are in any area of a foodservice or hotel operation should be protected from harm. Exterior and interior surveillance systems, in-room safes (to protect guests' valuables), and advanced systems designed to protect against identify theft are examples of the efforts undertaken by hospitality professionals to safeguard guests and their property.

In addition to guest protection, surveillance systems aid in the security of the operation's physical assets. Buyers choosing these systems generally select from one of two basic systems. The first involves using CD or DVD equipment to digitally record the activity within an area of the facility. For example, a restaurant could set up a security/surveillance camera that records the activity outside the liquor storeroom. Then if the storeroom was broken in to, a video recording would exist that could be useful in identifying the thieves. Parking lots, delivery areas, storage rooms, and areas near cashiers are the most commonly chosen areas for the use of surveillance systems.

The second type of security/surveillance commonly used in hospitality operations involves a **closed-circuit television (CCTV)** system. The potential uses of a CCTV system are many. It can be used, for example, in a multiple-entry property so activity outside each entrance can be monitored. It is important to remember that, to be most effective, a CCTV system must be monitored. Viewing monitors are typically placed in a central location and viewed, according to preset schedules, by an employee who is trained to respond appropriately to activities seen on the monitor. In some hospitality operations (such as casinos) a state regulatory agency may actually mandate the use of a CCTV system.

MONITORING ADVANCEMENTS IN HOSPITALITY-ORIENTED TECHNOLOGY

It can be very difficult to keep up with all of the hardware, software, and services advancements that can directly affect your business. However, it is critical that you do so. The choices available to you for continuing your education in this area are varied and depend on your own preference and geographic location. Most buyers in the hospitality industry can choose from one or more of the following methods:

- Professional associations/trade shows
- Publications and newsletters
- Current vendors
- Competitive vendors
- Technology-related classes
- Your own organization

Buyer's Guide to Purchasing Term

Closed-circuit television (CCTV)   A camera and monitor system that displays, in real time, the activity within the camera's field of vision. A CCTV consisting of several cameras and screens showing the camera's field of vision may be monitored in a single location (often the manager's office).

Professional Associations/Trade Shows

As a hospitality professional, you will likely elect to join one or more **professional trade associations.** These associations typically address a variety of certification, educational, social, and legislative goals that members feel are important. Associations typically hold annual gatherings and invite technology-related exhibitors (and others) who sell products and services of interest to their members. A feature of many of these gatherings is an area in which a variety of vendors display and talk about their latest product offerings. These events are an extremely efficient way to see the product offerings of a large number of advanced technology vendors in a very short time. Many trade associations also have both state and local chapters, some of which host their own smaller vendor showings.

Local chambers of commerce and other professional service organizations often hold meetings and schedule speakers who can update buyers on the newest business applications of technology. Membership in these organizations is generally well worth its modest cost.

Publications and Newsletters

Regular reading about the hospitality industry will help keep you abreast of the latest technological trends. In many cases technology and its application have become such a large part of the editorial interest of these publications that a special technology editor is employed to monitor changes that could be of interest to the publication's readers. Some printed publications are distributed free to qualified members of the hospitality industry, while others are not. Many publications and newsletters are available on the Internet. This delivery format is increasing in popularity and typically requires only that you supply a valid e-mail address to receive the e-publication.

Current Vendors

Your current suppliers of software, hardware, or technology services can be a valuable source of free information. Each will inevitably make improvements in their products and services as competition and the desire to grow drive their own development efforts.

An added advantage of working with your current technology suppliers is the fact that any new systems they develop are likely to be compatible with those systems your operation already owns and maintains. This can reduce staff training time and the errors that sometimes arise with new system implementation. In addition, current vendors may be more competitive when pricing their new offerings because, in most cases, they would very much like to expand the business they do with current clients.

Competitive Vendors

While current technology vendors can inform buyers of their own innovation efforts, competition in technology-related products and services in the hospitality industry is strong and getting stronger. Whether your interest is in software, hardware, or services, identifying your current vendor's strongest and best competitors is a good way to monitor advances in technology.

Buyer's Guide to Purchasing Term

Professional trade association   Voluntary membership organizations that serve the certification, educational, social, and legislative goals of their members.

Annual contacts, either in person or by telephone, can help purchasers quickly identify improvements in procedures and features that their own vendor may have overlooked or dismissed. Experienced buyers also contact small and start-up vendors they see advertised in publications or exhibiting at trade shows. Often these companies offer the most innovative and cutting-edge products and services available. Remember, however, that their small size may limit their ability to adequately service large accounts and those in distant locations. In many cases, however, they can be a tremendous source of new information.

Technology-Related Classes

Many community colleges and private training organizations offer instruction about technology that can be applied to the hospitality industry. For example, successfully completing an advanced course in word processing techniques using the Word program in Microsoft's Office suite of programs may allow a food operation to design and print its own daily specials menu. Similarly, a course in the applications of database programs (those programs designed to manipulate and store information such as street addresses, e-mail addresses, and telephone numbers) may allow the operation to develop its own direct-marketing programs more efficiently.

Current technology vendors may also be a source of free or reduced-cost instruction. Experienced buyers regularly contact the companies that currently provide their software, hardware, and services to learn if they offer free or low-cost classes that address current products or provide instruction on newer products.

Your Own Organization

International or national chains (and even large companies) may offer educational opportunities for their employees. Often, a large company produces newsletters, conducts in-service training, and/or holds regularly scheduled conferences that can be a good source of information about rapidly changing technology. All of these resources should be monitored and used if they are available. Sometimes a direct conversation with a buyer's supervisor regarding the technological changes affecting their own organization can be of tremendous value. Many times these professionals are in a very good position to see the technology advancements that could work best within the company.

As professionals, hospitality buyers know that they must continually be aware of changes in technology and be committed to implementing the best and most cost effective of these changes to benefit their organization and their own careers. Advances in technology will continue to change society and the hospitality industry as well. When these advances help buyers significantly improve their operations, the business, its employees, and its guests all benefit.

A good working relationship with current technology vendors helps purchasers learn about new technological advances that can affect their operations.

© MTPA Stock/Masterfile
www.masterfile.com

Buyer's Guide to Internet Resources: Technology Products and Services

Web Site	Topic
www.androtech.com	POS systems programmed in multiple languages
www.ncr.com	POS systems
www.actionsystems.com	Handwriting recognition systems for POS systems
www.epson.com	Handheld POS units (with printer capability)
www.berg-controls.com	Alcoholic beverage dispensing systems
www.manitowocfsg.com	Nonalcoholic beverage dispensing systems
www.takechargetech.com	Payment card processing services
www.securitysolutions.com	Surveillance systems
www.htmagazine.com	A technology-oriented hospitality publication
www.hftp.org	The Hospitality Financial and Technology Professionals (HFTP) Association

PURCHASE AND CONTROL OF ESSENTIAL SERVICES

While the decision to choose some of the technology-related products and services commonly used in the hospitality industry is not mandatory, some services you will purchase are simply a "must buy" for any operation. These essential services and some of the ways you can control the costs of buying them are the next topics of this chapter.

Essential Services Purchasing

All buyers must purchase some services simply to keep the doors of their operations open for business. One such group of essential services is **utilities.** For example, a supply of electricity sufficient to operate the business is fundamental to serving customers. Without electricity, the business could not open, and guests could not be served. Similarly, water supplies and the fuels needed to operate the business's **HVAC** system are essential.

In addition to the essential utilities they use, hospitality businesses generate solid waste products. These wastes must be removed from the business, and doing so can represent a significant cost. As a result, waste removal services are essential business services with which professional buyers must be familiar.

UTILITIES   Utility management is a tremendously important part of a hospitality business's overall operation. Utility costs include expenses for water bills; gas, electricity, or fossil fuel for heating and cooling the building; fuel for heating water; and in some cases, the purchase of steam or chilled water for heating and cooling.

It is important to recognize that some utilities costs involved in lighting, heating, and operating the equipment required to run a hospitality business will be incurred regardless of its revenue levels. While higher sales levels will result in some incremental increase in utility costs, as much as 80 percent of total utility

---

Buyer's Guide to Purchasing Terms

Utilities   Commodities and services such as electricity, water, and heating fuels that are usually provided by a public utility company.

HVAC   Industry term for a building's heating, ventilation, and air-conditioning equipment and systems.

costs for most hospitality businesses are fixed. A building's original design and construction, the age of its utility consuming equipment, its regular maintenance, and energy conservation techniques used by a business are all factors that affect utilities purchase and usage.

While the utilities needs of a hospitality business are, in part, determined by the menu items sold and the geographic location of the building, most hospitality buyers will find that they are responsible for ensuring adequate supplies of the following essential utilities:

Electricity

Water (including hot water)

HVAC-related utilities

Electricity   Electricity is the most common and usually the most expensive form of energy used in hospitality businesses. While some operations (e.g., large resort hotels) can make their own electricity by using a backup generator in an emergency when normal sources of electricity are interrupted, most businesses will rely totally on a local power provider to deliver electricity to their operations. As with other items they buy, professional purchasers should strive to buy only the amount of this essential service that is actually needed.

Electricity is expensive. In some areas electric bills account for well more than 50 percent (and sometimes as much as 80 percent) of a hospitality business's total utility costs. Electricity is used everywhere in the hospitality industry. It powers the business's administrative computers, operates fire safety systems, keeps food cold in freezers and refrigerators, and provides dining room lighting, to name but a few uses.

In many cases electrical usage is also tied directly to water and HVAC energy use. In a typical foodservice operation, electrical pumps move water from one area within the business to another. Also, electricity may heat the water used in dishwashing and for general cleaning. Electricity used by the HVAC system cools air and operates fans that provide fresh air to kitchen and dining areas. Even the lights illuminating parking areas operate on electricity. Clearly, electricity serves many roles in a hospitality business. It is no wonder, then, its purchase should not be taken for granted. This is especially true regarding electricity as the primary source of facility lighting. The lighting in a hospitality business is tremendously important to **curb appeal,** guest comfort, worker efficiency, and property security.

Lighting is sometimes referred to as illumination, and light intensity is measured in **foot-candles.** The electrical power required to generate various illumination levels varies by the type of light fixture used. Hospitality businesses require varying degrees of illumination in different locations, and the types of light fixtures and light bulbs used play a large role in producing the most appropriate, cost-effective light for each setting.

In many cases artificial light is produced to supplement natural (sun) light. Natural light is, of course, very cost effective and, when used properly, can have a positive effect on utility costs by limiting the amount of artificial light that must be

---

Buyer's Guide to Purchasing Terms

Curb appeal   The term used to indicate the first visual impression a business's parking areas, grounds, and external building create for an arriving customer.

Foot-candle   A measure of illumination. The greater the illumination level, the greater the measured number of foot-candles.

produced. Most businesses must supplement natural light, however, and when they do, they choose from two basic lighting options that directly affect the amount of electricity they will buy. The first of these is **incandescent** lamps. Incandescent lights are the type most buyers think of when they consider the light bulbs used in their own homes. Incandescent bulbs have relatively short life spans (two thousand or fewer operating hours) and must be frequently changed. They are also inefficient producers of foot-candles.

Incandescent lights are popular, however, because they are easy to install, easy to move, inexpensive to purchase, and have the characteristic of starting and restarting instantly. Incandescent lamp bulbs can also be manufactured to concentrate light in one area (these are known as spot or floodlights).

In cases where an incandescent light source is not the best for a specific lighting need, businesses can select an **electric discharge** lamp. Electric discharge lamps are characterized by longer lives (five thousand to twenty-five thousand operating hours) and higher foot-candle producing efficiency. The most common of this lamp type is the fluorescent, and it is frequently used where high light levels and low operating costs are a consideration. These are popular in restaurant storage areas, kitchens, and some dining areas.

Other types of electric discharge lamps include those for parking areas or security lighting. Sodium lamps are a popular choice as they are extremely efficient foot-candle producers and have very long lives. However, the initial costs to purchase and install these lights are usually greater than for incandescent lights.

In the late 1980s, compact versions of fluorescent lights (compact fluorescent lights, or CFLs) became popular in many hospitality businesses. These bulbs use at least two-thirds less energy than standard incandescent bulbs to provide the same amount of light, and they last up to ten times longer. These lights were designed to combine the energy efficiency and long life of a traditional fluorescent light with the convenience of an incandescent light. In many cases buyers have found that these lamps provide an excellent blend between operational efficiency (energy savings) and convenience. Hospitality buyers whose operations can benefit from the advantages of these bulbs should strongly consider purchasing them.

Water   While some hospitality businesses may own and use their own water wells, in most cases restaurants and institutional food facilities must purchase the water they use. Typically, local water utilities sell water to commercial accounts in one hundred- or one thousand-gallon increments.

Water prices vary nationally based on the scarcity of water in an area, seasonality, and the total quantity of water purchased per month. In some communities larger-volume users are given a discount for quantity purchases, but in other locations, volume users are penalized with increases in per-gallon prices as their water usage increases. Regardless of the pricing method the local water supplier uses, carefully controlling a business's water purchases is very cost effective. Conserving water

- reduces the number of gallons of water purchased.
- reduces the amount the business will pay for sewage (waste water disposal).

Buyer's Guide to Purchasing Terms

Incandescent (lamp)   A lamp type in which a filament inside the lamp's bulb is heated by electrical current to produce light.

Electric discharge (lamp)   A lamp in which light is generated by passing electrical current through a space filled with a special combination of gases (e.g., fluorescent, mercury vapor, metal halide, and sodium).

• (in the case of hot water) reduces water-heating costs because less hot water (e.g., the water used in automatic dishwashing machines) must be produced.

Water purchases can be significantly reduced if all members of a hospitality operation carefully monitor water usage. Some actions businesses can take to reduce water usage and, thus, water purchases will be examined later in this chapter.

HVAC-Related Utilities   Another significant consumer of electrical or other utilities is the foodservice operation's HVAC system. Heating, ventilation, and air-conditioning are considered together because they all use the operation's air treatment, thermostats, ducts (air passageways), and air handler systems. While it is not realistic to assume that buyers of hospitality products and services will be experts in HVAC operations, it is realistic to point out that a basic understanding of such systems is essential if buyers are to appreciate the effect HVAC operations will have on their utility purchases.

A properly operating HVAC system will deliver air to various parts of your building at a desired temperature. The efficiency at which an HVAC system operates, and thus the energy that must be purchased to heat or cool the operation's air space, is affected by several factors, including the following:

• The original temperature of the room
• The temperature of the new air delivered to the room
• The relative humidity of the new air delivered
• The air movement in the room
• The temperature-absorbing surfaces in the room

HVAC systems can be simple or very complex, but in most locations they will consist of components responsible for both heating and cooling. Therefore, professional utility buyers should understand both of these major component groups.

Heating components   An effective HVAC system heats air and water. While it is possible that all of a business's HVAC heating components are operated by electricity, this is not normally the case. Heating by electricity, especially in cold climates, is not generally cost effective. Businesses generally heat the air for at least some parts of their buildings using natural gas, liquefied petroleum gas (LPG), steam, or fuel oil (although electricity can be used to heat small areas).

In most businesses the heating of hot water is second in cost only to the heating of air. As a result, most hospitality operations require an effective furnace (or heat pump system) for heating air and a properly sized **boiler** for heating water.

Like furnaces, boilers may be powered by electricity, natural gas, LPG, or fuel oil. Regardless of the energy source(s) used in the HVAC system, fans or pumps use electricity to move warm air produced by a furnace or hot water produced by a boiler throughout the building.

Cooling components   Just as an operation must heat air and water, in many locations one or more parts of most restaurants must be cooled. Typically, the major cost of operating air-cooling or air-conditioning systems is related to electricity usage. Essentially, in an air-conditioning system, electrically operated equipment extracts heat from warm air and blows newly cooled air into

Buyer's Guide to Purchasing Term

Boiler   A large tank in which water is heated and stored as either hot water or steam. If relatively small, a boiler may be called a "hot water heater."

a designated space. The effectiveness of a cooling system, and thus the energy you will purchase to operate it, is dependent on several factors, including the following:

- The original air temperature and humidity of the room to be cooled
- The temperature and humidity of the cooled air delivered by the HVAC system
- The quantity of cooled air delivered by the HVAC system
- The energy efficiency of the air-conditioning equipment within the HVAC system

Some cooling systems are designed to produce small quantities of very cold air that are then pumped or blown into a room to reduce the room's temperature. Other systems supply larger quantities of air that are not as cold but because the quantity supplied is greater have the same room-cooling effect. The ability of a cooling system to deliver cold air (or water) of a specified temperature and in the quantity required determines the effectiveness of a cooling system. Many times, especially in hot, humid weather, the demands placed on a facility's cooling system are intense. Effective and continual maintenance on cooling equipment plays a crucial part in minimizing the energy purchases required to operate an air-conditioning system.

WASTE REMOVAL   The operation of a hospitality business inevitably results in the generation of waste materials. These waste products may be in liquid form (referred to as sewage), solid form, or a combination of both. Because liquid waste removal costs have historically been reported by hospitality businesses as part of their utility (water) bills, liquid waste removal is generally considered a utility cost and accounted for accordingly.

Solid waste (garbage and trash) removal, however, has not generally been considered a utility cost from a hospitality accountant's perspective (rather, it is considered an operations cost). Nevertheless waste removal expense is examined here because, like utilities costs, these expenses are related to an essential service, and their total costs must be properly controlled.

In some cases the liquid waste (including that disposed of in sinks, floor drains, and toilets) generated by a hospitality business will be processed in the business's own on-site (septic) sewage disposal system. A septic system is simply a small-scale sewage treatment system commonly used in rural areas with no connection to main sewerage pipes. In most cases, however, the liquid waste generated by a hospitality business will be pumped (or fed by gravity) into a larger municipally operated wastewater treatment (sewage) system. In the case of both a septic system and connection to a utility, there will be expenses associated with disposing of liquid waste. Charges for the removal of liquid wastes are generally assessed based on the number of gallons of waste removed.

In addition to liquid wastes, foodservice operations and lodging facilities generate a tremendous amount of solid waste, or trash. Sources of waste include packaging materials such as cardboard boxes, crates, and bags that were used in the shipping of food and supplies, kitchen garbage, restroom trash, and even yard waste generated from the business's landscaping efforts. In most cases waste removal charges for solid wastes are based on the number of times per week (or month) they are removed, the weight of the waste removed, or its volume (measured in cubic yards).

Increasingly, hospitality industry professionals, including buyers, have come to realize that excessive waste generation and poorly conceived waste disposal methods are harmful to the environment and represent a poor use of natural resources. In addition, as landfills become scarce, the cost of solid waste disposal has risen. As a result, all hospitality professionals have a heightened interest in minimizing their essential service (utilities) costs as well as properly controlling costs associated with waste disposal. Consequently, the wise management and conservation of essential services is a critical topic for buyers, and it is to that topic that we now turn your attention.

CONTROLLING ESSENTIAL SERVICE COSTS   Assume that a buyer for a foodservice operation purchased a large bag of carrots. Assume also that the carrots were not stored properly, resulting in a loss of 20 percent of the bag's contents. Further, assume that through poor preparation and cooking techniques, another 20 percent of the product was lost. Finally, assume that because of poor postproduction storage techniques, another 20 percent of the product was lost. In this example, more than half of the carrots purchased did not make it onto plates for the operation's guests. If such a food production situation actually existed, it would clearly be the job of management (likely assisted by those responsible for purchasing) to correct the problem. In a similar manner, if a business's financial resources are being needlessly spent on essential services such as utilities and waste removal, corrective action should be taken.

In the hospitality industry, some essential services costs can be controlled onsite. Through **source reduction**, however, these costs can be controlled even prior to the arrival of needed products.

As a result, a complete understanding of essential services cost control involves encouraging both source reduction and effective on-site conservation efforts.

Source Reduction   The removal of solid wastes is expensive. Many hospitality businesses have encouraged manufacturers who ship products to them to practice source reduction and have aggressively implemented creative programs to reduce the amount of solid waste they generate in their operations. Source reduction means decreasing the amount of materials or energy used during the manufacturing or distribution of products and packages. Because it stops waste before it starts, source reduction is the top solid waste priority of the U.S. Environmental

---

Did You Know? (12.2)

The focus of this text is the skills and knowledge needed by professionals buying items for use in the hospitality industry. Strictly speaking, then, all such professional buyers should be "conservationists" because they should want to buy no more of any product or service than that absolutely needed by their businesses. This includes natural resources.

Not only is conserving energy and reducing waste cost effective, but it is good for business because increasingly guests patronize those businesses that they believe are committed to preserving natural resources. This is evidenced by the growing concern among many guests (and restaurateurs) about filling local landfills with millions of plastic water bottles, the contents of which were perhaps only marginally superior to the water found in local utility company water lines.

Green is the generic term used for those programs and individuals in many areas of society who are concerned with conserving natural resources. In the hospitality industry, there is the Green Restaurant Association (GRA). To learn more about this group's philosophy and its goals, go to www.dinegreen.com. Also, click on "Find a Restaurant" to review a listing of participating properties.

Buyer's Guide to Purchasing Term

Source reduction   The effort by product manufacturers to design and ship products to minimize waste resulting from the products' shipment and delivery.

Protection Agency (EPA), the federal agency whose mission since its formation in 1970 is to protect human health and the environment.

Source reduction is not the same as recycling. Recycling is collecting already used materials and making them into another product. Recycling begins at the end of a product's life, while source reduction first takes place when the product and its packaging are being designed. Perhaps the best way to think about source reduction and recycling is as complementary activities: combined, source reduction and recycling have a significant effect on preventing solid waste as well as conserving natural (and financial) resources.

Source reduction conserves raw material and energy resources because smaller packages and concentrated products typically use fewer materials and less energy to manufacture, pack, and ship. The result is lower purchase prices for products. Source reduction also cuts back on what has to be thrown away, which helps keep solid waste disposal costs down.

Specific source reduction strategies that can be implemented by hospitality buyers include the following:

- *Purchasing concentrated products*   Many cleaning products, for example, have been reformulated to use less product to do the same job.
- *Buy the largest size container that can be used efficiently*   This is a good idea for many reasons. First, purchase unit prices for larger quantities of items are typically lower. Also, the amount of packaging materials used will be reduced, thus conserving natural resources. Finally, the cost of disposing of the packaging materials will be less.
- *Buy refill systems whenever possible*   These systems eliminate the shipping of duplicate dispensing products (self-dispensed hand soaps and disinfectants for employee hand washing are an example).

ON-SITE EFFORTS   Addressing energy conservation is important to profits, to the environment, and to your customers. According to the EPA, saving just 20 percent a year on energy operating costs can increase the profits shown on a restaurant's income statement by as much as one-third.

In many cases using simple preventive maintenance programs for equipment and remembering to turn off equipment and lights when they are not in use can significantly decrease utility bills. While professional purchasers wanting specific recommendations on how to conserve energy and reduce utility purchases will have no difficulty locating them (just enter "hospitality energy savings" into your favorite search engine), the following are examples of specific

Because many guests buy at peak times, energy-using equipment in busy restaurants such as this one can often be turned off or operated at reduced temperatures between each rush.

© acksonville Journal-Courier/The Image Works

utility conservation steps foodservice buyers can recommend and facility managers can easily implement.

Conservation of Electricity

✓ Replace old incandescent-bulb fixtures with ones that use fluorescent bulbs, which last longer and use less energy.

✓ Replace electrical cooking equipment and water heaters with gas units.

✓ Replace air-cooled (fan-cooled) ice machines with water-cooled units.

✓ Clean refrigerator and freezer condenser coils at least once every three months.

Conservation of Water

✓ Serve water to guests only on request.

✓ Install low-pressure prerinse spray valves in dishwashing areas.

✓ Thaw foods in the refrigerator rather than under running water.

✓ Install water-efficient (low-water-usage) toilets in guest and employee restrooms.

Conservation of HVAC-Related Utilities

✓ Have all HVAC equipment professionally serviced at least twice per year.

✓ Replace electric water heaters in dishwashers with gas heaters.

✓ Ensure walls, windows, ceilings, and foundations are properly insulated to avoid heat or cooling loss.

✓ Consider the installation of energy-management systems that automatically reduce thermostat settings when the operation is closed.

ESSENTIAL SERVICES BILLING

Like any other product or service, when professional buyers purchase essential services such as electricity, water, and HVAC fuels, they would like to pay what they owe, but no more. Unfortunately, for several reasons, purchasing an item

Buyers at Work (12.2)

"What are you reading, Pauline?" asked Eugene.

Eugene was the night foodservices supervisor at Oak Hills Regional Hospital, the largest medical facility in one of the rural areas of the Appalachian Mountains. The hospital had two separate dining rooms, connected to a common kitchen, one of which served staff, the other, hospital visitors. Eugene supervised dinner operations in the smaller room. Pauline was responsible for the larger dining area.

"Well," replied Pauline as she put down her copy of *Foodservice Director*, a monthly trade magazine read by many health-care foodservice professionals. "It's a fascinating article about energy loss due to worn or faulty refrigerator and freezer gaskets. The amount of energy that can be lost when doors don't fit tightly is incredible. Fixing them can save a lot of money."

"Who cares?" replied Eugene. "We don't pay for energy. There isn't even a line on our monthly departmental operating income statement for it. There's no way they can tell how much electricity we use in foodservice. It all comes in on one meter, so it's one bill, and the hospital pays it. Actually, we could use as much electricity as we want, and it wouldn't affect us."

Consider Eugene's response and assume that he was correct about the structure of his facility's income statement.

1. What would be your reply to Eugene if you were Pauline?
2. What would be your reply to Eugene if you were the individual responsible for the budget used to heat, cool, and power the hospital?
3. What would be your reply to Eugene if you were on the hospital's board of directors?

PROFESSIONAL PURCHASING PREVENTS PROBLEMS (12.4)

"Table for Two by the Window? . . . Right This Way"

A common problem: In some sunny climates, exterior windows allow for natural lighting and great scenery, but the same sunlight can cause significant heat buildup in the operation, greatly increasing air-conditioning costs.

In warmer climates exterior building windows can be attractive but can also significantly increase the costs of cooling the building. Draperies and blinds can block out the sun, but using them eliminates the guests' view of the outside. Architects address this problem by recommending the use of special Low-E window coatings. Low-E coatings are microscopically thin, virtually invisible materials used to cover exterior windows and reduce heat from the sun. Coating a glass surface with a Low-E material lowers the total heat flow through the window (and into the building). Low-E coatings are reasonably priced and are transparent in normal light; thus, they can often be an excellent option for hospitality buyers seeking to minimize facility utility costs while maximizing the use of natural lighting.

---

such as electricity is not as easy as buying a case of lettuce or a dozen wine goblets. For example, those who buy electricity do not actually see what they have purchased. The results of electricity consumption may be easy to see, but the product itself is invisible, so it is not always easy to know how much of the product was delivered. Second, while hospitality buyers are familiar with terms such as *cases, pounds, ounces,* and *dozens,* fewer buyers would immediately recognize the terms **KwH, CCF,** or **decatherm,** yet these are the most common purchase units for electricity, water, and natural gas, respectively.

It is also important to understand that utilities are an item in which the amount purchased is not completely in the hands of the buyer. Consider, for

---

Did You Know? (12.3)

ENERGY STAR is a joint program of the EPA and the U.S. Department of Energy designed to help save money and protect the environment through energy efficient products and practices. In 1992 the EPA introduced ENERGY STAR as a voluntary labeling program designed to identify and promote energy-efficient products. Computers and monitors were the first labeled products. Through 1995 the EPA expanded the label to additional office equipment products and residential heating and cooling equipment. In 1996 the EPA collaborated with the U.S. Department of Energy for specific product categories. The ENERGY STAR label is now on major appliances, office equipment, lighting, home electronics, and more. The EPA has also extended the label to cover new homes and commercial and industrial buildings. To learn more about specific ideas related to energy conservation, go to www.energystar.gov. When you arrive, click on "Buildings & Plants" and review their lists of specific recommendations (by category) for saving money through energy conservation.

Buyer's Guide to Purchasing Terms

KwH Short for kilowatt hour. It is the measurement used to calculate electricity usage. It may also be abbreviated as "kW·h" or "kWh."

CCF Short for "one hundred cubic feet." It is one measurement used to calculate water usage.

Decatherm The measurement used to calculate natural gas usage. One decatherm is equal to one million British thermal units (BTUs).

example, the foodservice guest who forgets and leaves the hot water in the restroom sink running after leaving that room. Alternatively, consider the chef who elects (improperly) to use running hot water to thaw frozen vegetable packages in a kitchen sink. In both cases the essential services consumption (electricity to operate the water pumps, the water itself, gas to heat the water, and sewage charges to dispose of the water) will rise needlessly.

Lastly, utilities such as electricity, water (and sewage services), and natural gas are typically metered products. Thus, the amount consumed is determined based on beginning and ending time period meter readings.

Electricity

The electric bills assessed to a hospitality business are determined by two main factors: (1) the amount of electrical usage and (2) the time period in which the electricity was used. Electricity usage is measured by the kilowatt hour. The formula for a kilowatt hour is as follows:

$$(\text{Number of watts generated} \times \text{Number of hours generated})/1,000$$
$$= \text{Kilowatt hours generated}$$

To illustrate, consider a restaurant with an exit sign. The sign is set up with two fifty-watt light bulbs (100 W total) and left on for ten hours per day. The exit sign will consume one thousand watt-hours, or one kilowatt hour per day [$(2 \times 50) \times 10)/1,000 = 1$].

If a power company charges $0.10 per KwH, then those two light bulbs will cost the operation $0.10 per day, or $0.70 over the course of a seven-day week. It is easy to see why products that are efficient users of energy (watts) and result in lower operational electric bills are highly desirable.

Electric bills are also affected by time. Unlike some other energy sources, electricity must be produced as it is needed. As a result, most electricity providers penalize (by charging higher rates) those users who consume large amounts of electricity during peak consumption periods. Rates charged per KwH used are often lower during nonpeak consumption periods.

Like most utility services, electricity is a metered product. As a result, the actual electricity bill received by a business will include the following information, all of which is important to the buyer responsible for billing accuracy and, thus, must be carefully examined:

Customer name   Just like other vendors, utility companies can make billing errors, including sending the wrong invoice to the wrong business, so this information should be carefully examined.

Billing date   The date this bill was printed.

Due date   The date your bill for the month is due. This is important because significant late payment charges will likely be added to overdue bills.

Type of service   Typically, a code that indicates the type of service (commercial, home, and the like) provided. An explanation of your code(s) will likely be found on the back of your bill.

Reading date   The date your meter was read (or estimated).

Number of days   The number of days between your present and previous meter readings. It shows the number of days of service covered by this bill and may vary by as many as two to seven days from the number of days in the prior billing period or that of the previous year (which must be considered before making prior year bill comparisons).

Meter readings   These numbers are the dial readings, which appear on the face of your meter. If this number has been estimated (because the meter was not actually read), the fact that it is an estimate will be noted by the utility provider.

Severe weather is just one of several potential reasons for the estimation of a utility meter reading.

AP Wide World Photos

Difference   The amount of electricity consumed. It is derived by subtracting the previous period meter reading from the present period meter reading.

Temperature differences (optional)   This column, when present, compares the average outdoor temperature of the current billing period to the average temperature of the previous month and year.

Usage differences (optional)   This column, when present, compares the actual usage by the operation during the current billing period to the average usage in the previous month as well as the previous year.

The electric bills generated by local utility companies are often difficult to read, yet it is critical that those responsible for ensuring their accuracy understand them well. A good place to begin is in the customer service department of the local utility, where the utility provider's representative and the operation's utility buyer should perform a line-by-line review of a typical monthly bill.

Water/Sewage

Water billings for hospitality operations typically consist of two main parts: the purchase unit and the price per unit. Hospitality buyers are likely to encounter one of two purchase units depending on the preference of the utility company supplying their water. Some buyers purchase water by the 100 CCF. (*Note:* One CCF equals 748 gallons of water, so for example, a water bill for usage of 1,525 CCF would represent 1,140,770 gallons of water [1,525 CCF × 748 gallons per CCF = 1,140,770 gallons]).

Alternatively, a local water provider may bill businesses based on the **Cgal,** a unit representing one hundred gallons. In the previous example of an operation using 1,140,770 gallons of water, the billing for that quantity would be 11,407 Cgals (1,140,770 gallons used / 100 gallons per Cgal = 11,407 Cgals used).

Like electricity, water is a metered product, so it is important that buyers periodically test the accuracy of water meters, replacing them if any questions arise about their precision. In most utility districts, sewage charges are not metered

---

Buyer's Guide to Purchasing Term

Cgal   Short for "hundred gallons"; a measurement to calculate water usage.

separately but, instead, are tied to water usage. The rationale for doing so is that, in a home or business, all water entering the building is likely to end up going down the drain at some point. Thus, sewage billings typically include a flat charge for sewage access and a sewage use charge tied directly to water usage. Due to the nature of billing sewage charges, it is easy to see why water used for landscaping or other purposes that will not require use of the utility entity's sewage treatment system be metered separately when the business is permitted to do so.

HVAC Fuels

In many geographic areas, natural gas or liquefied petroleum gas (also known as LPG, LP-gas, or even more commonly, propane) may be used to heat water and air. In foodservice operations, the overwhelming majority of chefs and cooks also prefer natural gas when cooking because of its rapid heat production and the degree of temperature control it allows. Managed properly, gas is an extremely safe and cost-effective source of energy.

Hospitality buyers purchasing natural gas may also encounter one of two different purchase units depending on the preference of their gas provider. Like electricity and water, gas is a metered product. On some meters, gas usage is measured by volume in **Mcf** (one thousand cubic feet) units.

Increasingly, however, gas consumers are demanding (and gas vendors are responding by supplying) gas bills metered in decatherms. This is important because

- the energy-producing ability of gas varies based on many product characteristics, including quality, origin, and purity.
- the volume of gas delivered is affected by the altitude at which it is delivered.
- the volume of gas delivered is affected by the temperature at which it is delivered.

As a result, most professional buyers believe gas bills measured in decatherms are a better indication of product usage for their hospitality operations than are those generated using Mcf.

Solid Waste

Solid waste removal charges (garbage, trash, and recycled materials) are generally dictated by at least three factors:

1. The number of waste containers supplied by the vendor
2. The size of waste containers supplied by the vendor
3. The frequency (number of times per week or month period) at which the waste containers are emptied

Effective buyers of waste removal services work with their vendors to manipulate the three factors above to minimize costs while optimizing service levels.

PURCHASING ADDITIONAL SERVICES

Some services such as electrical power, water, and other utilities must be purchased. Buyers have no choice. The purchase of some other services can, to a large degree, be viewed as optional. Consider the buyer for a restaurant located in the suburbs of a large Midwestern city. It is certainly not mandatory for the buyer to

---

Buyer's Guide to Purchasing Term

Mcf   Short for "one thousand cubic feet"; a measurement used to calculate natural gas usage.

select and employ a snow removal service. A decision not to secure such a service, however, is likely to meet with disaster the several times per winter when the restaurant's large parking area will be impassable due to significant snowfall. As this example illustrates, professional hospitality buyers will, of necessity, identify a variety of services that must be performed for or provided to their operations. Some additional examples include payroll processing, linen services, pest control, ventilation hood cleaning, window washing, exterior building maintenance, landscaping and/or lawn care, and parking lot lighting and maintenance.

For those buyers responsible for securing services such as the above, two issues are paramount. The first is the initial decision of whether to perform the service **in-house** or to outsource the same activity. Second, if the decision is made to outsource the service activity, buyers must then use a vendor identification process that results in the selection of a supplier who can consistently provide the needed service at required quality levels.

Considerations in Source Selection

When buyers consider the desirability of performing a required service in-house or contracting for that service with an outside vendor, three major factors must be evaluated:

1. Timing
2. Skill level requirements
3. Continuity requirements

TIMING   The quality of some required services is very dependent on the timing of service delivery. In the example of the Midwestern restaurateur securing snowplowing services, a delay of several hours (or days) in providing the plow service will make a significant difference in its quality because the need for plowing is immediate and cannot be delayed. Alternatively, however, if the same restaurant determined that its plants, shrubs, and trees required once-per-year fertilization, a service-delivery delay of days or even weeks may not be considered significant. Buyers evaluating the importance of service timing must firmly establish just how important timing of delivery will be to their ultimate evaluation of service quality.

SKILL LEVEL REQUIREMENTS   In many cases the delivery of a service requires highly skilled individuals and very specialized tools or equipment. Thus, for example, the tools and equipment needed to clean a kitchen's vent hoods may, in one geographic area, be owned and properly operated by only a few service providers. Because the service is needed only infrequently, it simply may not be in the best interest of the restaurant to invest in the equipment and training needed to perform this service in-house. Additional examples of areas in which technical complexity is so advanced that (in all but the largest of operations) services would likely be outsourced include computer and telephone systems repair; HVAC component repair and replacement; the servicing of kitchen equipment; provision of pest control services; cleaning of draft beer lines; and masonry, carpentry, and electrical work. Other outsourced services commonly include specialized tasks such as management recruitment, payroll processing, and legal and tax services.

Buyer's Guide to Purchasing Term

In-house (service)   The situation that exists when a business's employees are used to perform a needed service.

CONTINUITY REQUIREMENTS In some cases a hospitality buyer can move easily between performing a service in-house and using an outside vendor. Thus, for example, a restaurant may determine that in-house staff will perform minor spot cleaning of dining room carpets. The periodic complete cleaning of the carpets, however, may be subcontracted to an outside vendor. Both of the above activities could be undertaken without conflict. In cases such as payroll processing, however, frequently moving back and forth between in-house service delivery and the use of an outside vendor would be impractical.

In general, when an operation must make a significant investment in staff training and equipment acquisition to provide a service in-house, it will likely be most cost effective to continue providing the service in-house. When timing, skill level, and continuity requirements point to the use of an outside vendor, professional buyers must purchase those services. In these situations they must turn their attention to securing appropriate supplier bids followed by the selection of their preferred service provider.

Securing Service Provider Bids

The use of purchase specifications and a positive relationship with vendors are just as important when buying services as when you buy hospitality products. These two factors are interrelated. Service providers can only hope to fulfill buyers' expectations if they understand fully the work that they are expected to accomplish. When you buy services, a service specification that details precisely the service you seek, as well as any important contract terms related to the service, is crucial if a positive supplier relationship is to be established and maintained.

When professional buyers have thoroughly identified the services they seek, they should ask potential vendors to submit a written bid for supplying those services. A bid is simply an opportunity for potential suppliers to submit their charge for performing a particular service. In most cases buyers requesting bids

Buyers at Work (12.3)

In response to a telephone inquiry, Brenan's Arbor Services offered to trim the wind-damaged branches from a large oak tree on the lawn outside the entrance to the Outrigger Restaurant for a fee of $1,500.00. The service was needed because a recent storm had severely damaged the tree, and A.J., the restaurant's manager, was afraid the damaged branches still in the tree might fall and hit a guest, employee, or another person entering the restaurant.

A.J., again by telephone, agreed to the price quoted by Brenan's, as well as to a start date of Monday. At noon on Monday, Brenan's informed A.J. that the job was completed. The tree trimming went fine, and a large amount of wood, branches, and some leaves from the tree were left neatly piled near the tree's base. A.J. inquired about the removal of the debris and especially the dozen or so four-foot logs created by the removal of some of the largest damaged branches. The Brenan's representative stated that the removal of logs and branches had never been discussed and, thus, was not included in the quoted price.

A.J. agreed that the topic of waste removal was never discussed but stated that it is generally assumed that when a company trims a tree, it will remove the brush it generates; therefore, he refused to pay until all of the brush, including the logs, was removed.

1. Assume you were a small-claims court judge and this case appeared before you. In your opinion, which party to this service contract has the more valid argument? How would you resolve the issue between the two parties?
2. Based on your knowledge of procurement principles, what specific errors did A.J. make when entering into this services contract?

will use one of two alternative bid systems. A **closed-bid** system is one in which a potential supplier submits a formal, written, and confidential price quote to the buyer. Usually all closed bids are opened and reviewed by the buyer at the same time, with the job awarded to the lowest bidder who meets fully the bid's specifications. An **open-bid** system is more informal and is often used when time is a critical factor.

For example, assume that a broken pipe located on the second floor of a downtown building that houses a restaurant on the first floor results in severe flooding and damage to the restaurant. In such a case, the restaurant will likely seek the services of a water-extraction-services company. Time will likely be of the essence because the longer the water is in contact with the restaurant's ceiling, walls, carpets, carpet pads, and furnishings, the greater the damage to the facility. In such a case, the development of bid requirements followed by a formal closed-bid system is unrealistic. In this situation open bids, characterized by immediate response to the bid request, as well as immediate bidder selection would make more sense.

Selecting Service Providers

Professional hospitality buyers understand that, when selecting a service provider, price is an important factor. Price is, however, only one factor among many and, in the case of a service provider, price is rarely, if ever, the most critical selection factor. More important is the quality of service provided, the reputation of the vendor, and the willingness of service suppliers to stand behind, or warrant, their work.

As you learned in Chapter 1, warranties specify the conditions under which the service provider will make repairs or fix other problems that may arise at no additional cost to the buyer. A written warranty typically describes how long the warranty remains in effect as well as which repairs will be made, or services provided, at no extra charge. Most suppliers of services routinely warranty their work as part of their normal pricing. Experienced buyers, however, always make sure they are informed (in writing whenever possible) about the specific terms of the warranty.

EVALUATION OF SERVICE PROVIDERS

Buyers generally evaluate the quality of products they buy when the purchased items are delivered. In a similar manner, when vendors provide services, the quality of service provided must be evaluated. There are two reasons for doing so. First, before authorizing payment for the vendor's services, you must be sure the service purchased has been performed. While this might seem easy, in the case of some services (e.g., hood vent cleaning or ice machine preventive maintenance), it may not be so easy to determine if the work has been completed satisfactorily.

Secondly, when a purchased service will likely be purchased again in the future (e.g., lawn care, equipment repair, pest control, or tax preparation) the quality of service provided must be evaluated to assess the wisdom of reusing the same service provider.

Buyer's Guide to Purchasing Terms

Closed bid   A method of price solicitation in which confidential bids are submitted to be opened at a predetermined place and time. Also called a "sealed bid" or "confidential bid."

Open bid   A method of price solicitation in which bids are submitted and evaluated as they are received. In this system the buyer may evaluate price as well as speed of response when awarding the bid.

While professional buyers would agree on the necessity of evaluating service providers, they would also agree about the complexity of doing so. This is because the evaluation of services is generally more complex than the evaluation of products. The reason this is true are many and include the following:

Honest differences of opinion   In many cases the quality of a service cannot be easily measured, seen, or touched. Consequently, honest differences of opinion regarding quality levels can exist between service providers and those who receive the services. In the final analysis, however, the buyer must ultimately determine his or her own view of the quality provided.

Timing of delivery   In many cases a service is produced at the same time it is delivered. For example, the production and delivery of a window washer's service happens at the same time. Unlike a purchased product that can be inspected (and perhaps returned if the buyer is unsatisfied) quality inspection of services typically happens *after* the vendor has performed the work. In such situations it is not surprising that sometimes the vendor and the buyer may differ on whether the service has been delivered as they had agreed.

Irregular delivery   Service quality and consistency is subject to variation in delivery simply because they are delivered by *people* and human behavior is difficult to control. Professional buyers in the foodservice business are well aware that their own customers can sometimes experience uneven service levels when dining. In a similar manner, service vendors must employ individuals to deliver their services, and as a result, the quality of service delivered can vary by time of day (people get tired), experience, attitude, knowledge, style, and even friendliness of the vendor's staff.

To illustrate, consider two lawn-services companies. The first has well-groomed, friendly, and professionally dressed employees whose lawn care maintenance abilities are average. Employees of the second company are surly, slovenly in appearance, and often arrive one or two days later than their scheduled time. These employees, however, are not merely good at what they do, they are spectacular. For days after they trim the operation's landscaping, incoming customers make positive comments about how pretty the grounds are. Which company truly provides quality lawn care? As a professional buyer, you must make the decision.

Despite the challenges involved, all buyers must evaluate the quality of services provided by the vendors they choose. When you select a service provider, it is part of your job to follow through. Doing so ensures that the supplier has fully

The grooming and attire of service providers affects buyers' perceptions of service quality; a point that is well understood by managers in the hospitality industry.

Getty Images, Inc.

complied with the service specifications you established and that the work performed meets or exceeds your established quality standards.

Buyer's Guide to Internet Resources: Technology Products and Services

Web Site	Topic
www.dinegreen.com	Green Restaurant Association
www.epa.gov	Environmental Protection Agency
www.energystar.gov	Energy conservation information
www.ecomagination.com	Manufacturer's conservation site
www.aga.org	Advantages of gas use (American Gas Association)
www.hospitalitynet.org	Energy-saving tips for hospitality businesses
www.dulley.com	Energy-saving tips for all businesses
www.ase.org	Energy-efficiency activities worldwide
www.perfect.com	E-procurement systems
www.amazon.com	Books about evaluating service levels

Purchasing Terms

Field representative *336*

Buddy-punching *338*

Interfaced *339*

Credit card *343*

Debit card *343*

Merchant services provider (MSP) *343*

Closed-circuit television (CCTV) *345*

Professional trade association *346*

Utilities *348*

HVAC *348*

Curb appeal *349*

Foot-candle *349*

Incandescent (lamp) *350*

Electric discharge (lamp) *350*

Boiler *351*

Source reduction *353*

KwH *356*

CCF *356*

Decatherm *356*

Cgal *358*

Mcf *359*

In-house (service) *360*

Closed bid *362*

Open bid *362*

Make Your Own Purchasing Decisions

1. Some hospitality purchasers feel their companies should invest heavily in new technology to give their employees the most advanced work tools available. Other buyers express reservations about many of these new products, feeling they may be too complex for their employees to use easily. What specific factors will you consider as you determine when a new technology product is so valuable it is worth the training costs that may be required for that product's successful implementation?

2. Based on your knowledge of the hospitality industry, do you feel it leads or falls behind other industries in applying advanced technology products and services to its day-to-day operations? As a professional buyer, what role do you think a purchaser should play in influencing the technology-related purchasing decisions of the organization in which he or she works? Be prepared to defend your answers.

3. Older foodservice facilities are often less energy efficient than newer ones. Research and identify five specific energy-saving strategies that you, as a professional buyer of utilities, might recommend to the owners/managers of a foodservice facility that is more than twenty years old.

4. Some foodservice operators feel the implementation of energy-saving activities is justified only when the savings from such activities will exceed their costs. Others believe conservation is the responsibility of all businesses even if the amount spent on conservation activities exceeds potential savings. What is your position?

5. Some hospitality buyers feel it is appropriate to share one service vendor's open bid with another potential vendor who has yet to bid. Do you feel that position is ethical? Why or why not?

13

Purchasing Capital Equipment

Purchasing Pros Need to Know!

For most buyers, the day-to-day purchases made involve selecting the normal food and nonfood supplies required to produce the items on their operations' menus. From time to time, however, nearly all buyers will be confronted with the task of purchasing capital equipment.

In this chapter *capital equipment* refers to those items used by a business to generate income and that have an expected life of more than one year. Examples in the foodservice industry include items such as tables, chairs, light fixtures, and carpets in dining areas, and refrigerators, freezers, and cooking equipment in kitchen areas.

If you find it somewhat odd to think of a chair or a table as a piece of equipment, you are not alone. The types of capital equipment purchased vary, and many buyers use the term *capital* or *capital expenditure* when referring to any of these purchases. Other buyers prefer the industry shorthand term *FF&E* (furniture, fixtures, and equipment) when referring to their capital purchases. Regardless of the term you use, the buying of capital items is different from that of buying normal operating supplies, and in this chapter you will learn about some of these important differences.

Because capital items are most often more expensive than normal operating supplies, the manner in which they are financed when you buy them will likely be different. In some cases the decision will be made to pay cash for a capital item. In other situations a long- or short-term loan may be used to pay for the item. In still other cases, buyers may elect to lease rather than purchase a capital item. The chapter examines these strategies and the effect they have on the financial statements of the business.

In the concluding section of this chapter, you will learn that government entities write tax codes that directly affect business investments. As a result, tax considerations can often determine the wisdom of a specific capital purchase decision. Taxes are not voluntary contributions. Most businesspersons want to pay the taxes they owe but no more than they owe. To better understand the tax results of capital expenditures, this chapter (and the text) ends with an examination of how purchasing capital equipment can affect the amount of tax owed by a business.

■ ■ ■

Outline

Special Aspects of Capital Purchases
    Accounting for Capital Purchases
    Approval of Capital Purchases
Assessing Capital Equipment Needs
    Input on Decision Making
    Determining Replacement Needs
    Future Needs
    Influence of Competition
Furnishings, Fixtures, and Equipment Purchasing Goals

SPECIAL ASPECTS OF CAPITAL PURCHASES

Capital equipment refers to an item that is expected to benefit a business for more than one year. Thus, furniture, **fixtures,** and equipment **(FF&E)** are all considered capital purchases.

Technically, items such as metal spoons used in the kitchen or glassware used for serving guests are also considered capital equipment. Because the per-unit cost of these items is relatively small, however, they are typically considered capital equipment when they are first purchased, but their normal replacements (as spoons are lost or glasses are broken) are considered supplies rather than capital expenditures and are accounted for differently. Land and buildings are also capital purchases but are purchased only when first developing the typical food-service operation. In this chapter only those capital expenditures that do not include the purchase of land or buildings will be examined.

Accounting for Capital Purchases

In previous chapters you learned about purchasing foods, beverages, and services. These are most often considered normal operating costs and, for accounting purposes, are reported as an expense on the financial records of a business in the same month they are purchased. Thus, for example, prime ribs purchased in the month of December to be served at a banquet in that same month would be listed on the restaurant's December income and expense statement as an expense incurred in that month.

Consider, however, the cost of the oven used to roast the prime ribs. Because the oven has an expected life of more than one year (and perhaps as many as twenty or thirty years), hospitality accountants would list the cost and value of the oven on the company's balance sheet. For purposes of accounting for its monthly cost, the oven would be subject to the rules of **depreciation.** As a result, hospitality accountants recording the cost of the oven (like the costs of other capital equipment) would spread its expense over several years (rather than fully expense it in the month in which it was purchased).

Buyer's Guide to Purchasing Terms

Capital equipment   Assets with a useful life of more than one year that are used by the hospitality operation to produce products and/or provide services.

Fixture   Something that is permanently attached to a building as an essential or structural part (e.g., plumbing fixtures and lighting fixtures).

FF&E   Short for "furniture, fixtures, and equipment."

Depreciation   A method of allocating the cost of an asset over the useful life of the asset.

The net effect of using this depreciation-related generally accepted accounting principle **(GAAP)** is that capital expenditures have a different effect on an operation's financial statements and resulting tax liabilities than do normal operating expenses.

In addition to how they are treated for accounting purposes, there are other significant differences between capital expenditures and the purchase of normal operating supplies. For example, if a buyer purchases a fifty-pound bag of onions and finds the flavor of the onions to be inferior, it is not a big problem to change vendors to improve the quality of product in the future.

Consider, however, if the purchase involved an expensive machine used to slice or chop the onions. Assume a poor purchase choice was made and the machine chosen is inferior in operation and dependability when it is compared to other such machines. In this case the inferior piece of capital equipment will have to be used for many years or replaced at additional expense to the hospitality operation. Thus, decisions about capital purchases can have a very long-lasting positive or negative effect on the buyer's operation.

Approval of Capital Purchases

In business the term *capital* is synonymous with *money*. Those who invest their capital understand that, in most industries (including hospitality), investing money can be risky. Thus, effective capital purchasing seeks not only to secure quality products, but also to minimize business risk.

As you learned previously, capital expenditures are recorded on a business's balance sheet, while operating expenses are normally recorded on the income and expense statement. Capital expenditures typically are more costly than those related to daily operating expenses, and the owners of a business pay particularly close attention to them. In fact, because of their critical nature, in most cases only a company's owners can approve capital expenditures. As a result, even those buyers with a good deal of responsibility and authority will likely find their capital purchase expenditures closely reviewed by those responsible for providing the funds used to buy the equipment.

Buyers choosing capital equipment recognize that their purchase decisions have long-term effects because the equipment chosen will be used for many years.

Tim Hall/Photodisc/Getty Images

Buyer's Guide to Purchasing Term

GAAP   Short for "generally accepted accounting principle"; a set of accounting rules used to standardize financial reporting.

Did You Know? (13.1)

Most hospitality managers spend a good deal of time developing budgets. They are important because the management of a business's cash and other financial resources must be planned. If, for example, a foodservice manager knows that revenues will be high next month, it will be important to budget for more labor to serve higher guest counts. Similarly, that manager will need to purchase additional food and beverage products to ensure the operation does not run out of its menu items. It is easy to see why the ability to effectively budget revenue and operating expenses is a critical skill.

Capital budgets are a special form of budget that managers and buyers must also understand. A capital budget is a long-range plan that identifies capital expenditures that should be undertaken as well as when these expenses should be incurred. For example, the manager of a restaurant may be required to provide the operation's owners with answers to the following questions:

When should the parking lot be repaved?

When should dining room tables and chairs be replaced?

How often must bathroom areas be renovated?

How old should our ranges and ovens be before they are replaced?

Note that questions of this nature require buyers to understand customer perceptions and product quality concerns as well as issues about useful product life. For owners, too little investment of capital (too small a capital budget) can result in excessive labor costs, reduced sales, and negative customer perceptions of the property. Too much capital investment (too large a capital budget), however, can mean fewer profits are generated relative to the amount of money invested. To become truly valued advisers, professional hospitality buyers must learn to identify quality capital items, and they must also be able to advise owners about the right time to buy them.

ASSESSING CAPITAL EQUIPMENT NEEDS

Now that you know about capital expenditures, their importance, and how they vary from operational expenses, it is essential you understand why assessing the need for capital purchases is much more complex than assessing noncapital purchasing needs. The critical factors affecting capital purchases decision-making are, in very significant ways, different from those required for normal operating expenses.

Buyers responsible for selecting capital equipment will find the process is influenced by several unique factors, including the following:

- Input on decision making
- Determining replacement needs
- Future needs
- Influence of competition

Input on Decision Making

When hospitality buyers purchase items such as fresh produce and meats normally used in their foodservice operations or condiments placed on dining tables, few preapprovals are likely necessary. In fact, after purchase specifications have been established for products such as these, no one other than the buyer may need

Buyer's Guide to Purchasing Term

Capital budget A long-term plan identifying capital equipment and other assets to be purchased, as well as when to purchase them.

to authorize their purchase. When purchasing capital items, however, the individuals and groups that provide input can be diverse in perspective and influence. The most important of these include the following:

Owners You have learned that a business's owners are the ultimate providers of investment funds and, thus, the money required for capital expenditures. Because they must take ultimate responsibility for any capital purchase, it is logical that these individuals have a significant voice in the selection and approval of FF&E items. Buyers must understand that there are always pressures from managers, employees, customers, and potential vendors to improve or upgrade capital items. What manager, for example, would not want to have newer equipment, furnishings, and the latest in technological advancements? In the final analysis, however, the cost to purchase these items must be justified, and the individuals to whom they must be justified are the owners of the business.

Buyers As a professional buyer who is respected by your business's owners, you will have a significant voice in the selection of capital items. You must be knowledgeable about product quality and product life cycles and, when you show your understanding about these factors, your opinions about the wisdom of a specific capital purchase will be strongly considered.

End users In most cases it is highly advisable to seek the input of end users when contemplating a capital purchase. Consider, for example, the restaurant owner/operator who will be selecting a new range for use in the kitchen. The purchase price of the new range will be between $5,000 and $10,000. It would simply make sense to seek input about the best type of range (gas or electric) and its size, desirable features, ease of use, and cleaning concerns from those who will use the range. The cooks using the range should not determine which should be purchased, but professional buyers should seek, whenever possible, useful input from those workers who will be most affected by the capital purchase.

FF&E vendors It might seem unusual for vendors to be listed in a group of individuals from whom capital expenditure advice should be sought. However, information they provide can be important. For example, when buyers consider options related to warranties, service and repair availability, and compatibility with current equipment, vendors can be very helpful. Of course, professional buyers understand that the natural tendency of FF&E vendors will be toward increased, not decreased, capital expenditures. Despite that concern, knowledgeable buyers can take advantage of this valuable source of information and use what they learn to make better buying decisions.

Financial advisers Because capital purchases typically involve large sums of money, the input of a business's financial managers or accountants is often sought prior to making an FF&E purchase decision. Many hospitality businesses experience differences in cash flows (see Chapter 1) that make funds more available in some time periods than in others. When the timing of a capital expenditure significantly affects the amount of cash a business has to pay its other expenses such as payroll, utilities, taxes, and vendor invoices, the input of financial advisers can be critical. In addition to cash flow management, financial managers may be more experienced in negotiating with vendors about payment schedules, financing, and related payment terms.

Determining Replacement Needs

Because furnishings and equipment wear out, some FF&E purchases must be made simply to maintain predetermined quality levels. As a result, professional buyers must be aware of the condition of all their operation's FF&E items. Carpets, tables, chairs, booths, stools, bar tops, and kitchen equipment are examples of hospitality

Normal wear and tear will mean that this operation's tables, chairs, and carpets must be replaced on a regular basis if it is to maintain its elegant feel.

Jeff Greenberg/PhotoEdit Inc.

products that must periodically be replaced simply to maintain quality standards or, when necessary, to meet franchisor-mandated quality standards. Due to normal wear and tear, all hospitality buyers encounter the need to purchase FF&E products simply to replace and maintain their existing capital items.

Future Needs

Often when foodservice operations undertake significant FF&E renovations, it is because the operation is changing its concept (e.g., from one foodservice theme to another) or when a building is converted from a prior use to one involving the service of food and beverages. In such cases buyers are not replacing current FF&E items, but rather are purchasing the operation's future FF&E needs. This is a more challenging activity because much can be unknown about the actual FF&E needs of the business because it is not yet in operation.

Current and pending legislation may also affect future capital expenditure decisions. When considering remodeling and refurbishing costs, hospitality managers must consider the effect of changing building codes, laws such as the Americans with Disabilities Act (ADA), and other legislation that can directly influence what and when capital items must be purchased. For example, the ADA mandated many changes, including those related to the physical facilities of restaurants, hotels, and clubs. As a result, operators found that capital investments in parking lots, entrance areas, and seating facilities were often required to meet ADA requirements.

Influence of Competition

One of the most significant reasons for investing in FF&E items may be because other businesses do so. The hospitality business is competitive, and organizations that do not invest and reinvest in their physical facilities can discover that their products are perceived by consumers to be out of style or look worn out. Business owners must avoid such negative guest perceptions of their products.

Even when a business's FF&E items are not out of date or worn, they may still need to be replaced, updated, or complemented. For example, many industry observers believe the decision by McDonald's to invest in the coffee-making equipment needed to produce its own line of gourmet coffees was a direct result of the pressures they felt from other high-end coffee sellers such as Starbucks and Caribou Coffee.

Unless he or she is the business's owner as well as the buyer, a purchaser may not have the responsibility to monitor the competition for improvements that may result in the need for capital expenditures. However, monitoring the competition should be a responsibility of some individual or team within the hospitality organization. In some cases, however, it may be you, the professional hospitality buyer, who is given this responsibility.

FURNISHINGS, FIXTURES, AND EQUIPMENT PURCHASING GOALS

Professional buyers in the hospitality industry routinely purchase some FF&E items. The specific items purchased depend on a variety of factors, including the segment of the industry in which the buyer works. In all cases, however, effective FF&E purchasing has four main goals:

1. *A better-looking property*   In many cases FF&E items are purchased for show; that is, they are quite visible to guests. Entrance or lobby areas in restaurants (as well as dining rooms and bar areas) and club houses in private clubs are all examples in which FF&E items have a significant visual effect on guests. As a result, these areas must reflect a level of style, quality, and cleanliness that is in keeping with the image the business seeks to project.

2. *A more efficiently operating property*   In many cases FF&E upgrades improve business efficiency. This can occur because of changes in the design of FF&E products themselves (such as when standard toilets are replaced with those that make more efficient use of water that reduces utility bills) or when significant labor savings result. Professional buyers know that, in the final analysis, an FF&E purchase is a business investment. Business owners look more favorably on those investments that reduce costs, increase efficiency, and improve labor productivity than those that do not.

3. *Maximize the effect of FF&E expenditures*   Experienced hospitality managers agree that there never seems to be enough money in their annual FF&E budgets. Owners invest in businesses wisely. In most cases that means that FF&E resources will be expended only when there is a compelling reason to do so. Each dollar dedicated to FF&E replacement must be wisely spent to maximize its effect on the business.

4. *Increased business and more satisfied guests*   Businesses desire growth, and in the hospitality industry, that means serving more guests, serving

Visually stunning dining areas depend on both architectural design and complementary FF&E items.

Mira.com/Artist Name

PROFESSIONAL PURCHASING PREVENTS PROBLEMS (13.1)

"If It Ain't Broke . . . Consider Replacing It Anyway"

A common problem: Some buyers fail to realize the importance of maintaining back-of-house equipment at the same high quality levels as their front-of-house FF&E items.

It is relatively easy to know when the tables, chairs, and carpets in dining areas need to be replaced. It is more difficult for some buyers to recognize when back-of-house equipment has reached the end of its useful life. Dishwashers that are no longer energy efficient, refrigerators that consume excessive electricity, and ranges and ovens that waste energy cost an operation money when they are *not* replaced.

In all fields of production, skilled workers need the right tools if they are to produce high-quality products and perform their tasks efficiently. Too often, kitchen upgrades receive a low-priority status, using the faulty logic that kitchen-related equipment purchases do not produce a good return on the funds invested in them. Major pieces of equipment are sometimes not replaced until they simply cannot be repaired any longer, often resulting in excessive repair costs and lengthy periods of time when equipment is not available for use.

Experienced operators and culinary professionals recognize that it is the menu items produced in the back-of-house areas that keep guests returning to the front-of-house areas. Because that is true, savvy buyers understand both the front and back of house are of equal importance when planning capital equipment purchases.

---

them more frequently, and/or increasing sales to them. Word of mouth, the process of one customer recommending a facility to other customers, has long been recognized as one of the most powerful sources of new business. When FF&E items reflect positively on a business, constructive word of mouth is maximized. Unfortunately, when the appearance of FF&E items results in poor customer perceptions, negative word of mouth can also occur.

Business owners and buyers seeking to achieve their capital expenditure–related goals can view them most easily in terms of their **front-of-house** or **back-of-house** placement.

Front-of-house FF&E include those items found in public restrooms; dining room tables, chairs, and lighting fixtures; and the decor pieces that give a foodservice business its unique style or ambiance. FF&E items in these areas must be kept fresh looking, clean, and in good repair.

Back-of-house FF&E items include food production, cooking, refrigerating, and holding equipment as well as cleaning equipment. In many cases specialized equipment will be needed to support the menu. Then these specialized equipment items (e.g., barbecue meat smokers, rotisseries, and pizza ovens) must be carefully selected if the restaurant is to execute its menu properly.

Buyer's Guide to Purchasing Terms

Front of house Those areas within a food and beverage operation that are readily accessible to guests. Front-of-house areas include public restrooms, lobbies, dining rooms, and bar areas.

Back of house Those areas within a hospitality operation that are not typically accessible to guests. Back-of-house areas include employee locker rooms, kitchens, production areas, and offices. Sometimes called "heart of house."

Buyer's Guide to Internet Resources: Back-of-House Items

Web Site	Topic
www.traulsen.com	Blast chillers
www.vulcanhart.com	Broilers
www.blodgett.com	Convection ovens
www.lincolnfp.com	Conveyor ovens
www.alto-shaam.com	Cook-and-hold ovens
www.advancetabco.com	Custom stainless-steel fabrication
www.frymaster.com	Fryers
www.manitowoc.com	Ice makers
www.hobartcorp.com	Slicers and mixers (12-quart and larger)
www.wolfrange.com	Ranges
www.hennypenny.com	Rotisseries
www.groenkettles.com	Steam-jacketed kettles
www.clevelandrange.com	Steamers
www.truemfg.com	Reach-in refrigeration
www.kolpak.com	Walk-in refrigeration

CAPITAL PURCHASE FINANCING

When a hospitality buyer purchases common operating supplies such as food or beverages, it is typically assumed that the purchase will be paid for shortly after it is delivered. Payment is generally made in the form of an electronic funds transfer from the buyer's bank account, cash, or check and is generally for the full amount of the items' cost.

When purchasing capital items, however, owners can most often choose from a variety of payment or **financing** methods. Used in this manner, the word *financing* simply refers to the method of securing (providing) the money needed to purchase the capital item. Financing alternatives available to buyers include paying cash for their purchases, but several other financing alternatives to full-cash payments are available. A variety of issues can affect decisions regarding the best financing alternative for capital items. These include a fundamental understanding of the **time value of money** and of the earnings made on investments.

Time Value of Money

If you talk about the prices paid by consumers for goods and services with older persons, you will likely discover that many of them are shocked at the prices of today's products. Often they shake their heads in disbelief at their own children's or grandchildren's college tuition bills, the price of gasoline, or the cost of a restaurant meal. These examples all illustrate how the passage of time truly does change

Buyer's Guide to Purchasing Terms

Finance   To provide the money required to make a purchase.

Time value (of money)   The concept that money available for use now is worth more than the same amount in the future, due to its potential earning capacity.

people's view of the worth of a dollar, and they are one key to understanding the time value of money.

To illustrate, assume that you have just won $1,000,000 in a multi-state lottery. As a winner, your options for collecting the money are the following:

A. Receive $1,000,000 now

OR

B. Receive $1,000,000 in three years

If you are like most people, you would choose to receive the $1,000,000 now. This is because most people understand that it makes little sense to postpone a payment until some future time when they could have the exact same amount of money now. At its most basic level, the time value of money demonstrates that, all things being equal, it is better to have money now rather than have it later.

From an investment perspective, those in business also know they can do more with their money if they have it now because they can use it to earn even more money through wise investments. Thus, as a general rule, today's dollars are worth a good bit more than tomorrow's dollars both from a control aspect and from a potential earnings perspective. In fact, the further into the future dollars will be received, the less value they are considered to have. To illustrate further, assume that in 1975 you lent $12,000 to your best friend. The friend promised to pay you back in 2010 and did so. You would immediately recognize that the $12,000 you now have will buy you far less than the $12,000 you lent in 1975 (e.g., the average cost of a gallon of gas in the United States in 1975 was $0.55; the same gallon of gas now costs well more than $3.00).

Closely related to the time value of money is the concept of **return on investment (ROI)**. ROI is the reason investors invest. They wish to take the money they currently have and increase it. If, for example, an investor had $10,000 in cash and could make an investment (in this case, a loan to a business) that would result in the business paying back a total of $11,500 one year later, the investor would have made a $1,500 return on the investment. Such an investment could have been a good one for the business receiving the money, and it could be a good one for the investor (who was *returned* the original $10,000 that was invested plus an additional $1,500).

To illustrate ROI in relation to the purchase of capital equipment, assume a buyer is considering the purchase of a piece of cooking equipment for $5,000. Assume also that this equipment will save the restaurant $1000 per year for a five-year period. The ROI for the piece of equipment can be computed using the following ROI formula:

$$\frac{\text{Money earned on funds invested}}{\text{Funds invested}} = \text{ROI}$$

In this simplified example, the ROI for the piece of capital equipment would be computed as follows:

$$\frac{\$5,000 \text{ earned}}{\$5,000 \text{ invested}} = 1.00, \text{ or } 100\% \text{ over five years}$$

Buyer's Guide to Purchasing Term

Return on investment (ROI)   A ratio that describes the amount of money earned or saved by an investment, when compared to the amount of money originally invested.

On an annual basis, the ROI realized would be:

$$100\%/5 \text{ years} = 20.0\% \text{ per year}$$

In the previous example of the investor making a $10,000 loan to a business and receiving $11,500 one year later, the ROI would be calculated as follows:

$$\frac{\text{Money earned on funds invested}}{\text{Funds invested}} = \text{ROI}$$

or

$$\frac{\$1,500 \text{ earned}}{\$10,000 \text{ invested}} = 0.15, \text{ or } 15\%$$

Different business owners establish their own ROI requirements for capital investment based on their specific investment goals, and buyers should know these ROI minimums and the long-term goals owners have for their businesses. Most hospitality buyers understand that high levels of revenue do not necessarily result in high levels of profits. Very experienced buyers also recognize that high levels of profit are not the same as high levels of investment returns. Investors care much less about the profits achieved by a business than about the ROI the business produces because in some cases a restaurant that achieves a very good profit is still not a good investment for the restaurant's owner. In other cases a restaurant that achieves a less spectacular profit may be a much better investment.

To illustrate, assume two restaurant owners have generated $200,000 in profits after a year of operating their respective restaurants. The first owner has a very nice facility in a modest part of town and has invested $2,000,000 in the operation. The second owner has a much more upscale facility in a more exclusive area of town. This owner has invested $4,000,000 in the business.

In this example the first owner achieved an ROI of 10 percent ($200,000 earned ÷ $2,000,000 invested = 10% ROI), while the second owner achieved an ROI of 5 percent ($200,000 earned ÷ $4,000,000 invested = 5% ROI). It is for this reason that some suggestions about capital expenditures that seem to be good ones (because they will likely increase the profits of the business) must still be carefully evaluated for their likely ROI results.

Now that you have learned about the time value of money and ROI, you are better prepared to understand how these two concepts work together to influence investment decisions, including those involving capital expenditures. To see how, consider Allisha and Ralph. From previous investments, both these investors are owed $1,000. Allisha collects the money owed to her on January 1, while Ralph collects the $1,000 owed to him on December 31 of the same year.

After thoroughly evaluating her new investment opportunities, Allisha takes her money on January 1 and invests it in a company that will pay her a 10 percent annual rate of return. As a result, on December 31 Allisha would have $1,100, as calculated by the following total-value-of-investment formula:

$$\text{Money earned on funds invested} + \text{Original funds invested} = \text{Total value of investment}$$

In this example:

$100 earned + $1,000 original investment = $1,100 total value of investment

As a result of her investment, on December 31 (the end of the year), Allisha's $1,000 has grown to $1,100; while the $1,000 Ralph will collect on that day is still worth only $1,000.

Assume further that Allisha wants to continue investing her money. If she does so, she may be able to increase the future value of her money even further by earning investment returns over an even longer period of time. For example, if, in

Buyers at Work (13.1)

"I don't understand why we can't just get a new one," said Sandy. "Where I worked before, we had a new POS, and it was much faster than this one. This is such a waste of time."

Sandy was talking to Peggy, her coworker at the very popular Richard's Seafoods and Steaks, an independently owned and managed restaurant whose menu featured fresh seafood, prime steaks, and fine wines.

Sandy and Peggy were servers, and their jobs required that they enter guests' orders into one of two available dining room POS terminals. The touch screen terminals used in the restaurant's POS systems sometimes didn't work well, requiring the servers to tap the screens several times to get the machine to accept the order. Also, the computer processor that managed the data was an older one and on busy nights, such as tonight, when servers were lined up two deep to get to the machines, it significantly slowed down guest order entry.

"I don't see why the owners don't just buy a new POS," continues Sandy. "They make them with handheld entry systems now. And fast. I could have had all my orders entered and be back in the dining room taking care of my guests and making sure they like the food and service enough to leave a good tip instead of just standing around here waiting."

"It is frustrating," replied Peggy. "Hey, Sandy, maybe you should talk to the manager and suggest that they replace this whole thing. If you do, perhaps we'll get a new system."

1. Do you think a new POS system would increase revenue levels in this business?
2. Identify at least three capital equipment–related issues that are evident from this on-the-job operational problem.
3. As a professional buyer, how would you advise the owners of this restaurant to assess the pros and cons of investing in a new POS system?

the coming years, Allisha reinvested both the original $1,000 and all of the earnings from it; her investment would grow as follows:

Year 1	$1,000 + ($1,000 × 0.10) = $1,100
Year 2	$1,100 + ($1,100 × 0.10) = $1,210
Year 3	$1,210 + ($1,210 × 0.10) = $1,331
Year 4	$1,331 + ($1,331 × 0.10) = $1,464

Viewed another way, Allisha's multi-year investment returns can be displayed as shown in Figure 13.1.

As you can see, reinvestment of funds at consistent rates of return will cause investments to grow rapidly in value. In fact, the total rate of return for Allisha in this example is 46.4 percent ($464 returned ÷ $1,000 invested = 46.4%), an annual average return of 11.6 percent (46.4% return ÷ 4-year investment period = 11.6% per year).

Because of the time value of money and the importance of ROI, you can easily see why savvy investors carefully assess both of these issues before they elect to make a long-term investment in a capital equipment purchase. This is because few, if any, investors will continue to invest in a hospitality operation if their ROI is less than what they could achieve with other investment opportunities offering the same or even less risk.

Investment Value	Year 1	Year 2	Year 3	Year 4
Beginning Value	$1,000	$1,100	$1,210	$1,331
Investment Earnings	100	110	121	133
Year End Total Value of Investment	$1,100	$1,210	$1,331	$1,464

FIGURE 13.1 Illustration of Allisha's Multi-year Investment Returns

Financing Alternatives

Professional buyers understand that most business owners seek to maximize the returns on their investments. In the majority of cases, it is only after investors determine that a capital purchase should in fact be made that they next turn to determining the best way to finance the investment.

To illustrate the process in a practical way, assume you are shopping for a new car. Your first task is to find the vehicle that suits your purpose and is offered for sale at a price you believe is reasonable. After you have done so, you can then determine the best way to finance it.

If your credit is good, it is likely that financing alternatives for your car purchase could range from paying the full purchase price in cash to borrowing 100 percent of the purchase price. Paying all cash at the time of purchase is known as 100 percent **equity** funding because, when used, buyers have 100 percent free and clear ownership of the item.

If you did not have the cash required to buy the car, or if you simply preferred to do so, you could consider borrowing the car's full purchase price. If you applied for and received a loan for the car's full purchase price, the result would be 100 percent **debt financing.** A third realistic option for your car purchase would be the use of some of your own money (equity funding) combined with the use of some borrowed money (debt financing).

In the hospitality industry, large FF&E purchases are frequently financed with both equity and debt. The precise manner in which financing is secured will have a major effect on the ROI investors ultimately achieve. This is because, with nearly all investments, the greater the **financial leverage**, the greater the ROI achieved by the investor.

Financial leverage is most easily understood as the use of debt to be reinvested to generate a higher ROI than the interest paid on the debt.

To illustrate, consider the case of LeLani. She is the owner of an off-site catering company. LeLani calculates that, for an additional investment of $50,000 in trucks and equipment, she would increase her profits by $8,000 per year. Applying the ROI formula you learned earlier, her ROI would be calculated as follows:

$$\frac{\text{Money earned on funds invested}}{\text{Funds invested}} = \text{ROI}$$

or

$$\frac{\$8,000}{\$50,000} = 16\%$$

Assume, however, that because of its excellent credit rating, LeLani's business has the ability to borrow money at her local bank at an annual interest rate of less than 16 percent. For example, assume that LeLani could borrow money at 10 percent interest per year. In that case the cost of her loan would be $5,000 per year ($50,000 borrowed × 10% annual interest = $5,000 loan cost). In this case the use of borrowed money not only allows her to conserve her own cash (or use it for alternative investments), but it also creates a profit of $3,000 (the difference

---

Buyer's Guide to Purchasing Terms

Equity   Free and clear ownership of an asset (also, the difference between the value of an item and the amount of money owed on the item).

Debt financing   The purchase of an asset using borrowed money.

Financial leverage   The amount of a purchase funded by debt; also called "leverage."

Source of Funds	Investment Amount	Investment Return	ROI
Lender (debt)	$25,000	$2,500	10%
LeLani (equity)	$25,000	$5,500	22%
Total	$50,000	$8,000	16%

FIGURE 13.2   Illustration of LeLani's $50,000 Leveraged Investment Returns with $8,000 Additional Profits Achieved

between the cost of the borrowed funds and the money she will make reinvesting those funds in her business).

Now consider the case in which LeLani elects to fund half of her purchase with her own money (equity funding) and half with borrowed funds. Figure 13.2 shows the results that would be achieved assuming that LeLani realizes the additional profits she has projected. In this case the lender would receive the first $2,500 of additional profit (the interest due on the loaned money) and LeLani would receive the $5,500 remaining profits ($8,000 total profit − $2,500 interest on bank loan = $5,500 remaining profit).

Given the above example of LeLani and her achieved 22 percent (rather than 16 percent) ROI, buyers may ask, "Why not fund 50 percent or even more of every investment using debt?" The answer to this question lies in repayment of debt. Those who supply debt funding must be repaid before those who have provided equity funding. If LeLani does *not* achieve $8,000 in additional profits, the bank will still require its payment of $2,500 interest.

To illustrate, assume that LeLani created only $2,500 in additional profits with the $50,000 investment. In that case the bank would still receive its $2,500. As shown in Figure 13.3, LeLani's ROI in this case would be 0% despite the fact that the entire investment returned 5 percent ($2,500/$50,000 = 5% ROI).

Just as investors maintain minimum ROI requirements prior to considering an investment to be a good one, lenders will analyze a borrower's projected profits and ability to repay debt when they determine the risk they are willing to assume when lending to an investor. It is also important to recognize that those who seek debt funding but whose projects do not demonstrate the proven ability to create significant additional profits, will most often find that the only money lent to their project will come at a higher cost because of a higher interest rate. Because most lending institutions consider businesses in the hospitality industry to be high risk, many will provide debt financing for no more than 50 percent to 70 percent (or even less) of a capital expenditure's total cost and are likely to require the capital asset acquired be used as **collateral** for the loan.

As a professional buyer, it is important that you have good understanding of the effects of alternative debt/equity approaches to FF&E financing because, in today's complex financial world, owner/buyers can often choose from literally hundreds of different debt/equity investment options.

Source of Funds	Investment Amount	Investment Return	ROI
Lender (debt)	$25,000	$2,500	10%
LeLani (equity)	$25,000	$0	0%
Total	$50,000	$2,500	5%

FIGURE 13.3   Illustration of LeLani's $50,000 Leveraged Investment Returns with $2,500 Additional Profits Achieved

Buyer's Guide to Purchasing Term

Collateral   Property used as security for a loan and forfeited if the loan is not repaid.

As the Owner	As the Lessee
1. Right to Use the Property Unlimited use in any legal manner they see fit	Use is strictly limited to the terms of the lease
2. Treatment of Cost Property is depreciable in accordance with federal and state income tax law	Lease payments are deductible as a business expense, according to federal and state tax laws
3. Ability to Finance The property can be used as collateral	The property may not generally be used to secure a loan
4. Nonpayment of Lease Retains rights to the property	Loses right to keep the property

FIGURE 13.4   Four Selected Legal Considerations of Buying versus Leasing Property

Returning now to our example of your new car, if you wished, you could even investigate and ultimately choose to **lease** rather than purchase it. Leasing allows a person or business to use an asset without immediately requiring all of the cash needed to buy it. It is often an excellent way for those with restricted or limited funds to gain immediate possession and use of a needed capital asset.

Just as a business owner's decision to vary the debt/equity ratio funding of a project directly affects ROI, so too will ROI be affected by a decision to lease rather than purchase capital assets. Leasing can provide distinct advantages for **lessors** as well as for the **lessee.**

In a lease arrangement, lessors receive immediate income from their property while still maintaining ownership of the property. Lessees enjoy specific property rights (e.g., they can use but not sell the property), distinct financial and tax advantages, and the right in many cases to buy the property at an agreed-on price at the end of the lease's term.

It is important to recognize that, from a legal as well as a financial perspective, buying a capital asset is much different than leasing it. Figure 13.4 details some significant differences between the legal rights of lessors (the property's owners) and the lessees of that same property.

Despite the significant differences in the legal treatment of owned and leased property, in most cases the decision to lease rather than purchase property is a financial rather than legal one. The financial and tax consequences of leasing assets rather than buying them are significant and, as a result, those buyers considering such decisions should consult with their organization's tax advisers. This is suggested because many factors affect the desirability of leasing, including the purchase price of the item, the cost and length of the lease, and the treatment of the asset at the end of the lease period.

Effect on Financial Statements

You have learned that capital equipment purchases are important to help a business remain competitive. You have also learned that capital equipment purchases are an investment that should be undertaken only after serious consideration of

Buyer's Guide to Purchasing Terms

Lease   A legal contract allowing for the exclusive possession of another's property for a specific time in exchange for an agreed-on payment.

Lessor   The entity that owns a leased asset.

Lessee   The entity that leases an asset.

The owner's/buyer's decisions to lease or purchase significant amounts of capital equipment such as that required by this operation will often be legally and financially complex.

[Photographer]/Photographer's Choice/Getty Images

Did You Know? (13.2)

Having enough cash on hand is a persistent problem in many foodservice operations, so it might seem leasing would often be the best way to finance capital purchases. Despite their many advantages, however, leases can have distinct disadvantages. The first is cost. In almost all cases, leasing then buying equipment is more expensive in the long term than buying it in the first place. More important, however, with some equipment, changing technology may make leased equipment obsolete before the lease term is expired, and typically, significant penalties are incurred if a lessee seeks to terminate the lease before its original expiration date. The important point to remember is that each lease situation must be considered separately before you decide if it is the best way to proceed.

---

the investment returns that are likely to be achieved. As a professional buyer, you should also be aware that the methods used to acquire capital equipment have a significant effect on the three most important financial statements (summaries) prepared by businesses:

1. Balance sheet
2. Income statement
3. Statement of cash flows

The purchase of capital equipment effects each of these important financial statements in a different way. An understanding of the statements and the manner in which they are changed when capital equipment is acquired can help you better understand and communicate with the owners of the business about the best ways to acquire FF&E items.

BALANCE SHEET   As you learned earlier in this text, the balance sheet is an important financial document. It details the worth of a business (its assets), the amount owed by the business (its liabilities), and the amount of any free and clear ownership (equity) held by the owners of the business. (*Note:* Recall that equity is the amount of an item owned free and clear of debt.) Thus, the formula for a balance sheet can be simply expressed as follows:

Company assets = Company liabilities + Owner's equity in the company

Stated in another way, the formula could be expressed as follows:

Company assets = What is OWED + What is OWNED

To illustrate the effect of a capital purchase on a balance sheet, consider Lea. She is the owner of a pizza business with a value of $2,000,000. The balance sheet

	Total Value	=	Amount Owed	+	Amount Owned
Initial balance sheet	$2,000,000		$1,000,000		$1,000,000
Capital purchase with borrowed money	$2,050,000		$1,050,000		$1,000,000
Capital purchase with personal money	$2,050,000		$1,000,000		$1,050,000

FIGURE 13.5 Effect of Capital Purchases on Lea's Balance Sheet

for her business reflects, however, that she does not own the business free and clear; that is, she has some loans and other liabilities that must be repaid over time. She does have $1,000,000 equity in the business. Thus, an accurate balance sheet for her business would show the following:

$$\text{Value of Lea's company} = \text{Amount OWED} + \text{Amount OWNED}$$

In this example:

$$\$2,000,000 = \$1,000,000 + \$1,000,000$$

It should be easy to see that if Lea made a purchase of a piece of capital equipment worth $50,000, the value of her company (assets) would increase by the worth of the new equipment, and the amount owed (if Lea borrowed the money for the purchase) or the amount owned (if Lea paid the full purchase price from her personal money not already invested in the business) would increase as well. These two alternatives are shown in Figure 13.5.

The financial effect of a decision to lease rather than buy capital assets also has an effect on the balance sheet of a business. The most critical of these is that an agreement to lease a capital asset creates a liability for a business. That is, the business agrees to pay the lease and establishes a debt (liability) that will be recorded on the balance sheet.

INCOME STATEMENT You have learned that the itemized record of a business's income, expense, and profit (or loss) during a specific time period is known as the income statement (see Chapter 6). The technical name for this financial summary statement is the statement of income and expense, but it is commonly known as the profit and loss, or P&L, statement.

The income statement provides details about a business's revenue, expenses, and profit for a specified accounting period. It details how much money (revenue) the business brought in during a specific period of time, how much it spent (expense), and finally, how much, if any, money (profit) remained after the expenses were paid. Thus, the formula for an income statement can be simply expressed as follows:

$$\text{Income} = \text{Expenses} + \text{Profit (or Loss)}$$

To illustrate, Figure 13.6 shows the three possible financial outcomes for Lea's business if her income statement is prepared at the end of a month's operation in which her business achieved $150,000 in sales.

In most cases for income statement purposes, loan payments for capital purchases are treated differently than would be lease payments for the same items. Various capital asset acquisition and purchasing strategies will affect the income statement of a business, and often these effects are so complex, they are best determined by the business's owners, financial managers, tax accountants, and legal advisers. Professional buyers should understand, however, that decisions regarding the acquisition of capital items can have a significant effect on the income statement of a business. They should also recognize that an income statement is, in most cases, used to evaluate the effectiveness of the managers operating a business. As a result, the managers will be very interested in the methods used to

FIGURE 13.6 Effect of Profits or Losses on Lea's Income Statement

Lea's income statement with a sample profit of $25,000:	
Revenue	$150,000
Less expense	$125,000
Profit	$ 25,000

Lea's income statement with a sample loss of $25,000:	
Revenue	$150,000
Less expense	$175,000
Profit	($ 25,000)

Lea's income statement with no profit or loss:	
Revenue	$150,000
Less expense	$150,000
Profit	$ 0

acquire capital assets, especially if the methods used make the profits of the business appear smaller than they would be under alternative acquisition strategies.

STATEMENT OF CASH FLOWS   The third financial statement affected by capital acquisition strategies is less well known than either the balance sheet or the income statement. It is called a **statement of cash flows.** In Chapter 1 you learned that cash flows refer to the total amount of money received and spent by a business during a specific time period.

There are actually three distinct business activities that will affect a business's overall cash flow, and the statement of cash flows details each one. The three activities are as follows:

1. *Operating activities*   These include the revenues generated by sales and the expenses required to generate those sales. When revenues exceed expenses, operating activities will generate cash. When expenses exceed revenues, cash levels are reduced.
2. *Investing activities*   When assets such as land, buildings, or equipment are purchased for cash, cash levels decrease. When assets are sold for cash, cash levels increase.
3. *Loan (financing) activities*   When loans are received by the business, cash levels increase. As these loans are repaid, cash levels will decline.

There are several other asset acquisitions and sales activities that will affect a business's cash position. Some of these are shown in Figure 13.7.

Activity	Decrease Cash	Increase/Conserve Cash
FF&E assets are purchased and paid for in cash	X	
FF&E assets are purchased and paid for by loans to the business		X
Equipment or other capital assets are leased		X
Assets are sold		X
Repayments of loans	X	

FIGURE 13.7   Business Activities That Affect Cash Flows

Buyer's Guide to Purchasing Term

Statement of cash flows   A summary of the change in cash available to a business during a designated accounting period.

Buyers at Work (13.2)

"Well, I don't like it at all. It just isn't fair," said Sean, the assistant restaurant manager. He was talking to Ericka, the unit manager for the Pancake Palace, one in a chain of fifteen privately owned units that featured breakfast items all day long. All Pancake Palace operations were open seven days a week, and it was not unusual for there to be many diners waiting for a table on Saturday and Sunday mornings. Business was good, but that was part of the problem.

"Well, it does make sense actually," replied Ericka. "The hot water heater for our store is pretty old and gets constant use. You know we need to take care of that. A new unit with the ventilation that would meet the current building codes in our area would cost $3,000. A replacement of the worn-out heating coil and refurbishing the electrical box on our old unit is only $1,500, and the service technician tells me if we make that repair, it will be "good as new.""

"Did the technician also mention that equipment repairs are reported on our monthly income statement and with a $1,500 charge this month, we won't make our bonuses?" asked Sean angrily.

"I'm sorry, Sean," said Ericka. "I know our performance bonuses are set pretty high. That's true of all the company stores and for all the managers and assistants. I also realize that with an unbudgeted $1,500 expense this month, we won't make the numbers we need to max out our bonuses. It's a hit to us personally, but what would you do if you owned the company?" asked Ericka.

"I would tell the technician to replace the whole unit. Replace, not repair. Then there is no repair bill on this month's P&L, we get our bonuses, and our restaurant gets a new hot water heater that the company can depreciate. Everybody wins."

1. If Sean is correct and the cost of a new hot water heater does not affect the income statement, what financial statement(s) would it affect?

Assume you were Ericka:

2. Would you be persuaded by Sean's rationale? Why or why not.
3. How do you think the owner of the company would respond to Sean's statement that, under his recommendation, "everybody wins"?

Because so many capital purchase-related decisions affect a business's cash position and because of the importance of cash management, buyers must understand the effect of their capital purchase recommendations on the statement of cash flows as well as other measures of a business's financial performance. This is especially so because of the favorable tax-related laws affecting the depreciation of capital assets.

Effect on Tax Obligations

Those who understand the very complex tax laws under which their businesses operate can make decisions to help ensure that the taxes paid are exactly the amount owed. This is important because, when the correct amount of tax is paid, the owner's ROIs will be maximized and the business owners will reap the maximum return on their investment.

Taxing entities such as the federal, state, and local governments generally assess taxes to individuals and businesses based on these entities' definitions of taxable income. The manner in which capital purchases are made and recorded can directly affect taxable income levels and, thus, the taxes a business must pay. Hospitality buyers are not expected to be experts in tax accounting, nor must they have detailed knowledge of all the laws related to the taxes a business must pay.

Taxable Income Greater Than	Not Greater Than	Tax Rate
$0	$50,000	15%
50,000	75,000	25%
75,000	100,000	34%
100,000	335,000	39%
335,000	10,000,000	34%
10,000,000	15,000,000	35%
15,000,000	18,333,333	38%
18,333,333+		35%

FIGURE 13.8 Corporate Income Tax Rates (Federal)
Source: www.smbiz.com/sbrl001.html

They must, however, understand the effect of their capital purchase decisions on tax obligations. The information in Figure 13.8 can be a helpful reminder in recalling why the amount of taxable income reported by a business is important. It provides an example of federally imposed business tax rates for corporations. While the actual rates contained in federal taxation legislation vary somewhat from year to year, the important point to notice is that, as business income rises, taxes due and payable rise as well.

The Internal Revenue Service (IRS) is the taxing authority with which hospitality buyers will likely be most familiar. The IRS is a division of the U.S. Department of Treasury. Its goal is to provide taxpayers with top-quality service by helping them understand and meet their tax responsibilities and by applying the tax law with integrity and fairness. This includes business owners and their tax liabilities. As a result, the IRS's Web site (www.irs.gov) is a good source of information regarding the allowable treatment of expenses related to the purchase of capital equipment and the tax-related results of using various FF&E purchase strategies.

A business's net income is also subject to tax at the state and even local levels. In addition to income taxes, the federal government and some states impose a tax on gains from the sale of property, which normally includes FF&E items.

With literally thousands of federal, state, and local agencies, departments, offices, and individuals charged with setting or enforcing tax policy, it is not possible for typical hospitality buyers to be completely knowledgeable about all the tax requirements that could significantly affect their capital purchase decisions. Professional buyers selecting capital equipment should confer with the tax specialists employed by their companies or the owners of the business before making significant capital equipment acquisition commitments.

Did You Know? (13.3)

Current business tax policy in the United States is heavily biased in favor of those businesses that invest in capital assets by purchasing them. When they own (rather than lease) their assets, companies are allowed to reduce their taxable incomes by the amount of legally allowable asset depreciation. Lower taxable incomes for most businesses mean reduced tax levels.

The laws surrounding allowable depreciation rates are complex, and professional buyers would do well to notify their business's tax advisers when decisions related to capital asset purchases are to be made. In some cases the manner in which depreciation rates are calculated will have such a significant effect on capital equipment purchasing that they will be the single most important factor in such decisions.

> ## PROFESSIONAL PURCHASING PREVENTS PROBLEMS (13.2)
> ### "When New Isn't Better"
>
> *A common problem:* Some buyers fall short of maximizing the effect of their FF&E purchases by failing to consider used or reconditioned equipment purchases.
>
> One characteristic of the restaurant business is that many manufacturers building heavy-duty equipment such as broilers, ovens, dishwashers, fryers, and steamers as well as other kitchen items build them to last for many years. Many restaurants, however, do not last as long. The result is that, at any given time, foodservice buyers may be able to locate and purchase high-quality pieces of preowned equipment at very reasonable prices.
>
> Sources of used equipment include local restaurant supply houses that routinely accept these items as trade-ins for new equipment or purchase them from owners closing their businesses. Additional sources include auctions and direct public sales held by owners who wish to liquidate their restaurants.
>
> Buyers choosing to purchase used, previously leased, or reconditioned equipment must consider issues such as the lack of warranties and reduced levels of choice when making their selections. The cost advantages of purchasing preowned pieces of equipment with long remaining useful lives, however, often far outweigh the benefits of buying new.

Buyer's Guide to Internet Resources: Front-of-House Items

Web Site	Topic
www.theinteriorgallery.com	Restroom fixtures
www.andreuworldamerica.com	Restaurant tables and chairs
www.springusa.com	Front-of-house serving equipment
www.neo-metro.com	Restroom furnishings
www.modernoutdoor.com	Outdoor patio furniture

Purchasing Terms

Capital equipment *366*
Fixture *366*
FF&E *366*
Depreciation *366*
GAAP *367*

Capital budget *368*
Front of house *372*
Back of house *372*
Finance *373*
Time value (of money) *373*

Return on investment (ROI) *374*
Equity *377*
Debt financing *377*
Financial leverage *377*

Collateral *378*
Lease *379*
Lessor *379*
Lessee *379*
Statement of cash flows *382*

Make Your Own Purchasing Decisions

1. As a buyer, in what ways do capital purchase expenditures differ from normal operating expenditures? As an owner, in what ways do capital expenditures differ from normal operating expenditures?

2. Some buyers believe that purchasing equipment with a low equity/high debt financing structure will maximize an owner's ROI. Others believe the opposite (high equity/low debt) provides the best returns. Explain the rationale for the differences in these two common viewpoints.

3. Leasing FF&E items is more popular in some segments of the hospitality industry than in others. Identify three reasons you would advise a buyer

in any foodservice segment to consider leasing a high-cost FF&E item rather than buying it. Also, identify three reasons purchasing high-cost FF&E items might be better than leasing them.

4. Some foodservice buyers have great success in identifying and purchasing preowned FF&E items. What are some FF&E items that you would be comfortable buying used? What are some items you would consider purchasing only when they are new? Explain the reason for your two answers.

5. The decision to lease (rather than buy) FF&E items has many long-lasting effects on a business. Draft a short paragraph that would clearly explain to a nonaccountant the effects on a business's cash reserves and ownership claims when it leases, rather than buys, an expensive piece of capital equipment.

INDEX